D0410541

8

UNIVERSITY OF LUTON
PARK SQ. LIBRARY

3401048158

621.78

TEM

SEVEN DAY LOAN

UNIVERS
PARK

FLEXIBLE MANUFACTURING SYSTEMS

WILEY SERIES IN SYSTEMS ENGINEERING

Andrew P. Sage

FLEXIBLE MANUFACTURING SYSTEMS
Decision Support for Design and Operation

HORST TEMPELMEIER
Technical University of Braunschweig
HEINRICH KUHN
Technical University of Braunschweig

A Wiley-Interscience Publication
JOHN WILEY & SONS, INC.
New York / Chichester / Brisbane / Toronto / Singapore

This text is printed on acid-free paper.

Copyright © 1993 by John Wiley & Sons, Inc.

All rights reserved. Published simultaneously in Canada.

Reproduction or translation of any part of this work beyond
that permitted by Section 107 or 108 of the 1976 United States
Copyright Act without the permission of the copyright owner
is unlawful. Requests for permission or further information
should be addressed to the Permissions Department,
John Wiley & Sons, Inc., 605 Third Avenue,
New York, NY
10158-0012.

Library of Congress Cataloging-in-Publication Data:
Tempelmeier, Horst, 1952–
    Flexible manufacturing systems: decision support for design and
operation / Horst Tempelmeier, Heinrich Kuhn.
        p.   cm. —(Wiley series in systems engineering)
    Includes bibliographical references and indexes.
    ISBN 0-471-30721-1 (alk. paper)
    1. Flexible manufacturing systems—Planning. I. Kuhn, Heinrich,
Dr. II. Title. III. Series.
TS155.6.T473   1993
670.42′7—dc20   93-1461

Printed in the United States of America

10 9 8 7 6 5 4 3 2 1

To Barbara, Jacqueline and Jenny

— H.T.

To Marion and Julius

— H.K.

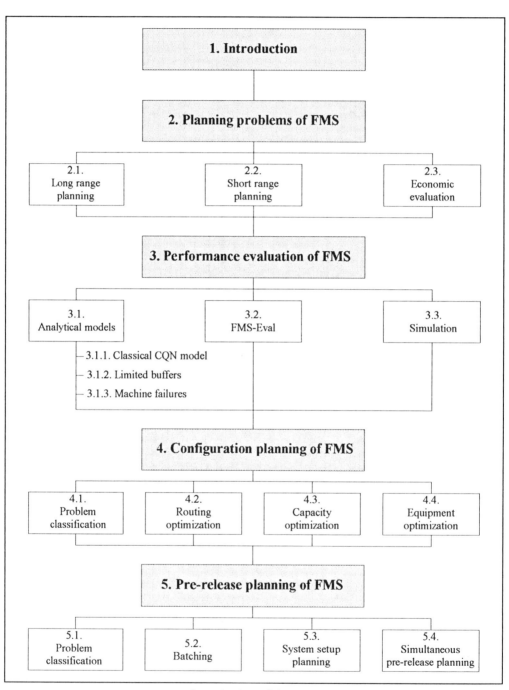

Organization of the book

Contents

Preface

In the past decade enormous technological advances have led to sophisticated hardware solutions in manufacturing technology. Increased international competition with shortening of product lifetimes and diminishing reaction times to changes in the marketplace has forced companies to make massive investments into flexible manufacturing systems (FMSs). According to forecasts, at the end of the century there will be more than 2000 FMSs worldwide.

Considering the impressive advantages promised by the FMS concept (short lead times, low inventory, high adaptability to changing production requirements) in industrial practice, however, there seems to be a disillusion about the economic advantages associated with this technology. The reason for this is that the design and operation of an FMS cannot be properly accomplished with intuition, rules-of-thumb, or trial-and-error approaches that are often found in industrial practice.

The design and operation of an FMS require a large amount of planning knowledge. This is dispersed in the areas of industrial engineering, computer science, business administration, operations management and management science. Unfortunately this is very often documented in books and scientific journals that are rarely available to the industrial planner of an FMS, who normally has access to a limited number of publications.

To compile this knowledge and present it in a comprehensive way to the reader is the main purpose of this book. A structured survey over the many types of problems, modelling and solution approaches in the design of an

FMS configuration and the operation of an already installed FMS is given. The approaches marking the basic line of development in each problem area are discussed in great detail and illustrated with numerical examples. In order to make the material more comprehensible we have inserted a large number of graphical illustrations.

This book aims at several heterogenous groups of readers. First, it could be used as supporting material for graduate level university courses in operations management, industrial engineering, systems engineering, and operations research. There is a high probability for *students* of these fields to come into contact with some sort of flexible production technology during their industrial career—if not as a systems planner, operator, or software engineer, then hopefully as a decision maker.

The second group of readers we have in mind are *decision makers* in industrial practice facing FMS related problems. For this kind of reader it would be interesting to be informed about the many types of problems and their very complex interdependencies as well as the available solution approaches. Only if the variety of decision variables and their complex interactions are known, the optimal decision may be taken. In this way the decision maker can avoid common (and very expensive) pitfalls in the design and operation of an FMS.

Last but not least the book is intended to be part of the desktop accessories for every professional concerned with the planning of the design or the operation of an FMS. This *FMS planner* may be employed in an FMS manufacturer's marketing department confronted with the task to send an offer for a specific FMS design alternative to a prospective customer as well as in an FMS user's production planning department. He/she may also be a software engineer responsible for the design of FMS control software.

In the technical parts of this book it is assumed that the reader is familiar with the fundamental methodologies of operations research, such as mathematical programming, queueing theory, and probability theory. There is a large number of excellent textbooks available in these fields.

This book first appeared in German in March 1992. The English edition has been translated by Edward Cabot. Due to the rapid development of the knowledge in the FMS field we have included the most noticeable contributions that came to our knowledge up to March 1993 in order to keep the book as up-to-date as possible.

We would like to acknowledge the corrections and suggestions we received from all the people, with which we had many discussions about FMSs during the last years. First of all these are our former students of industrial engineering and computer science at the Technical University of Darmstadt (F.R.G.), who supported us through the implementation of numerical solution procedures in the acquisition of the insights into this complex field of research.

We also thank Dr. Ulrich Tetzlaff for his support during the conceptional phase of the book as well as for providing some numerical results and for numerous critical comments.

HORST TEMPELMEIER
HEINRICH KUHN

FLEXIBLE MANUFACTURING SYSTEMS

1. INTRODUCTION

1.1. DEFINITION OF A FLEXIBLE MANUFACTURING SYSTEM

A flexible manufacturing system (FMS) is a production system consisting of a set of identical and/or complementary *numerically controlled machines* which are connected through an *automated transportation system*. Each process in an FMS is controlled by a *dedicated computer* (FMS cell computer). This is often imbedded in a large hierarchical network of computers. An FMS is capable of processing workpieces of a certain workpiece-spectrum in an arbitrary sequence with negligible setup delays between operations. This is possible since in an FMS a set of preadjusted tools is available through a centralized tool magazine with short access time and/or through local tool magazines at the machines with direct access. Furthermore, workpieces are clamped on pallets at separate setup tables thus allowing them to be quickly positioned at the machines. Due to the automation of tool exchange operations, the usually time-consuming interruptions for tool exchanges (including tool preparation, if necessary) are performed while the machine is operating. While a workpiece is being machined by a given tool, the next tool is already picked up by a robotic arm from the tool magazine. After completion of the process it is exchanged with the previous tool. This procedure generally requires only a few seconds. In the case of a workpiece exchange, this time is necessary anyway while the new NC program required to control the next operation to be performed at the machine is loaded.

It is customary to process workpieces of several different product types and production orders simultaneously in an FMS. Usually the workpieces are mounted on pallets with the help of fixtures. Every workpiece is characterized by its specific process advancement, which continuously has to be updated and stored individually by the control system of the FMS. Intermediate storing of unfinished workpieces between operations can be accomplished at central storage areas (central buffer) or, if possible, at local storage areas at the machines.

A set of (ca. 20-200) local tools is assigned to each of the CNC machines[1] (machining centers) in an FMS for direct access. They can be stored in cassettes, drums, discs or chain magazines. For processing parts which require tools not available at the local tool storage, external supply is necessary. In general, this is achieved by exchanging tools which are no longer required. This tool exchange can involve a single tool, or it can involve complete cassettes or discs armed with those tools which are next required at the machine. The exchange procedure can be performed either automatically, through a tool supply system, or manually. Figure

---

[1] Computer Numerical Control. For a survey of FMS hardware see **Bonetto** (1988); **Greenwood** (1988); **Lenz** (1989).

(1) shows a machine with a tool chain magazine and single tool exchange via an automated tool transportation system.

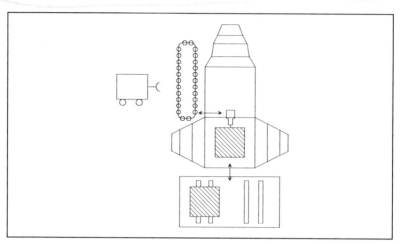

Figure 1: CNC machine with tool chain magazine

Machines with tool *chain magazines* require a (short) tool setup time when changing from one part spectrum to another, because a tool storage chain is not capable of supplying the spindle during the external tool exchange. Machines with tool cassettes or exchangeable tool discs, however, are more flexible, since subsets of tools can be exchanged without interfering with processing and thus can prepare the machine for the next workpiece.

If *tool cassettes* are used [figure (2)], one or more cassettes are assigned to a machine. In contrast to tool chain or tool disc magazines, supplying the spindle with a tool does not require the simultaneous movement of the whole tool set. Rather, a local transportation mechanism[2] is used to pick up the tool from the cassette and to transfer and pass it over to the twin arm[3] which brings the new tool to the spindle. In preparing for a tool cassette exchange (exchange of the tools necessary for two different workpieces) the tools can be presorted with the help of an appropriate control system.

The exchange of a tool cassette can be performed manually (with the help of transportation devices) or automatically through a tool transportation system. In some FMSs the same transportation system is used for workpieces as well as for tools. In this case considerable control problems emerge in synchronizing part and tool flow, however.

The large number of tools used at a single machine leads to a high degree of *functional integration*. Thus, it is found that in an FMS the number of different

---

2   The correct positioning of tools at tool chain magazines is performed by advancing the chain or, at tool disc magazines, by turning the disc. Depending on the size of the magazine, considerable force might be required.

3   **Kusiak** (1990), p. 41. A twin arm is also applied at tool chain magazines.

types of machines is less than in comparable conventional job shops[4]. Simply through the exchange of tools a machine can fulfill a completely different function.

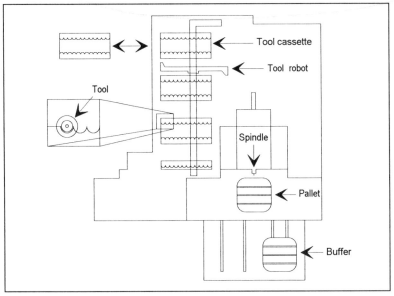

Figure 2: CNC machine with tool cassette magazines

Figure (3) shows the layout of an FMS with several CNC machines which are provided with tool cassettes through a centralized tool supply system. The tools of the cassettes are preadjusted and prepared for operation at a tool setup area. Afterwards they are either stored at a central tool magazine or, if they are to be used immediately, transported to a local tool magazine at a machine. The transportation of the tool cassettes to the machines is achieved in this case through a separate tool transportation system. Obviously, the design of such a tool supply system requires special consideration of the capacity of the tool transportation system so that processing delays due to late tool supply may be avoided. Central buffers are placed around and with their backs oriented toward the center positioned machines. Two setup tables (load/unload stations) are located at the left hand side. They represent the interface between the FMS and its production environment.

Worldwide roughly 1200 FMSs[5] existed at the beginning of 1989. In previous years the rate of growth had been around 20-25% per annum. According to forecasts, around 2500-3500 FMSs will be operating in the year 2000.

---

4   **Kusiak** (1990), p. 20
5   **Ranta/Tchijov** (1990). It should be noted that the published numbers of existing FMSs depend on the definition of the term FMS.

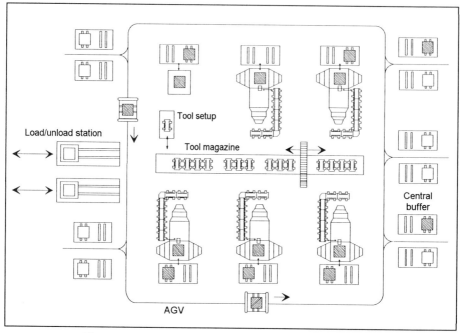

Figure 3: FMS with two AGV carts and a central tool magazine

Flexible production systems come in different forms, yet there does not exist a generally accepted classification in the literature[6]. In the following we base our considerations on the classification shown in figure (4).

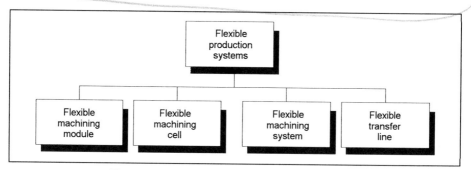

Figure 4: Classification of flexible production systems

- *Flexible machining modules* (FMM; also: flexible machining centers) consist of a *single* CNC machine equipped with a tool/workpiece exchange mechanism.

---

6   One reason for this might be the fact that vendors' and FMS-users' publications tend to broaden their definition for public relations purposes.

The automated tool exchange mechanism makes it possible to perform several different operations in one setup configuration with short tool exchange times. FMMs often possess local input/output buffers, which allow intermediate storage of unprocessed (input) and processed (output) parts. Because of limited workpiece storage capabilities FMMs can only work for a short period of time without external supply. Machining centers are the smallest self-contained production units and constitute the basic components of larger and more highly integrated production systems. FMMs with local buffer spaces are shown in the figures (1)-(3).

- **Flexible machining cells** (FMC) are a combination of an FMM with a setup station, machine independent workpiece storage (central storage), and an automated tool transportation system. This enables the cell to run for a longer period of time with little or no supervision. Figure (5) shows a flexible cell in which the local input/output buffer has been replaced by a pallet storage carousel with room for eight pallets and an integrated workpiece transportation mechanism.

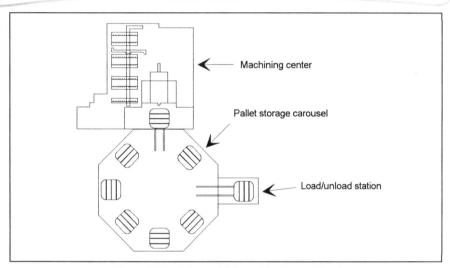

Figure 5: Flexible machining cell with one FMM

- **Flexible manufacturing systems**[7] (FMS) consist of several identical and/or complementary machining centers as well as machine-independent workpiece and possibly also tool storage. All components are connected through automated workpiece, tool, and information flows. FMSs can be configured to be *process*- or *product*-oriented. In the latter case, the FMS consists of different FMMs and possibly also washing machines, burring machines, gaging machines, centralized tool magazines, etc. Therefore, such a system may be used for the *complete processing* of workpieces. If the FMS is configured to be pro-

---

7   **Bonetto** (1988)

cess-oriented, then it is only capable of performing one operation for a specific workpiece spectrum, though that operation may be quite complex and require numerous different tools. In figure (6) two identical FMMs are combined with one specialized machine to build an FMS. Workpieces for which there is no room at the local machine buffers are stored in the central buffer. The latter consists of several pallet storage areas. The flow of workpieces is accomplished through an automatic rail-guided vehicle.

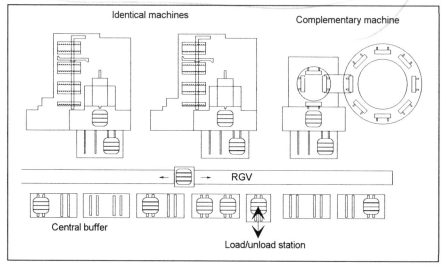

Figure 6: Flexible manufacturing system

The above FMS is quite small. It does, however, show all the characteristic features of an FMS. In reality, much larger FMSs can be found. A selection of different FMS layouts is presented and commented upon in *Carrie*[8].

- *Flexible transfer lines*[9] consist of several CNC machines, and their layout is process-oriented. The flow of material is paced with an inside interlinkage, i.e. the workpieces are transferred simultaneously in a fixed sequence through the operation area of the machines. A flexible transfer line can process a limited spectrum of different workpieces in an arbitrary order. The flow of material, however, is not arbitrary. Its direction is predetermined by the transport mechanism. A new setup for a change from one workpiece spectrum to another can only be achieved by shutting down the whole transfer line. This requires considerable setup time and thus causes a severe interruption in production.

8   **Carrie** (1988); see also **Maleki** (1991), pp. 27-41; **Dupont-Gatelmand** (1982)
9   **Bonetto** (1988), pp. 73-75

Further designations for certain configurations of flexible production systems of a more complex order can be found in the literature, e.g. *flexible manufacturing group, flexible production system*[10]. Within the framework of this book, emphasis is placed on flexible manufacturing systems because here the below mentioned problems for planning and operating come clearly into focus.

There exists considerable uncertainty both in theory and in practice about the *economic advantages* of FMSs in comparison to conventional production systems. According to *Ranta and Tchijov*[11], small simply structured FMSs (with 2-4 machines) and large complex FMSs (with 15-30 machines) tend to be the most advantageous. This observation can be explained as follows: small FMSs, e.g. FMSs with identical universal machines which perform only one (though complex) operation, can be easily installed and operated with simple planning procedures. Because of limited functional demands, the expenditures for the development of planning and control software are low. In comparison to the conventional job shop, the positive results considerably outweigh the additional costs for more complex planning software. Medium sized FMSs require far more planning. Here all the basic features of a complex planning and control system have to be integrated, even if each one of them is required only for a single machine type. The resulting costs are sometimes not compensated for by corresponding benefits. As the size of the FMS increases, software with the basic planning and control features for medium sized systems can still be used. The costs for software comprise a large portion of the fixed costs and can only be offset by positive effects when applied in larger systems. It can be assumed, however, that with further increases in size negative effects caused by increasing complexity may again outweigh these positive effects.

1.2. SUBSYSTEMS OF A FLEXIBLE MANUFACTURING SYSTEM

An FMS consists of several closely interconnected subsystems, including the *technical system*, the *human operator system* and the *information system* [see figure (7)[12]].

* **Technical system**

The *technical system* consists of the *processing system*, the *workpiece supply system* and the *tool supply system*. In addition it comprises special logistic subsystems such as the energy system and the auxiliary system, responsible for the supply of lubricants and coolants, and the waste disposal system [see figure (8)].

---

10   **Kusiak** (1985a)
11   **Ranta/Tchijov** (1990)
12   **Kuhn** (1990), p. 6

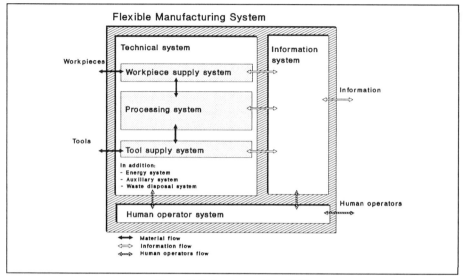

Figure 7: Subsystems of an FMS

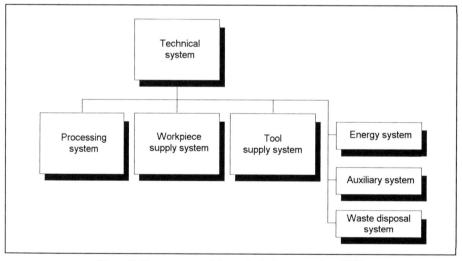

Figure 8: Components of the technical system of an FMS

• **Processing system**

The *processing system* of an FMS consists of *machines*, *local tool exchange* and *tool storage systems*, *quality control* (measuring) *stations* and *washing machines* [see figure (9)]. The machines are generally computer numerical controlled machines

(NC machines)[13]. These machines work according to the following principle: after a workpiece has been tightly positioned, the tool and workpiece can be moved relative to each other. All these movements are controlled by an NC program.

Numerically controlled machine tools have gone through several stages of development. During the first stage, the control of the machine was achieved through a permanently wired control system (*NC machines*[14]).

CNC machines[15] allow an NC program to be downloaded into the machine control unit. Microprocessor controlled systems (MCNC systems) and multiple processor systems are currently used. A CNC machine which is connected to a dedicated FMS computer (cell or system computer) from which the required programs are downloaded is called a *DNC machine*[16]. When workpiece changes are necessary, downloading a new NC program takes less than a minute. However, if workpiece and thus program changes occur often, considerable time delays will result. Such negative impacts on the productivity of the machine can be avoided through appropriate system setup planning.

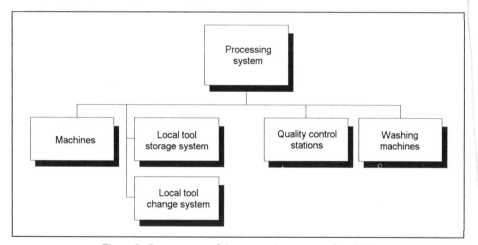

Figure 9: Components of the processing system of an FMS

According to their capabilities, machine tools can be classified into universal machines (often machining centers) or specialized machines. *Universal machines* are machine tools which can perform several different types of cutting operations (e.g. drilling, milling and turning) with the workpiece in a single clamped position, i.e. without refixturing the workpiece. This is possible through a tool exchange and, if necessary, through a change of the NC program. Such a possibility does not exist for *specialized machines* (e.g. drilling machines, grinding machines,

---

13   **Talavage/Hannam** (1988), p. 13-35
14   Numerical Control
15   Computerized Numerical Control
16   Direct Numerical Control

washing machines). At first glance it seems that universal machines offer considerable advantages in achieving a higher utilization over specialized machines.
Further examination is necessary, however. The large number of tools stored at
and used by CNC machines has a considerable value[17], yet only one tool can be
used at any given point in time. The machine is highly utilized but its tools are
not, thus there is always a part of the invested capital which is not in use. Furthermore, specialized machines which are only partly utilized are often included
in an FMS, even within an optimal configuration.

Universal machines are most frequently used in FMSs. As shown in a 1985 study[18], 55% of the machines in an FMS were universal, and 45% were specialized
machines (lathes, milling machines, drilling machines, grinding machines and
other single purpose machines). 73% of the examined FMSs contained between 2
and 10 machines, while only 8% were larger than 15 machines.

Depending on the operation to be performed by the machine, FMSs can be classified into systems with *identical* or *complementary* machines as well as *combined
systems*[19]. Identical machines can perform identical operations. If they are equipped with identical tools, they can be used alternatively for an operation and thus
offer a choice in the processing of a workpiece. It should be kept in mind, however, that identical machines cannot automatically be used in an alternative
fashion because they generally have different sets of tools available in their local
tool storage magazines. First a tool exchange has to take place at the local tool
storage. This requires a certain setup time. Section 5. presents decision models of
loading problems which allow setup times to be reduced using a sophisticated
loading strategy.

A local *tool magazine* can be a cassette, drum, disc or chain magazine. A tool
magazine can be set up with a large number of different tools, though there may
be more than one of each type. If, after the end of an operation or after the end
of a tool's life, a new tool is required, the old tool is taken off the spindle and replaced through a tool exchange mechanism by a new tool from the tool magazine.
The number of available tools at the local tool magazine depends largely on the
type and size of the magazine. In general there are between 20 and 200 tools.
Since most tools are quite expensive ($1000 and more) there is a tendency to
have only one tool (or only a few tools) of each type in the FMS. This strategy,
however, requires frequent tool exchanges and thus might jeopardize the system's production rate if the tool supply system becomes a bottleneck.

· **Workpiece supply system**

The workpiece supply system consists of a *transportation system*, a *storage system*,
a *setup system* and a *handling system* [see figure (10)].

---

17   Their value can be up to several hundred thousand dollars.
18   **Mertins** (1985)
19   See section 1.1.

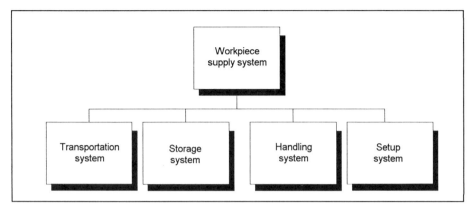

Figure 10: Workpiece supply system

The *workpiece transportation system* governs the flow of workpieces between the machining stations, the storage system and the setup system. Two different types of interlinkages can be distinguished: inside and outside interlinkages. If an *inside interlinkage* is used, the flow of material is directed through the operating area of the machines, whereas at an *outside interlinkage* it passes around the outside of the operating area. An inside interlinkage requires a paced transportation system with high machine reliability or an appropriate number of buffers between the machines. Inside interlinkage is found particularly in transfer lines. FMSs use primarily outside interlinkages. Inside interlinkages are used only for certain machines, such as washing machines.

The workpieces are transported on pallets. In practice, continuous and discontinuous material flow systems can be distinguished[20]. Both are found in roughly equal numbers, as was shown in the above-mentioned study[21]. Among the continuous material flow systems, powered roller conveyors are most common; whereas discontinuous material flow systems are dominated by automatic wire-guided vehicles (AGV) or rail-guided vehicles (RGV).

The *workpiece storage system* has the task of storing the workpieces (which are already clamped on pallets) between operations at different machines. The available buffer areas within an FMS can be distinguished according to their location as either local or central *buffer* areas. *Local buffer areas* are assigned to a certain machining station (or a setup station) as input/output buffers. Therefore, they are only available to workpieces at that station. On the other hand, *central buffer areas* are available to all workpieces. They are used when no more local buffer capacity is available.

The *workpiece setup system* is intended to manage the clamping and unclamping of workpieces onto and off of the pallets. In addition, setup tables are often used for reorienting workpieces on pallets to allow machine access to formerly hidden

20 **Talavage/Hannam** (1988), p. 103-136
21 **Mertins** (1985)

surfaces. The required operations are generally performed manually at a setup station. From the perspective of a workpiece, the setup station represents the entrance and exit of the FMS. Rotational-symmetric workpieces for horizontal turret lathes are generally supplied unclamped on a pallet or in a container to the machines. Prismatic workpieces are clamped on the pallet with special fixturing devices[22]. If clamping blocks are used, several identical or different workpieces can be clamped on a pallet at one of the up to five sides of the block.

Pallets are generally standardized and dedicated to a certain class of workpieces whose fixture is mounted on the pallet. For the clamped workpieces, the operating setup is identical to the transportation setup. If multi-side processing is required, the workpiece orientation must be changed at a setup station. Unclamped workpieces, however, are moved by a robotic arm to the operating area of the machine and are fixed there automatically.

The *workpiece handling system* is responsible for specific changes in the position and orientation of workpieces and/or pallets between the machining, transportation and setup systems. Whereas a transportation task performs a change of a workpiece's location, a handling operation performs an additional change of orientation. A typical handling operation is the transfer of a pallet from a local buffer to the operating area of a machine.

·   **Tool supply system**

Similar to the workpiece supply system, the tool supply system transports, prepares, and stores the tools required for the processing of workpieces. Tools have to be exchanged after the tool life has been exhausted. They are also exchanged when the workpiece mix to be processed in the FMS within a certain time period is changed - if the tool requirements are different. Tool supply systems can be distinguished according to whether the supply of the local tool magazine with new tools is achieved manually (decentralized tool supply) or automatically (centralized tool supply). In a *decentralized tool supply system* a manual setup of the local tool magazines is performed from time to time, for example when a cassette with preset tools is exchanged at a machine with the help of a tool transportation vehicle. During the exchange procedure the operation of the machine is often restricted and processing must be interrupted. The resulting loss of processing time through this manual exchange is a major incentive for processing workpieces with similar or identical tool requirements in *batches*. Production of a batch size "1" is often inadequate because of restrictions caused by the tool supply system.

With a *centralized tool supply system* an exchange of tools at the local tool magazine is often possible without interrupting the currently running process at the machine. The tool supply is drawn from a centralized tool storage area with the help of an automated tool transportation and handling system. Often a direct exchange of a single tool is also possible. The automated supply of local tool maga-

---

22   Bidanda/Muralikrishnan (1992)

zines allows the simultaneous production of almost all workpiece types which can be processed in the FMS. In this case, the tool setup times are shorter than in the decentralized case. In practice, however, the tool supply system tends to become the bottleneck of the whole FMS.

- **Human operator system**

The *human operator system* includes all the personnel directly required for the operation of the FMS. In many design approaches for FMSs found in the literature the operator system is not mentioned explicitly. This gives the impression that an FMS can be operated without any personnel at all. In fact, this can only be accomplished during a limited time (an unmanned shift). The operator system is responsible for workpiece and tool preparation, the supervision of the operating system, and the maintenance and repair of the mechanical system as well as of the computerized control system. The current standard of FMS control software also often requires manual interactions. For example, a decision as to which workpiece will be transported next to a machine for processing is often left to the system supervisor who controls the FMS from a graphical computer terminal. Besides the system supervisor, the operator system requires personnel to setup workpieces, preadjust tools and to maintain the system. The current trend is to reduce the task segregation between the members of the operator system. This then has consequences for internal staff training.

- **Information system**

The information system takes over all the functions [see figure (11)], which are required for the control of the production process. It can be further subdivided into the *short-term planning and control system* and the *data management system*.

The *data management system* stores and keeps easily accessible all the data relevant to the planning and control of workpiece processing in the FMS, such as the status and process history of each workpiece currently residing in the FMS. This function comprises the administration of the process plan (including tool requirements for given operations as well as NC programs) and the process advancement of a workpiece. It also manages the tool magazines and controls the status of the tools (remaining lifetime). To facilitate the diagnosis and prevention of breakdowns a detailed recording, registration and interpretation of the causes is necessary.

The *short-term planning and control system* embodies all planning and control functions which are necessary to ensure the well coordinated performance of the processing, handling and transportation operations in the FMS. The *planning system*, after taking into consideration the current status of the FMS, loads orders released from the central production planning and control system (PPC system) into the FMS and assigns them to the machines. The planning procedures described in section 5. can be applied here.

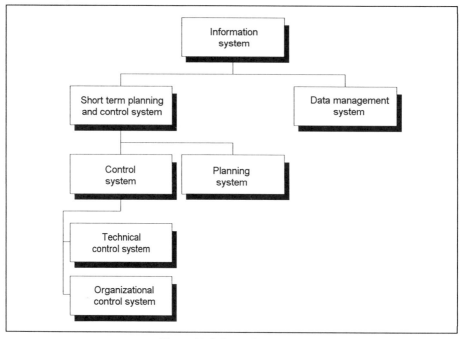

Figure 11: Information system

The *control system* can be further subdivided into the technical and the organizational control systems. The *technical control system* supervises, among other things, the transfer of NC programs, the control of the workpiece and tool supply systems (e.g. coordination of the positions of AGVs to avoid collisions), the synchronization between the control of the machine and transportation systems, and the control of each individual machine. Specialized dedicated process computers are used[23] to manage the large amount of data. Because of the rapid process advancement, all components of the FMS have to be linked online with the process computer. This allows the process computer to respond quickly to new control demands. On the other hand, the *organizational control system* is responsible for dispatching and loading (loading of machines and vehicles, rescheduling in case of breakdowns) and data collection. Whereas the latter is often neglected in conventional production systems, it is an indispensable requirement for the operation of an FMS.

---

23   In many FMSs the control of the transportation vehicle is assigned to a separate personal computer.

1.3. FLEXIBILITY AS A CHARACTERISTIC OF A FLEXIBLE MANUFACTURING SYSTEM

Numerous economic goals are pursued when an FMS is introduced. For example, it is expected that personnel costs can be reduced and that the utilization of a machine can be improved through production during an unmanned third shift or on Sundays and holidays. Furthermore, reduced processing time for orders and the associated lower inventory and capital costs are beneficial and allow a greater adaptability to short-term changes. At the same time, a high adaptability to changing long term production tasks is also ascribed to FMSs. A higher product quality is expected through the reduction of human interference in the production process[24].

The high *flexibility* of the FMS makes the accomplishment of these goals possible. The term flexibility cannot be described in one dimension, however. It has numerous aspects. There is also no uniform definition in the economic and engineering literature[25]. Flexibility means the availability of degrees of freedom in a certain decision making situation. This situation can arise out of *disturbances* of a currently running process or by new *opportunities* presented by the environment.

Keeping in mind the above definition of an FMS, in the following those issues concerning the *time, cost and capacity aspects* of the flexibility of an FMS during changes in product mix and production volumes will be emphasized. Flexibility can be achieved in very different ways. The most widespread form of flexible production in industry is the *conventional job shop*. Here short-term changes in the production task can be accomplished through changing the setup of the machines. Since with each new setup procedure productive machining time is lost, the production volume per period (i.e. the portion of capacity which is used productively) of a conventional job shop decreases with an increasing utilization of this potential flexibility. Furthermore, with increasing setup times productivity decreases even more rapidly. According to this example, a machine is flexible if it can change to another production task *without loss of time*.

Flexibility of a production system can also be achieved with several parallel *flow shops*. For example, it would be possible to install a dedicated flow line for each product or for each process plan and to produce the product quantities when required on these lines. A change from one product to the other could be simply achieved through a change from one line to the other. For the production of single units or small batches such a procedure is obviously not economical. Since the flow lines would be utilized at a very low level, flexibility of this kind is not found in industrial practice. This extreme case, however, shows that aside from time, the *costs of flexibility* play an important role.

The *FMS concept* aims at the combination of the advantages of a conventional job shop (quick change of production tasks with low investment costs) with the efficiency of a flow shop (high production capacity with low unit costs when the production capacity is used to a high degree). However, it should be emphasized

---

24   See empirical results from Japan in **Murata/Tajima** (1990), p. 253.
25   For an overview see **Sethi/Sethi** (1990); see also **Rao/Mohanty** (1991).

that an FMS is only flexible within the framework of the product mix for which it was designed. Universal FMSs which can process any possible workpiece spectrum do not exist. To elucidate the major aspects of flexibility, the most important types of flexibility found in the literature are presented below[26].

• *Machine flexibility*

  Machine flexibility describes the ease, with which a machine can be switched over from one operation to another. In an FMS this is achieved through an automatic tool exchange.
  Machine flexibility is a quality of a *machine*. It is affected by the dimensions of the local tool magazine[27].

• *Material handling flexibility*

  Material handling flexibility is the ability of the FMS's material handling system to transport and to locate workpieces of different types and sizes. The larger the material handling flexibility the better the machines can be supplied with workpieces, thus the flexibility of the machines is not hindered by the limitations of the material handling system.
  Material handling flexibility is a quality of the *material handling system*. It can be influenced by its technical design and by the layout of the transportation paths.

• *Operation flexibility*

  Operation flexibility is available to a workpiece if it can be processed with different technological sequences of operations (process plans). The larger the operation flexibility of a workpiece, the better the workload can be balanced among the machines, thus increasing the potential production volume of the FMS.
  Operation flexibility is a quality of a *workpiece* (i.e. the workpiece type). It is affected through the generation of different process plans for a single workpiece type.

Machine, material handling and operation flexibility describe properties of machines, of the material handling system and of the workpiece types processed by an FMS respectively. Each of these flexibilities concerns only *one element* of the FMS. The following types of flexibilities concern *several elements* of an FMS simultaneously.

• *Expansion flexibility*

  Expansion flexibility describes by how much and whether or not an FMS can be expanded through an increase or decrease in the number of machines, setup stations, etc. An expansion might be necessary if, because of changes in

---

26   **Browne/Dubois/Rathmill/Sethi/Stecke** (1984); **Sethi/Sethi** (1990); **Kochikar/Narendran** (1992)
27   The capability of a tool magazine to store different tools is also called magazine flexibility. **Köhler** (1988), p. 6

production requirements, a set of identical machines becomes a bottleneck and must be expanded by one machine. A change of the FMS configuration is also necessary if new workpiece types are to be processed by the FMS requiring operations which cannot be performed with the machines currently available to the system.

Closely related to expansion flexibility is *reconstruction flexibility*, in which components are exchanged to adapt the system to new production requirements.

Expansion flexibility is an attribute of the whole system. It can be improved by a forward-looking layout planning (leaving empty space for machines to be included in the FMS in the future) and modular hardware and software concepts.

- *Production flexibility*

  If one considers instead of expanding an existing FMS the possibility of *changing its setup*, then the term production flexibility becomes relevant. Production flexibility concerns the set of products which can be processed by the FMS without further investments.

  Production flexibility is a capability of *all components* of the FMS. It is influenced by the technical design of the machines and the degree to which these machines are identical or complementary. It can be observed that FMSs with complementary machines have a higher potential production flexibility than FMSs which primarily consist of identical machines.

- *Process flexibility*

  Process flexibility describes the short-term flexibility of an FMS *without* allowing the possibility of an extension or a *new setup*. It concerns the set of different workpiece types which can be processed on the FMS without any major setup disruptions. The larger this set, the smaller the inventory required to ensure a certain delivery time for the customers, because all these workpiece types can be produced immediately without changing the setup.

  Process flexibility is primarily a characteristic of the *machines and their tools* within the system.

- *Routing flexibility*

  Routing flexibility applies when a workpiece with a given process plan can follow different routes through an FMS. This is the case when several identical machines can be alternatively used for performing an operation. It is especially important when machines break down.

  Routing flexibility is a property of the *machines* in the FMS. It depends in particular on the number of identical machines and on how quickly the desired tools can be supplied.

- *Volume flexibility*

  Volume flexibility describes the ability of an FMS to work *economically* at different output levels. An FMS with a high volume flexibility shows an extremely flat curve for the costs per workpiece.
  Volume flexibility is a property of the *FMS as a whole*.

Further reading for section 1.:

Bonetto (1988)
Carrie (1988)
Greenwood (1988)
Kusiak (1985a), (1990)
Lenz (1989)
Maleki (1991)
Sethi/Sethi (1990)
Talavage/Hannam (1988)
Tempelmeier (1992a)

2. PLANNING PROBLEMS OF FLEXIBLE MANUFACTURING SYSTEMS

This section presents an overview of the diverse decision problems encountered in the design and operation of an FMS. These problems can be divided into long-term and short-term problems. Structural changes of the equipment, such as investment decisions, are considered in the discussion of *long-term* planning problems in section 2.1., while section 2.2. reviews *short-term* problems associated with the operation of the equipment.

A question closely related to long range planning is the *economic justification* of an FMS design. A large number of approaches for the treatment of this question have been developed in investment theory. They are introduced in section 2.3.

2.1. LONG RANGE PLANNING OF FLEXIBLE MANUFACTURING SYSTEMS

2.1.1. The Structure of the Planning Process

The decision of a company to invest in an FMS can be regarded as a strategic decision. This is due to the high investment expenses (between $5-100 million) and the long lifetime of such a system (in general several product lifecycles). The long-term planning of an FMS is part of a company's long-term product and capacity planning and thus a consequence of a *technology strategy* concentrating on a process of technological innovation. Because of the high investment volume a close relationship to finance and investment planning is necessary.

The process of making a decision regarding the implementation of an FMS can be initiated for different reasons:

- If the top management finds it necessary to invest in modern production technology to *ensure future competeveness and participation in the rapid technological advancements in production*, primary emphasis is placed on strategic arguments regarding the development of production technology. Even if economic arguments do not favor the introduction of an FMS, an early entry into this new technology might prevent the need to make a larger technological jump later.

- *Cost considerations* which require the replacement of old production technology with the newest developments to keep up with increased market demands in quality and delivery time[28] may also be important.

---

28   **Boer/Hill/Krabbendam** (1990), p. 6

- *New investments* demanded by the growth of the company are also economically motivated. The required capacity can be established based on a long
  range production plan. This is done by comparing the required with the available capacity. If there is a *capacity gap* for certain products, efforts must be
  made to close this gap.
  This can be achieved by increasing the capacity, by buying the required products externally from outside vendors or by increasing the utilization of existing capacity. If an *increase in capacity* is necessary, the type of production
  system to be selected must be investigated. In the case of an FMS, a conventional job shop or a flexible transfer line are usually other possible production
  alternatives. Aside from the capabilities of the system, financial issues such as
  budget restrictions are also of importance for such a decision.

The issues mentioned above might lead to the decision to consider an FMS as a
possible alternative and to begin the planning process. The planning process consists of three steps[29]. Its structure is outlined in figure (12).

At the beginning of the process the workpiece spectrum must be examined. According to given geometrical and technological criteria, those workpiece types
which can be produced on an FMS are selected from the set of all workpiece
types produced by the company. Technological criteria include the *required quality level* or the *number of workpiece type variations*.

The types of workpieces which can be produced on an FMS are described
through their process plans (in many cases these are redefined according to the
capability of the FMS technology under consideration) and their production requirements in a given period of time. Based on this data it is possible to determine the equipment necessary for the FMS: machining centers, setup stations,
washing and gauging machines, material handling systems, pallets, and fixtures.

Based on the requirements given by the above-mentioned part type descriptions
the following questions must be answered:

- *Which part types should be produced on the FMS?*

  The answer to this question describes the necessary capacity and flexibility
  which the FMS and its components must deliver.

- *Which components should be integrated into the FMS?*

  This question describes the investment requirements and operating costs of
  the system.

These two questions are largely interdependent. The configuration of an FMS is
influenced by the production requirements of the products to be produced. On
the other hand, the specific structure of an FMS configuration may present certain advantages for the production of a particular workpiece type.

---

29   **Browne/Chan/Rathmill** (1985); see also **Suresh** (1990); **Tetzlaff** (1990), (1992b)

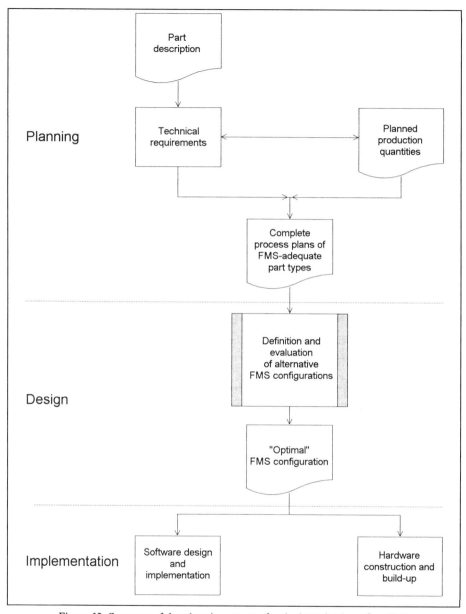

Figure 12: Structure of the planning process for the introduction of an FMS

The complexity of the problem considered is further increased since the work-piece spectrum, the process plans and the production quantity will normally vary during the lifetime of the FMS. These changes, and thus the production requirements, can not be anticipated with certainty. This gives the problem a stochastic character.

In the process of evaluating possible FMS alternatives numerous *technical, economic* and *social goals* must be considered[30]. Many of them are non-quantifiable. In order to evaluate an FMS design alternative all these goals have to be assessed in an *integrative* fashion and aggregated within the *systematic framework* of the general decision process. This results in a ranking of FMS configuration alternatives. The classical Multi-Attribute Decision Model can be used as a problem structuring aid[31]. In a simplified form it is often used to evaluate strategic decision alternatives. A specialized concept for the evaluation of production systems is given by *Troxler and Blank*[32].

During the configuration phase, a system planner might come to the conclusion that for the given workpiece spectrum even the best FMS alternative is not satisfactory. In this situation the possibility of changing the planned workpiece spectrum and thus returning to the technical planning phase should be considered. It is obvious that such a situation requires technical as well as economic expertise.

The long range planning of an FMS ends with a decision about the installation of the best possible system alternative. Afterwards, a detailed planning stage begins in which the technical details, such as the layout of the FMS, are determined, the design of the software and hardware is developed, and the project planning and realization begins.

2.1.2. Decision Problems in the Design of a Flexible Manufacturing System

The decision problems which arise during the design of an FMS are based upon the available decision *variables*, the pursued *objectives*, and the given *constraints*.

• Decision variables

When planning an FMS, a large number of decision variables have to be quantified. The basic variables are the *workpiece spectrum* and its relevant features (production volumes and process plans) and the possible *components* of the FMS (machines, pallets, transportation vehicles, etc.) Thus the following issues have to be reviewed:

*   *Subset of part types to be produced on the FMS:*
    *   Part types
    *   Production volume
    *   Sequence of operations (routes, process plans)

---

30   **Padmanabhan** (1989), p. 197
31   **Reeve/Sullivan** (1990)
32   **Troxler/Blank** (1989); see also section 2.3.

- Mix of process plans, in case a product can be produced by alternative process plans with different workloads at the machines.

- *Components of the FMS*:
  - Type and number of CNC machines
  - Type and number of load/unload stations (setup stations)
  - Type and capacity of the transportation systems for parts and tools
  - Type and number of buffer areas and the storage system
  - Type and capacity of the tool supply system
  - Type and number of pallets and fixtures

- *Layout of the FMS*

- *Type of the computer system and structure of the planning and control system*

- *Number and qualifications of personnel*

An FMS configuration alternative is characterized by a specific *combination of the above decision variables*. From an economic point of view, the *workpiece spectrum* and the *types and numbers of FMS components* (resources) are especially important. Many of these variables are interdependent, for example the type and number of parts to be produced by the FMS determine the type and number of operations to be performed and thus the type and number of machines and the transportation capacities required.

• Constraints

The feasible configurations, i.e. those which satisfy the given constraints, have to be selected from the large number of possible FMS configurations. The constraints are defined by the requirements the system must fulfill. They can be divided into the requirements concerning the *output* and those concerning the *input* of the FMS. In the output of the FMS restrictions are given by the required production volume per unit time, i.e. the production rate, and the diversity of the product types to be manufactured. An input related restriction is set by a limit on the possible investment volume. In general it can be assumed that the relevant restrictions derive from decisions taken on higher hierarchy levels of management.

Aside from restrictions arising from previous planning processes, *technical restrictions* might also apply. They are defined by the technological requirements for manufacturing the given product spectrum as well as by the technological properties of the potential equipment for the system. The latter is especially important, since in most systems the components come from different manufacturers.

Finally, restrictions in space should be mentioned. This in many cases limits available options since an FMS is often integrated into an existing production environment. If it must be installed into an already existing building, only limited space may be available for the new machines, buffer spaces, etc.

It should be clear that many of these aspects can only be treated by or with the help of a technically well trained system planner. In a concrete planning situation, there will exist numerous feasible FMS configurations which could meet all requirements of the given restrictions. From these alternatives, an ordering with respect to the following objectives has to be generated.

• Objectives

With the introduction of an FMS many objectives are pursued, most of which cannot be quantified. In the following, two different classes of objectives are considered. *Original objectives* are those which are pursued through the introduction of an FMS instead of a conventional job shop. *Derived objectives* include those associated with the configuration and those pursued during the planning process, i.e. during the optimization process. The following objectives are mentioned in the literature[33]:

Original objectives:

• Higher adaptability to changes of product type and demand
• Low labor cost
• Higher product quality through more precisely reproducible processes
• Higher productivity through better utilization of resources

Derived objectives pursued during the design of an FMS configuration:

• High production volume and short lead times
• High utilization of resources
• Low work-in-process inventory
• Low investment costs

Obviously the decision problem is one with multiple objectives. Furthermore, many of the above-mentioned goals cannot be quantified. In this book, only a subset of the above objectives is considered. This subset must be integrated later on into the framework of a general planning process[34]. The quantitative procedures for the performance evaluation of an FMS configuration introduced in the remainder of this book are designed with respect to these derived objectives.

2.2. SHORT RANGE PLANNING OF FLEXIBLE MANUFACTURING SYSTEMS

Short range (operational) planning and control governs the details in the sequence of production events in an existing FMS. It has to be integrated into the planning processes for the whole production function in a firm, which is in turn

---

33   **Padmanabhan** (1989); **Troxler/Blank** (1989); **Suresh** (1990)
34   See also section 2.3.

supported by a computerized production planning and control system (PPC system).

2.2.1. Relationship between Short Range Planning for Flexible Manufacturing Systems and Production Planning and Control

2.2.1.1. Production planning and control

A typical production planning and control system works according to a multi-stage, successive planning strategy[35] and is structured as shown in figure (13).

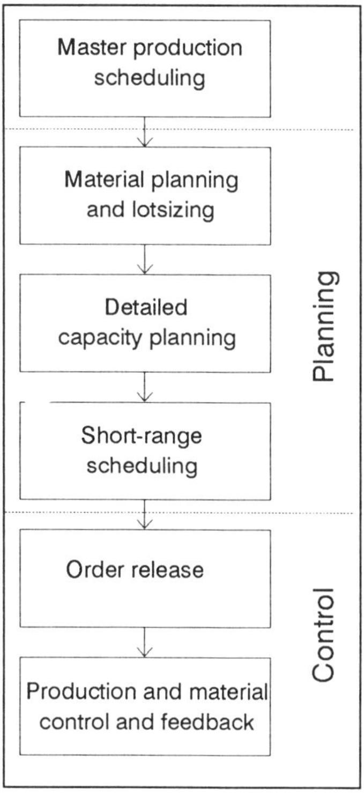

The process of *production planning* is divided into the phases of master production scheduling, material planning and lotsizing, detailed capacity planning, and short-range scheduling. *Production control* can be divided into order release and production and material control and feedback.

The starting point for all planning considerations is the aggregate production plan for the next 1-2 years. During the aggregate planning procedure a compromise between the conflicting goals of a "low inventory" and a "smooth production level" has to be found[36].

Master production scheduling transforms this aggregate information based largely on product families and product groups into disaggregated planning data. Based on detailed product related sales forecasts considering both potential customer orders and the available inventory, the products to be produced are defined according to type, volume and due date. Most available computerized production planning and control systems[37] do not support the aggregate production planning and master production scheduling functions.

Material planning and lotsizing follow the master production scheduling phase. To be able to achieve the planned production volume, material requirements planning determines the amount of raw material, the number of components, and the subassemblies with their respective due dates while considering the inventory on hand over time.

Figure 13: Production planning and control system

---

35   Scheer (1991), p. 19
36   Hax/Candea (1984); Silver/Peterson (1985), pp. 531-573
37   In figure (13) this point is emphasized with the upper dotted line.

Material requirements planning procedures can be either deterministic (based on the product documentation which describes the product structure, i.e. the inter-relationships between components, subassemblies and the finished products) or stochastic (using forecasts derived from historical data of past material require-ments)[38]. *Lotsizing* then aggregates the time-phased requirements into procure-ment or production batches considering the trade-off between inventory and set-up costs (i.e. ordering costs). Production lead times or procurement lead times as well as existing inventory have to be considered.

Dates for beginning and completing production have to be set during the *detailed capacity planning* (capacity requirements planning) for the production orders scheduled in the material requirements planning and lotsizing phase. Here the operation sequences based on technological considerations as well as the planned production lead times are taken into account. It is then reviewed whether or not the available capacity is sufficient to produce the scheduled orders on time. If the available capacity in a given period is overloaded, one of two strategies can be chosen. Either the capacity can be adjusted through measures which are effective in the short-term, or the timing of the production orders can be shifted within the slack times in order to more evenly distribute the workload over time.

The purpose of *short-range scheduling* is to definitively fix the production plan. In this stage the assignment of individual operations and available resources is de-fined. Decisions are also made regarding the sequence of production orders at the individual machines. Operation scheduling is also often considered part of the production control phase. Whether or not that makes sense depends on to what degree planning and control tasks can be taken over by the shop floor per-sonnel. Technical aids which can help in this process include planning boards and, more recently, electronic Leitstands. These offer user-friendly support in the interactive generation of schedules and an interface for the processing of pro-duction control data.

The *production control* phase parallels the processing of the orders. The availa-bility of machinery and material is reviewed during the *order release*. The *order and capacity monitoring* follows the production process in order to be able to react to order changes desired by customers or to interruptions in the production process (e.g. machine breakdowns).

Computer supported PPC systems are the planning core of a computer inte-grated factory. This has been discussed under the term CIM[39] for some time both in industrial practice and in academics. The production planning and control takes on an important role aside from the technical functions (CAD[40], CAP[41], CAQ[42] and CAM[43]) in that the economic efficiency of production stands or falls with the quality of the planning results [see figure (14)].

---

38   **Tempelmeier** (1992b)
39   Computer Integrated Manufacturing; **Scheer** (1991)
40   Computer Aided Design (product planning and design)
41   Computer Aided Planning (operations planning)
42   Computer Aided Quality Control (quality assurance)
43   Computer Aided Manufacturing (machining and assembly)

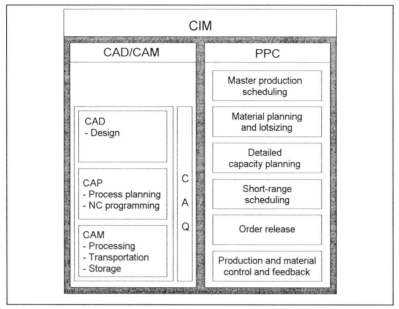

Figure 14: The CIM concept[44]

Between the production planning and control and the technical functions there exist extensive data interconnections which must influence the organization of all production related processes as a prerequisite for the successful realization of the CIM concept in industrial practice[45].

An FMS, as part of the CIM concept and with respect to its technical aspects, can be considered to be an element of the CAM field. The resulting short-term planning problems are part of production planning and control (PPC).

2.2.1.2. Production planning and control in the use of a flexible manufacturing system

The introduction of an FMS has various effects on the production planning and control system. These are not restricted to copying NC programs from the CIM database or to the automated data processing and feedback. From the point of view of the central PPC system, the FMS functions as a self-contained unit. This is in contrast to conventional machine tools. In an FMS *numerous production orders* are processed *simultaneously*, and decidedly smaller orders (lot sizes) can be produced due to *short delays caused by setup changes*. When production of an order is begun on an FMS the completion time can be determined with relatively

---

44   **Hackstein** (1985)
45   **Scheer** (1991)

high accuracy. *Short-term changes* in the lot size or the due date of an order can, for the most part, be realized on an FMS.

Through the introduction of an FMS instead of the conventional job shop, the entire planning process for the central PPC system is simplified. The FMS operates as a decentrally controlled manufacturing isle which only receives order related due dates and production quantities from the PPC system and is supposed to deliver the finished products in time.

Important planning and control tasks are thus transferred from the PPC system to the level of the FMS. For the production planning and control within the FMS, however, a number of *new aspects* can be observed which are not found in conventional job shop production processes:

- The machining centers can carry out numerous different operations without considerable setup time losses. The number of operations which can be carried out at a given machining center at one time is prescribed by the preparation of each machine's tool magazine with tools.

- The tool magazines at the machines can generally accept only a limited number of tools. The number of different workpieces that can be simultaneously processed by an FMS is, therefore, limited. In contrast to the often expressed opinion that a lot size of "1" can be easily realized through the introduction of an FMS, when the tool magazines are limited, processing a group of several identical workpieces is more sensible. In addition, it is important to choose workpieces with common tool requirements.

- For each type of tool there is only a limited number of tools available. This also reduces the routing flexibility that is essentially there but limited by the actual outfitting of the tool magazines.

- The proximity of the different machines and the availability of an automated transportation system make it possible to determine the physical path of a workpiece through the FMS in real time when the current state of the system is precisely known.

- The number of workpieces circulating in an FMS is limited by the number of available pallets. This may lead to occasional idleness at the machines.

- Also the workpiece specific fixtures for connecting the workpieces to the pallets are often only available in limited numbers. Thus, the number of workpieces of a particular type that can circulate in an FMS is restricted for this reason too.

- The use of clamping blocks can make it possible to clamp a number of different workpieces on a single pallet, however the independent mobility of the individual workpieces is thereby reduced.

These facts must be considered in the short-term production planning and control of an FMS. The replacement of a conventional job shop production system with an FMS results on the one hand in an *increased planning complexity*[46]. On the other hand, however, *reductions in the planning complexity* arise due to the improved structure and transparency of the production process. The latter is based on the following observations:

- Since FMS machining centers integrate the technological functions of several conventional machine tools, the number of different machines, and thus the number of planning objects to be considered in the production process, is significantly less than that of conventional job shop production[47].

- The associated reduction in the number of operations to be performed on a single workpiece decreases the number of production stages and thus the number of assignments of orders to specific machines that have to be observed. Here, the result is also a reduction in the problem complexity.

- The integration of the automated production facilities into a computer network improves data processing and provides up to date planning data.

The *increase in planning complexity* affects primarily the *planning process within the FMS*, whereas the *reduction in planning complexity* affects primarily the central *PPC system*. A decentralized organization of the overall production planning and control system in which the FMS acts as a subsystem would, therefore, be advantageous. In a decentralized PPC system, planning is centrally oriented only down to a specific planning level. Further instructions for the decentralized production segments are then derived from the results of the central planning stage. Each production segment is responsible for planning and control within given parameters in that particular segment.

An important question is clearly how to divide the production planning and control responsibilities between the *central* and *decentral* levels. The answer to this question depends on the degree to which workpieces in addition to their processing by the FMS need to be further processed outside of the system. These additional operations can be performed before or after processing inside the FMS, or the FMS processing can be interrupted and a workpiece removed for external processing. In the case of this intermediate external processing[48], workpieces are processed in the FMS, then removed from the system (for surface treatment, for example) and then returned for further processing to the FMS. As the number of operations that have to be carried out outside of the FMS in comparison to the total number of operations performed on a workpiece increases, the need to integrate the production planning of the FMS into the central production planning and control increases as well, and the degree of autonomy of the planning system of the FMS decreases. Thus, the central PPC system must provide for the continuous supply of workpieces, tools and supplementary materials to the FMS, since otherwise idle time resulting from planning errors could result.

---

46 **Stecke/Solberg** (1981a), pp.7-8
47 **Kusiak** (1990), p. 19
48 These intermediate operations often are used for surface treatment, e.g. hardening, galvanizing, painting.

If we look at the planning phases shown in figure (13) it is clearly possible to assign responsibility for the *master production scheduling* and the *material requirements planning* to the central PPC system. In contrast, the assignment of responsibility for *lotsizing* is not as obvious. On the one hand, lotsizing must be an integral part of material requirements and lot size planning. On the other hand, decisions about the order size (the actual use of the FMS-inherent process flexibility) in an FMS are influenced by the pre-release planning. As will be described in more detail in section 5., decisions regarding the release of orders or workpieces in the FMS are influenced to a large degree by the supply of tools to the processing machines. In this context the reduction of setup times and costs, normally considered in the material requirements and lot size planning phase, becomes particularly important. The goal of minimizing inventory costs is generally not significant in an FMS since the number of workpieces (pallets) is practically constant.

It is therefore necessary that the central PPC system, in the context of the material requirements planning, transfer the time-phased production requirements to the FMS without combining them into larger production orders.

If additional production segments exist aside from the FMS in which pre-processing, post-processing, or intermediate-processing of workpieces takes place, or which can even be used as an alternative to FMS production[49]; then *time-phased capacity planning* can be carried out in aggregate form by the central PPC system. At this planning level it is necessary to decide, for example, which orders should be delegated to the conventional workshop and which to the FMS[50]. The results of this planning phase are scheduled orders with planned production quantities and due dates for the manufacturing process. These orders are then assigned to a specific manufacturing segment, such as the FMS. The operation scheduling and the production control for these orders is then carried out in the decentralized planning and control system of the particular manufacturing segment.

The division of responsibilities described above is further supported by the fact that the automated processes performed in an FMS require an integrated scheduling and control. Furthermore, a detailed schedule for the supplying of all the resources necessary to the production process, including the appropriate control data (e.g. NC programs), is necessary in order to prevent possible interruptions in production. Insufficient planning cannot be made up for through improvisation on the part of the shop floor operators as in the case of the conventional job shop. Due to the limited storage capacity, it is no longer possible to make up for production delays resulting from insufficient workload balancing by building up extra stocks.

All of these issues taken together show the necessity for a specific planning and control system that can be directly dedicated to the FMS in the form of a *Leitstand*. The purpose here is to free the central PPC system from subsystem specific coordination and optimization tasks as well as from the administration of basic data. Both of these tasks can be more effectively and more efficiently car-

---

49 This can be a conventional job shop or another FMS.
50 **Avonts/Gelders/Van Wassenhove** (1988); **Liang/Dutta** (1992)

ried out in a decentralized planning concept. Production orders released by the central PPC system would then be transferred to the Leitstand. Data transfer between the Leitstand and the PPC system would be necessary when orders were completed or when the planned due dates could not be realized by the FMS. Such a hierarchical, structured, and decentrally organized production planning and control concept is schematically illustrated in figure (15).

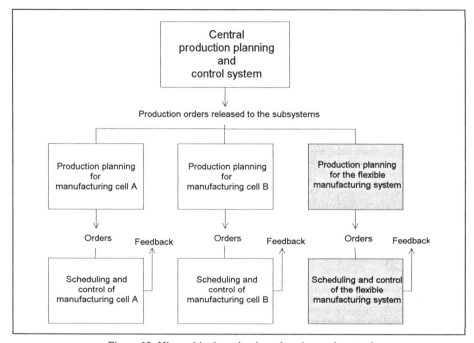

Figure 15: Hierarchical production planning and control

The manufacturing cells shown could include a conventional job shop, a manufacturing cell organized along the principals of group technology, or another FMS[51] that would be used for the processing of another product spectrum.

2.2.2. Planning Phases in the Operation of a Flexible Manufacturing System

Assuming an FMS to be integrated in a hierarchical planning concept as described above, the central planning considerations will end with releasing time-phased requirements which are assigned to one of the manufacturing segments.

---

51 In the literature several concepts of hierarchical planning and control systems for FMSs are proposed. **Warnecke/Kölle** (1979), p. 637; **Suri/Whitney** (1984), pp. 67-68; **Kusiak** (1985a), p. 1062; **Jones/McLean** (1986); **Kusiak** (1986), p. 339; **Van Looveren/ Gelders/Van Wassenhove** (1986), p. 6; **Morton/Smunt** (1986), pp. 155-162; **Villa/Rossetto** (1986); **Sharit/Eberts/Salvendy** (1988); **Solot** (1990b)

In the central PPC system the requirements from different periods are not combined into a larger production order. Instead the net requirements necessary to manufacture a product in an FMS are transferred directly as a fixed production requirement to the FMS. This method is preferred when the FMS supplies the input to a conventional production process, and when it can be assumed that the lost setup time in the conventional processes determines the minimum order size. If the FMS is not integrated into the production process and operates instead as an isolated manufacturing segment, then there is no need for coordination with the other production units controlled by the central PPC system.

2.2.2.1. Pre-release planning

The starting points for the planning and control of an FMS are production orders released by the central production planning and control system. These are characterized by *workpiece identification*, *quantity required*, the earliest *availability date* for the *raw materials* and the *due date* of the order. The release of these orders into the FMS is determined by the planning system of the FMS. The structure of the planning process is represented in figure (16).

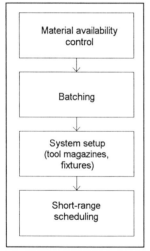

Figure 16: Pre-release planning

In the first stage of this planning process it is necessary to carry out an *availability check* on the raw materials, tools, NC programs, etc. Only after this has been completed are the relevant orders and the corresponding part types for the next planning period known. These, however, cannot generally be manufactured simultaneously in an FMS. This restriction is dependent on limited machine capacity and on the fact that the machines and pallets are provided with workpiece-specific tools and fixtures respectively. An arbitrary release of orders in an FMS would cause difficulties in meeting due dates and a loss of productive time due to unnecessary setup changes. Setups in an FMS can be often carried out parallel to a running operation, but the capacity limits of the tool supply and setup systems have to be observed.

It is, therefore, important to determine when and with which other orders a production order can be released in an FMS. At the same time, it is necessary to determine how the local *tool magazines* will be equipped and how the fixtures will be assigned to the pallets. The problem of order release in an FMS is usually so complex that it is impossible to find the globally optimal solution for problems of practically relevant sizes. In the literature it is therefore suggested that the planning problem be divided into a *batching* phase and a *system setup* phase[52].

Batching[53] involves grouping various orders for common and simultaneous processing in an FMS.

System setup planning describes the process of determining to which of the available identical machines the necessary tools should be provided for processing the batches. Only when the necessary tools have been supplied can the required operations be performed. In this planning stage the degree to which various functionally identical machines should be equipped with the same tool set for a given operation must be determined. The advantage of identically tooled machines being able to easily replace each other becomes clear when a machine breaks down, since the routing flexibility of the workpieces is increased.

At this point the complexity of the pre-release planning for an FMS is apparent. In contrast to job shop manufacturing, there may exist *no predetermined assignment of an operation to a particular machine* since several identical machines may exist in an FMS. A possible assignment is defined only by the availability of the necessary tools. Tool availability is, however, accompanied by certain restrictions. At the same time the capacity utilization must be precisely balanced, since a limited amount of buffer space is available in an FMS. The possibility to provide extra workpiece inventory in order to avoid machine idleness is given only in limited cases.

The assignment of fixtures to the pallets is a further aspect of system setup planning. This too is dependent on batching and tool assignment. Here the number of identical workpieces circulating in the system at any given time is determined.

Following batching and setup planning, the *sequence of the workpiece-release* has to be determined for the orders included in a given batch. It is not sufficient to simply integrate all the orders in a particular batch in one release sequence. Each workpiece of an order has to be identified as a single object and handled separately. The complete release of all workpieces of an order would present the danger of a potentially unequal capacity utilization in that the predetermined production ratios between the part types could not be maintained.

This illustration of the function of pre-release planning shows that the originally high degree of flexibility of an FMS is successively reduced. Thus, the *pre-release planning* stage plays a *key role* in assuring the efficient and effective function of an FMS (prevention of process-dependent idle times, limiting setup time losses, meeting due dates.)

Nof et al.[54] show the importance of batching in a simulation study in which they determine the throughput (number of processed workpieces per unit time) as a function of the number of simultaneously manufactured workpiece types in an FMS [see figure (17)]. The production volume in an FMS progressively sinks be-

---

52 **Suri/Whitney** (1984), pp. 64-65; **Whitney/Gaul** (1985), p. 302; **Kusiak** (1986), pp. 339-340; **Van Looveren/ Gelders/Van Wassenhove** (1986), pp. 9-12; **Bastos** (1988), pp. 232-233; **Kuhn** (1990)

53 Batching must not be confused with the long-term decision problem selecting the part type to be produced in the FMS.

54 **Nof/Barash/Solberg** (1979), pp. 482-483; **Buzacott/Shanthikumar** (1980), p. 344

ginning at a particular number of different workpiece types, i.e with increasing heterogeneity of the workpiece mix. The cause of this phenomenon is found in two opposing developments. On the one hand, more numerous workpiece types can better balance out the different machine requirements and through a more balanced machine workload lead to a higher production rate. On the other hand, the demands on the tool supply system are increased by more diverse workpiece types, and this can cause bottlenecks in the FMS. Since the machines have to be setup more frequently, idle time can result which again leads to a reduction in the throughput.

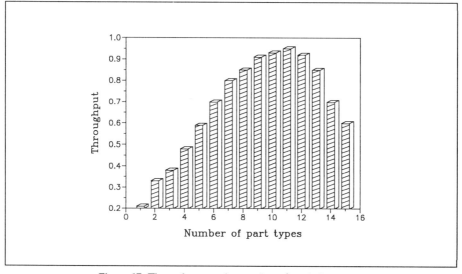

Figure 17: Throughput vs. the number of workpiece types

The tool equipment of the machines also affects the production rate of an FMS. When several machines are equipped with the same set of tools, the number of concurrent workpiece types in an FMS is restricted and thus potentially the production rate as well. At the same time, however, the increased routing flexibility of the workpiece types improves the potential for a high utilization of the identical machines[55]. Aside from these affects the changed tool demand and setup difficulties must be considered.

The assignment of the available fixtures to the pallets determines the relationship of the circulating workpiece types in the system. Here too there can be found an optimal relationship[56], as illustrated in figure (18). All together these relationships underline the importance of pre-release planning for the successful management of an FMS.

55   **Buzacott/Shanthikumar** (1980), p. 344
56   **Nof/Barash/Solberg** (1979), pp. 483-484

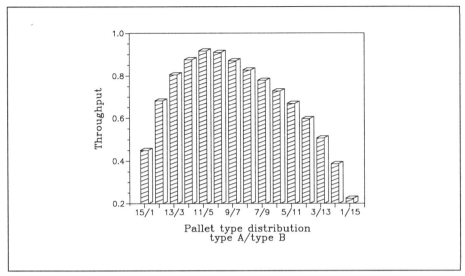

Figure 18: Throughput vs. the distribution of pallets between two workpiece types

2.2.2.2. Scheduling and control

The scheduling and control phase begins immediately after the pre-release planning phase in an FMS [see figure (19)][57]. In the control phase decisions have to be made regarding the spatial and temporal structure of the manufacturing process in an FMS with respect to the current state of the system (including all machines, tools, vehicles, pallets, fixtures and workpieces). It may be possible here to fall back on the order sequence established in the last stage of the pre-release planning. If no such sequence was determined, or if the sequence must be revised due to the current state of the system, it would then be necessary to make a decision about the sequence in the control phase.

For the workpieces circulating in an FMS it is necessary to determine, within the given limitations, which of the required operations are to be carried out by which machine (operational control). A choice of the most appropriate means of transportation is also necessary at this point.

Alongside the decisions which must be made during the operation of the system, the equipment (machines, tools, vehicles, pallets, fixtures) and the progress of the workpieces and orders also has to be monitored. In the case of an interruption in the production process due to a machine breakdown, this becomes important in order to be able to choose among available alternatives to adapt to the new situation.

---

57   **Stecke** (1985), pp. 9-11; **Escudero** (1989)

Various approaches to these planning and control problems can be found in the literature[58]. At this point the approaches to sequencing and operational control will be briefly reviewed, whereas approaches to pre-release planning will be discussed in more detail in section 5.

Sequencing is the last planning phase before actually beginning the production process. Decision models designed for this level assume an empty FMS and attempt to devise a production plan which explicitly allows for the precedence relationships[59] between the operations to be performed on a workpiece. It is further assumed that a fixed assignment of operations to machine tools has been established during the previous planning level. In contrast to the classical job shop scheduling problem, in an FMS the limited buffers must also be considered. *Hitz*[60] suggested a branch-and-bound method for the solution of flow shop scheduling problems (flexible production line, FPL). This method determines periodical release plans with respect to the goal of minimizing idle times at the bottleneck machine[61]. *Erschler et al.*[62] modified and further developed this approach in the context of an heuristic procedure for FMSs.

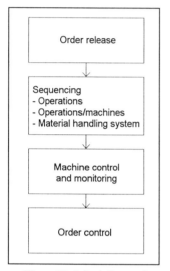

Figure 19: Scheduling and control of an FMS

Sawik[63] suggested a two-level heuristic method for the solution of the FMS sequencing and dispatching problem in which the minimization of lateness is the central objective.

In the *operational control phase* upcoming decisions are normally made on the basis of priority rules. Every order waiting to be processed is assigned a specific priority number that is used to select the next order to be assigned to one of the system's resources. Depending on the information which has been used to calculate the priority number, priority rules can be described as local or global and as static or dynamic. Local rules are derived exclusively from information relating to a particular resource, whereas global rules are based on any relevant information about the state of the entire system. Static rules arise from information that is independent of the particular state of the system at any given time, but dynamic rules, in contrast, process the

58   For an overview see **Buzacott/Yao** (1986); **Van Looveren/Gelders/Van Wassenhove** (1986); **Kusiak** (1986); **Zijm** (1988).
59   This problem is equivalent to the static deterministic job shop scheduling problem. **Baker** (1974); **French** (1982); **Hax/Candea** (1984)
60   **Hitz** (1979), (1980); for a literature review on scheduling problems in flowshops and hybrid flowshops see **Voß** (1993).
61   **Nemhauser/Wolsey** (1988), p. 355
62   **Erschler/Lévêque/Roubellat** (1984); **Erschler/Roubellat/Thuriot** (1985)
63   **Sawik** (1990)

most recent information available regarding the system's state. Dynamic rules can be further distinguished based on whether they include future developments or whether their parameters change only on the basis of past values[64].

Expert, or *knowledge based systems* are the logical extensions of priority rules. In these systems, FMS-specific knowledge based on past experience is stored in a knowledge base in the form of declarative facts and procedural heuristic knowledge (rules). When a decision has to be made, it is possible to explain a certain state of the FMS with the help of the facts and rules known and also to derive a proposal for further action. Some expert systems include a knowledge acquisition component so that the knowledge base can be enlarged through the application of the system as experience grows[65].

Ben-Arieh[66] as well as *Subramanyam and Askin*[67], among others, suggest an expert system for the operational control phase of an FMS. These systems primarily make decisions regarding the application of available priority rules. *Ben-Arieh*'s expert system attempts to evaluate a potential solution alternative in advance with the help of a simulation model.

In contrast to the pre-release phase, the control phase is of less importance. In this phase it is nearly impossibly to compensate for insufficient planning in preceding phases. The primary task of system control must be to maintain the previously set production ratios between the product types and to react to production disturbances, such as breakdowns. This has been shown in a number of different simulation studies[68]. Furthermore, *Co et al.*[69] have shown in the context of a simulation study that priority rules in FMSs are only of limited use. The effectiveness of these rules is restricted due to the limited number of pallets in the system. Only short workpiece queues exist at the relevant decision making points in the system, and thus the number of available alternatives is relatively small.

Further reading for sections 2.1. to 2.2.:

Avonts/Gelders/Van Wassenhove (1988)
Buzacott/Yao (1986)
Kalkunte/Sarin/Wilhelm (1986)
Kuhn (1990)
Mazzola/Neebe/Dunn (1989)
Stecke (1985)
Tempelmeier (1992b)
Tetzlaff (1990), (1992b)
Zijm (1988)

---

64 Hax/Candea (1984), pp. 314-321; Haupt (1989)
65 Applications of expert systems in PPCs are described in Tou (1985); Morton/Smunt (1986).
66 Ben-Arieh (1986)
67 Subramanyam/Askin (1986); see also Schmidt (1989)
68 Nof/Barash/Solberg (1979), pp. 485-487; Stecke/Solberg (1981b), pp. 486-487
69 Co/Jaw/Chen (1988)

2.3. PROBLEMS IN THE ECONOMIC EVALUATION OF A FLEXIBLE MANUFACTURING SYSTEM

It is the intention of this book to present some guidelines for solving the many problems encountered in the configuration and use of an FMS. Among the economic considerations, questions of *economic viability of an FMS* stand out as the most important. Indeed, in industrial practice this question is of supreme significance. It is a difficult one to answer, however, because the economic viability of an FMS is dependent on a number of factors whose future variations may be difficult to predict with any accuracy. Making a general evaluation of the economic viability of an FMS has, nevertheless, been often attempted. A conclusion as to whether or not an FMS presents an economically viable production system alternative in any specific case can only be reached when the *optimal* FMS configuration alternative is known. That means:

> A thorough understanding of the *technical performance capabilities* of the system is the central prerequisite for an *economic evaluation* of any FMS configuration alternative under consideration.

A large number of publications have addressed the problems of economic evaluation of FMSs (or more generally, automated production systems)[70]. For the most part, the same methods used for ranking other investment proposals can also be used in the evaluation of the economic viability of an FMS. In that these have been discussed in detail in the *finance and investment literature*, only those procedures suggested for or actually used in the evaluation of FMSs will be briefly reviewed here.

With respect to the decision situation, considerable emphasis is laid on the *time aspect* of the decision and the *degree of uncertainty* of the available planning data in a particular scenario. Figure (20) illustrates how the various procedures used for the economic evaluation of an FMS can be differentiated.

a) *Single-level procedures* supporting a one time decision for or against an FMS design alternative

 - Dynamic investment analysis under certainty

   The classical dynamic procedures for the evaluation of isolated investment proposals (the present value method, the internal rate of return method, the annuity method) are based on the characterization of an FMS design alternative by a deterministically known time *series of payments* (net cash flows). The payments are made comparable with one another in that they are all discounted with respect to a particular point in time, generally time 0. Procedures of this kind are commonly used in practice. The present value (with respect to time 0) of an investment proposal described by a series of payments is given by equation (1).

---

70   **Canada/Sullivan** (1989); **Liberatore** (1990); **Swamidass/Waller** (1990); **Krinsky/Miltenburg** (1991)

$$K_0 = \sum_{t=0}^{T} e_t \cdot (1+r)^{-t} \tag{1}$$

annual discount rate

net cash flow in period t

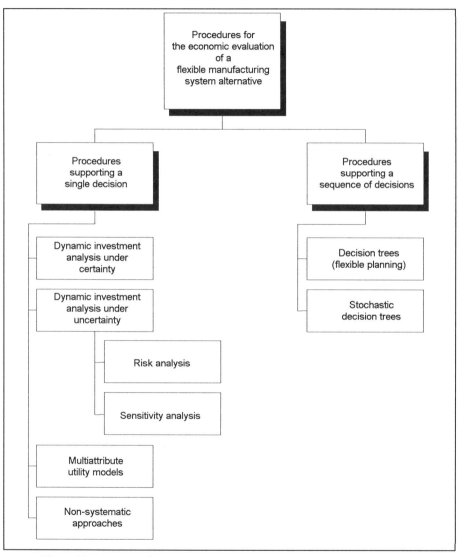

Figure 20: Procedures for the economic evaluation of an FMS design alternative

The components of the series of cash flows [initial investment, e_0; net cash flow during period t of the investment project, e_t ($t = 1,...,T-1$); salvage value e_T] are described by their expected values.

In addition to the challenges associated with assumptions about the *accurateness of future expectations*, the estimation of a period's net cash flow is also difficult. This is primarily due to the fact that an investment project (i.e. the flexible manufacturing system) affects the firm both vertically and horizontally over time in ways that are difficult to isolate.

Horizontal effects over time arise from the fact that an FMS does not exist in a vacuum, rather it is embedded in a company-wide production strategy whose goal, as understood by the CIM concept, is to increase the degree of automation of production. It is, therefore, quite difficult to separate all the positive, and possibly also negative, consequences resulting directly from a specific FMS design alternative.

Vertical effects over time arise from the fact that an investment in an FMS often results in further follow-up investments at a later time, e.g. the inclusion of new machining centers in order to enlarge the scope of the production possibilities of the FMS. Investment alternatives which develop over time can, therefore, not be considered independent of each other. The case of the installation of a "small" FMS with limited capabilities which can be expanded later, for example, is not considered in the classical investment analysis procedures.

- Procedures for investment analysis under uncertainty

When using these procedures it is taken explicitly into consideration that the components of the series of payments related to the FMS investment project are not known with certainty. However, it is understood that they are determined by stochastic variables whose future effects at the point in time at which the investment decision has to be realized are not predictable with certainty. For example, in general the future earnings from a product manufactured in an FMS are not precisely known. At most, rough estimates of the expected value of the turnover in a particular time period may be available. If the economic consequences of an FMS investment project are evaluated using only deterministic methods of investment appraisal, then a key aspect of an investment decision is neglected: the risk. The degree of riskiness involved in a particular FMS proposal, however, is generally not unimportant to the decision maker.

- *Risk analysis*

Numerous methods have been proposed in the literature which attempt to take the condition of uncertainty into account. According to the concept of *risk analysis*[71] the development of an investment project over time is considered as a stochastic process - as a series of realizations of stochastic variables - such as the time series of the cash in-

---

71   Hertz (1964); Miltenburg (1987); Reeve/Sullivan (1990)

flows and outflows associated with the installation and operation of an FMS. Each stochastic variable is assigned a probability distribution. With the help of analytic enumeration methods, or more often with the use of a computer (Monte Carlo) simulation, numerous realizations of the stochastic process are generated. Each realization represents a possible form of the payment series of the observed investment project. After discounting the elements of the payment series and statistically analyzing the individual present values, a *probability distribution of the present value of the project* is calculated. With respect to the subjective risk preferences of the decision maker, this can be used to help in the evaluation of the investment project.

A simple example may serve to introduce the basic principle of risk analysis more clearly. The object of the investigation is assumed to be an FMS configuration which involves investment expenses with different degrees of certainty. In addition to those outlays for FMS hardware that are deterministically fixed in the buying contract with the FMS supplier, the amount of outlays for FMS software and training costs for personnel cannot be precisely forecasted. It is assumed that the sum of the payments due at time 0 will be equal to $12.8 million ($14 million, $15.3 million) with a probability of 20% (60%, 20%). It is furthermore expected that with the products produced by the FMS, stochastic earnings will result that depend on the production quantities and the selling prices of the products. The turnover is governed by the market price, which is expected to be $100 ($110) with a probability of 80% (20%), and the quantity sold. These are both determined by conditions in the marketplace. It is assumed that with a probability of 50% (50%) 50,000 (60,000) units of the product could be sold. There are also only subjective estimates available for the variable unit costs (especially material costs). Thus it is assumed that the variable unit costs will be $10 ($15, $25) with a probability of 20% (60%, 20%). It is also assumed that the useful life of an FMS in the defined configuration is a random variable due to the unknown length of the product life-cycle. It is assumed to be equally probable that this be 5, 6, 7 or 8 years. After the end of the useful life certain components of the FMS are removed. Some parts (e.g. foundations, supply and removal systems for coolants and waste materials, engines at the machining centers, load/unload stations, pallets, and fixtures) are retained and reintegrated into a newly installed FMS. This can save between $400,000 and $600,000 in new investments. An annual discount rate of 10% is assumed for this example. It is clearly important to note that the decision maker is not only interested in the size of the *expected* present value, but also in the probability that the present value will be negative.

The example described above can be modelled with the help of a gene-ral-purpose simulation language. In this case SIMAN IV is used[72]. The complete simulation model is presented in the figures (21) and (22). The analysis and evaluation of the simulation model on a PC results in the probability distribution for the present value of the investment project depicted in figure (23). As can be observed, the probability that the present value will be positive - that the FMS will be economi-cally advantageous - is relatively high. The expected present value is $5.368 million. There does exist a remote, though possibly important, risk that the project will have a negative present value. If this would happen, the FMS project would not be the best option in comparison to possible alternative investments at the assumed interest rate.

Model definition:

```
BEGIN;
;
; Risk analysis of an FMS
;
START    CREATE:1,1000;
;
; Initial outlay
;
         ASSIGN:PRESVAL=0;
         ASSIGN:AO=DISC(0.2,128, 0.8,140, 1.0,153);
         ASSIGN:PRESVAL=PRESVAL-AO*100000;
;
; Useful life
;
         ASSIGN:UTILTIME=DISC(0.25,5, 0.5,6, 0.75,7, 1.0,8);
         ASSIGN:TIME=UTILTIME;
GOON     ASSIGN:TIME=TIME-1;
         BRANCH,1:
            IF,TIME.LE.0,FINI:
            ELSE,NEWTIME;
;
; Compute the net cash flow of the actual time period
;
NEWTIME  ASSIGN:QUANT=DISC(0.5,50000, 1.0,60000);
         ASSIGN:PRICE=DISC(0.8,100, 1.0,110);
         ASSIGN:COST=DISC(0.2,10, 0.8,15, 1.0,25);
;
; Compute present value of the net cash flow
;
         ASSIGN:PRVOLD=(QUANT*(PRICE-COST))/(1.1)**TIME;
         ASSIGN:PRESVAL=PRESVAL+PRVOLD:NEXT(GOON);
;
FINI     ASSIGN:SALVAL=DISC(0.8,400000,1.0,600000)/(1.1)**UTILTIME;
         ASSIGN:PRESVAL=PRESVAL+SALVAL;
         TALLY:1,PRESVAL:DISPOSE;
END;
```

*Figure 21: Risk analysis with a SIMAN IV simulation model
(model definition)*

72   **Pegden/Shannon/Sadowski** (1990); **Tempelmeier** (1990); see also section 3.3.

Experimental frame:

```
BEGIN;
PROJECT,FMS;
TALLIES:1,Present Worth,1;
REPLICATE,1;
VARIABLES:PRESVAL:COST:PRVOLD:UTILTIME:TIME:PRICE:QUANT:AO:SALVAL;
END;
```

*Figure 22: Risk analysis with a SIMAN IV simulation model
(experimental frame)*

The decision maker has to decide now if he or she is prepared to accept the limited though ever present risk of a possible loss after the realization of the FMS investment project. The ability to quantify this risk is the advantage offered by a risk analysis. However, the quality of the results of a risk analysis are obviously dependent upon the accuracy of the assumptions regarding the input probability distributions.

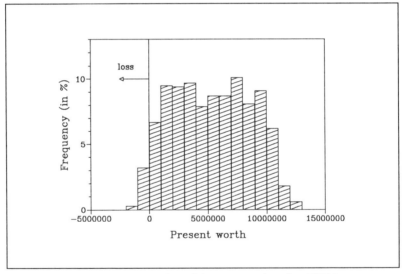

*Figure 23: Probability distribution of the present value of an FMS investment
project*

Sensitivity analysis

A simpler and - due to the limited computing power needed - generally less costly method is a *sensitivity analysis*. Here the key factors affecting the success of an investment project are considered as parameters and varied by the analyst, and their effect on the target quantities is measured. A sensitivity analysis defines ranges within which the key quantities may vary without forcing a revision of the basic decision for or against the project. Sensitivity analysis can thus be used to determine *critical values* for the central factors affecting the success of an investment. In order to reduce the dependency on the accuracy of input probability distributions, the problem common in risk analysis, a sensitivity analysis and a risk analysis may be combined. In this case, the input data (the probability distributions) to the risk analysis are systematically varied, and their influence on the resulting distribution is calculated. In this way, the sensitivity of the present value distribution in reaction to variations of assumptions represented by the input data can be analyzed.

- Methods built on *the basic model of multi-attribute utility theory*[73]

  These methods support the evaluation of individual FMS alternatives with regard to a particular set of objectives and then compile the results in a *results matrix*. The multidimensional results are then transformed on a point scale. Each FMS alternative is then evaluated by an aggregate score. Since scoring methods are relatively easy to understand, such procedures are frequently both suggested and applied in management practice[74].

- *Non-theoretical methods*

  Some non-theoretical methods use a *balance of arguments* approach. Here all the advantages and disadvantages of a particular FMS configuration alternative are listed in tabular form so that they may be easily compared. Such a balance of arguments, however, can be quite long. The balance of arguments results in a numerical superiority of either the positive (assets) or negative (liabilities) arguments. The central advantage of a balance of arguments lies, as is the case for most checklists, in the clear manner in which the many objectives associated with a particular investment alternative are presented. This makes a rough ranking of FMS alternatives possible. It is, however, important to note the particular difficulties associated with having to weight each of the positive and negative arguments.

b) *Multi-level, sequential methods* which explicitly consider the possibility of making successive decisions (accounting for vertical interdependencies over time)

This group of methods centers around the fact that an investment decision has long term consequences and is often only the beginning of a series of decisions that have to be made in the aftermath of the initial decision. It is, for example, possible to install a "small" FMS when future demand growth is unknown and then decide later whether or not the system should be expanded depending on developments in the marketplace. One method of handling

73   **Reeve/Sullivan** (1990)
74   **Canada/Sullivan** (1989)

such sequences of decisions under conditions of uncertainty is the concept of flexible planning that can be applied using *Magee's* decision tree.

- Flexible planning with the decision tree[75]

A decision tree is a graph with an arborescent structure comprising two kinds of nodes. A square node represents a decision, and a circular node represents a chance event outside of the control of the decision maker. The nodes are arranged so as to clearly emphasize the temporal structure of the sequence of decisions. The decision tree includes information on both the expected future developments in the relevant environment and on issues which may arise at different points in time as the decision making process evolves. Figure (24) shows a decision tree for a case in which at time 0 a decision must be made to install a large FMS immediately or to install a smaller system and wait to see how product demand develops. Following the decision in favor of the small FMS an option is made available, at time 1 to expand the system *if there has been a positive development in demand by that time*.
As can be seen in the decision tree shown, the investment project "FMS" beginning at the decision node 1 could follow different development paths to the four different end-points B, C, D, and E.

Path	Description
1-A-B:	At time 0 the small FMS is installed; since only limited demand develops, no further decision is necessary: end-point B.
1-A-2-C:	At time 0 the small FMS is installed; although significant demand develops, it is decided at time 1 not to expand the system: end-point C.
1-A-2-D:	At time 0 the small FMS is installed; since significant demand develops, at time 1 it is decided to expand the system: end-point D.
1-E:	At time 0 a large FMS is installed. No further decisions are necessary: end-point E.

The presentation of the problem using a decision tree makes it clear that the potential success of an investment project depends both on the decisions made and on developments in its relevant environment, i.e. the demand for the products to be produced with the FMS under consideration. Each path from node 1 to the end-points B, C, D and E represents a combination of the possible alternative courses of action and the developments in the environment.
A probability distribution for the net cash flows (discounted from time 2) that accrue during the development of the project is assigned to each of the four end-points. The level of these payments is, of course, determined by the development of the environment and by the particular decisions made. The *roll-back method* is one good way to evaluate the decision tree.

---

75   **Magee** (1964); **Mao** (1968); **Whitehouse** (1973), pp. 198-202; **Canada/Sullivan** (1989), pp. 341-352

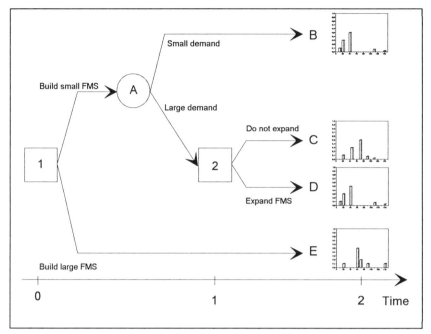

Figure 24: Decision tree

- Stochastic decision tree[76]

A decision tree such as that described here can only be used when the points in time at which decisions have to be made are deterministically fixed. Furthermore, the graphic representation can become quite inconvenient when too many environmental factors are considered. In both cases, a *risk analysis* could be used in conjunction with the decision tree[77] in which the intervals between different events are presented in a model as stochastic variables.

The concepts based on investment theory described above all attempt to summarize quantitatively the *financial effects* (cash inflows and outflows) of an FMS alternative. During the early stages of the planning process the desired production quantity is fixed, and the optimal FMS configuration - the one with the lowest investment costs - that can produce this desired quantity is chosen. In order to find the best configuration, however, it is necessary to have methods available to evaluate the capabilities of each of the FMS alternatives considered. In section 3. several different methods and models will be presented that can be used to accomplish this task.

76   **Miltenburg** (1987)
77   **Hespos/Strassmann** (1965); **Whitehouse** (1973), pp. 224-228; **Canada/Sullivan** (1989), pp. 356-357

Aside from the methods available for the performance evaluation of a *given* FMS configuration, there exist also decision models that can help a system planner determine the design alternatives which should be more carefully studied from among the large set of technically possible FMS configurations. This is done simply by evaluating the quality of the different FMS alternatives with respect to a *specific partial objective*. Methods of this kind are presented in section 4.

In the following, it is assumed that the decision to install an FMS is a *multi-criteria decision*[78]. It is generally characterized by a large number of FMS alternatives that must be evaluated. This evaluation is carried out based on a system of quantifiable and non-quantifiable, monetary and non-monetary objectives. The developments in the relevant environment are uncertain. At best only subjective estimations of probabilities are available. Taking into consideration all the relevant objectives, the optimal FMS alternative has to be found.

An FMS alternative can be explicitly formulated by a system planner. However, it could also be the result of a pre-optimization process. In this case an optimization model is used to choose from a set of FMS alternatives implicitly defined by a system of constraints to be met that alternative that optimizes a specific partial objective function.

The techniques for performance evaluation and the determination of the "optimal" system configuration presented in the following sections can either be used for the evaluation of a *given FMS alternative* or for finding the best of a number of FMS alternatives in terms of a *quantifiable goal*. Both groups of approaches are building blocks in an integrated design and evaluation process in which all criteria relevant to an overall evaluation of an FMS are taken into consideration.

The structure of a multi-criteria decision problem under uncertainty can be presented in a three-dimensional matrix in which the dimensions represent *alternatives, objectives, and environmental states* [see figure (25)]. The future state of the relevant environment can evolve in different ways. Each possible development in the environment is represented by an environmental state U_k which may occur with a known probability $P\{U_k\}$. For each state the effects of the FMS alternative under consideration with respect to the desired (qualitative and quantitative) objectives Z_j are summarized in a *results matrix*.

The *performance evaluation models* to be presented in section 3. can be used to fill in *individual elements of the results matrix*. In this case the element e_{ijk} of the results matrix could represent the average production rate (column j) of the FMS alternative A_i (row i) that is achieved when it is assumed that in the environmental state U_k a specific quantity and type of product mix is produced in the FMS. The calculation of the resulting quantity can be extremely complicated. When objectives cannot be quantified, an FMS alternative must be judged subjectively.

---

78   An overview over multi-criteria decision approaches for automated production systems is provided by **Canada/Sullivan** (1989).

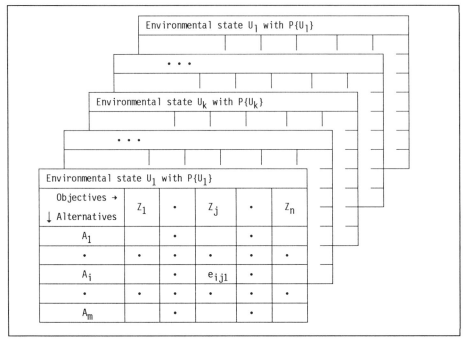

Figure 25: Three-dimensional results matrix

The *optimization models* described in section 4. can be used to reduce the number of FMS alternatives explicitly included in the results matrix (rows in the results matrix) through a pre-selection process.

Further reading for section 2.3.:

Canada/Sullivan (1989)
Kakati/Dhar (1991)
*Krinsky/*Miltenburg (1991)
Liberatore (1990)
Meredith/Suresh (1986)
Miltenburg (1987)
Miltenburg/Krinsky (1987)
Stam/Kuula (1991)
Suresh/Meredith (1985)

3. MODELS FOR THE PERFORMANCE EVALUATION OF AN FMS CONFIGURATION

After having analyzed the decision problems associated with the introduction and use of an FMS in section 2., now the methods available for the *performance evaluation* of an FMS will be discussed. In the literature these methods are mainly described in the context of *configuring* an FMS (the first-time installation or expansion of an FMS). In recent years there has been an increasing number of proposals to use these performance evaluation models to evaluate the feasibility of a short-term production plan[79]. Due to the dominance of long-term issues, however, these will be emphasized in the following presentation.

Before the evaluation of a flexible manufacturing system and a firm's decision about its installation, numerous issues related to the specific technical design and dimensions of the FMS have to be addressed. When reviewing the entire mix of products (workpiece spectrum) produced by a firm, it is important first to consider, on the basis of *technical criteria*, which product types would be appropriate for processing in the planned FMS. Such an analysis can often result in quite a large number of product types[80]. Those product types which also satisfy the relevant *economic criteria* for processing in an FMS must then be selected from this group. Economic considerations are influenced by the workload imposed on the individual machines through the assignment of specific product types and by the resulting effects on the other FMS components.

It is possible that a particular product type could *technically* be produced on the planned FMS with the appropriate special tools and machines, but that it is *economically* not favorable. This would apply when the product type is rarely produced and the special tools and machines cannot be used for other product types and would therefore be low utilized. Thus it may be more sensible to produce such a product in a conventional job shop.

Theoretically, the components of an FMS described in section 1.2. could be combined in any of a large number of FMS configurations. However, not every combination can offer the required level of performance, i.e. not every combination is capable of producing the planned production quantity. On the other hand, not every combination that is technically capable of performing up to standard can be considered advantageous with respect to the investment volume and the operating costs. Many industrial users have already had to learn these lessons the hard way.

Thus when introducing a new FMS an appropriate configuration must be chosen that satisfies both the technical and economic *requirements*. These requirements

---

79 See **Kuhn** (1990), who uses a closed queueing network model to approximate the makespan of a batch in the pre-release planning stage.

80 **Kiran/Schloffer/Hawkins** (1989)

can be divided into those associated with the input side (*operating costs and capital expenditures*) and those associated with the output side (e.g. *production quantity*) of the FMS. The configuration which best satisfies the objectives of the introduction of the FMS can then be chosen from the set of defined and evaluated alternatives.

A variety of approaches and models are available to support this decision process [see figure (26)]. The various approaches can be classified into those which assess a given FMS alternative (*performance evaluation models*) and those which generate new configuration alternatives (*optimization models*). The generating process is governed by an objective function, but it must use some method of evaluation as well.

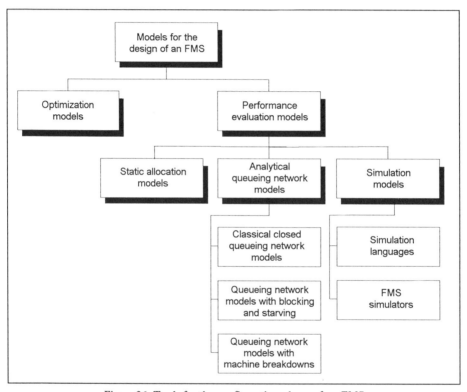

Figure 26: Tools for the configuration phase of an FMS

The evaluative approaches can be subdivided into static allocation models, analytical models based on queueing theory, and simulation models. *Static allocation models* neglect the queueing phenomena arising in an FMS. Instead, the bottleneck in the system is identified, and the performance of the other system components is derived from the limited performance of the bottleneck. In contrast, both queueing models and simulation models are able to analyze the queueing processes that arise from the dynamic relationships between workpieces and the resources of the FMS. The approaches based on *analytical queueing theory* compute in a finite number of steps the key parameters needed for the performance evaluation of an FMS. This process is based on theoretical results from queueing theory, especially from the theory of closed *queueing networks*. A *simulation* model attempts to present a more or less detailed picture of the FMS alternative under consideration and to mimic and observe the dynamic performance of the system over time. The relevant evaluation criteria (average flow time of the workpieces, frequency distributions of queue lengths) are then derived from these dynamic observations. Simulation approaches can be subdivided into general *simulation languages* and special purpose *FMS simulators*. While simulation languages allow the user to build an unlimited variety of different models, FMS simulators are pre-structured programs designed specifically for the simulation of FMSs. In order to use a simulator only a small number of parameters describing the particular FMS to be simulated must be specified by the analyst.

Queueing models are distinguished based on the level of detail which is used to describe the characteristics peculiar to a given FMS. The *classical (product-form) closed queueing network* model (CQN model) is of fundamental importance. This model is based on several key assumptions which may not hold in industrial FMS practice. Whereas the assumption of exponentially distributed processing times does not pose severe problems, the assumption of *limited local buffers* does. However, several queueing theory based approaches are available which allow for the fact that *blocking* and *starving* situations may occur in many FMSs due to limited local workpiece buffers at the machines, and that the automated components of the FMS will sometimes *fail*. In addition, specialized approaches exist which take into account the availability of a separate tool supply system[81].

Evaluative approaches play an important role in optimization in that they provide the basis for the *ranking of different feasible solutions*. Optimization models determine the *optimal FMS configuration* in terms of the relevant objectives through a finite (preferably small) number of computational steps. The idea is essentially to evaluate (explicitly or implicitly) and rank a series of feasible FMS configuration alternatives. Here again one can distinguish between the *mathematical optimization* approaches and those which are based on concepts of *artificial intelligence* (knowledge-based or expert systems).

The various *mathematical optimization* approaches proposed in the literature cover a wide range of different decision variables. An algorithmic optimization procedure, however, can often only be used with a model representation of an FMS that has some well-behaved mathematical characteristics. For example, a necessary pre-requisite to finding an optimal solution to a problem is often that the objective function have no local optima.

In contrast to the mathematical optimization methods, the concepts of *artificial intelligence* offer the FMS planner nothing more than support in finding the best path to an optimal solution. They offer an environment within which proposals for individual FMS variations can be further investigated. The proposals are

---

81   **Tetzlaff** (1992a)

based on a collection of knowledge, stored in a *knowledge base*, of the basic relationships between the decision variables and the objective criteria. This knowledge is stored in the form of *rules* which refer to the characteristics of FMS and
their interdependencies. An example of such a rule could read, "*When* the utilization of all the machines and the transportation system in the FMS is less than
80% *and* the production rate is to be maximized, *then* increase the number of
pallets". If the system planner accepts this advice he or she must re-evaluate the
changed FMS configuration and continue the dialog with the expert system, if
necessary. This interactive process of searching for the best FMS configuration is
not an exception since it also requires methods for calculating the quantitative
performance characteristics of the FMS. Current developments suggest that expert systems which largely automate the step-by-step search for the optimal FMS
will emerge[82].

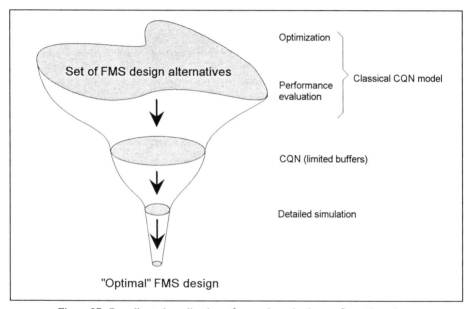

Figure 27: Coordinated application of procedures in the configuration phase

Whether an optimization model is applied, an expert system is used, or an expe-
rienced system planner chooses a path toward the optimal FMS the same prerequisite remains central: a quick and precise evaluation has to be made as to
whether a certain configuration alternative can satisfy the relevant performance
criteria. The entirety of section 3. is dedicated to this question. *Analytical models*
for rapid performance estimations that allow increasingly precise evaluations of a

---

82   **O'Keefe** (1986); **Mellichamp/Wahab** (1987); **Floss/Talavage** (1990); **Mellichamp/Kwon/Wahab** (1990); **Wang/Bell** (1992)

real FMS will be treated first. Directly thereafter the use of *simulation models* as instruments for the detailed investigation of an FMS configuration is described.

The evaluation procedures that will be presented in this book are intended to complement each other in a successive planning process [see figure (27)]. In the early stages of the planning process it is possible to use performance evaluation procedures that can quickly provide a rough estimation of an FMSs performance. It thus becomes possible to eliminate a large number of non-promising configuration alternatives early on with relatively little computational effort. Such procedures are often based on the classical closed queueing network model (CQN model). For the most part, the optimization models presented in section 4. would be appropriate for this purpose.

As the planning process continues there will remain progressively fewer FMS configurations that have to be investigated in more detail. Those alternatives still considered to be good candidates towards the end of the process can be analyzed in detail with the help of a simulation model. In order to maintain a high degree of efficiency in the planning process, it is necessary that unsuitable alternatives be identified and rejected as early as possible in order to prevent the loss of time through unnecessarily detailed investigations.

3.1. ANALYTICAL MODELS FOR THE PERFORMANCE EVALUATION OF AN FMS CONFIGURATION

Analytical models for the performance evaluation of an FMS are based on models and methods taken from queueing theory. Queueing problems arise when "customers" make demands on "service facilities" without exactly synchronizing the arrival process with the service process[83]. The "customers" in an FMS are the pallets on which the workpieces are fixed. The service facilities are the machines, load/unload stations, etc. A queue arises when the intervals between the customer arrivals and the service times are stochastic or when service times are deterministic but vary significantly for different workpieces. The latter is normally the case in an FMS.

A *queueing system* consists of the following components [see figure (28)]:

- A *calling source* from which customers arrive.

- A *waiting line* in which the customers can wait until they are processed. The order in which the customers will be serviced follows certain ranking criteria (service discipline).

- A *service system* (service channel) which can include one or more service facilities.

---

[83] A good introduction to queueing theory is given by **Taha** (1989).

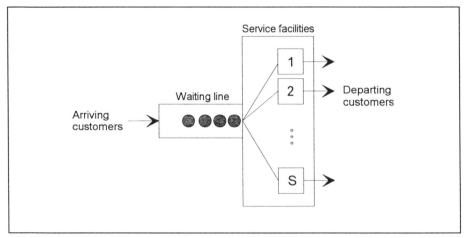

Figure 28: Components of a queueing system

The components of a queueing system can all take different forms. The *calling source*, for example, can be described in various ways according to the character- istics of the customer reservoir (limited, unlimited), customer arrival (individuals, groups), arrival behavior (can be influenced, cannot be influenced), interarrival time (deterministic, stochastic), or customer access (conditional unconditional). Similar distinctions can be made for *waiting lines* and *service facilities*. A queueing model is designed to calculate the key parameters of a queueing system as defi- ned by the above-mentioned characteristics. The *Kendall/Lee/Taha*-notation in the form (a/b/c):(d/e/f) is commonly used to describe the characteristics of a queueing system[84]. The parameters used in this notation include the arrival time distribution (a), the service time distribution (b), the number of parallel servers (c), the service discipline (d), the maximum number of customers allowed in the system (in service and waiting) (e), and the customer reservoir (f). One particular queueing model used in connection with the analysis of queueing networks is the M/M/c-model. In this model the interarrival times and the service times are ex- ponentially distributed (M) and c service facilities work parallel with one another, all being supplied by the same queue. {FCFS[85], ∞, ∞} is assumed to re- present the parameters d, e, and f. The most interesting characteristics to observe in such a queueing system include the length of the queue, the queueing delay and a customer's flow time.

Models for the evaluation of the performance of an FMS are often based on the theory of *closed queueing networks*. This theory is relatively well developed in its application to the configuration of computer systems[86]. Models of this kind are applied to investigate the *stationary* behavior of a closed queueing network. *Jack-*

84   **Taha** (1989), p. 608
85   First-Come-First-Served
86   For computer performance evaluation see **Bruell/Balbo** (1980); **Lazowska/Zahorjan/Graham/Sevcik** (1984)

son[87] was one of the first researchers to analyze queueing networks. He showed that, under certain conditions, the stationary probability distribution of "customers" at the nodes (stations) in an *open queueing network*, $P\{\underline{n}\}$, can be represented by the product of state probabilities of the individual nodes, $P_m\{n_m\}$[88]. It is thus possible to analyze the individual nodes of the network independently of one another with the help of an M/M/c-queueing model[89] and to multiply the resulting state probabilities:

$$P\{\underline{n}\}=P\{n_1,n_2,\dots,n_M\}=P_1\{n_1\}\cdot P_2\{n_2\}\cdot\dots\cdot P_M\{n_M\} \tag{2}$$

The form of the equation (2) is called a *product form*. *Gordon and Newell*[90] considered a *closed queueing network* and showed that here too the probability distribution of the "customers" at the nodes could be described by the product of station specific factors $f_m(n_m)$ (m = 1,...,M)[91]. Since the number of customers is constant, $N = \Sigma_m n_m$, in a closed system, the individual factors are related to each other through an integrating quantity called the normalization constant, g(N,M) [see equation (3)]. The normalization constant assures that the sum of the probabilities of the number of customers being at the nodes of the network is exactly equal to one.

$$P\{\underline{n}\}=P\{n_1,n_2,\dots,n_M\} = \frac{1}{g(N,M)}\cdot f_1\{n_1\}\cdot f_2\{n_2\}\cdot\dots\cdot f_M\{n_M\} \tag{3}$$

Buzen[92] developed the concept of the closed queueing network further by introducing a central server through which a customer must pass every time it moves through the system.

Solberg[93] was the first to use the *classical* model of a closed queueing network for the analysis of a flexible manufacturing system. His work provides the basis for the following presentation.

3.1.1. Performance Evaluation of an FMS with the Classical Closed Queueing Network Model (CQN Model)

3.1.1.1. The classical CQN model for universal pallets

Consider the representation of an FMS as a classical closed queueing network model (CQN model). This representation was first used by *Solberg* and implemented in a computer program that has become widely known as *CAN-Q*[94]. The

---

87   **Jackson** (1957)
88   **Bruell/Balbo** (1980) p. 14
89   **Gross/Harris**(1985), pp. 229-236; **Taha** (1989)
90   **Gordon/Newell** (1967); **Gross/Harris** (1985), pp. 236-243
91   The factors $f_m(n_m)$ are defined in section 3.1.1.1.2.
92   **Buzen** (1973)
93   **Solberg** (1977); see also **Stecke/Solberg** (1981a). For a short overview of closed queueing network models applied to FMSs see **Buzacott/Yao** (1986); **Buzacott/Shanthikumar** (1993).
94   A version of the FORTRAN program is reprinted in **Leimkühler** (1984).

FMS is modelled as a set of M interconnected single-stage queueing systems (stations). A station includes one or more *service facilities* (processing machinery, load/unload stations, measuring devices, vehicles, etc.) and a *waiting room* with *unlimited* capacity [figure (29)].

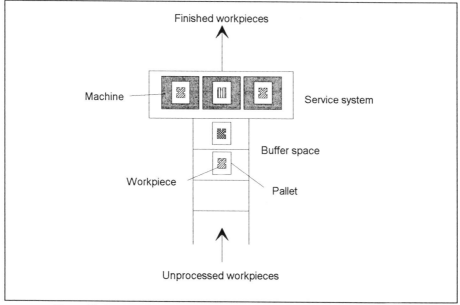

Figure 29: Station of an FMS, represented as a single-stage queueing system

The network considered is composed of several such single-stage queueing systems. It is *closed* in the sense that at any given time precisely *N universal pallets* are circulating inside the system. A *universal pallet* is one that is equipped so as to be able to transport all the different workpiece types being processed in the FMS. *Special pallets*, on the other hand, are capable of transporting only a limited set of the workpiece spectrum. Special pallet types are often distinguished by their dimensions or by the fixtures associated with them[95].

Figure (30) shows a representation of an FMS as a closed queueing network. The stations 1 to (M-1) include the processing machinery and the setup areas (load/unload stations which are the physical entrance and exit of the system). Every station includes one or more servers (machines, setup areas, vehicles). Identical machines of a particular type are considered to be part of one station even if they are physically located far apart. As far as the CQN model is concerned, the only uniting characteristic is that they are supplied from the same queue.

---

95   The CQN model for special pallets will be described in section 3.1.1.2.

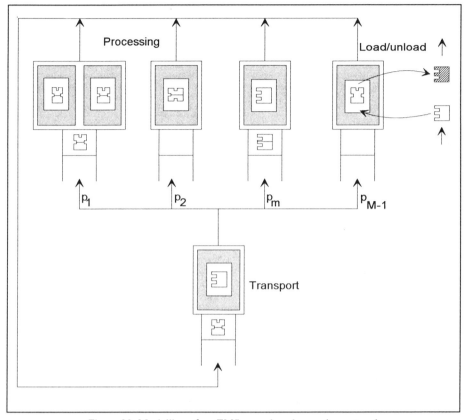

Figure 30: Modelling of an FMS as a closed queueing network

The *material flow system* is also considered to be a station (M). This station has a special function in that it takes over the roll of a *central server* in the closed queueing network. This means that after each individual operation at a machine the transportation system is activated. When a workpiece passes one time through the network while completing an operation it includes both *a transportation process* and an *operation* at a processing machine (or at a setup area). The production rate of the transportation system (the number of transported workpieces per unit time) is thus the sum of the production rates of all the machining stations and setup stations. "Customers" in the queueing network are the *pallets* on which the workpieces are mounted. The workpieces themselves do not appear in a representation of an FMS as a closed queueing network. They are simply assumed to be present on the pallets.

The quantities p_m (m = 1,2,...,M-1) represent the pallets' relative arrival frequencies at the individual stations in an FMS after completing a transportation process. They arise from the process plans of the product types[96] and from the planned production quantities.

As soon as a workpiece has been fully processed (when it has been removed from the pallet at an load/unload station) it is taken out of the FMS and immediately replaced by a new workpiece. This happens without a time lag since the time for removing the workpiece from the pallet has already been accounted for in the load time (see below). A necessary prerequisite to the smooth functioning of this process is that new workpieces be available at all times. A sufficiently sized storage area for unprocessed parts at the entrance to the FMS could satisfy this requirement for a constant supply. Similarly, space must also be available for the processed workpieces that are removed from the FMS.

In the diagram in figure (30) the *workpiece exchange* does not take place inside the network. Instead it is assumed to be a logical operation that takes place outside the network. From the point of view of the queueing network, after leaving the setup area the pallet begins a new run through the system. Time losses at a setup area can be considered to have the same effect on the performance of the system as time losses during any other operation.

If more than one product type is processed in an FMS, as is normally the case in industrial practice, then the next product type to be loaded is determined stochastically based on the preset production ratios of the product types. These ratios can be derived from the overall production plan. If, for example, an average of 100 workpieces of product type A and 400 workpieces of product type B are to be produced per period, then the production ratios are $\alpha_A = 0.2$ and $\alpha_B = 0.8$ respectively. Unprocessed parts have to be fed into the system, or fixed on the universal pallets, at a ratio of A:B = 1:4. After evaluating the key performance criteria of the queueing network, the total production rate of the FMS with respect to the universal pallets can be broken down using the production ratios.

In the classical CQN model every station, including the transportation station, is assigned a waiting room that is large enough to give room for all N pallets and associated workpieces that are circulating in the FMS at any given point in time. This means that no delays can result from a limited capacity at a station's workpiece buffer. When the waiting room is large enough, then each workpiece is assured of being able to leave a machine or a vehicle and enter the next queue immediately after processing or transportation. The buffers (waiting rooms) of the machines or of the transportation system are large enough to accept each newly arriving workpiece. Blockages at the machines due to limited local buffer capacities are thus impossible. It is also critical to ensure that when a workpiece is intended to be processed by a newly freed machine it is in fact physically able to do so. This too is guaranteed when sufficient buffer capacities are available since a workpiece is only assigned to a machine when the *transportation process immediately preceding the operation is complete*.

These assumptions can generally be considered *fulfilled* under the following conditions:

---

96   see section 3.1.1.1.1.

- There are numerous local *input buffers or output buffers* available at the stations, such as in the case of round table pallet buffers which can be directly connected to a machine.

- All stations have access to a central buffer, and delays due to idle trips or load trips to and from this buffer are insignificantly small.

At least one of these conditions is found in practice in many FMSs. This is especially true when the central buffer areas are distributed throughout the FMS, and when unprocessed workpieces are always stored near their next machining station thus reducing the transportation distance between a machine and the current location of the next workpiece to be processed.

According to the assumptions in the classical CQN model, the processing times at all stations follow *exponential distributions* whose average values can be derived for each station from the process plans of each of the product types circulating through the system. The assumption of exponential distribution appears at first sight to be quite restrictive because the duration of the individual operations performed on a workpiece - excluding failures - is deterministically known. From the point of view of the machine, however, a large number of different operations on different workpieces all requiring different processing times have to be performed. Thus the assumption of exponential distribution for this purpose seems to be legitimate.

Figure (31) describes the sequence of operations of a typical workpiece flow in an FMS with two processing operations. It is important to note that the two operations "load" and "unload" in fact represent *one single operation* whose operation time is made up of the combination of the two. It is not interrupted by a transportation process and the associated waiting time.

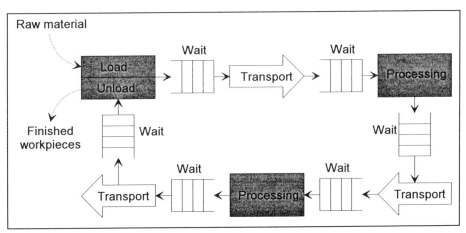

Figure 31: Workpiece flow in the CQN model

3.1.1.1.1. Data preparation

The data describing the product types to be produced and the planned FMS configuration provide the basis for building the classical CQN model of the FMS under consideration. These data are gathered in the early planning phases of the project. The product types to be manufactured can be described by their

- *process plans*

and their

- *planned production quantities.*

Operation Nr.	Station Nr.	Name	Operation time[97]	Operation frequency
Product type 1: production ratio $\alpha_1 = 0.2$				
1	1	L/UL	90.0	1.0 ↔
2	3	M1	428.0	1.0
3	1	L/UL	90.0	1.0
4	3	M1	57.0	1.0
5	1	L/UL	90.0	1.0
6	3	M1	57.0	1.0
7	1	L/UL	90.0	1.0
8	3	M1	57.0	1.0
9	1	L/UL	90.0	1.0
10	3	M1	351.0	1.0
11	1	L/UL	90.0	1.0
12	2	M2	229.0	1.0
Product type 2: production ratio $\alpha_2 = 0.2$				
1	1	L/UL	90.0	1.0 ↔
2	3	M1	470.0	1.0
3	1	L/UL	90.0	1.0
4	2	M2	639.0	1.0
Product type 3: production ratio $\alpha_3 = 0.4$				
1	1	L/UL	90.0	1.0 ↔
2	3	M1	185.0	1.0
3	1	L/UL	90.0	1.0
4	3	M1	130.0	1.0
Product type 4: production ratio $\alpha_4 = 0.2$				
1	1	L/UL	90.0	1.0 ↔
2	3	M1	47.0	1.0
3	1	L/UL	90.0	1.0
4	3	M1	223.0	1.0
5	1	L/UL	90.0	1.0
6	2	M2	19.0	1.0
↑ m_{ko}		↑ t_{ko}		↑ f_{ko}

Table 1: Process plans for four product types (example 3-1)

---

97   minutes

Table (1) shows process plans for an FMS in which four product types are to be manufactured. The process plan for the product type k (k = 1,2,...,K) includes several operations. In addition to the operation number o, the corresponding station (including its number m_{ko} and its name) and the processing time t_{ko} are also indicated for each operation. In the last column (operation frequency) the proportion f_{ko} of the workpieces that has to go through this particular operation is given. If, for example, according to a quality control strategy every other workpiece is checked on a measuring device, a value of 0.5 would represent the operation frequency for the operation "measure". The planned production quantities are given as relative quantities in the form of production ratios α_k based on the average planned production rate per period. The symbol "↔" represents a workpiece exchange.

The transportation processes that occur between operations are not explicitly included in the process plans. Since these process plans provide the foundation for the sample calculations that follow, it is further assumed that the average *transportation time* for a one-time transportation process is 5.9 minutes. In other words, a workpiece occupies a vehicle between two operations for an average of 5.9 minutes. In order to compute the total load on the transportation system of a fully processed workpiece, it is necessary to account for the average number of transportation processes (= the average number of operations).

When modelling an FMS as a closed queueing network the system and product data are treated in the following manner [see figure (32)]. The *product dependent* information included in the process plans is aggregated to produce station dependent *arrival frequencies* and *processing times*. These then provide the data base for the numerical determination of the key performance indicators of a particular FMS configuration alternative considered by a system planner.

A more specific description of the aggregation procedure follows. K product types are supposed to be processed by the FMS. A process plan and a share of the total production quantity (production ratio) of the FMS is given for each product type. The *process plan* of product type k is specified by a sequence of station numbers $\{m_{k1},m_{k2},...\}$. Since not every operation is performed on every workpiece of a particular product type, the *proportion* of the workpieces that have to pass through a particular operation is also given: $\{f_{k1},f_{k2},...\}$[98]. Every machining operation requires a specific *processing time* at a machine: $\{t_{k1},t_{k2},...\}$.

The transportation system is always activated between two operations in that it is always necessary to transport the workpiece from one station to the next. The exchange of an already processed workpiece for an unprocessed workpiece (loading and unloading) is considered to be *a single* operation since no transportation is performed between the two operations[99]. A processing operation is always marked on both sides by transportation operations.

---

[98]   If a measuring device checks every other workpiece, then $f_{ko} = 0.5$.

[99]   In reality, a process plan generally includes a load operation (at the beginning of the process plan) and an unload operation (at the end of the process plan). These must be combined into a single operation.

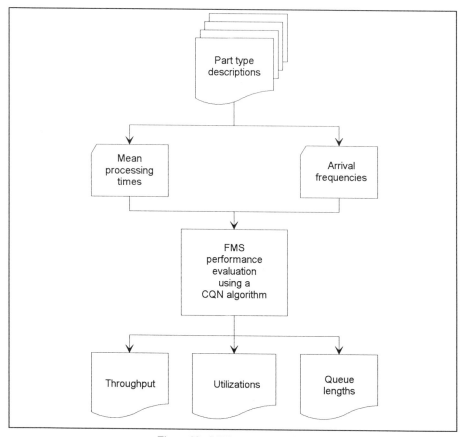

Figure 32: CQN model data flow

The distribution of the various product types over the whole production quantity of the FMS is described by *production ratios* α_k (k = 1,2,...,K). The sum of all the production ratios is equal to one. All the symbols used for the "input data" are summarized in table (2).

α_k	production ratio of product type k
f_{ko}	proportion of workpieces of product type k passing through operation o
k	product type index
K	number of product types
m	index of stations (groups of identical machines)
M	number of stations (including transportation station)
m_{ko}	station number of the o-th operation of product type k
t_{ko}	processing time of the o-th operation of product type k

Table 2: Symbols used in the description of the process plans

The data required by the following procedure for the evaluation of a closed queueing network can be derived from these descriptions of the products manufactured by an FMS[100]:

- **Product type specific evaluation of process plans**

The first step is to count how many times a workpiece visits station m while circulating through the FMS as prescribed by the process plan.

- *Average number of operations on a workpiece of product type k at station m* (per cycle through the FMS):

$$v_{km} = \sum_{\{o\,|\,m_{ko}=m\}} f_{ko} \qquad\qquad k=1,2,\ldots,K;\ m=1,2,\ldots,M-1 \qquad (4)$$

The quantity v_{km} is thus the average number of operations that are carried out upon a workpiece of product type k at station m during the workpiece's residence in the FMS.

The average processing time per operation of a workpiece of product type k at station m is obtained by adding up the entire time a workpiece resides at the station and then dividing this by the number of operations carried out on the workpiece at that particular station.

- *Average processing time of a workpiece of product type k at station m* (per operation):

$$b_{km} = \frac{1}{v_{km}} \cdot \left(\underbrace{\sum_{\{o\,|\,m_{ko}=m\}} f_{ko} \cdot t_{ko}}_{\text{total processing time of a workpiece of product type k at station m}} \right) \qquad k=1,2,\ldots,K;\ m=1,2,\ldots,M-1 \qquad (5)$$

The data specific to the product types and stations are computed in this way. The results computed up to now for example 3-1, as described above, are presented in table (3).

The classical CQN model for *universal pallets* is based on the assumption that *only one type of workpiece* (customer) is circulating in the queueing network. All of the product type specific data must, therefore, be aggregated. It must also be remembered, however, that every product type is supposed to have a specific share α_k of the total number of workpieces being processed in the FMS. This share (production ratio) can be derived from the planned production quantities.

Product type	Station number	Number of visits	Processing time per	
			Workpiece	Operation
1	1 2 3	6 1 5	540.0 229.0 950.0	90.0 229.0 190.0
2	1 2 3	2 1 1	180.0 639.0 470.0	90.0 639.0 470.0
3	1 3	2 2	180.0 315.0	90.0 157.5
4	1 2 3	3 1 2	270.0 19.0 270.0	90.0 19.0 135.0
		$\uparrow$ v_{km}		$\uparrow$ b_{km}

Table 3: Intermediate results after the first aggregation step
(example 3-1)

- *Aggregation of the product type specific data:*

When the product and station specific numbers of operations of the workpieces are weighted according to the production ratios of the different product types, the average number of visits at station m of the *aggregate of all product types* can be found. This could be said to be based on an average workpiece - one that is representative of the entire workpiece mix:

- *Average number of operations at station m* (per cycle of an average workpiece through the FMS; visit frequency):

$$v_m = \sum_{k=1}^{K} \alpha_k \cdot v_{km} \qquad\qquad m=1,2,\ldots,M-1 \qquad\qquad (6)$$

The average processing time of an average workpiece (pallet) at station m can be found by taking the total time spent by all workpieces at this station (over all visits) and dividing that by the average number of visits.

- *Average processing time of a workpiece at station m* (per operation):

$$b_m = \frac{1}{v_m} \cdot \left(\sum_{k=1}^{K} \alpha_k \cdot v_{km} \cdot b_{km} \right) \qquad\qquad m=1,2,\ldots,M-1 \qquad\qquad (7)$$

After the first aggregation step applied to example 3-1 we get the results shown in table (4).

m	v_m	b_m
1	3.0	90.00
2	0.6	295.67
3	2.4	193.33

↑ mean processing time per visit
of a workpiece at station m

↳ mean number of visits at station m

| total | 6.0 | |

*Table 4: Intermediate results after the second aggregation step
(example 3-1)*

The mean *transportation time* b_M is given as an average value independent of the routes followed and the workpieces to be transported. It can be estimated, in the case of an already roughly laid out FMS, based on the distances between stations, taking into account the times for the transfer of the pallets between a vehicle and a station. A method for estimating the average transportation time is presented during the discussion of starving in a later section[101] where, in addition to the trips performed to supply processing stations with workpieces (supply trips), idle trips and trips to the central buffer (disposal trips) are taken into consideration. These latter types of trips are not accounted for in the classical CQN model.

Next relative arrival frequencies at the stations are calculated from the relationship between the average number of visits of a typical workpiece at station m to the total number of visits of the workpieces at all stations (average number of operations).

- *Relative arrival frequency of a workpiece at station m* (per movement of the workpiece between two operations, i.e. after the completion of a transportation process):

$$p_m = v_m / \left(\sum_{i=1}^{M-1} v_i \right) \qquad\qquad m=1,2,\ldots,M-1 \qquad (8)$$

↳ number of operations of a typical workpiece per cycle through the entire FMS

= number of visits of a workpiece at the processing stations per cycle through the entire FMS

= number of transportation processes of a typical workpiece per cycle through the entire FMS

$$p_M = 1 = \sum_{m=1}^{M-1} p_m \qquad\qquad (9)$$

The quantity p_m ($m = 1,2,\ldots,M-1$) can be interpreted as the probability that a given pallet or workpiece will be transported to the station m after leaving any station. This is also called the *visit ratio* since it describes the relative frequency of arrivals

101 see section 3.1.2.5.

of a workpiece at the station m per arrival at the station M (the transportation station)[102]. The sum of all the relative arrival frequencies over all (M-1) machining stations is equal to 1. This can be clearly shown using equation (8). The quantity p_M is also assumed to be equal to 1 since every movement of a workpiece through the FMS necessarily activates the transportation system as well.

While b_m represents the average time the station m is occupied during the processing of a workpiece, it is important to clarify, as shown by the multiplication of p_m and b_m, that a workpiece is not transported to station m after every transportation process. The flow fraction of station m is only equivalent to p_m. Thus the average *workload* of the station m for an individual circulation of a workpiece through the queueing network can be determined as follows.

- *Average workload of station m* (per circuit through the queueing network):

$$w_m = p_m \cdot b_m \qquad\qquad\qquad m=1,2,\ldots,M-1 \qquad\qquad (10)$$

       ⌐ mean processing time per operation

    ⌐ relative arrival frequency

- *Average workload of the transportation system* (per transportation process):

$$w_M = p_M \cdot b_M \qquad\qquad\qquad\qquad\qquad\qquad\qquad\qquad (11)$$

       ⌐ mean transportation time

    ⌐ = 1

The station-dependent workloads for example 3-1 are shown in table (5).

m	v_m	p_m	w_m	
1	3.0	0.5	45.000	L/UL
2	0.6	0.1	29.567	M2
3	2.4	0.4	77.333	M1
Σ	6.0	1.0		
4	6.0	1.0	5.900	Transportation

Table 5: Intermediate results after the third aggregation step
(example 3-1)

The flow of the workpieces or pallets through the FMS is described by the relative arrival frequencies at the stations, p_m (m = 1,2,...,M-1), as derived from the process plans. It is assumed in the CQN model that these are independent of the current state of the system, i.e. that the probability of a workpiece arriving at station m after a given transportation process does not depend on the processing status (progress) of the workpiece. This means that the FMS here is considered to be in a *stationary condition*, and that the observations are not made on a spe-

---

102   **Buzacott/Yao** (1986), p. 10

cific workpiece, but rather on *a representative workpiece* mounted on a *universal pallet*.

The processing and transportation times are both based on a single circuit through the queueing network. This is important for the determination of the key performance measures of the FMS in that a workpiece normally requires several operation and transportation processes for its complete manufacture[103].

The quantity p_m has, up to now, been considered to represent the *arrival probability* of a workpiece at a station m. This reflects an input oriented approach to the analysis of material flow, i.e. an approach emphasizing the input side of the stations. It is also possible to use an output oriented approach and to describe the material flow using the *transition probabilities of the workpieces between stations j and m*, r_{jm}. The relationship between the arrival probabilities p_m and the transition probabilities r_{jm} is illustrated in the system of equations (12).

$$p_m = \sum_{j=1}^{M-1} p_j \cdot r_{jm} \qquad\qquad m=1,2,\dots,M-1 \qquad (12)$$

$\quad\quad\ \ \uparrow$ probability that a workpiece will be transported to station m after leaving station j (transition probability between j and m)

It is possible to calculate the transition probabilities r_{jm} with the help of equation (13). Here the sum of the workpiece movements between the upstream station j and the downstream station m (weighted appropriately according to the product dependent production rates) is divided by the total number of workpieces leaving the station j.

$$r_{jm} = \frac{\sum\limits_{k=1}^{K} \sum\limits_{\{o\,|\,m_{ko}=j,m_{k,o+1}=m\}} \alpha_k \cdot f_{ko}}{\sum\limits_{l=1}^{M} \sum\limits_{k=1}^{K} \sum\limits_{\{o\,|\,m_{ko}=j,m_{k,o+1}=l\}} \alpha_k \cdot f_{ko}} \qquad\qquad j,m=1,2,\dots,M-1 \qquad (13)$$

If the *layout* and distances between the stations in the planned FMS configuration are known, then the transition probabilities can be used to approximate the *average transportation times*. This is accomplished by multiplying the transition probabilities by the distances, adding these values together, and then dividing the total by the average vehicle speed and by the number of machining stations (M-1).

When the process plans from table (1) are evaluated in this way (excluding the transportation processes) the results can be summarized in the matrix presented in table (6). The exchange of finished for unfinished workpieces takes place outside the system and is thus not included in this representation of the closed queueing network.

---

103 In example 3-1 a workpiece needs a mean number of 6 operations (6 circulations through the queueing network) to be completely processed.

From \ To	1 (L/UL)	2 (M2)	3 (M1)	Total:
1 (L/UL)	0	1·0.2 + 1·0.2 + 1·0.2 = 0.6	5·0.2 + 1·0.2 + 2·0.4 + 2·0.2 = 2.4	3.0
		r_{12}=0.2	r_{13}=0.8	1.0
2 (M2)	1·0.2 + 1·0.2 + 1·0.2 = 0.6	0	0	0.6
	r_{21}=1.0			1.0
3 (M1)	5·0.2 + 1·0.2 + 2·0.4 + 2·0.2 = 2.4	0	0	2.4
	r_{31}=1.0			1.0
Total:	3.0	0.6	2.4	

Table 6: Transition probabilities between machining and load/unload stations
(example 3-1)

The quantity p_m in equations (12) describes the relative arrival frequency of a workpiece at station m (m = 1,2,...,M-1). The material flow system is also excluded from consideration, for the moment. The system of equations (12) is made up of M-1 variables and M-1 linear dependent equations. There exists, therefore, an *infinite number of solutions*, each being distinguished from the others by a constant factor. The system of equations can be solved when an additional equation, including one or more of the variables, is introduced.

One obvious possibility is to set the sum of the p_m values equal to one. In this way p_m can be interpreted as the probability that a given workpiece will be processed next at station m after leaving any station in the system. The system of equations and its solution work out to be:

$$p_1 =   0·p_1 + 1.0·p_2 + 1.0·p_3$$
$$p_2 = 0.2·p_1 +   0·p_2 +   0·p_3$$
$$p_3 = 0.8·p_1 +   0·p_2 +   0·p_3$$
$$1 =   p_1 +   p_2 +   p_3$$

Solution: p_1=0.5; p_2=0.1; p_3=0.4

It is easy to show that even when another constant factor is taken, such as $p_1 = 1$, the p_m values in the solutions are always in a ratio of 5:1:4.

If the transportation system (AGV) is included in the analysis, then it must be remembered that a transportation process is necessary *after every operation*. There are no direct transitions from one processing station to another. Transitions take place only between the material flow system and the machining and load/unload stations. This is shown in table (7).

From \ To	1 (L/UL)	2 (M2)	3 (M1)	4 (AGV)	Total:
1 (L/UL)	0	0	0	6·0.2 + 2·0.2 + 2·0.4 + 3·0.2 = 3.0	3.0
				r_{14}=1.0	1.0
2 (M2)	0	0	0	1·0.2 + 1·0.2 + 1·0.2 = 0.6	0.6
				r_{24}=1.0	1.0
3 (M1)	0	0	0	+ 5·0.2 + 1·0.2 + 2·0.4 + 2·0.2 = 2.4	2.4
				r_{34}=1.0	1.0
4 (AGV)	6·0.2 + 2·0.2 + 2·0.4 + 3·0.2 = 3.0	1·0.2 + 1·0.2 + 1·0.2 = 0.6	5·0.2 + 1·0.2 + 2·0.4 + 2·0.2 = 2.4	0	6.0
	r_{41}=0.5	r_{42}=0.1	r_{43}=0.4		1.0
Total:	3.0	0.6	2.4	6.0	

Table 7: Transition probabilities between the material handling system (AGV) and the machining and load/unload stations (example 3-1)

If the system of equations shown above is expanded by one variable (p_4) and one equation, and p_4 is set to 1.0, the following results:

$$
\begin{aligned}
p_1 &= 0 \cdot p_1 + 0 \cdot p_2 + 0 \cdot p_3 + 0.5 \cdot p_4 \\
p_2 &= 0 \cdot p_1 + 0 \cdot p_2 + 0 \cdot p_3 + 0.1 \cdot p_4 \\
p_3 &= 0 \cdot p_1 + 0 \cdot p_2 + 0 \cdot p_3 + 0.4 \cdot p_4 \\
p_4 &= 1.0 \cdot p_1 + 1.0 \cdot p_2 + 1.0 \cdot p_3 + 0 \cdot p_4 \\
p_4 &= 1.0
\end{aligned}
$$

Solution: p_1=0.5; p_2=0.1; p_3=0.4; p_4=1.0

The arrival probabilities can now be directly derived from the transition probabilities since there are now transitions only between the transportation station and the processing stations.

The queueing networks which correspond to both variants of material flow representation described are shown graphically in figure (33).

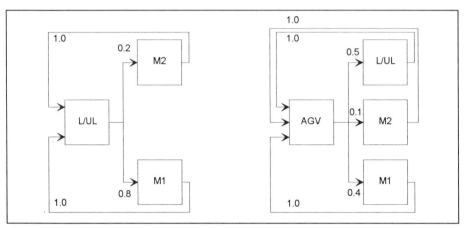

Figure 33: Transition probabilities with and without consideration of the material handling system (example 3-1)

It is not necessary to determine the transition probabilities r_{jm} between the individual nodes of the closed queueing network in order to use the classical CQN model for the evaluation of an FMS. This is true because the arrival probabilities p_m can be directly derived from the products' process plans. In other areas in which CQN models are used, such as the performance evaluation of communication or computer networks, the transition probabilities are known, from which the arrival probabilities for the individual stations in the queueing network can be derived. The transition probabilities must, however, be calculated for the analysis of FMSs with limited local buffers in order to quantify blocking conditions[104].

In the literature the arrival probabilities at the stations (setup areas, machines, etc.) are occasionally quantified in such a way that their sum is not equal to the arrival probability at the transportation station[105]. This form of quantification results when the central transportation system of the FMS to be modelled is not activated after every machining operation.

---

104   This is discussed further in section 3.1.2.
105   **Solberg** (1977)

3.1.1.1.2. Model evaluation

When the input data have been aggregated as described in the previous section, all the product types are essentially combined into one representative product group. An average workload for each station based on the product dependent process plans was calculated. The workpieces in this product group are now moved through the FMS mounted on N *universal pallets*.

In order to calculate the key performance parameters of the FMS, such as production rates, flow times, queue lengths, etc., it is necessary to know the *spatial distribution of all pallets* in the FMS at any given time in the stationary phase of the operation of the system. Let the vector $\underline{n} = (n_1, n_2, ..., n_M)$ describe a state of the FMS (queueing network) where n_m is the number of pallets (or workpieces) that are currently at the station m (either in the queue or being processed).

The set of possible states $S(N,M)$ of the CQN is dependent on the number of stations (M) and the number of pallets (N), as described by equation (14).

$$S(N,M) = \{(n_1, n_2, ..., n_M) \mid \text{with} \sum_{m=1}^{M} n_m = N; \ n_m \geq 0, \ m = 1, 2, ..., M\} \qquad (14)$$

where the annotations indicate:
- number of stations
- number of pallets in the FMS
- number of pallets at station m

In order to calculate the number of possible states of the FMS, each state can be represented by a binary number[106] including M groups (some may be empty) out of a total of N ones separated by M-1 zeros. The states of the FMS are described then by the positions of the zeros within the binary numbers. In the case of M = 3 stations and N = 6 pallets, for example, the state $(n_1 = 3, n_2 = 2, n_3 = 1)$ is described by the following binary number:

```
11101101
```
with n_1, n_2, n_3 indicated.

For the state $(n_1 = 0, n_2 = 0, n_3 = 6)$ we have

```
0 0111111
```
with n_1, n_2, n_3 indicated.

---

106 **Denning/Buzen** (1978), p. 247

The number of different states of the FMS is thus equal to the number of different possibilities for placing M-1 zeros in a total of N+M-1 possible positions (the rest are filled with the N ones). This number is given by the binomial coefficient

$$\begin{bmatrix} N+M-1 \\ M-1 \end{bmatrix}$$

An FMS with three stations (including the transportation station) and 4 pallets could take on any one of the following 15 states. Each of those is here represented with an M-tupel and the corresponding binary numbers:

$$S(4,3) = \begin{cases} (0,0,4) & 001111 \\ (0,1,3) & 010111 \\ (0,2,2) & 011011 \\ (0,3,1) & 011101 \\ (0,4,0) & 011110 \\ (1,0,3) & 100111 \\ (1,1,2) & 101011 \\ (1,2,1) & 101101 \\ (1,3,0) & 101110 \\ (2,0,2) & 110011 \\ (2,1,1) & 110101 \\ (2,2,0) & 110110 \\ (3,0,1) & 111001 \\ (3,1,0) & 111010 \\ (4,0,0) & 111100 \end{cases}$$

number of workpieces at station 3 (n_3)

number of workpieces at station 2 (n_2)

number of workpieces at station 1 (n_1)

The probability that a particular state will exist, i.e. that there will be a particular combination of pallets at the various stations (including the transportation station), is given by equation (15)[107].

$$P\{\underline{n}\} = P\{n_1, n_2, \ldots, n_M\} = \frac{1}{g(N,M)} \cdot \prod_{m=1}^{M} f_m(n_m) \tag{15}$$

The term g(N,M) defines the normalization constant over the state space S(N,M). Since the sum of the probabilities of all states must be equal to one, the following must also be true:

$$\sum_{\underline{n} \in S(N,M)} P\{\underline{n}\} = \frac{1}{g(N,M)} \cdot \sum_{\underline{n} \in S(N,M)} \prod_{m=1}^{M} f_m(n_m) = 1 \tag{16}$$

The normalization constant is thus defined by equation (17).

$$g(N,M) = \sum_{\underline{n} \in S(N,M)} \prod_{m=1}^{M} f_m(n_m) \tag{17}$$

---

107 **Gordon/Newell** (1967); **Bruell/Balbo** (1980), p. 33; **Gross/Harris** (1985), pp. 236-238

The quantity $f_m(n_m)$ depends, aside from the average workload w_m of the station m, both on the number of workpieces at the station and on the number of identical machines that are supplied from the common queue of this station.

This is defined in equation (18) for the case of a single server *(one machine per station[108])*.

$$f_m(n_m) = w_m^{n_m} \qquad\qquad m=1,2,\ldots,M; \; n_m=0,1,2,\ldots,N \qquad (18)$$

If a station comprises *several* (S_m) *identical machines* (multiple server), then equation (19) applies.

$$f_m(n_m) = \frac{w_m^{n_m}}{A_m(n_m)} \qquad\qquad m=1,2,\ldots,M; \; n_m=0,1,2,\ldots,N \qquad (19)$$

The denominator in equation (19), $A_m(n_m)$, depends on whether the number n_m of workpieces at the station is sufficient to keep all S_m machines busy. It allows for the fact that a station with S_m machines *busy* has a service rate S_m times as high as that of an individual machine. If fewer than S_m workpieces are present at the station m, then some machines remain idle and the production rate of the station is limited by the number of workpieces. Hence it is only n_m times as high as that of an individual machine. Only when enough workpieces are present at a station can this station reach its maximum production rate, i.e. the rate limited only by the number of parallel machines. This is expressed in equation (20).

$$A_m(n_m) = \begin{cases} n_m! & n_m \leq S_m \text{ or } N \leq S_m \\ S_m! \cdot S_m^{(n_m-S_m)} & n_m > S_m \end{cases} \qquad m=1,2,\ldots,M \qquad (20)$$

It is not difficult to show that equation (19) reduces to equation (18) for the case of a single machine since $\{A_m(n_m)=1!=1 \mid S_m=1; \; n_m=0,1,\ldots,N\}$. If the number of machines (servers) at a station is at least as large as the total number of pallets in the FMS, i.e. when $N \leq S_m$, then a workpiece will never have to wait. As a result, the flow time of a pallet at the station is equal to its processing time. This is important for modelling a transportation system that is layed out in the form of a continuous *conveyor system*. In such a case the transportation process can begin immediately after the completion of an operation.

Sample calculations of the product $f_m(n_m)$ are presented in table (8) for $n_m=4$ pallets at a station and with different numbers of machines, S_m. The individual quotients in the table $[w_m/\min\{S_m,n\}; \; n=1,\ldots,n_m]$ show that a station at which n machines are in use has a production rate n times as high as that of a single machine.

---

108 **Kleinrock** (1975), p. 102; **Bruell/Balbo** (1980), p. 33

$n_m=4$, $S_m=1$	$n_m=4$, $S_m=5$	$n_m=4$, $S_m=2$
$f_m(n_m)=\dfrac{w_m}{1}\cdot\dfrac{w_m}{1}\cdot\dfrac{w_m}{1}\cdot\dfrac{w_m}{1}$	$f_m(n_m)=\dfrac{w_m}{1}\cdot\dfrac{w_m}{2}\cdot\dfrac{w_m}{3}\cdot\dfrac{w_m}{4}$	$f_m(n_m)=\dfrac{w_m}{1}\cdot\dfrac{w_m}{2}\cdot\dfrac{w_m}{2}\cdot\dfrac{w_m}{2}$

Table 8: Computation of the product $f_m(n_m)$

Buzen[109] proposed a procedure for calculating the normalization constant. It involves recursively filling in a matrix $\underline{G}$ (with N rows and M columns) with the elements g(n,m). The matrix element g(n,m) is the normalization constant for a closed queueing network with only n customers (workpieces) and m stations. When the procedure is completed, the matrix element g(N,M) represents the normalization constant for the entire network.

The algorithmic structure of *Buzen's* procedure is based on the following transformation[110] of equation (17). If only the first station (m = 1) is considered, the number of possible states is significantly reduced. For a given value of n this station can only take on one state[111]. Thus the following results from equation (17):

$$g(n,1) = \sum_{\underline{n}\in S(n,1)} \prod_{i=1}^{1} f_i(n_i)$$

$$= \sum_{\underline{n}\in\{n\}} f_1(n)$$

$$= f_1(n) \qquad\qquad\qquad\qquad n=0,1,\ldots,N \qquad\qquad (21)$$

With respect to several stations (m > 1) equation (17) can be revised as follows:

$$g(n,m) = \sum_{\underline{n}\in S(n,m)} \prod_{i=1}^{m} f_i(n_i)$$

$$= \sum_{k=0}^{n} \left[\sum_{\substack{\underline{n}\in S(n,m)\\ n_m=k}} \prod_{i=1}^{m} f_i(n_i) \right]$$

With this transformation all possible states of station m are considered separately.

$$= \sum_{k=0}^{n} f_m(k)\cdot \underbrace{\left[\sum_{\underline{n}\in S(n-k,m-1)} \prod_{i=1}^{m-1} f_i(n_i) \right]}_{= g(n-k,m-1)}$$

Now from the remaining state space the states of station m are removed, with k pallets located at station m. The set of states of the residual network is reduced by these k pallets and by station m.

$$= \sum_{k=0}^{n} f_m(k)\cdot g(n-k,m-1) \qquad m=2,3,\ldots,M; \; n=0,1,\ldots,N \qquad (22)$$

---

109 **Buzen** (1973); **Bruell/Balbo** (1980), pp. 36-46; **Denning/Buzen** (1978), pp. 252-253; **Gross/Harris** (1985), pp. 240-243. Closed form expressions for the normalization constant of a network of single server queues are given by **Harrison** (1985) and **Gordon** (1990).

110 **Bruell/Balbo** (1980), p. 37; **Kuhn** (1990), p. 126

111 The first column of the matrix $\underline{G}$ represents the states with 0,1,2,...,N pallets at the station.

In this way, the normalization constant for a closed queueing network with n customers and m stations can be derived recursively using the normalization constant from a network with (m-1) stations. When m = 1 (for the left column in the matrix $\underline{G}$) the normalization constant as defined in equation (21) is used. Figure (34) shows the flow of values during the computation of the matrix element g(n,m).

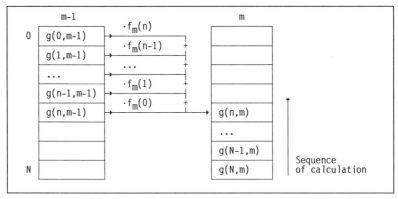

Figure 34: Flow of values in the computation of g(n,m) for stations with several machines

The first row of the Matrix $\underline{G}$ (n = 0) is described by equation (23).

$$g(0,m) = \sum_{\underline{n}\in S(0,m)} \prod_{i=1}^{m} f_i(0)$$

$$\uparrow = 1$$

$$= \sum_{\underline{n}\in\{0,\ldots,0\}} \prod_{i=1}^{m} 1$$

$$= 1 \hspace{4cm} m=1,2,\ldots,M \hspace{2cm} (23)$$

The values in the first row of the Matrix $\underline{G}$ can be explained by the fact that in a network in which zero customers are present, only one state (0,0,...,0) with a probability of 1 can exist.

As can also be seen in figure (34), only a *one-dimensional* array of length N + 1 is necessary to calculate the matrix $\underline{G}$. In order to calculate the element g(n,m) (column n) the elements [g(k,m-1), k = 0,...,n-1] are needed. These are still stored in the lower array elements. After calculating the element g(n,m) its value can be written in place of the previous element g(n,m-1).

The procedure for the numerical calculation of the array elements is depicted in figure (35) for the case of multiple server stations.

```
Initialize G(0)=1.0; G(n)=0.0, n=1,...,N

for m=1 to M do                         (column m: multiple server)
  for n=N to 1 do
    TMP=G(0)
    for k=1 to n do
      TMP=G(k)+TMP*wm/min(Sm,n-k+1)
    endfor
    G(n)=TMP
  endfor
endfor

{Note: After each assignment "G(n)=TMP" the array G(0) to G(n-1)
       contains the matrix elements g(0,m-1) to g(n-1,m-1)
       and the array G(n) to G(N) contains the matrix elements
       g(n,m) to g(N,m)}
```

*Figure 35: Procedure of Buzen for the computation of the normalization constant
(for multiple server stations)*

To make the calculations perfectly clear, equation (22) is here shown in detail, where $f_m(n_m)$ is replaced according to equation (19).

$$g(n,m) =$$

$$= \frac{w_m^0}{A_m(0)} \cdot g(n-0,m-1) \qquad\qquad k=0$$

$$+ \frac{w_m^1}{min(S_m,1)} \cdot g(n-1,m-1) \qquad\qquad k=1$$

$$+ \frac{w_m^2}{min(S_m,1)\cdot min(S_m,2)} \cdot g(n-2,m-1) \qquad\qquad k=2$$

$$+ \ldots + \qquad\qquad\qquad \ldots$$

$$+ \frac{w_m^n}{min(S_m,1)\cdot\ldots\cdot min(S_m,n)} \cdot g(n-n,m-1) \qquad\qquad k=n \qquad (24)$$

Through a further revision, the recursive structure of the equation becomes apparent:

$$g(n,m) = g(n,m-1)+\frac{w_m}{min(S_m,1)} \cdot \left[g(n-1,m-1)+\frac{w_m}{min(S_m,2)} \cdot \left[g(n-2,m-1)+ \ldots \right] \right] \qquad (25)$$

The meaning of the temporary variables TMP used in the description of the procedure in figure (35) can be recognized in the following formulation:

$$g(n,m) = g(n,m-1) + \frac{w_m}{\min(S_m,1)} \cdot \left[\quad \right]$$

$$\uparrow$$

$$g(n-1,m-1) + \frac{w_m}{\min(S_m,2)} \cdot \left[\quad \right]$$

$$\uparrow$$

$$g(n-2,m-1) + \frac{w_m}{\min(S_m,3)} \cdot \left[\quad \cdots \quad \right]$$

$$= \text{TMP}(N-2)$$

$$= \text{TMP}(N-1)$$

$$= \text{TMP}(N) \tag{26}$$

The term TMP(.) represents the summation of the elements in column (m-1) multiplied by the f_m-values, as shown in figure (34).

The calculation can be significantly simplified for *stations with a single machine*. In this case equation (27) applies[112].

$$f_m(k) = w_m^k \qquad\qquad k=0,1,\ldots,N; \; m=1,2,\ldots,M; \; S_m=1 \tag{27}$$

Solving equation (27) with reference to equation (22), the following is obtained:

$$g(n,m) = \sum_{k=0}^{n} w_m^k \cdot g(n-k,m-1)$$

$$= w_m^0 \cdot g(n,m-1) + \sum_{k=1}^{n} w_m^k \cdot g(n-k,m-1)$$

$$= w_m^0 \cdot g(n,m-1) + w_m \cdot \sum_{k=1}^{n} w_m^{k-1} \cdot g(n-k,m-1)$$

$$\uparrow \left[\quad = \sum_{k=0}^{n-1} w_m^k \cdot g(n-1-k,m-1) \right.$$

$$\uparrow \quad = g(n-1,m)$$

$$= g(n,m-1) + w_m \cdot g(n-1,m) \qquad\qquad n=1,2,\ldots,N; \; m=2,3,\ldots,M; \; S_m=1 \tag{28}$$

The simplified flow of values in the calculation of $g(n,m)$ for stations with a single machine (single server) is shown in figure (36).

---

112 **Bruell/Balbo** (1980), p. 37

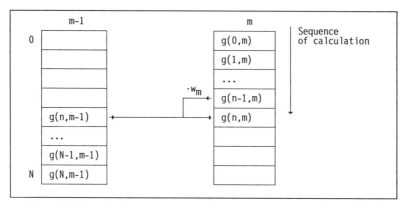

Figure 36: Flow of values in the computation of g(n,m) for stations with one machine

All the necessary quantities can be stored in this simplified case in a one-dimensional array of length $N+1$[113]. Figure (37) summarizes the description of the procedure.

```
Initialize G(0)=1.0; G(n)=0.0, n=1,2,...,N

for m=1 to M do                        (column m: one machine)
  for n=1 to N do
    G(n)=w_m·G(n-1)+G(n)
  endfor
endfor

{Note: G(n-1) contains the matrix element g(n-1,m) and
       G(n) contains the matrix element g(n,m-1)}
```

Figure 37: Procedure of Buzen for the computation of the normalization constant (for single-server stations)

For the example 3-1, in which every station contains only one machine, the matrix $\underline{G}$ shown in table (9) applies.

113 **Denning/Buzen** (1978), p. 253

w_m	45.00	29.567	77.333	5.90
n\m	1	2	3	4
0	1	1	1	1
1	45.00 $=45.00^1$	74.567 $=45.00+29.567\cdot1$	151.900 $=74.567+77.333\cdot1$	157.800 $=151.900+5.90\cdot1$
2	2025.000 $=45.00^2$	4229.723 $=2025+29.567\cdot74.567$	15976.620	16907.640
3	91125.000 $=45.00^3$	216182.800	1451708.000	1551463.000 $=G(N-1)$
4	4100625.000 $=45.00^4$	10492430.000	122757900.000	*131911500.000* $=G(N)$

Table 9: Matrix $\underline{G}$ (example 3-1)

The average workloads at the stations [see table (5)] are given in the first line of table (9). The calculation of the matrix proceeds from one column to the next. A column m in the table (for $n=0$ to $n=4$) is stored in the one-dimensional array $G(N)$. After the first column (for station 1) and the first row ($n=0$) have been completely filled in, the matrix elements $g(n,m)$ $(m>1,n>0)$ are calculated. Two variables are needed to calculate $g(n,m)$: the quantity $g(n,m-1)$ from the array element $G(n)$ in the calculations for column m-1; and the quantity $g(n-1,m)$ for the current column m as stored in the array element $G(n-1)$. At the end of the procedure the array G includes information exclusively from the last column in the table. All other values have been written over. The array element $G(N)$ thus contains the desired normalization constant.

A FORTRAN implementation of the procedure for the calculation of the matrix $\underline{G}$ is shown in figure (38)[114]. Both the simplified form of the calculation for a station with one machine and the general form for stations with several identical machines are shown.

---

114 This FORTRAN routine was extracted from the program CAN-Q; see **Steckc/Solberg** (1981a), p. 298; see also **Leimkühler** (1984)

```
              SUBROUTINE NORMKN(NN,MM,W,NS)
C
C             Computation of the normalization constant
C
C NN - number of pallets
C MM - number of stations (incl. material handling system)
C NS - number of servers per station
C W  - workloads
C
              DIMENSION W(50),NS(50),G(100)
            ┌ DO 140 J=1,NN
            │    G(J)=0.
      140   └ CONTINUE
            ┌ DO 147 I=1,MM
            │    IF (W(I).LE.0.) GOTO 146
            │    TMP=1.
            │    IF (NS(I).GT.1) GOTO 142
C           │
C           │ single server stations
C           │
            │  ┌ DO 141 J=1,NN
            │  │    TMP=W(I)*TMP+G(J)
            │  │    G(J)=TMP
      141   │  └ CONTINUE
            │    GOTO 145
C           │
C           │ multiple server stations
C           │
      142   │    CONTINUE
            │  ┌ DO 144 J=1,NN
            │  │    JJ=NN-J+1
            │  │  ┌ DO 143 K=1,JJ
            │  │  │    A=FLOAT(NS(I))
            │  │  │    CHK=FLOAT(JJ-K+1)
            │  │  │    IF (CHK.LT.A) A=CHK
            │  │  │    TMP=(W(I)*TMP)/A+G(K)
      143   │  │  └ CONTINUE
            │  │    G(JJ)=TMP
            │  │    TMP=1.
      144   │  └ CONTINUE
      145   │    CONTINUE
      146   │    CONTINUE
      147   └ CONTINUE
              RETURN
              END
```

Figure 38: FORTRAN subroutine for the computation of the normalization constant
following the procedure of Buzen

As the values for example 3-1 in table (9) show, the normalization constant can (especially in a case with many pallets and many stations) be either quite large or quite small. Certain numerical problems can arise from this fact (floating point overflow). Several modifications have been proposed in the literature to prevent these problems from arising[115]. *Stecke and Solberg*[116] scale the average workloads at the stations w_m by dividing the workload of one station by the average workload of all machines (servers) in the FMS [see equation (29)].

---

115 **Reiser** (1981), pp. 12-13. With the algorithm of Reiser numerical problems are largely avoided. A pseudo-code formulation of this procedure is presented in **Yao/Buzacott** (1985).

116 **Stecke/Solberg** (1981a), pp. 72-73; see also **Kuhn** (1990), p. 128; **Tetzlaff** (1990), pp. 42-43.

$$w_m^\star = \frac{w_m}{\sum\limits_{m=1}^{M} w_m} \cdot \sum\limits_{m=1}^{M} S_m \qquad\qquad m=1,2,\ldots,M \qquad\qquad (29)$$

Table (10) shows that in the case of example 3-1 the scaled workloads are significantly smaller than the original values. Since the w_m values are one factor used for the calculation of the normalization constant, the above-mentioned numerical problems tend to come up later (with a larger number of pallets).

m	w_m	$w_m^\star$
1	45.000	1.140
2	29.567	0.748
3	77.333	1.960
4	5.900	0.148
Σ	157.800	3.966 $\approx$ 4

Table 10: Scaled workloads of the stations (example 3-1)

After completing the procedure for the calculation of the normalization constant, the parameters relevant to the evaluation of the FMS can be derived as follows with the help of the matrix elements g(N,M) and g(N-1,M), or the array elements G(N) and G(N-1)[117].

- *Probability distribution of the number of workpieces (pallets) at station m:*

The probability distributions of the numbers of workpieces or pallets n_m (m = 1,2,...,M) at the stations (either in a queue or being processed) can be determined with the help of the elements of the matrix $\underline{G}$ and the workloads of the stations as follows.

The probability that precisely n workpieces will be found at station m results from the consideration of all the states in the set S(N,M) in which n workpieces are present at station m. This is expressed in equation (30).

$$P\{n_m=n,N\} = \sum\limits_{\substack{\underline{n}\in S(N,M)\\ n_m=n}} P\{n_1,\ldots,n_m=n,\ldots,n_M\} \qquad\qquad n=0,1,\ldots,N \qquad (30)$$

When equation (15) is taken into account, the relationship expressed in equation (30) can also be rewritten as shown in equation (31)[118]. Here the factor $f_m(n_m=n)$ particular to station m is isolated so that only the states of the FMS in which n workpieces are found at station m are considered.

---

117 Denning/Buzen (1978), pp. 252-253; Solberg (1977), pp. 1265-1275; Bruell/Balbo (1980), pp. 48-53
118 Solberg (1977); Bruell/Balbo (1980), pp. 46-49

$$P\{n_m=n,N\} = \frac{f_m(n_m=n)}{g(N,M)} \cdot \underset{\substack{n\in S(N,M) \\ n_m=n}}{\Sigma} \underset{\substack{j=1 \\ j\neq m}}{\overset{M}{\Pi}} f_j(n_j) \qquad m=1,2,\ldots,M; \; n=0,1,\ldots,N \qquad (31)$$

↑
└ normalization constant for the queueing network which has been
reduced by **station m** and **n workpieces** residing there

= normalization constant for the queueing network
without station m with (N-n) circulating workpieces

The quantity $f_m(n_m=n)$ is defined by equation (19). Analogous to equation (17), the sum described by equation (31) can be understood to be the normalization constant of the original queueing network from which the station m and its n pallets have been removed. In the remaining network only (N-n) workpieces are circulating. In the following the normalization constant of such a reduced queueing network is represented by the term $g^{(m)}(N-n,M)$ [see equation (32)].

$$g^{(m)}(N-n,M) = \underset{\substack{n\in S(N,M) \\ n_m=n}}{\Sigma} \underset{\substack{j=1 \\ j\neq m}}{\overset{M}{\Pi}} f_j(n_j) \qquad m=1,2,\ldots,M; \; n=0,1,\ldots,N \qquad (32)$$

The removal of the last station (M) in the queueing network is equivalent to eliminating the last column of the matrix $\underline{G}$. Therefore, the following must be true:

$$g^{(M)}(k,M) = g(k,M-1) \qquad\qquad\qquad k=0,1,\ldots,N \qquad (33)$$

The normalization constant of a network with M stations and n workpieces from which the station M has been factored out is thus equal to the normalization constant of the network with M-1 stations and n workpieces.

The probability that exactly n workpieces will be found at station m is given by equation (34).

$$P\{n_m=n,N\} = \frac{f_m(n_m=n)}{g(N,M)} \cdot g^{(m)}(N-n,M) \qquad m=1,2,\ldots,M; \; n=0,1,\ldots,N \qquad (34)$$

The numerical evaluation of equation (34) can be extended to cover the entire network by using the normalization constant as calculated above. To do this the indexing of the station would have to be changed such that the station m, whose probability distribution is to be determined, receives the index M. In this case the required value for $g^{(m)}(N-n,M)$ is found in the column M-1 of the matrix $\underline{G}$. The disadvantage of this method, originally suggested by *Buzen*[119], is that the normalization constants repeatedly have to be recalculated for different station indexing.

---

119 **Buzen** (1973)

Bruell and Balbo[120] have suggested a method with which the repeated calculation of the normalization constants can be prevented. Since the sum of all the probabilities that any number of workpieces will be present at a station at a given time is always equal to one, it is also possible to represent the probability that exactly n workpieces will be present at station m with equation (35).

$$\sum_{k=0}^{N} P\{n_m=n,N\} = \sum_{k=0}^{N} \frac{f_m(n_m=k)}{g(N,M)} \cdot g^{(m)}(N-k,M) = 1 \qquad m=1,2,\ldots,M \qquad (35)$$

After rearranging equation (35), the following results:

$$g(N,M) = \sum_{k=0}^{N} f_m(n_m=k) \cdot g^{(m)}(N-k,M)$$

$$= \underbrace{f_m(0)}_{=1} \cdot g^{(m)}(N,M) + \sum_{k=1}^{N} f_m(n_m=k) \cdot g^{(m)}(N-k,M) \qquad m=1,2,\ldots,M \qquad (36)$$

A further rearrangement produces the following:

$$g^{(m)}(N,M) = g(N,M) - \sum_{k=1}^{N} f_m(n_m=k) \cdot g^{(m)}(N-k,M) \qquad m=1,2,\ldots,M \qquad (37)$$

or more generally,

$$g^{(m)}(n,M) = g(n,M) - \sum_{k=1}^{n} f_m(n_m=k) \cdot g^{(m)}(n-k,M) \qquad m=1,2,\ldots,M; \; n=1,2,\ldots,N \qquad (38)$$

When the last column in the matrix $\underline{G}$ for the entire network has been calculated and stored, then the equations necessary for the determination of the probabilities can be iteratively computed. The following is taken as a starting value:

$$g^{(m)}(0,M) = 1 \qquad m=1,2,\ldots,M \qquad (39)$$

Both the normalization constant g(N,M) and the previously determined auxiliary variables [$g^{(m)}(k,M)$; $k=0,\ldots,n-1$] are used to calculate $g^{(m)}(n,M)$. This is shown in the following illustration:

---

120   **Bruell/Balbo** (1980), pp. 47-48

$g^{(m)}(0,M) = 1$

$\llcorner$ ⟶

$g^{(m)}(1,M) = g(1,M)-f_m(1)\cdot g^{(m)}(0,M)$

$\llcorner$ ⟶

$g^{(m)}(2,M) = g(2,M)-[f_m(1)\cdot g^{(m)}(1,M)+f_m(2)\cdot g^{(m)}(0,M)]$

etc.

The factors corresponding to station m are removed on the basis of the last column in the matrix $\underline{G}$.

Equation (38) is simplified for the case of a station with a single machine (single server) as follows:

$$g^{(m)}(n,M) = g(n,M)-\sum_{k=1}^{n} f_m(n_m=k)\cdot g^{(m)}(n-k,M)$$

$$= g(n,M)-w_m\cdot \underbrace{\sum_{k=1}^{n} f_m(k-1)\cdot g^{(m)}(n-k,M)}$$

$$\underset{\bigl\uparrow\;=\; g(n-1,M)}{}$$

$$= g(n,M)-w_m\cdot g(n-1,M) \qquad\qquad m=1,2,\ldots,M;\ n=1,2,\ldots,N \qquad (40)$$

Combining equation (40) with equation (34), the following result applies to *stations with one machine* (single server stations):

$$P\{n_m=n,N\} = \frac{w_m^n}{g(N,M)}\cdot[g(N-n,M)-w_m\cdot g(N-1-n,M)] \qquad m=1,2,\ldots,M;\ n=0,1,\ldots,N \qquad (41)$$

where

$$g(n,M)=0 \qquad\qquad\qquad\qquad n<0 \qquad\qquad\qquad\qquad (42)$$

The probability distribution of the number of pallets at station $m=1$ (L/UL) in example 3-1[121] when $N=4$ pallets are circulating in the system is presented in table (11).

---

121 In this example every station consists of a single machine. Therefore, equation (41) applies.

$P\{n_1=0\}$	$w_1^0/g(N,M)\cdot[g(N-0,M)-w_1\cdot g(N-1-0,M)]$ $=1/131911500\cdot[131911500-45.0\cdot1551463]$	0.4707
$P\{n_1=1\}$	$w_1^1/g(N,M)\cdot[g(N-1,M)-w_1\cdot g(N-1-1,M)]$ $=45/131911500\cdot(1551463-45.0\cdot16907.640)$	0.2697
$P\{n_1=2\}$	$w_1^2/g(N,M)\cdot[g(N-2,M)-w_1\cdot g(N-1-2,M)]$ $=2025/131911500\cdot[16907.640-45.0\cdot157.800]$	0.1505
$P\{n_1=3\}$	$w_1^3/g(N,M)\cdot[g(N-3,M)-w_1\cdot g(N-1-3,M)]$ $=91125/131911500\cdot[157.800-45.0\cdot1]$	0.0779
$P\{n_1=4\}$	$w_1^4/g(N,M)\cdot[g(N-4,M)-w_1\cdot g(N-1-4,M)]$ $=4100625/131911500\cdot[1-45.0\cdot0]$	0.0311
$P\{0\le n_1\le4\}$		0.9999[122]

Table 11: Probability distribution of the number of workpieces at station 1 (L/UL)

Figure (39) shows the probability distributions of the numbers of workpieces at the individual stations for the example 3-1. As can be clearly seen, station M1 is the bottleneck. Since station M1 carries the largest workload and consists of only one machine, a relatively long queue will build up at this station. Indeed, there exists a non-negligible possibility that *all* the workpieces circulating in the FMS could be *waiting* at this station *simultaneously*.

For this reason, it would be worthwhile during the planning stage of the FMS to consider placing the central buffer area as close as possible to station M1. In this way the time for the transfer of workpieces between the machine and the central buffer could be kept to a minimum. Depending on the desired production rate, it may even be desirable to integrate more M1 type machines into the FMS. This is a typical conclusion drawn from an evaluation of a particular FMS design alternative based on the CQN model.

---

122 Because of rounding errors the probability numbers do not add up to one.

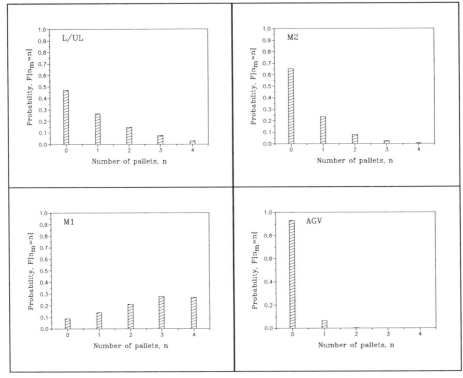

Figure 39: Probability distributions of the number of workpieces at the stations (example 3-1)

- *Average number of workpieces at the station m:*

The average number of workpieces at a station can be calculated according to equation (43) using the probability distributions of the numbers of workpieces at the stations. These quantities provide information for determining the size of the local buffers at the stations.

$$Q_m(N) = \sum_{n=1}^{N} n \cdot P\{n_m = n, N\} \qquad\qquad m=1,2,\ldots,M \qquad\qquad (43)$$

Obviously, the sum of the workpieces at each station in the system must be equal to the total number of circulating workpieces, N [see equation (44)]. This means that the work-in-process inventory with a given number of pallets is constant.

$$\sum_{m=1}^{M} Q_m(N) = N \qquad\qquad (44)$$

- *Average production rate of station m:*

The average production rate[123] of a station is described by the number of finished workpieces produced per unit time. It is influenced by the number of machines (servers) at the station, the speed of production of a machine and the number of workpieces at the station. The production rate of a busy machine is equal to the reciprocal of the average processing time, $\mu_m = 1/b_m$ (service rate). If there is no workpiece available at a machine, then its production rate is zero. With respect to all S_m machines, the service rate of the station m is then described by equation (45).

$$\mu_m(n) = \begin{cases} n/b_m & n \leq S_m \\ S_m/b_m & n > S_m \end{cases} \qquad m=1,2,\ldots,M \qquad (45)$$

The *production rate of the station m* can thus be derived as follows by observing all possible states[124] of the station:

$$X_m(N) = \sum_{n=1}^{N} P\{n_m=n,N\} \cdot \mu_m(n) \qquad m=1,2,\ldots,M \qquad (46)$$

By combining equations (34) and (46) the following results:

$$X_m(N) = \sum_{n=1}^{N} \frac{f_m(n_m=n)}{g(N,M)} \cdot g^{(m)}(N-n,M) \cdot \mu_m(n) \qquad m=1,2,\ldots,M \qquad (47)$$

A rearrangement of equation (19) leads to[125]:

$$f_m(n_m) = \begin{cases} \dfrac{p_m^{n_m}}{\prod\limits_{k=1}^{n_m} \mu_m(k)} & n_m=1,2,\ldots,N \\ 1 & n_m=0 \end{cases} \qquad m=1,2,\ldots,M \qquad (48)$$

Equation (48) could also be written recursively:

$$f_m(n_m=n) = \frac{p_m}{\mu_m(n)} \cdot f_m(n_m=n-1) \qquad m=1,2,\ldots,M; \ n=1,2,\ldots,N \qquad (49)$$

The production rate of station m can then be determined by combining equations (49) and (47):

$$X_m(N) = \sum_{n=1}^{N} \frac{p_m}{\mu_m(n)} \cdot \frac{f_m(n_m=n-1)}{g(N,M)} \cdot g^{(m)}(N-n,M) \cdot \mu_m(n)$$

---

123 **Bruell/Balbo** (1980), p. 50
124 i.e. the number of workpieces at the station
125 **Bruell/Balbo** (1980), p. 33

$$= \frac{p_m}{g(N,M)} \cdot \sum_{n=1}^{N} \frac{1}{\mu_m(n)} \cdot f_m(n_m{=}n{-}1) \cdot g^{(m)}(N{-}n,M) \cdot \mu_m(n)$$

$$= \frac{p_m}{g(N,M)} \cdot \underbrace{\sum_{n=0}^{N-1} f_m(n_m{=}n) \cdot g^{(m)}(N{-}1{-}n,M)}_{= g(N-1,M)}$$

$$= p_m \cdot \frac{g(N-1,M)}{g(N,M)} \qquad\qquad m=1,2,\ldots,M \qquad\qquad (50)$$

The production rate of a station can thus be relatively easily derived from the normalization constant. If the workloads at the stations have been scaled according to equation (29), then it is necessary to recall this fact when calculating the production rates.

- **Production rate of the transportation system:**

The production rate of the transportation system can also be found using equation (50). If the stationary arrival probability of the transportation system is $p_M = 1$, then we obtain:

$$X_M(N) = \frac{g(N-1,M)}{g(N,M)} \qquad\qquad\qquad\qquad (51)$$

- **Production rate of the FMS:**

The production rate of the *entire FMS* is described by the number of workpieces finished per unit time. If there is only one *load/unload station* in the FMS at which each operation is equivalent to a workpiece exchange, then the production rate of this station is equal to that of the FMS. If the load/unload station is also used for re-fixturing of workpieces (to change the position of a workpiece on a pallet), as in example 3-1, then this identity is no longer true. In general, it is possible to determine the production rate of an FMS using equation (52). Here the production rate of the transportation system is divided by the average number of operations (or transportation processes) which are carried out on a workpiece.

$$X(N) = \underbrace{[g(N-1,M)/g(N,M)]}/\underbrace{v_M} \qquad\qquad (52)$$

‎   ↑ production rate of the transportation system   ↑ mean number of operations per workpieces

The results of this analysis as applied to example 3-1 ($v_M = 6$) are presented in table (12).

Production rate of the transportation system	Production rate of the FMS
g(N-1,M)/g(N,M)	[g(N-1,M)/g(N,M)]/v_M
1551463/131911500 =0.0117614	0.0117614/6 =0.0019602

Table 12: Production rate of the transportation system and the FMS (example 3-1)

The overall production rate based on universal pallets (i.e. a representative work-piece type) can be used to calculate the production rates of the individual product types when multiplied by the production ratio of each product type. This is shown in equation (53).

$$X_k(N) = \alpha_k \cdot X(N) \qquad\qquad k=1,2,\ldots,K \qquad (53)$$

- *Utilization of station m:*

The utilization of station m is found by multiplying the production rate of the station m by the average processing time and then dividing by the number of machines (servers) at the station [see equation (54)].

$$U_m(N) = b_m \cdot X_m(N)/S_m \qquad\qquad m=1,2,\ldots,M \qquad (54)$$

             └ number of machines at station m

        └ production rate of station m

    └ mean processing time at station m per operation

A summary of the production rates and workloads for example 3-1 with N=4 pallets in the FMS is given in table (13).

m	Production rate $X_m(4)$	Utilization $U_m(4)$
1	0.5·0.011761=0.005881	0.005881·90= 0.529
2	0.1·0.011761=0.001176	0.001176·295.6667=0.347
3	0.4·0.011761=0.004704	0.004704·193.3333=0.909
4	1.0·0.011761=0.011761	0.011761·5.9= 0.069

Table 13: Production rates and utilizations (example 3-1)

The product specific production rates of the FMS have been put together in table (14).

Product type k	1	2	3	4
Production rate (Pieces/minute)	0.2·0.0019602 = 0.0003920	0.2·0.0019602 = 0.0003920	0.4·0.0019602 = 0.0007841	0.2·0.0019602 = 0.0003920

Table 14: Production rates per product type (example 3-1)

- *Average flow time of a workpiece at station m:*

The average flow time of a workpiece at station m is, according to *Little's law*[126], equal to the number of workpieces at the station divided by their production rates [see equation (55)].

$$D_m(N) = \frac{Q_m(N)}{X_m(N)} \qquad\qquad m=1,2,\ldots,M \qquad (55)$$

In table (15) the average number of workpieces at the stations and the average flow times for example 3-1 are shown.

m	Number of workpieces $Q_m(4)$	Flow time $D_m(4)$
1	0.929	0.929/0.005881=157.97
2	0.497	0.497/0.001176=422.62
3	2.500	2.500/0.004704=531.46
4	0.074	0.074/0.011761= 6.29

Table 15: Number of workpieces and flow times at the stations (example 3-1)

- *Average flow time of a workpiece through the entire FMS:*

Equation (56) describes the average flow time of a workpiece through the FMS from the first operation to the last. Little's Law is applied here to the entire FMS. The number of pallets N is divided by the production rate of the FMS.

$$D(N) = \frac{N}{X(N)} \qquad\qquad m=1,2,\ldots,M \qquad (56)$$

In the case of example 3-1 with four pallets in circulation, the average flow time of a workpiece is

$D(4) = 4/0.001960 = 2041$ minutes.

The symbols that have been used up to now are summarized in table (16).

---

126 **Little** (1961)

b_{km}	mean processing time of a workpiece of product type k at station m
b_m	mean processing time of a workpiece at station m
$D(N)$	mean flow time of a workpiece through the entire FMS
$D_m(N)$	mean flow time of a workpiece at station m
$g(n,m)$	element of the matrix $\underline{G}$
k	product type index $(k=1,2,\ldots,K)$
$\mu_m(n)$	service rate of station m (depending on the number of workpieces at station m)
m	station index $(m=1,2,\ldots,M)$
N	number of (universal) pallets or workpieces circulating in the FMS
$\underline{n}$	vector to describe the spatial distribution of workpieces at the stations
n_m	number of workpieces at station m (waiting or in process)
$P\{.\}$	probability distribution
p_m	relative arrival frequency of an arbitrary workpiece at station m
$Q_m(N)$	mean number of workpieces at station m
r_{jm}	probability that a workpiece upon completion of processing at station j will next be processed at station m
$S(N,M)$	set of states of the closed queueing network
$U_m(N)$	utilization of station m
v_{km}	mean number of visits of product type k at station m
v_m	mean number of visits of a typical workpiece (pallet) at station m
w_m	mean workload of station m
$X(N)$	production rate of the FMS
$X_m(N)$	production rate of station m
$X_M(N)$	production rate of the transportation system

Table 16: Summary of symbols used

This concept of a classical closed queueing network, including the *Buzen* procedure for the calculation of the normalization constant, has been implemented by *Solberg* in a FORTRAN program called CAN-Q. This program has already been used in numerous studies and analyzes of FMSs[127], though the rather restrictive assumptions underlying the classical CQN model were generally not all satisfied. The results nevertheless tended to be similar to those of simulation analyzes carried out parallel to the use of CAN-Q[128].

In the following comparison the degree to which the most important of the fundamental assumptions underlying the classical CQN model[129] could apply in an FMS is reviewed.

127 **Stecke/Solberg** (1981a), pp. 294-305; **Duffau/Bloche** (1985); **Co/Wysk** (1986); **Tempelmeier** (1988)

128 see also section 3.1.1.3. Explanations for this phenomenon are also given by "operational analysis"; see **Denning/Buzen** (1978)

129 **Stecke/Solberg** (1981a), pp. 66-70

Assumptions of the classical CQN model:	Situation in a real-life FMS:
There are always exactly N pallets with workpieces circulating in the FMS.	This assumption holds, if the supply of unprocessed workpieces is permanently ensured. This can be accomplished through the installation of a raw material storage area located near the load/unload station of the FMS.
Each station is assigned a waiting room large enough to accept all N pallets residing in the FMS, if necessary. Through this assumption blocking and starving of machines due to limited local buffers is avoided. Thus upon completion of a given workpiece a machine is immediately ready to process the next workpiece waiting in the queue.	This assumption will *approximately* hold, if there are several local buffer spaces at a station (e.g. a round-table buffer with six pallet locations) or if the FMS includes a central buffer and the transportation system is relatively fast and low utilized. In this case, the central buffer behaves as a virtual local buffer.
A station may comprise several servers (identical machines, vehicles). In this case the waiting line is common to all servers.	This assumption can be considered fulfilled if a central buffer is present and if the transfer times between the machines and the central buffer are negligible, and if during the operation of the FMS the machines remain functionally identical with respect to their tool magazine setup.
At all stations the FCFS queueing discipline is used.	In industrial practice the FCFS discipline is most widely used when a decision is made as to which workpiece should be taken out of the central buffer and sent to a given station. Observe that the main purpose of the CQN model is the analysis of long-term running conditions. Therefore the priority rules used are of minor relevance.
All operation times are exponentially distributed.	From a workpiece's point of view the operation time at a station is deterministically given. From a machine's point of view, however, many different workpieces arrive stochastically with different operation times. The exponential distribution can then serve as a rough approximation.
The workpiece flow through the network is governed by the stationary arrival probabilities p_m ($m = 1,2,...,M$).	The performance evaluation results are used for long-term considerations. Therefore, it is legitimate to confine one's attention to typical production requirements arising from a representative workpiece in the long run.

3.1.1.1.3. Sensitivity analysis

The equations described in the preceding sections can be used in a sensitivity analysis to examine the functional relationships between the key configuration variables and the performance of an FMS alternative. It is possible to perform a sensitivity analysis on any of the input data in a CQN model. The analysis of the production rate of an FMS should not be restricted to the influence of the

- *Number of pallets.*

A whole series of other factors which influence the performance of an FMS must be evaluated in order to make a rational decision about the optimal FMS configuration:

- *Number of machines, setup areas, and vehicles*[130].
- *Production ratios* of the different product types.
- Structure of the product-specific *process plans*.
- *Processing times.*
- Distribution of the planned production quantity of one product type among *alternative process plans*[131].
- *Capacity* of the *local workpiece buffers* (a rarely discussed topic since it is unknown in the classical CQN model)[132].

Each of these decision variables influences the performance of an FMS configuration, and they are often considered as givens after the technical planning phase has been completed. The following discussion is limited to an investigation of the influence of the number of pallets on the relevant performance parameters of an FMS.

- **Production rate of the FMS vs. the number of pallets:**

Suri[133] has shown that under the assumptions of the classical CQN model of a queueing network with universal pallets, the production rate is a non-decreasing function of the number of pallets. This is only true, however, if the service rate at all stations does not decrease as the number of workpieces increases.

That means,

If $\mu_m(n+1) \geq \mu_m(n)$, then $X_m(n+1) \geq X_m(n)$ m=1,2,...,M; n=0,1,...   (57)

---

130 A numerical example illustrating the influence of the number of servers on the production rate of an FMS is presented by **Leimkühler** (1984).

131 see section 4.2.2.

132 see section 3.1.2.

133 **Suri** (1985); **van der Wal** (1989); **Buzacott/Shanthikumar** (1993), pp. 374-376

The condition expressed in equation (57) would be satisfied by a closed queueing network with exponentially distributed service rates at the stations and unlimited local buffer capacities. If there is only one machine per station, then the service rate is independent of the station's queue length. If a station is made up of more than one machine, then the service rate increases as the number of workpieces increases - as long as the number of pallets n_m is not larger than the number of machines. If the number of machines is less than the number of workpieces, the service rate remains constant. In both cases the service rate is a *non-decreasing* function of the number of workpieces at a station.

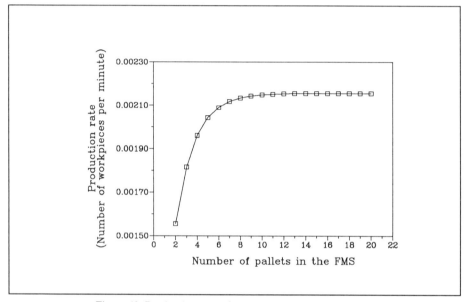

Figure 40: Production rate of the FMS vs. number of pallets

Returning to example 3-1, figure (40) shows that here too this correlation holds true. The more pallets circulating in the FMS, the higher the average production rate will be. It is important, however, to note the diminishing increase of the production rate, and that it asymptotically approaches an upper bound. The size of this upper bound is determined by the *bottleneck station*. This will be discussed below in more detail.

- **Queue lengths at the stations vs. the number of pallets:**

When the number of pallets reaches a certain level, a further increase results only in an insignificant improvement in the performance of the FMS, yet the lengths of the queues at the stations increase. This is shown in figure (41).

It can be seen that the lengths of the queues, particularly of the one at the bottleneck machine, increase from a specific number of pallets onward. Since the inventory of unfinished workpieces in the FMS (work-in-process inventory) is directly related to the number of circulating pallets, and since certain costs are associated with every pallet (cost of the pallet itself, cost of the buffer space to be provided for the pallet in the FMS, cost of the capital invested in the workpieces), the number of pallets will be held as low as possible as long as the desired production rate is met.

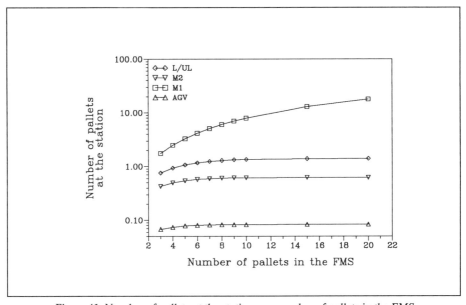

Figure 41: Number of pallets at the stations vs. number of pallets in the FMS

• **Utilizations of the stations vs. the number of pallets:**

A similar phenomenon can be observed in the utilization of the stations when the number of pallets is varied [see figure (42)]. When more pallets are present in the FMS, the utilizations of the machines will be higher. On the other hand, according to *Little's law* the average flow time of a workpiece will increase with the number of pallets as well. *Gutenberg*[134] called this the *scheduling dilemma* and described it as the conflict between the goals of maximizing the utilization and minimizing the flow time.

---

134 **Gutenberg** (1983)

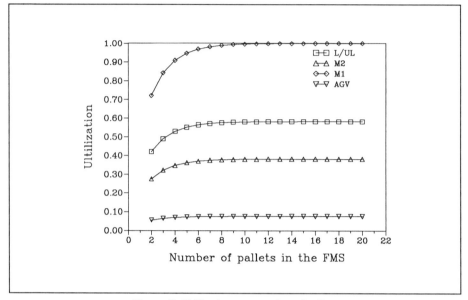

Figure 42: Utilizations vs. number of pallets

• **Asymptotic behavior of the production rate for large numbers of pallets:**

A closed queueing network exhibits an interesting behavior when it contains a large number of pallets. The number of pallets in the FMS eventually reaches a point at which the queue at a certain station, the bottleneck, increases so much that the station reaches full utilization. The *bottleneck station* e is the station with the largest average workload per machine (server) [see equation (58)].

$$e = \arg \max_{m} \{ \frac{p_m \cdot b_m}{S_m} \} \tag{58}$$

In the example above, the bottleneck occurs at station 3 (machine M1). If the number of pallets is increased such that the bottleneck station is always busy processing a workpiece, i.e. that the station is fully utilized, then the production rate of the bottleneck station e is equal to the product of the number of machines at this station and the service rate (μ_e) of each machine. This is also equal to the quotient of the number of machines divided by the average processing time of a workpiece at the station. This is shown in equation (59).

$$x_e^{max} = S_e \cdot \mu_e = \frac{S_e}{b_e} \tag{59}$$

Referring to equation (50), which described the production rate of a station as a function of the number of pallets in the FMS, the *production rate of the bottleneck station* for the limiting case of an infinite number of pallets is given by equation (60)[135]:

$$X_e^{max} = \lim_{N \to \infty} X_e(N) = \lim_{N \to \infty} p_e \cdot \frac{g(N-1,M)}{g(N,M)} = \frac{S_e}{b_e} \qquad (60)$$

Figure (43) illustrates the increase in the production rate of the bottleneck station 3 (M1) as the number of pallets circulating in the FMS is enlarged. The maximum production rate of this station is $X_3^{max} = 1/193.33 = 0.005172$.

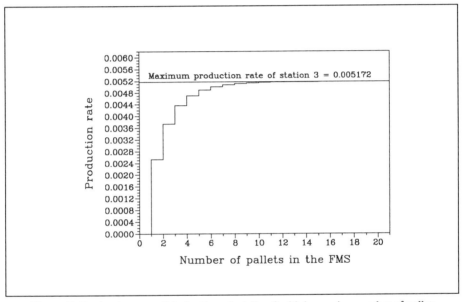

Figure 43: Production rate of the bottleneck station 3 with increasing number of pallets

The conclusion to be drawn from this discussion is that it is possible to use static allocation models to analyze an FMS with a relatively large number of pallets[136]. In this case the performance of the FMS can be derived from the performance of the bottleneck station, which is assumed to be 100% utilized. In industrial practice this bottleneck-oriented static analysis of the FMS is often the only performance evaluation technique used. In this case the bottleneck station is determined using equation (58) and its production rate is determined with the help of equation (59). The production rates and the utilizations of the nonbottleneck stations can then be calculated using equations (61) and (62) respectively.

$$X_m(N) = p_m \cdot X_M(N) \qquad\qquad m=1,2,\dots,M \qquad (61)$$

---

135 Secco-Suardo (1978), p. 20
136 Tetzlaff (1990), pp. 55-57; see also section 4.

$$U_m(N) = \frac{b_m \cdot X_m(N)}{S_m} \qquad\qquad m=1,2,\ldots,M \qquad (62)$$

Returning to example 3-1, the results of this approach are shown in table (17). For purposes of comparison, results from the use of the classical CQN model, assuming that $N=4$ pallets are circulating in the FMS, are given as well.

Station	CQN model		Static analysis	
	X_m	U_m	X_m	U_m
L/UL	0.005881	52.93%	0.006466	58.19%
M2	0.001176	34.77%	0.001293	38.23%
M1	0.004704	90.95%	0.005172	100.00%
AGV	0.011761	6.94%	0.012931	7.60%

Table 17: Comparison of the results from the use of the CQN model with the results from the bottleneck-oriented static analysis (example 3-1)

As can be seen in the table, the utilization of the stations, all of which have only one machine in this example, is proportional to the workload. This is also true when the number of pallets is limited ($N < \infty$).

The example shows that the static analysis makes a relatively optimistic estimation of the performance of the FMS under consideration. The reason for this is that the queueing processes in the CQN model, which can occasionally cause the bottleneck station to be idle since all the workpieces are under processing or waiting at other stations, are not allowed for in the static analysis. The results for the other stations are extrapolated from the overestimation of the production rate at the bottleneck station. This overestimation of the performance of an FMS alternative may be that much more serious since even the estimates of the classical CQN model tend to be optimistic[137]. The error associated with the use of the static analysis compared to the CQN model increases with decreasing difference between the utilizations of the bottleneck and the station with the second-highest utilization.

It is essentially possible to carry out a sensitivity analysis with respect to the other data that describe an FMS. It might be possible, for example, to consider varying the *production ratios* such that the proportion of product types that mainly impute workload on the stations which are not fully utilized would be increased, while the proportion of those product types concentrated at the bottleneck in the system would be reduced. Such considerations assume, however, that it is possible to shift production from the FMS to an alternative production system, such as a conventional job shop, still under operation in the factory. Another possibility would be to change the process plans so that those operations carried out at the bottleneck machines could be transferred to another machine which is not so heavily loaded. Changing the *processing times*, if possible, may be another way to reach a more balanced utilization of the FMS components.

---

137   see section 3.1.2.

If, after the investigation process described above, an FMS configuration has been found that fits the relevant performance criteria, then a system planner could transform this information into a concrete design proposal. Figure (44) shows one possible layout of an FMS for example 3-1[138].

Figure 44: FMS design proposal

Further reading for section 3.1.1.1.:

Bruell/Balbo (1980)
Buzacott (1989)
Buzacott/Shanthikumar (1992), (1993)
Buzacott/Yao (1986)
Buzen (1973)
Dallery (1986)
Denning/Buzen (1978)
Kleinrock (1975)
Kuhn (1990)
Proth/Hillion (1990)
Solberg (1977)
Stecke/Solberg (1981a)
Tempelmeier (1988)
Tetzlaff (1990)

---

138 **Tetzlaff** (1990), p. 6

3.1.1.2. The classical CQN model for special pallets

In the previous section 3.1.1.1. it was assumed that only one pallet type was circulating in the FMS. All product types could be affixed to these universal pallets. It was thus possible to draw conclusions about the performance of the FMS with respect to a single aggregated product group. This section is concerned with FMSs in which several dedicated pallet types circulate. The pallets may come in various sizes or have different fixtures attached to them. They are designated to be used by product types from several different product groups. These pallets are called *special (or dedicated) pallets*. It is possible to evaluate the key parameters for a closed queueing network with several (C) pallet types using the procedure described in section 3.1.1.1. based on the calculation of a normalization constant[139]. The normalization constant in this case, however, is dependent on the number of stations and the number of pallets of each *pallet type*. In this case a state of an FMS represents the distribution of the pallets of the various pallet types among the stations of the closed queueing network.

The description of the probability distribution of the customers in a closed queueing network with C customer classes and M stations is significantly more complicated[140] [see equation (63)].

$$P\{\underline{n}\} = P\{\underline{n}_1, \underline{n}_2, \ldots, \underline{n}_M\} = \frac{1}{g(N_1, N_2, \ldots, N_C, M)} \cdot \prod_{m=1}^{M} f_m\{\underline{n}_m\} \tag{63}$$

Not only the normalization constant, but also the factors $f_m(\underline{n}_m)$ are now defined with respect to several customer classes. In order for equation (63) to hold true, a fundamental prerequisite must be met: for a station following the FCFS queueing discipline, all pallet types must have exponentially distributed processing times with the same mean values.

FMSs in which special pallets circulate can also be investigated on the basis of a closed queueing network using the *mean value analysis* (MVA), as developed by *Reiser and Lavenberg*[141]. This is a method for calculating the key parameters of a queueing network that omits the complicated process of determining the normalization constant $g(N_1, N_2, \ldots, N_C, M)$.

Several different procedures can be found in the literature which are based on the mean value analysis. An *exact* MVA algorithm for the determination of the performance parameters of an FMS can be used[142]. This requires, however, that the assumptions of the classical CQN model apply and that the average processing times for all pallet types at a station with FCFS queueing discipline are the same.

---

139 **Bruell/Balbo** (1980), pp. 55-76
140 **Bruell/Balbo/Afshari** (1984)
141 **Reiser/Lavenberg** (1980)
142 For the exact MVA see **Bruell/Balbo** (1980), pp. 135-149; **Lazowska/Zahorjan/Graham/Sevcik** (1984), pp. 112-117

There also exists a number of *heuristic* procedures which are particularly suitable to the analysis of problem-specific aspects of an FMS. The following will concentrate on the heuristic MVA variation proposed by *Shalev-Oren, Seidmann and Schweitzer*[143] which is particularly useful for the analysis of FMSs.

3.1.1.2.1. Data preparation

Just as in the case of an FMS with only universal pallets, the first step in the analysis of the performance parameters of the FMS is to prepare the data available with the processing plans for the product types to be produced. C different *pallet types* (product groups) are distinguished from which N_c pallets circulate in the FMS. A specific set of product types (product group) is assigned to each pallet type. The criteria for this assignment usually have to do with the size of the workpieces or with the special fixtures for attaching workpieces to the different pallet types. The set of product types that can be fixed to type c pallets is represented by the index set K_c. The planned distribution of the production quantities among the members of product group c is given by the production ratios $ß_k$ ($k \in K_c$). The sum of the production ratios *within a single product group* must be equal to 1 [see equation (64)].

$$\sum_{k \in K_c} ß_k = 1 \qquad\qquad c=1,2,\ldots,C \qquad (64)$$

Product type k	1	2	3	4	5	6	7	8
Production ratio	$ß_1$	$ß_2$	$ß_3$	$ß_4$	$ß_5$	$ß_6$	$ß_7$	$ß_8$
Product group c		1				2		

Figure 45: Relationship between product types and dedicated pallet types

This grouping for eight products and two product groups (pallet types) is shown in figure (45). As is the case for a system with universal pallets, the production ratios *within a product group* must be maintained at the load/unload station by loading the workpieces appropriately on the pallets. The relative production ratios *among the product groups* (or pallet types), and thus for products of different product groups, cannot be determined in advance. They are dependent on the number of pallets of each type circulating in the FMS and on the characteristics of the products associated with each type, especially the workloads[144]. They result from the fact that the various pallet types move through the FMS at differing speeds. Pallets with workpieces that visit few stations for relatively short periods can move through the system significantly faster than pallets with work-

---

143 **Shalev-Oren/Seidmann/Schweitzer** (1985); **Suri/Hildebrant** (1984)
144 **Solot** (1990a); **Newman/Boc/Denzler** (1991).

pieces which visit numerous stations, have long processing times, or must wait for long periods at a heavily utilized station.

Example 3-2 illustrates these considerations in a more concrete fashion. The processing plans for the product types which are to be manufactured in the FMS are summarized in table (18). For purposes of simplicity, it is assumed that precisely one product is assigned to each pallet type ($\beta_k = 1$, k = 1,2,3). It is possible, however, to expand this method to include an unlimited number of products for each pallet type.

Operation no.	Station no.	name	Processing time[145]	Operation frequency
Product type 1: production ratio β_1=1.0 pallet type 1				
1	1	L/UL	15.0	1.0 ↔
2	2	M4	28.0	1.0
3	1	L/UL	15.0	1.0
4	3	M1	12.0	1.0
Product type 2: production ratio β_2=1.0 pallet type 2				
1	1	L/UL	15.0	1.0 ↔
2	4	M2	30.0	1.0
3	1	L/UL	15.0	1.0
4	5	M3	5.0	1.0
Product type 3: production ratio β_3=1.0 pallet type 3				
1	1	L/UL	15.0	1.0 ↔
2	5	M3	15.0	1.0
3	1	L/UL	5.0	1.0
4	2	M4	10.0	1.0
5	1	L/UL	10.0	1.0
6	3	M1	15.0	1.0
↑ m_{ko}			↑ t_{ko}	↑ f_{ko}

Table 18: Process plans for three product groups
(example 3-2)

If one examines the processing plans of the three product groups more closely it can be seen that each one generates different demands on the load/unload station and the machines. The relationships between the product groups are shown in figure (46). An edge between two product group nodes indicates that competition for capacity exists between them. Whereas station M2 is only used by product group 2 [represented in figure (46) by the small circle associated only with product group 2], the load/unload station (L/UL) is a point of competition for all three groups.

---

145 minutes

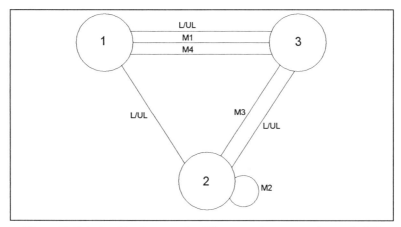

Figure 46: Relationships between the different product groups (example 3-2)

Again parallel to the procedure described for FMSs with universal pallets, the data within each product group must first be aggregated[146]. The results of this step provide the input data for further aggregations. The average transportation time is assumed to be 2.5 minutes. The symbols used for the input data are shown in table (19).

β_k	production ratio of product type k with respect to the production rate of its product group (pallet type)
b_{km}	mean processing time of a workpiece of product type k at station m
c	product group (pallet type) index (c=1,2,...,C)
k	product type index (k=1,2,...,K)
K_c	index set of product types assigned to pallet type c
m	station index (incl. transportation station) (m=1,2,...,M)
v_{km}	mean number of visits of a workpiece of product type k at station m

Table 19: Symbols used in the description of the process plans

The following relationships will now hold for each group:

• *Average number of operations for product group c at station m* (per circulation of an average workpiece of product group c through the FMS, pallet type specific visit frequency):

$$v_{cm} = \sum_{k \in K_c} \beta_k \cdot v_{km} \qquad\qquad c=1,2,\ldots,C;\ m=1,2,\ldots,M-1 \qquad (65)$$

∟ mean number of operations on a workpiece of product type k at station m

---

146   see section 3.1.1.1.1.

The product dependent number of operations v_{km} results from equation (4). Since a transportation process must follow every machining operation, the number of workpiece movements of the pallet type c is equal to

$$v_{cM} = \sum_{m=1}^{M-1} v_{cm} \qquad\qquad c=1,2,\ldots,C \qquad\qquad (66)$$

Table (20) shows the visit frequencies that result from the evaluation of the processing plans in example 3-2.

v_{cm}		c		
		1	2	3
m	1 (L/UL)	2.0	2.0	3.0
	2 (M4)	1.0	0.0	1.0
	3 (M1)	1.0	0.0	1.0
	4 (M2)	0.0	1.0	0.0
	5 (M3)	0.0	1.0	1.0
	6 (AGV)	4.0	4.0	6.0

Table 20: Visit frequencies per workpiece circulation through the FMS (example 3-2)

• **Average processing time of a workpiece of product group c at machine m** (per operation):

$$b_{cm} = \frac{1}{v_{cm}} \cdot \left(\sum_{k \in K_c} \beta_k \cdot v_{km} \cdot b_{km} \right) \qquad\qquad c=1,2,\ldots,C;\ m=1,2,\ldots,M-1 \qquad\qquad (67)$$

The product dependent processing time b_{km} is defined by equation (5). The processing times at the stations are now defined with respect to the different pallet types. The relevant values for example 3-2 are summarized in table (21). The identical average transportation times for all pallet types is also given in the last row of the table.

b_{cm}		c		
		1	2	3
m	1 (L/UL)	15.0	15.0	10.0
	2 (M4)	28.0	0.0	10.0
	3 (M1)	12.0	0.0	15.0
	4 (M2)	0.0	30.0	0.0
	5 (M3)	0.0	5.0	15.0
	6 (AGV)	2.5	2.5	2.5

Table 21: Mean processing times per pallet type and station (example 3-2)

- *Relative arrival frequency of a workpiece of product group c at machine m* (per movement of the workpiece between two operations, i.e. after the completion of a transportation process):

$$p_{cm} = \frac{v_{cm}}{\displaystyle\sum_{i=1}^{M-1} v_{ci}} \left.\right\} \begin{array}{l} \text{\ \ \ } \end{array} \qquad\qquad c=1,2,\ldots,C;\ m=1,2,\ldots,M-1 \qquad (68)$$

number of operations of a typical workpiece of product group c per cycle through the entire FMS

$$p_{cM} = 1 \qquad\qquad\qquad\qquad c=1,2,\ldots,C \qquad\qquad (69)$$

Here again, as in the case of universal pallets, it is assumed for the calculation of the arrival probabilities for the different pallet types that a transportation process is always performed between two operations. Table (22) shows the relative arrival frequencies for example 3-2.

p_{cm}		c		
		1	2	3
m	1 (L/UL)	0.500	0.500	0.500
	2 (M4)	0.250	0.000	0.167
	3 (M1)	0.250	0.000	0.167
	4 (M2)	0.000	0.250	0.000
	5 (M3)	0.000	0.250	0.167
	6 (AGV)	1.000	1.000	1.000

Table 22: Mean relative arrival frequencies per pallet type and station (example 3-2)

3.1.1.2.2. Model evaluation

The calculation of the performance parameters for an FMS can now be made based on the input data preprocessed in the previous section 3.1.1.2.1. Let the vector $\underline{N} = \{N_1, N_2, \ldots, N_C\}$ describe an externally *predetermined distribution* of the pallets among the individual pallet types. These pallets circulate through the FMS according to the process plans of the product types assigned to them. As soon as a workpiece has completed its processing it will be exchanged without delay for an unprocessed workpiece of the same product group already waiting outside the system. This sequence of events moves along just as in a system with universal pallets, with the exception that the individual pallet types move on their own *separate paths* through the system and often at differing speeds.

Figure (47) shows a closed queueing network in which two different pallet types are circulating. For each of the pallet types the stationary arrival probabilities p_{cm} ($c=1,2$; $m=1,2,3,4$) peculiar to that station are given. The different pallet types impose differing loads on the stations. This is marked by the varied shading in the rectangles in the figure. The various pallet types compete for the stations' capacities. They also influence each other via their flow through the queueing network. A change in the process plan for pallet type 1 can affect the average flow times of the other pallet type. This will be discussed further in section 3.1.1.2.3.

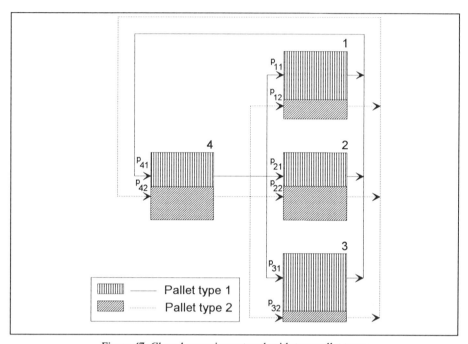

Figure 47: Closed queueing network with two pallet types

A great number of computational procedures are available for determining the performance parameters of an FMS modelled in this way. They can, for the most part, be categorized as either exact or heuristic procedures. An exact evaluation procedure will be presented first because this is the basis for the derivation of an heuristic procedure[147]. The discussion is limited to the single server case (one machine at each station and one vehicle)[148].

The *exact form* of the *MVA* is based on the following relationships between the mean flow times, queue lengths and production rates of the stations in the closed queueing network considered[149].

147 The distinction between exact and heuristic procedures is not intended to suggest that the former are more accurate and thus provide results that are always more useful for the performance evaluation of a particular FMS. The CQN models providing the basis for the heuristic procedures generally fit the reality of an FMS better than the CQN model that can be evaluated with an exact algorithm. A crucial assumption underlying the exact procedures is that the mean processing times at a specific station be the same for all pallet types. This assumption will rarely hold in real-life FMSs.
148 For the mean value analysis for queueing networks with parallel server stations see **Reiser/Lavenberg** (1980); **Bruell/Balbo/Afshari** (1984)
149 **Lazowska/Zahorjan/Graham/Sevcik** (1984), p. 139; see also **Van Doremalen** (1986)

· *Average flow time of pallet type c at station m:*

First, the point of view of a type c workpiece is examined *immediately before its arrival* at station m. At this point in time $A_{cm}(\underline{N})$ pallets are located at the station. Upon arrival at the station the workpiece will join the end of the queue (FCFS queueing discipline). The time span from its arrival to its departure after being processed is equal to the processing time of the workpiece considered plus the time the station needs for processing all the other workpieces in the line. Assuming that *all the pallet types* at a station m require the *same average* (exponentially distributed) *processing time* (i.e. when $b_{1m}=...=b_{Cm}=b_m$), then the average flow time of a workpiece of product group c at station m can be described by equation (70).

$$
\begin{array}{c}
\text{total processing time of all workpieces waiting at station m} \\
\downarrow \qquad \text{processing time of the arriving workpiece} \\
\downarrow
\end{array}
$$

$$D_{cm}(\underline{N}) = b_m \cdot A_{cm}(\underline{N}) + b_m \qquad\qquad c=1,2,\ldots,C;\ m=1,2,\ldots,M \qquad (70)$$

mean number of pallets at station m upon arrival of a pallet of type c

mean processing time of a pallet at station m (station dependent)

mean flow time of a pallet of type c at station m

It must be remembered, however, that

$$b_{cm}=b_m \qquad\qquad c=1,2,\ldots,C;\ m=1,2,\ldots,M \qquad (71)$$

The calculation is *simplified* when it can be assured that every incoming workpiece is processed immediately on arrival, i.e. without delay. If, for example, a continuously moving *conveyor system* is used for the transportation of workpieces in the FMS, then it can be assumed that a workpiece will be transported to the next station immediately after completion of a machining operation. For stations at which there are no queueing delays (delay server stations), equation (70) could be replaced with equation (72)[150].

$$D_{cm}(\underline{N})=b_m \qquad\qquad c=1,2,\ldots,C \qquad (72)$$

· *Average production rate for type c pallets at station m:*

Little's law, which provides for a stationary queueing system a relationsship between the expected number of customers, the arrival rate and the expected residence time, can be used for the calculation of the production rates[151]. In the current context, it states that the number of pallets in the system is equal to the product of the average production rate X and the flow time D. For an FMS with only one pallet type, this relationship is described in equation (73).

---

150   In the following we will mainly concentrate on stations where queueing processes play a role.
151   **Little** (1961); **Gross/Harris** (1985), p. 78

Here only a single circuit (transportation and machining operation) of a pallet through the queueing network is considered.

$$N = X \cdot D \qquad \text{or} \qquad X = N/D \qquad\qquad \textbf{Little's formula} \qquad (73)$$

- mean flow time
- mean production rate
- (mean) number of pallets in the FMS

The average production rate for type c pallets at station m can be found as follows. First, *Little's* law has to be applied to the entire network with respect to pallet type c:

$$X_c(\underline{N}) = \frac{N_c}{D_c(\underline{N})} \qquad\qquad c=1,2,\ldots,C \qquad (74)$$

- mean flow time of pallet type c

Since the number of type c pallets circulating in the system is constant (N_c), only the flow time $D_c(\underline{N})$ specific for each pallet type has to be determined. The average flow time of a type c pallet for one circuit through the network (transportation and machining operation) is a result of the sum of the station dependent flow times weighted by the relative arrival frequencies:

$$D_c(\underline{N}) = \sum_{m=1}^{M} p_{cm} \cdot D_{cm}(\underline{N}) \qquad\qquad c=1,2,\ldots,C \qquad (75)$$

Substituting equation (75) into equation (74), we obtain:

$$X_c(\underline{N}) = \frac{N_c}{\left. \sum_{m=1}^{M} p_{cm} \cdot D_{cm}(\underline{N}) \right\}} \qquad\qquad c=1,2,\ldots,C \qquad (76)$$

- mean flow time of pallet type c

When the production rates $X_c(\underline{N})$ specific for each pallet type (=production rate of the transportation system for pallet type c) are multiplied with the station specific relative arrival frequencies p_{cm}, the production rate of an individual station m can be determined:

$$X_{cm}(\underline{N}) = p_{cm} \cdot \frac{N_c}{\sum_{j=1}^{M} p_{cj} \cdot D_{cj}(\underline{N})} \qquad\qquad c=1,2,\ldots,C; \ m=1,2,\ldots,M \qquad (77)$$

- **Average number of type c pallets at station m:**

When *Little's* law is applied to a node in the network, equation (78) can be used to find the average number of pallets of type c at station m.

$$Q_{cm}(\underline{N}) = X_{cm}(\underline{N}) \cdot D_{cm}(\underline{N}) \qquad\qquad c=1,2,\ldots,C; \ m=1,2,\ldots,M \qquad (78)$$

$\quad$ mean flow time of a pallet of type c at station m

$\quad$ mean production rate for pallet type c at station m

$\quad$ mean number of type c pallets at station m (waiting or in process)

A distinction between two terms in this discussion is quite important. The first is the average number of pallets, $Q_m(\underline{N})$, present at the station m *over a certain time period*. The second is the average number of pallets that are present at the station m at a *specific point in time* - immediately before the arrival of a type c pallet, $A_{cm}(\underline{N})$. The following relationship between these two different quantities allows a recursive evaluation of the above equations:

$$A_{cm}(\underline{N}) = Q_m(\underline{N}-\underline{1}_c) \qquad\qquad c=1,2,\ldots,C; \ m=1,2,\ldots,M \qquad (79)$$

$\quad$ mean number of pallets at station m (time average)

$\quad$ mean number of pallets of type c at station m upon arrival of a type c pallet (arrival average)

$\underline{1}_c$ is a zero vector with a one at the cth position. Equation (79) should be understood so that each pallet which arrives at the station considers the rest of the queueing network *as if it were not a member of that network itself*. $Q_m(\underline{N})$ describes the time-average number of pallets at station m over all pallet types:

$$Q_m(\underline{N}) = \sum_{c=1}^{C} Q_{cm}(\underline{N}) \qquad\qquad m=1,2,\ldots,M \qquad (80)$$

The interactions between these equations and the resulting flow of values are summarized in figure (48).

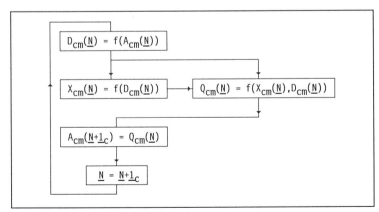

Figure 48: Flow of values in the mean value analysis procedure

The exact mean value analysis procedure for special pallets starts with the vector $\underline{N} = \{0,0,...,0\}$, i.e. with an empty queueing network. The above equation is then solved by making single unit step-by-step increases in one element from $\underline{N}$ on until the desired vector, $\underline{N} = \{N_1,N_2,...,N_C\}$, is achieved[152] [see figure (49)].

The recursive relationship between the arrival-average number of pallets present at the time of a workpiece's arrival and the time-average number of pallets present at a station in a given period for a pallet population decreased by one unit results in high memory requirements, which is exponentially related to the number of different pallet types. In a FORTRAN implementation, for example, for an FMS with 8 stations and 2 pallet types, each of which includes 10 pallets, it is necessary to define an array $Q(8,11,11)$ (968 memory spaces). If a third pallet type with 15 pallets is considered, then the dimension of the array increases to $Q(8,11,11,16)$ (15488 memory spaces). The demand for memory and computation time are clearly dependent on the product $(M \cdot N_1 \cdot N_2 \cdot ... \cdot N_C)$. Thus these factors, especially the memory requirements, can pose restrictions on the practical use of the exact MVA[153] algorithm.

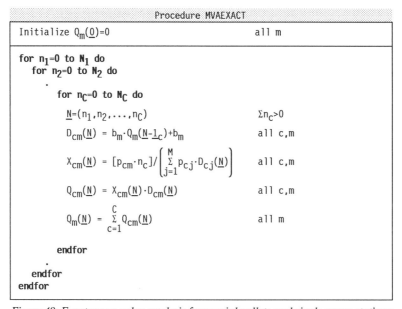

Figure 49: Exact mean value analysis for special pallets and single server stations

In a case with universal pallets and single server stations, and when the input data have been aggregated identically, one arrives at the same results whether using the exact MVA algorithm or the convolution procedure described in section 3.1.1.1. for the calculation of the normalization constant $g(N,M)$. This is de-

152 **Bruell/Balbo** (1980), pp. 143-147; **Reiser/Lavenberg** (1980)
153 **Reiser/Lavenberg** (1980), p. 320

monstrated for the *example 3-1 with universal pallets* (with one product group $C=1$). The input data are summarized in table (23).

station m	processing time	arrival frequency
1 (L/UL)	90.0000	0.5
2 (M2)	295.6700	0.1
3 (M1)	193.3333	0.4
4 (AGV)	5.9000	1.0
	$\uparrow b_m$	$\uparrow p_{1m}$

Table 23: Input data for the exact MVA procedure
(example 3-1)

The individual steps which must be carried out are described below. The basic procedure consists of increasing the pallet population in single-unit steps and then deriving the relevant parameters for n pallets based on the results for n-1 pallets.

Procedure MVAEXACT - example 3-1

Step 0: $n_1=0$

$\underline{N}=(0)$

m	1	2	3	4
$Q_{1m}(0)$	0.0	0.0	0.0	0.0

All stations are empty, as no pallet is circulating in the FMS. The time-average number of pallets, $Q_{1m}(0)$, with $n=0$ pallets is equal to the arrival-average number of pallets, $A_{1m}(1)$, found by a newly arriving (here the only one present in the FMS) pallet at a station.

Step 1: $n_1=1$

$\underline{N}=(1)$

m	1	2	3	4
$D_{1m}(1)$	90.000	295.670	193.333	5.900

$D(1)=157.80$

As all queues are empty the mean flow times at the stations are equal to the mean processing times.

The mean total flow time of a pallet through the entire FMS (all operations) is equal to the sum of the station-specific flow times. These are weighted by the relative arrival frequencies [denominator in equation (77)].

m	1	2	3	4
$X_{1m}(1)$	0.003169	0.000634	0.002535	0.006337

Mean production rates

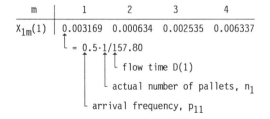

$= 0.5 \cdot 1 / 157.80$

flow time D(1)

actual number of pallets, n_1

arrival frequency, p_{11}

m	1	2	3	4	
$Q_{1m}(1)$	0.285	0.187	0.490	0.037	Mean number of pallets. Due to a rounding error the sum is only 0.999.

$$\uparrow$$
$$\mathrel{\rule{0pt}{0pt}}\!\!= 0.003169 \cdot 90.0$$

Step 2: $n_1 = 2$

$\underline{N} = (2)$ Mean flow times

m	1	2	3	4
$D_{1m}(2)$	115.650	350.960	288.066	6.118

$$\uparrow$$
$$\mathrel{\rule{0pt}{0pt}}\!\!= 0.285 \cdot 90.0 + 90.0$$

$D(2) = 214.266$ Mean total flow time

m	1	2	3	4	Mean production rates
$X_{1m}(2)$	0.004667	0.000933	0.003734	0.009334	

m	1	2	3	4	Mean number of pallets. The sum is 2.
$Q_{1m}(2)$	0.540	0.327	1.076	0.057	

Step 3: $n_1 = 3$

$\underline{N} = (3)$ Mean flow times

m	1	2	3	4
$D_{1m}(3)$	138.600	392.354	401.359	6.236

$D(3) = 275.315$ Mean total flow time

m	1	2	3	4	Mean production rates
$X_{1m}(3)$	0.005448	0.001090	0.004359	0.010897	

m	1	2	3	4	Mean number of pallets. The sum is 3.
$Q_{1m}(3)$	0.755	0.428	1.750	0.068	

Step 4: $n_1 = 4$

$\underline{N} = (4)$ Mean flow times

m	1	2	3	4
$D_{1m}(3)$	157.950	422.217	531.666	6.301

$D(4) = 340.164$ Mean total flow time

m	1	2	3	4	Mean production rates. The production rate of the transportation system (station 4) is equal to the sum of the production rates of the stations 1 to 3.
$X_{1m}(4)$	0.005880	0.001176	0.004704	0.011759	

m	1	2	3	4	Mean number of pallets. The sum is 4.
$Q_{1m}(4)$	0.929	0.497	2.501	0.074	

End of procedure MVAEXACT - example 3-1

Apart from the slight deviations due to rounding off, the results agree with those from the calculation of the normalization constant in section 3.1.1.1.2. In addition to using equations (70)-(78) to find the flow times, the production rates, and the number of pallets at the stations, after completion of the recursive procedure MVAEXACT the following parameters of the FMS can be derived as well:

· **Production rate of the FMS for product group c:**

The production rate of the FMS for product group c can be found by dividing the production rate of the transportation system by the average number of transportation processes (or machining operations) required for the manufacture of a workpiece [see equation (81)]. In contrast to the variable $X_c(\underline{N})$ from equation (74), the full course of the workpiece through the FMS is considered (all operations) instead of a one-time circuit through the queueing network.

$$X_c(\underline{N}) = \frac{X_{cM}(\underline{N})}{v_{cM}} \qquad\qquad c=1,2,\ldots,C \qquad (81)$$

$\overset{\uparrow}{L}$ = mean number of operations for product group (pallet type) c

Thus for example 3-1, the production rate of the FMS (recall that $v_{1M}=6$) would be equal to $0.011761/6=0.001960$ workpieces per minute.

· **Utilization of station m due to product group c:**

The utilization of station m attributable to a specific pallet type is defined, according to equation (82), as the product of the production rate X_{cm} and the average processing time b_{cm}, since there is only one machine present at each station.

$$U_{cm}(\underline{N}) = X_{cm}(\underline{N}) \cdot b_{cm} \qquad\qquad m=1,2,\ldots,M \qquad (82)$$

The results of this calculation for example 3-1 are presented in table (24).

Station m	Utilization	Number of pallets at the station	Flow time
1	0.529	0.929	157.97
2	0.347	0.497	422.62
3	0.909	2.500	531.46
4	0.069	0.074	6.29

Table 24: Exact MVA results for example 3-1

A FORTRAN implementation of the exact MVA version as described above for the case of universal pallets is illustrated in figure (50). The program can be easily modified for a situation with a station of unlimited capacity (delay server). It would only be necessary to change "D(M)=B(M)*..." into "D(M)=B(M)" in the row for the calculation of the flow time for this station [see equation (72)].

```
          SUBROUTINE MVAEX (NN,MM,B,P)
C
C         Exact MVA; universal pallets; single server stations
C
C NN - number of pallets
C MM - number of stations (incl. transportation station)
C B  - mean processing times
C P  - relative arrival frequencies
C
          DIMENSION Q(100),D(100),X(100)
          DIMENSION P(100),B(100)
          REAL L
       ┌ DO 10 M=1,MM
       │   Q(M)=0.0
    10 └ CONTINUE
C
C      Iteration
C
       ┌ DO 40 N=1,NN
       │   SD=0.0
       │ ┌ DO 20 M=1,MM
C      │ │   flow time at station M
       │ │   D(M)=B(M)*(1.0+Q(M))
C      │ │   total flow time
       │ │   SD=SD+D(M)*P(M)
    20 │ └ CONTINUE
       │ ┌ DO 30 M=1,MM
C      │ │   production rate of station m
       │ │   X(M)=P(M)*N/SD
C      │ │   mean number of pallets at station M
C      │ │   (time persistent queues; for N pallets)
       │ │   Q(M)=D(M)*X(M)
    30 │ └ CONTINUE
    40 └ CONTINUE
          RETURN
          END
```

Figure 50: FORTRAN program of the exact MVA for universal pallets and single server stations

The algorithm could also easily be implemented with the help of a PC spreadsheet software package.

In *Lazowska/Zahorjan/Graham/Sevcik*[154] a FORTRAN version of the exact MVA for special pallets is described. The exact determination of the relevant parameters with the MVA procedure for special pallets is only possible under the restrictive condition that all the pallet types at a station have the same average processing time. That means that the pallet types can only be distinguished based on their flow through the network (i.e. on their transition probabilities or their stationary arrival probabilities). This condition is almost never satisfied in FMSs. Furthermore, the exact recursive evaluation of the above equations for many pallet types and many pallets - as already indicated - requires large memory and long computation times. For these reasons a number of *heuristic* procedures have been developed[155]. The central idea of most of these procedures is to replace the equations (70) (flow time) and (79) (queues at a given point in time) with a non-recursive approximation.

---

154 Lazowska/Zahorjan/Graham/Sevcik (1984), pp. 398-402
155 Schweitzer (1979); Hildebrant (1980); Chandy/Neuse (1982); Van Doremalen (1986); Zahorjan/Eager/Sweillam (1988)

Schweitzer[156] proposed the approximation described in equation (83) for the average number of pallets at station m on arrival of a type c pallet. Here the entire pallet population at a station is reduced by a proportion due to the pallet which is just arriving at the station. According to *Zahorjan, Eager and Sweillam*[157], this kind of approximation is called *proportional estimation* (PE).

$$
A_{cm}(\underline{N}) \approx \frac{(N_c-1)}{N_c} \cdot Q_{cm}(\underline{N}) + \sum_{\substack{j=1 \\ j \neq c}}^{C} Q_{jm}(\underline{N})
$$

<!-- annotation arrows -->
         └ number of pallets of the other pallet types

└ number of pallets of type c at station m

$$
= \sum_{j=1}^{C} Q_{jm}(\underline{N}) - \frac{Q_{cm}(\underline{N})}{N_c}
\qquad\qquad c=1,2,\dots,C; \; m=1,2,\dots,M \quad (83)
$$

Since the analysis of real-life FMSs is the focus of this study, certain heuristic variations of the MVA are particularly interesting. They include those which make it possible to observe *product group specific processing and queueing times* and *parallel servers* at a given station[158].

The approximative mean value analysis variation proposed by *Shalev-Oren, Seidmann and Schweitzer* for FMS performance evaluation will now be discussed in more detail[159]. Here the basic relationships between the key parameters of an FMS are not described based on a pallet's flow time at a station (D_{cm}). Instead the flow times of the different pallet types are broken down into their components (queueing time, processing time) and each is approximated individually. By explicitly *approximating the queueing time* at a station it is possible to account for the influence of different *queueing disciplines* at the machines on the performance of the FMS.

The average flow time of a workpiece on a type c pallet that arrives at any given time at the station m is made up of a number of different components[160] :

156 Schweitzer (1979); see also Schweitzer/Seidmann/Shalev-Oren (1986)
157 Zahorjan/Eager/Sweillam (1988)
158 Suri/Hildebrant (1984); Seidmann/Shalev-Oren/Schweitzer (1986)
159 Shalev-Oren/Seidmann/Schweitzer (1985)
160 see also Cavaille/Dubois (1982)

Mean *flow time* D_{cm}

=

Mean *waiting time* W_{cm}

=
Mean *residual service time* $W0_{cm}$ of the workpiece currently being processed, that will leave the station next
+
Mean *total processing time* $W1_{cm}$ *of all workpieces already waiting* for service at station m (from all product groups)

+

Processing time b_{cm} of the arriving workpiece (pallet)

Figure 51: Break-down of the mean flow time of a pallet of type c
at station m

Figure (52) illustrates the composition of the flow time of a workpiece at a station with only one machine at which two pallet types can be processed.

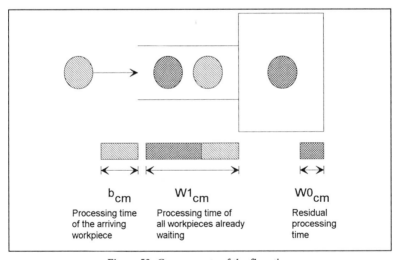

Figure 52: Components of the flow time

The processing times corresponding to the workpieces are represented by rectangles. In the case depicted here the machine is currently busy. The workpiece that has just arrived must, therefore, wait until the piece being processed is finished (residual processing time). In addition the arriving workpiece must wait until the workpieces already in the queue have been processed. These considerations can also be extended to the multiple server case, in which several parallel machines working at one station are supplied by a single queue. This extension would only affect the time required for the pieces already in line to be processed and the estimation of the residual processing time for the pieces currently being processed. According to figure (52), the average flow time of a workpiece of product group c at station m is described as follows:

$$D_{cm} = b_{cm} + W0_{cm} + W1_{cm} \qquad\qquad c=1,2,\ldots,C;\ m=1,2,\ldots,M \qquad (84)$$

- total processing time of the workpieces already waiting
- residual service time of the workpiece currently being processed, that will leave the station next
- processing time of the arriving workpiece
- mean flow time of a pallet of type c at station m

The break-down of a pallet's flow time at a station, as described above, allows a detailed analysis and approximation of its component parts. This will be taken up in the following section.

- *Average total processing time of the workpieces already waiting:*

The *average total processing time* $W1_{cm}$ of all the *workpieces awaiting processing* upon arrival of a type c pallet can be estimated as follows[161], assuming an FCFS queueing discipline. In what follows, the quantity S_m describes the number of parallel identical machines, and QW_{cm} represents the length of the queue of type c pallets at station m.

$$W1_{cm} \approx \frac{1}{S_m} \cdot \left(\sum_{j=1}^{C} b_{jm} \cdot QW_{jm} - \frac{b_{cm} \cdot QW_{cm}}{N_c} \right) \qquad c=1,2,\ldots,C;\ m=1,2,\ldots,M \qquad (85)$$

- queue length of pallet type j at station m

The correction term $(b_{cm} \cdot QW_{cm}/N_c)$ is intended to represent the share of the average queue length at station m taken up by the type of the newly arriving pallet. According to equation (86), the length of the queue for type c pallets at station m is equal to the production rate multiplied by the average queueing time.

$$QW_{cm} = X_{cm} \cdot W_{cm} \qquad\qquad c=1,2,\ldots,C;\ m=1,2,\ldots,M \qquad (86)$$

- *Residual service time:*

The residual service time describes the time period from the arrival of a workpiece at a station to the point in time when the next workpiece is taken out of

---

161 In a similar manner it is also possible to account for situations where the pallet types have different known priorities. See **Shalev-Oren/Seidmann/Schweitzer** (1985); **Van Doremalen** (1986)

the queue and passed on to a machine for processing. The (conditional[162]) residual service time of a workpiece being processed when another workpiece arrives at the station can be derived with the help of results provided by *renewal theory*. If $\sigma\{B_{cm}\}$ represents the standard deviation of the processing times of a type c pallet at station m, then the (conditional) *average residual service time* br_{cm} is given by equation (87)[163].

$$
\begin{aligned}
br_{cm} &= \frac{b_{cm}^2 + \sigma^2\{B_{cm}\}}{2 \cdot b_{cm}} \\[2em]
&= b_{cm} \cdot \frac{1 + \left[\dfrac{\sigma\{B_{cm}\}}{b_{cm}}\right]^2}{2}
\end{aligned}
\qquad c=1,2,\ldots,C; \; m=1,2,\ldots,M \qquad (87)
$$

The second summand in the numerator of equation (87) is the squared coefficient of variation of the processing times. Since under the assumption of exponentially distributed processing times the average value b_{cm} is equal to the standard deviation $\sigma\{B_{cm}\}$, the expected value of the residual service time is equal to the average processing time of a workpiece.

Residual service time can only exist when upon a pallet's arrival at a station all machines are busy processing other workpieces[164]. The expected (conditional) residual service time must, therefore, be multiplied by the *probability that the station will be fully utilized*.

This procedure is carried out differently depending on the number of machines at a station[165].

• *Stations with a single machine*

If the station comprises only one machine (single server), then the probability that it will be processing a workpiece at any given moment is equal to its average *utilization*[166]. In this case the approximation of the average residual service time as described in equation (88) can be used. Here the total utilization of the station m is represented by the pallet type specific utilizations U_{jm}. The proportion of the mean residual service time that can be assigned to the pallet type under consideration is subtracted from the sum of residual service times.

---

162 The residual service time can be derived based on results provided by renewal theory only under the assumption that the machine is always busy. This is meant by the term "conditional".

163 **Kleinrock** (1975), p. 173; **Cavaille/Dubois** (1982); **Tijms** (1986), p. 8. In the terminology of renewal theory this is called the *residual life time*.

164 Otherwise the arriving workpiece could immediately be processed by an idle machine.

165 **Shalev-Oren/Seidmann/Schweitzer** (1985)

166 The utilization is equal to the fraction of a time period when the machine is busy. This is equal to the probability that an arriving workpiece will find the machine busy and consequently its processing will be delayed.

$$
WO_{cm} \approx \sum_{j=1}^{C} U_{jm} \cdot b_{jm} - \frac{U_{cm} \cdot b_{cm}}{N_C} \qquad\qquad c=1,2,\ldots,C; \; m=1,2,\ldots,M \,|\, S_m=1 \qquad (88)
$$

conditional mean residual processing time for pallet type j (with exponentially distributed processing times)

mean utilization of station m with respect to pallet type j

= P{machine is busy with pallet type j}

- *Stations with several identical machines*

In the case of several identical machines at a station (multiple server) the probability that the station will be fully utilized upon arrival of a pallet (PB_{cm}) is estimated by use of the $(M/M/S_m):(GD/N_{max(m)}/\infty)]$ queueing model with the average *arrival rate*

$$
\lambda_{cm} = \sum_{j=1}^{C} X_{jm} - \frac{X_{cm}}{N_C} \qquad\qquad c=1,2,\ldots,C; \; m=1,2,\ldots,M \qquad (89)
$$

and the average *processing time*[167]

$$
b_{cm}^{b} = \frac{\displaystyle\sum_{j=1}^{C} X_{jm} \cdot b_{jm} - \frac{X_{cm} \cdot b_{cm}}{N_C}}{\lambda_{cm}} \qquad\qquad c=1,2,\ldots,C; \; m=1,2,\ldots,M. \qquad (90)
$$

The term $N_{max(m)}$ represents the maximum number of pallets that could be present at station m when a new pallet arrives. It can be derived from the product's process plans. $N_{max(m)}$ is described in equation (91) as the total number of pallets minus one of those pallet types that visit station m. This is the maximum number of pallets that could simultaneously be waiting for processing at station m.

$$
N_{max(m)} = \left(\sum_{\substack{c=1 \\ v_{cm}>0}}^{C} N_C \right) -1 \qquad\qquad m=1,2,\ldots,M \qquad (91)
$$

The abbreviation GD (general discipline) stands for the three queueing disciplines: "First-Come-First-Served", "Last-Come-First-Served" and "Service-in-Random-Order". The *average residual service time* of a workpiece about to be processed after the arrival of a type c pallet at a fully utilized machine can be found by dividing the average processing time at the station by the number of machines [see equation (92)].

$$
RB_{cm} \approx \frac{b_{cm}^{b}}{S_m} \qquad\qquad c=1,2,\ldots,C; \; m=1,2,\ldots,M \qquad (92)
$$

---

167 **Taha** (1989), pp. 625-627

This quantity RB_{cm} is then multiplied by the probability that an arriving workpiece will find all the machines at the station occupied (PB_{cm}). The following approximation of the *average residual service time* $W0_{cm}$ at a station with several machines thus results:

$$W0_{cm} \approx PB_{cm} \cdot RB_{cm} \qquad\qquad\qquad c=1,2,\ldots,C; \ m=1,2,\ldots,M \,|\, S_m>1 \qquad (93)$$

                    └ period of time between the pallet's arrival at the busy station m
                       and the point in time when the next machine is freed

        └ probability that all machines are busy upon arrival of a pallet

  └ mean waiting time until a workpiece currently being processed will leave the station

The probability that all the machines at a station will be occupied can be calculated with equation (94).

$$PB_{cm} = \sum_{l=S_m}^{N_{max}(m)} P_m\{l\} \qquad\qquad\qquad c=1,2,\ldots,C; \ m=1,2,\ldots,M \qquad (94)$$

        └ probability that l pallets are found at station m[168]

The average queueing time of an arriving type c pallet at station m can thus be found using equation (95).

$$W_{cm} = W0_{cm} + W1_{cm} \qquad\qquad\qquad c=1,2,\ldots,C; \ m=1,2,\ldots,M \qquad (95)$$

The utilization of the station m by the pallet type c is given as follows:

$$U_{cm} = \frac{X_{cm} \cdot b_{cm}}{S_m} \qquad\qquad\qquad c=1,2,\ldots,C; \ m=1,2,\ldots,M \qquad (96)$$

The average number of type c pallets at station m results from the addition of the queue length QW_{cm} and the average number of workpieces currently being processed:

$$Q_{cm} = QW_{cm} + U_{cm} \cdot S_m \qquad\qquad\qquad c=1,2,\ldots,C; \ m=1,2,\ldots,M \qquad (97)$$

        └ mean number of workpieces under processing

These relationships[169] provide the basis for the successive substitution procedure illustrated in figure (53), which is carried out until variations of the estimates of the average queue lengths remain within a given tolerance level $\in$.

---

[168] The computation of this probability for the M/M/c-queueing model is illustrated in **Taha** (1989), pp. 625-627.
[169] **Shalev-Oren/Seidmann/Schweitzer** (1985)

Procedure MVAHEU

Iteration 0:

Initialize

Mean flow times,	e.g. $D_{cm}=b_{cm}$	all c,m
Mean queue lengths,	e.g. $QW_{cm}=N_c/M$	all c,m
Mean waiting times,	$W_{cm}=0$	all c,m
Tolerance level	ϵ	

Iteration 1:

Mean production rates:

$$X_{cm} = [p_{cm} \cdot N_c] / \left(\sum_{j=1}^{M} p_{cj} \cdot D_{cj} \right) \qquad \text{all c,m}$$

Mean waiting times:

$$W_{cm} = W0_{cm} + W1_{cm} \qquad \text{all c,m; } p_{cm} > 0$$

Mean flow times:

$$D_{cm} = b_{cm} + W0_{cm} + W1_{cm} \qquad \text{all c,m; } p_{cm} > 0$$

Mean queue lengths

$$QW_{cm} = X_{cm} \cdot W_{cm} \qquad \text{all c,m}$$

Convergence test:

If the mean queue lengths changed less than the tolerance level ϵ, STOP; otherwise perform a further iteration.

Figure 53: Approximate mean value analysis for FMSs with special pallets and multiple server stations

For purposes of illustration, the MVAHEU procedure will be applied to example 3-2. The FMS alternative in the example is assumed to contain three pallet types with $N_1 = 8$, $N_2 = 2$ and $N_3 = 4$ pallets, respectively. It is further assumed that there is only one machine at each station. The tolerance level which will trigger the end of the procedure is fixed at $\epsilon = 0.1$.

Procedure MVAHEU - example 3-2

Iteration 0 (Initialization):

$\epsilon=0.1$ Tolerance level

D_{cm}:   The mean processing times are taken as
                                                                      initial values for the mean flow times.

	1	2	3
1	15.000	15.000	10.000
2	28.000	0.000	10.000
3	12.000	0.000	15.000
4	0.000	30.000	0.000
5	0.000	5.000	15.000
6	2.500	2.500	2.500

QW_{cm}:   Mean queue lengths: as a starting point the
                                                                      type c pallets are equally distributed
                                                                      among all stations.

	1	2	3
1	1.3333	0.3333	0.6667
2	1.3333	0.3333	0.6667
3	1.3333	0.3333	0.6667
4	1.3333	0.3333	0.6667
5	1.3333	0.3333	0.6667
6	1.3333	0.3333	0.6667

Iteration 1:

	1	2	3
	20.00	18.75	14.18

$$= 0.500 \cdot 10.0$$
$$+0.167 \cdot 10.0$$
$$+0.167 \cdot 15.0$$
$$+0.167 \cdot 15.0$$
$$+1.000 \cdot 2.5$$

$\underset{p_{3j}}{\uparrow}\quad\underset{D_{3j}}{\uparrow}$

Auxiliary variables: sum of the flow times weighted with the arrival probabilities; denominator from equation (77) for the mean production rates.

X_{cm}:   Production rates according to equation
                                                                      (77). The production rates of the transpor-
                                                                      tation station are equal to the sum of the
                                                                      production rates of the processing stations.

	1	2	3
1	0.2000	0.0533	0.1410	$\leftarrow = 0.5 \cdot 4/14.18$
2	0.1000	0.0000	0.0471
3	0.1000	0.0000	0.0471
4	0.0000	0.0267	0.0000
5	0.0000	0.0267	0.0471
6	0.4000	0.1067	0.2821

auxiliary variable
$\underset{N_3}{\uparrow}$
$\underset{p_{13}}{\uparrow}$

U_{cm}:   Auxiliary variables: utilizations according to
                                                                      equation (96)

	1	2	3
1	3.0000	0.7995	1.4100	$\leftarrow = 0.1410 \cdot 10.0$
2	2.8000	0.0000	0.4710
3	1.2000	0.0000	0.7065
4	0.0000	0.8010	0.0000
5	0.0000	0.1335	0.7065
6	1.0000	0.2668	0.7053

$\underset{X_{13}}{\uparrow}\quad\underset{b_{13}}{\uparrow}$

$$= 0.2821 \cdot 2.5$$
$\underset{X_{36}}{\uparrow}\quad\underset{b_{36}}{\uparrow}$

WO_{cm}:

Residual service times according to equation (88)

	1	2	3
1	65.4675	65.0963	67.5675
2	73.3100	0.0000	81.9325
3	23.1975	0.0000	22.3481
4	0.0000	12.0150	0.0000
5	0.0000	10.9313	8.6156
6	4.6178	4.5968	4.4894

$\leftarrow \; = \; 3.0000 \cdot 15.0$
$+ \; 0.7995 \cdot 15.0$
$+ \; 1.4100 \cdot 10.0$
$- \; 1.4100 \cdot 10.0 / 4$

$\mathsf{L} \; = \; 1.0000 \cdot 2.5$
$+ \; 0.2668 \cdot 2.5$
$+ \; 0.7053 \cdot 2.5$

$\mathsf{L} \; U_{j6} \quad \mathsf{L} \; b_{j6}$

$- \; 0.7053 \cdot 2.5 / 4$

$\mathsf{L} \; U_{36} \quad \mathsf{L} \; b_{36} \quad \mathsf{L} \; N_3$

$W1_{cm}$:

Total processing times of the waiting workpieces according to equation (85)

	1	2	3
1	29.1661	29.1663	29.9993
2	39.3329	0.0000	42.3327
3	24.0002	0.0000	23.5000
4	0.0000	4.9995	0.0000
5	0.0000	10.8338	9.1669
6	5.4166	5.4166	5.4166

$\leftarrow \; = \; 1.3333 \cdot 15.0$
$+ \; 0.3333 \cdot 15.0$
$+ \; 0.6667 \cdot 10.0$
$- \; 0.6667 \cdot 10.0 / 4$

$\mathsf{L} \; = \; 1.3333 \cdot 2.5$
$+ \; 0.3333 \cdot 2.5$
$+ \; 0.6667 \cdot 2.5$

$\mathsf{L} \; QW_{j6} \quad \mathsf{L} \; b_{j6}$

$- \; 0.6667 \cdot 2.5 / 4$

$\mathsf{L} \; QW_{36} \quad \mathsf{L} \; b_{36} \quad \mathsf{L} \; N_3$

W_{cm}:

Waiting times according to equation (95)

	1	2	3
1	94.6336	94.2626	97.5668
2	112.6429	0.0000	124.2652
3	47.1977	0.0000	45.8481
4	0.0000	17.0145	0.0000
5	0.0000	21.7651	17.7825
6	10.0344	10.0134	9.9060

$\leftarrow \; = \; 67.5675$
$+ \; 29.9993$

$\mathsf{L} \; = \; 4.4894 + 5.4166$

$\mathsf{L} \; WO_{36} \quad \mathsf{L} \; W1_{36}$

D_{cm}:

Flow times; sums of processing and waiting times according to equation (84)

	1	2	3
1	109.6336	109.2626	107.5668 ← = 97.5668
2	140.6429	0.0000	134.2652 + 10.0
3	59.1977	0.0000	60.8481
4	0.0000	47.0145	0.0000
5	0.0000	26.7651	32.7825
6	12.5344	12.5134	12.4060

$$\llcorner = 9.9060 + 2.5$$
$$\llcorner w_{36} \quad \llcorner b_{36}$$

QW_{cm}:

Queue lengths according to equation (86). Obviously these values are not very precise. The sum of the queue lengths for a particular pallet type over all stations is larger than the number of pallets.

	1	2	3
1	18.9267	5.0242	13.7569 ← = 0.1410·97.5668
2	11.2643	0.0000	5.8529
3	4.7198	0.0000	2.1594 $\llcorner x_{31}$ $\llcorner w_{31}$
4	0.0000	0.4543	0.0000
5	0.0000	0.5811	0.8376
6	4.0138	1.0684	2.7945

$$\llcorner = 0.2821 \cdot 9.9060$$
$$\llcorner x_{36} \quad \llcorner w_{36}$$

Σ   38.9246   7.1280 25.4013

convergence test:

Several (at least one) queue lengths have changed more than ∈. Therefore another iteration is performed.

$$\max_{(all\ c,m)} \{Abs(QW^1_{cm} - QW_{cm})\} = 17.5934 > \mathrm{E} = 0.01$$

$$\llcorner \quad \llcorner = 1.3333$$
$$\llcorner = 18.9267$$

Iteration 2:

	1	2	3
	117.3114	85.5896	104.2480

Auxiliary variables: sum of the weighted flow times

$$\llcorner = 0.500 \cdot 107.5668$$
$$+0.167 \cdot 134.2652$$
$$+0.167 \cdot 60.8481$$
$$+0.167 \cdot 32.7825$$
$$+1.000 \cdot 12.4060$$

$$\llcorner p_{3m} \quad \llcorner D_{3j}$$

X_{cm}:

Production rates

	1	2	3
1	.0341	.0117	.0192
2	.0170	.0000	.0064
3	.0170	.0000	.0064
4	.0000	.0058	.0000
5	.0000	.0058	.0064
6	.0682	.0234	.0384

etc.

After completion of the last iteration the results can be summarized as follows:

Pallet type specific results:

Pallet type   1: ─────────────────────────────────────

    Production rate: .019918 parts/min
                        1.1951 parts/hour
                        9.5608 parts/day
    Flow time: 401.6396 min

Station No.	Name	Utilization U_{1m}	Number of pallets Q_{1m}	Flow time (min.) D_{1m}
1	L/UL	.5976	5.881	147.6344
2	M4	.5577	1.394	69.9892
3	M1	.2390	.374	18.7816
4	M2	.0000	.000	0.0000
5	M3	.0000	.000	0.0000
6	AGV	.1992	.317	3.9742

$$\Sigma\ 7.966 \approx 8$$

Pallet type   2: ─────────────────────────────────────

    Production rate: .005781 parts/min.
                        .3469 parts/hour
                        2.7749 parts/day
    Flow time: 345.9559 min

Station No.	Name	Utilization U_{2m}	Number of pallets Q_{2m}	Flow time (min.) D_{2m}
1	L/UL	.1734	1.686	145.7946
2	M4	.0000	.000	0.0000
3	M1	.0000	.000	0.0000
4	M2	.1734	.190	32.8999
5	M3	.0289	.040	6.9358
6	AGV	.0578	.091	3.9563

$$\Sigma\ 2.007 \approx 2$$

Pallet type   3: ─────────────────────────────────────

    Production rate: .007187 parts/min.
                        .4312 parts/hour
                        3.4497 parts/day
    Flow time: 556.5649 min.

Station No.	Name	Utilization U_{3m}	Number of pallets Q_{3m}	Flow time (min.) D_{3m}
1	L/UL	.2156	3.141	145.6988
2	M4	.0719	.404	56.1801
3	M1	.1078	.156	21.7570
4	M2	.0000	.000	0.0000
5	M3	.1078	.119	16.5852
6	AGV	.1078	.171	3.9648

$$\Sigma\ 3.991 \approx 4$$

Table 25-1: Results of the procedure MVAHEU for example 3-2

Station specific results:			

Station No.	Name	Utilization	
1	L/UL	.9866	
2	M4	.6296	
3	M1	.3468	
4	M2	.1734	
5	M3	.1367	
6	AGV	.3648	

Production rates:			

Product No.	Name	Production rate per minute	hour	shift
1	P1	.019918	1.1951	9.56
2	P2	.005781	.3469	2.77
3	P3	.007187	.4312	3.45

Table 25-2: Results of the procedure MVAHEU for example 3-2

When the procedure is applied as described to example 3-2, 19 iterations are necessary to reach a point at which the solution is stable, i.e. when successive queue lengths do not vary more than $\in = 0.1$. One way to accelerate the convergence of the procedure is to transform the queue lengths QW_{cm} as suggested by *Bard*[170]. This generally leads to a significant reduction in the number of iterations. In the previous example the solution could have been reached after only 12 iterations. A graphical representation of both variations of the MVAHEU procedure - with or without the convergence inducement - is shown in figure (54) based on the length of the queue at station 1 (L/UL). It can be clearly seen that the oscillations reduce significantly faster when the convergence inducement is used than in the original variation of the procedure described above.

However, there are situations when convergence is very slow. This is especially the case when the number of pallets is very large and there are several stations with nearly the same utilization as the bottleneck.

---

170 **Bard** (1981)

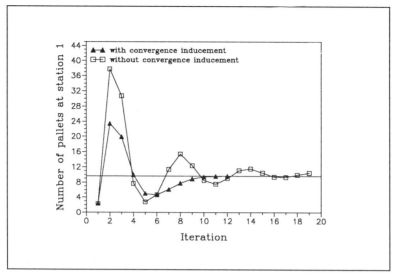

Figure 54: Development of queue length at station 1 during the iterations with and without the Bard convergence inducement procedure

The utilizations are graphically represented in figure (55).

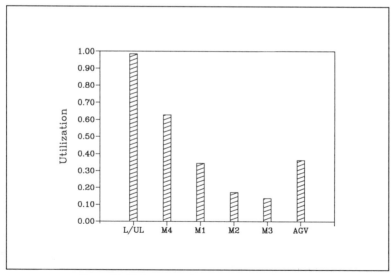

Figure 55: Utilizations of the stations (example 3-2)

As can be clearly seen in figure (55), the station L/UL (setup area) is the bottle-neck in the FMS configuration presented in example 3-2. The other stations are relatively less utilized. It is, therefore, necessary to consider whether or not a change in the configuration of the FMS could improve its performance.

Table (26) offers an overview of the progress of an experiment in which first the capacity of the stations (setup areas, machines, vehicles) and then the number of pallets were changed.

	Number of machines or carts						Number of pallets		
	L/UL	M4	M1	M2	M3	AGV	N_1	N_2	N_3
Variant 1	1	1	1	1	1	1	8	2	4
Utilizations:	.9866	.6296	.3468	.1734	.1347	.3648			
Variant 2	∇ 2	1	1	1	1	1	8	2	4
Utilizations:	.8436	.9484	.5408	.4292	.2596	.6251			
Variant 3	∇ 3	∇ 2	1	1	1	1	8	2	4
Utilizations:	.7372	.6779	.7693	.4201	.3336	.8251			
Variant 4	3	2	1	1	1	1	∇ 10	2	4
Utilizations:	.7672	.7424	.8064	.4048	.3055	.8466			
Variant 5	3	2	1	1	1	1	10	∇ 3	∇ 5
Utilizations:	.7846	.7005	.7914	.5091	.3522	.8737			
Variant 6:	3	2	1	1	1	∇ 2	10	∇ 4	∇ 7
Utilizations:	.9315	.7451	.9159	.6990	.5046	.5305			
Variant 7:	3	2	1	1	1	2	10	4	∇ 10
Utilizations:	.9324	.7038	.9483	.6680	.5944	.5467			

Table 26: Utilizations changing with the FMS variants (example 3-2)

Beginning with the first variant, in which the utilizations [figure (55)] are unbalanced and thus significant machine capacity is wasted, the first step in adjusting the configuration is to increase the capacity of the bottleneck station (L/UL) by one unit. As could be expected, a reduction in the average utilization of this station results, but now station M4 becomes the bottleneck station. In the next step the capacities of both station L/UL and station M4 are increased by one unit each. The utilizations of the stations L/UL and M4 have been reduced through the increase of the total capacity of the FMS. However, the entire system is at a relatively low level of utilization. Since the number of pallets has remained constant throughout this process, the next step would be to increase the number of pallets as well.

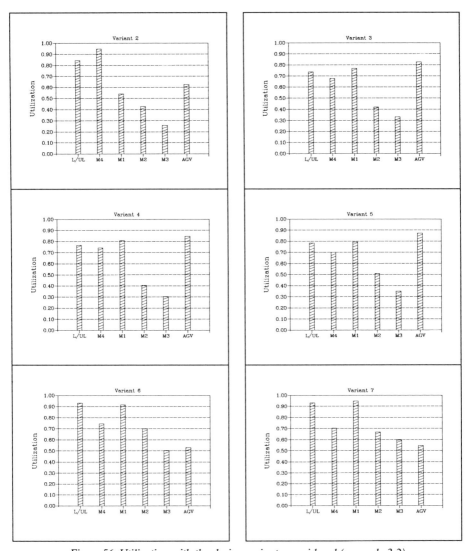

Figure 56: Utilization with the design variants considered (example 3-2)

The further adjustments are intended to increase the utilizations of the stations M2 and M3. This can be accomplished by increasing the number of type 2 and type 3 pallets, since both of these pallet types are processed primarily at stations

M2 and M3. As the increase in the number of pallets also increases the load on the transportation system, the transportation capacity is enlarged by two vehicles in FMS design variant number six. The changes in the utilization that arise when varying the configuration of the FMS are summarized in figure (56). Through a series of step by step changes in the FMS configuration the average utilization of all stations is increased, and differences in the utilizations of the various stations are decreased.

Figure (57) illustrates the changes in the production rate of the FMS resulting from the changes in its configuration. It can be seen that the largest increases result from increases in the capacities (number of servers), whereas increases in the number of pallets tend to bring about relatively small changes in the production rate. Particularly noteworthy is the fact that the introduction of a second setup area almost doubled the production rate of the FMS. This is due to the significantly improved use of unoccupied machine capacities that are now more efficiently supplied with workpieces.

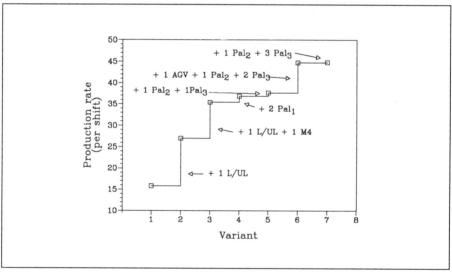

Figure 57: Production rate changing with the FMS variants
(example 3-2)

Aside from the purely technologically oriented output analysis conducted, each adjustment in the FMS configuration also has consequences for the economic efficiency of the FMS. It must be assured that the *costs* of introducing further machines or pallets are compensated by the possible *additional earnings* (value of the additionally produced and sold workpieces)[171].

The symbols used in this section are summarized for convenience in table (27).

---

171   see also **Leimkühler** (1984)

β_k	production ratio of product type k with respect to its pallet type
ϵ	tolerance level
$\sigma\{.\}$	standard deviation
$A_{cm}(.)$	mean number of workpieces at station m upon arrival of a type c pallet
b^b_{cm}	mean processing time of a workpiece at station m with respect to pallet type c, as used in the $(M/M/S_m)$ model
b_{cm}	mean processing time of a workpiece of pallet type c at station m
b_{km}	mean processing time of a workpiece of product type k at station m
br_{cm}	mean residual processing time of a workpiece of pallet type c at station m
c	pallet type index $(c=1,2,\dots,C)$
D	mean flow time
$D_{cm}(.)$	mean flow time of a workpiece of pallet type c at station m
K_c	set of product types assigned to pallet type c
m	station index $(m=1,2,\dots,M)$
N_c	number of type c pallets
$N_{max}(m)$	maximum number of pallets waiting at station m
P_{cm}	relative arrival frequency of a workpiece of pallet type c at station m
$Q_{cm}(.)$	mean number of pallets of type c at station m per period
QW_{cm}	mean queue length of pallet type c at station m
RB_{cm}	mean residual processing time of a workpiece at a busy station m upon arrival of a type c pallet (approximated)
$U_{cm}(.)$	utilization of station m by pallet type c
v_{cm}	mean number of operations on a workpiece of pallet type c at station m
v_{cM}	mean number of transportations of a workpiece of pallet type c
v_{km}	mean number of operations on a workpiece of product type k at station m
$W0_{cm}$	mean residual processing time of a workpiece upon arrival of a pallet of type c at station m
$W1_{cm}$	mean total processing time of all workpieces waiting at station m upon arrival of a pallet of type c
W_{cm}	mean waiting time of a type c pallet at station m
X	mean production rate
$X_c(.)$	mean production rate of the FMS for pallet type c
X_{cm}	mean production rate of station m for pallet type c

Table 27: Symbols used

3.1.1.2.3. Sensitivity analysis

If several pallet types are circulating in an FMS, then their production rates will be determined by the speed at which the individual workpieces can move through the system. These speeds depend primarily, aside from the processing times of the workpieces, on the degree of competition between the different workpiece types for processing capacity at the stations. The greater the competition for capacity, especially at the bottleneck station, the more the different workpiece types will influence one another.

Increasing the number of pallets of one type while holding the other pallet types constant causes changes in the distribution of the total available production capacity among the different product groups. The more pallets of a particular type there are circulating in an FMS, the greater the probability that a machine which becomes free will next process a workpiece of this type. This is made clear in figures (58) and (59)[172]. Here the production rates for types 1 and 2 pallets from example 3-2 are shown for different numbers of type 2 pallets as a function of the number of type 1 pallets.

When the number of type 1 pallets increases, the rate of production for this pallet type also increases, but it does so at a progressively decreasing rate [see figure (58)]. The production rate is higher when fewer type 2 pallets circulate in the system. It was assumed in this case that only one type 3 pallet was circulating in the FMS.

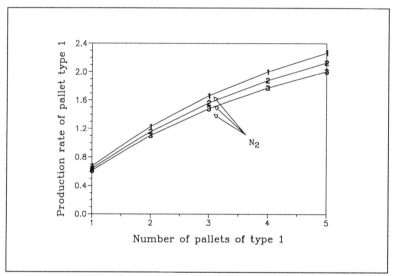

Figure 58: Production rate of pallet type 1 vs. number of pallets of type 1 (example 3-2)

The reverse relationship is true for the production rate of type 2 pallets [see figure (59)]. An increase in the number of type 1 pallets causes a redistribution of the available production capacity. The production rate of the type 2 pallet is thus reduced, though the actual level of the production rate depends on the number of pallets of this type in the system.

As might be expected, the production rate for pallet type 1 increases as the number of pallets of this type increases. Yet at the same time the production rates of the other pallet types decline[173]. These relationships suggest that there is an *optimal combination* of the numbers of pallets of the different pallet types. A decision model could be formulated with the objective function containing the sum of the weighted production rates and the constraints defining a minimum production quantity for each product group. The effects of an increase in the number of pallets from any product group, N_c for example, on the other product

---

172 see also **Canals/Frabolot** (1988)
173 see also **Solot** (1990a)

groups could then be investigated to see whether or not such an increase would be advantageous from an economic point of view. As long as the minimum production quantities are achieved, it would be only worthwhile to increase N_c when the increase in the production value associated with the change in the number of type c pallets outweighs the decrease in the production value in the other product groups and the costs associated with the additional pallets.

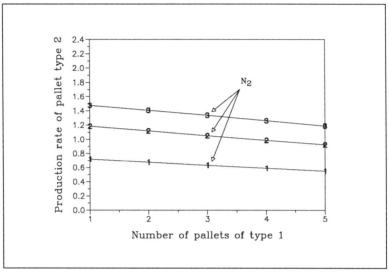

Figure 59: Production rates of pallet type 2 vs. number of pallets of type 1
(example 3-2)

3.1.1.3. Numerical results for the classical CQN model

In this section the accurateness of the classical CQN model based procedures for the performance evaluation of real-life FMSs of varying complexity will be discussed. The characteristics of the FMSs to be studied are such that the assumptions of the classical CQN model are largely satisfied. The data have all been taken from practical examples. The quality of the performance approximations will be checked with detailed and specially developed SIMAN IV simulation models[174]. In this model, all the setup, machining and transportation processes to be performed in an FMS are simulated as deterministic processes so that they closely parallel reality. This is especially true for the workpieces' use of the material flow system. Idle trips as well as trips between machines and the central buffer locations are all taken into consideration in the simulation. Disruptions due to machine breakdowns, broken tools, insufficient supplies of material, etc. are not included.

---

174 Simulation models are discussed in section 3.3.

Three FMSs and a flexible transfer line are investigated[175]. The FMSs can be distinguished from one another in two general ways [see figure (60)]. In all three systems the material flow is based on fixed predetermined process plans with deterministic processing times and operation sequences. A typical path of a workpiece through the FMS might include the following operations: *(load)-(operation machine_1)-(change_setup)-(operation machine_2)-(wash)-(unload)*. The average transportation times were estimated based on experiences the system planners had made with similar FMS configurations.

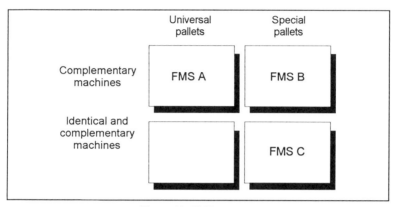

Figure 60: FMSs studied

• **FMS A: Universal pallets, complementary machines**

The *FMS A* is identical with the example 3-1 introduced in section 3.1.1.1. It is made up of two complementary machines (single-server stations) and a setup table for loading, unloading, and reloading the workpieces onto and off of their pallets. The layout of the FMS is schematically represented in figure (61).

Four product types with different production ratios are processed in this system. No local buffers are planned for the machines or the setup area, so only one pallet can be present there at a time. The only buffer capacity in the system is offered by a central pallet storage with space for three pallets. Four universal pallets circulate in the FMS. A rail-guided vehicle is used for transportation. Its average transportation time is very short in comparison to the setup and processing times.

---

175   see also **Tempelmeier** (1988)

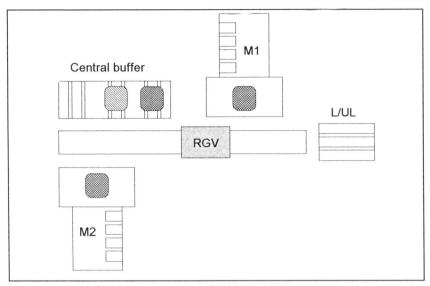

Figure 61: Layout of FMS A

Since there is only one pallet type (universal pallets) circulating in this system, the convolution approach described in section 3.1.1.1.2. using the normalization constant g(N,M) can be applied. Table (28) provides an overview of the results of this analysis[176].

	Sim	CQN	Diff
Production rate	0.002004	0.001960	-2.20%
Flow time	1986	2041	+2.72%
Utilization Machine 1	0.93	0.91	-.02
Utilization Machine 2	0.36	0.35	-.01
Utilization L/UL	0.54	0.53	-.01
Utilization RGV	0.14	0.07	-.07

Table 28: Results for FMS A

• **FMS B: Special pallets, complementary machines**

The *FMS B* includes three complementary machining centers, two pallet type specific load/unload stations, and a central buffer with space for four pallets. The workpieces are transported by a rail-guided vehicle. Figure (62) illustrates the layout of this system.

---

176   The differences concerning the production rates and flow times are relative values, whereas the differences concerning the utilizations are absolute percentage points.

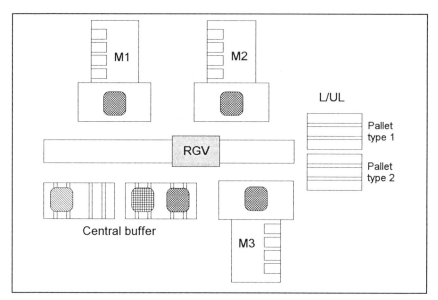

Figure 62: Layout of FMS B

15 different product types are processed on *two pallet types*. Product types 1-3 and 4-15 are mounted on pallet types 1 and 2, respectively. Two type 1 pallets and three type 2 pallets circulate in the FMS. The production ratios of the product groups associated with each of the two pallet types are fixed and predetermined. A setup table is exclusively assigned to each of the two pallet types.

Since there are several pallet types being observed in this case, the heuristic mean value analysis (MVAHEU) is used. In table (29) the results are compared with those of the simulation.

	Sim	MVAHEU	Diff
Production rate 1	0.001050	0.001010	-3.81%
Production rate 2	0.006456	0.007046	+9.14%
Flow time 1	1902	1981	+4.15%
Flow time 2	463	426	-7.99%
Utilization Machine 1	0.93	0.95	+.02
Utilization Machine 2	0.87	0.83	-.04
Utilization Machine 3	0.39	0.39	.00
Utilization L/UL 1	0.19	0.16	-.03
Utilization L/UL 2	0.11	0.09	-.02
Utilization RGV	0.20	0.14	-.06

Table 29: Results for FMS B

- **FMS C:** Special pallets, identical and complementary machines

The *FMS C* is made up of *four identical load/unload stations*, one machine group with *five identical machines*, several complementary machines and a central buffer. Variations of three product types are moved through the FMS on two pallet types. Two automatic wire-guided vehicles are used for transportation. The wires are laid out in a manner providing sufficient maneuverability for the vehicles so that collisions and deadlocks are not to be expected - provided appropriate vehicle control is exercised. The layout of the system is shown in figure (63).

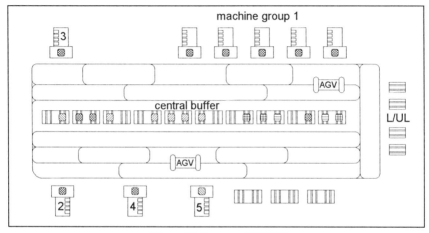

Figure 63: Layout of FMS C

It is assumed that in this FMS there are twenty type 1 pallets and nine type 2 pallets. The results of the MVAHEU procedure are compared with those of the detailed simulation in table (30).

	Sim	MVAHEU	Diff
Production rate 1	0.03153	0.03326	+5.49%
Production rate 2	0.00721	0.00801	+11.10%
Flow time 1	632	601	-4.91%
Flow time 2	1242	1123	-9.58%
Utilization Machine 1	0.58	0.61	-.03
Utilization Machine 2	0.57	0.63	+.06
Utilization Machine 3	0.57	0.59	+.02
Utilization Machine 4	0.39	0.39	.00
Utilization Machine 5	0.93	0.98	+.05
Utilization L/UL	0.26	0.27	+.01
Utilization AGV	0.31	0.30	-.01

Table 30: Results for FMS C

The results observed for all three FMSs suggest that based on the classical CQN model analysis, estimates can be made for the performance of the system that are sufficiently accurate for the decision problems posed in the configuration phase. It is particularly interesting to note that in the classical CQN model the processing times are assumed to be exponentially distributed, while in the detailed simulation models the process plans are deterministically set. The general conclusion drawn from these results is consistent with most statements made in the literature[177], although the latter are primarily based on hypothetical FMSs.

· **Flexible transfer line**

The flexible transfer line considered includes 25 stations. Two variations of one product type, each with a production ratio of 50%, are manufactured on it. Deterministic processing times are given for each product variation at the stations. The transportation of the workpieces is accomplished through a power-and-free conveyor. The distances between the stations are so large that there is space for between 6 and 10 pallets. All together 100 pallets circulate in this flexible production system. Figure (64) offers an overview of the layout of the flexible transfer line.

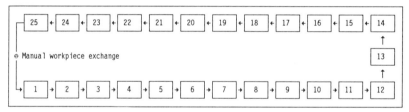

Figure 64: Flexible transfer line

Two *special aspects* of this production system distinguish it from the FMSs which have been discussed up to now: the *material flow is linear*, and the pallets are transported by the central *transportation* system immediately - *without queueing* time - to the next station. The flow time through the transportation system between two machining operations consists exclusively of transportation time.

The key parameters of the flexible transfer line can be calculated with the help of the CQN model for universal pallets. The calculation of the normalization constant for $N > 30$ pallets according to the *Buzen* procedure described in section 3.1.1.1.2. breaks down, however, due to a numerical value overflow[178]. This is also the case when the input data are standardized beforehand, as proposed by *Stecke* and *Solberg*[179]. These kinds of numerical problems do not come up when the mean value analysis is used for the computation of the performance indicators. Indeed, both the exact and the heuristic variations can be used. The results

177 **Solberg** (1977); **Shalev-Oren/Seidmann/Schweitzer** (1985); **Co/Wysk** (1986); **Seidmann/Schweitzer/Shalev-Oren** (1987); **Solot/Bastos** (1988)
178 see also **Reiser/Lavenberg** (1980), p. 319
179 Equation (29)

from the exact and the heuristic mean value analyzes are compared with those of the simulation in table (31) and figure (65).

		Sim	MVAHEU	MVAEX
Production rate		112	107	109
	1	0.4455	0.4189	0.4246
	2	0.9620	0.8976	0.9099
	3	0.6361	0.5984	0.6066
	4	0.7060	0.6582	0.6672
	5	0.6358	0.5984	0.6066
	6	0.9988	0.9575	0.9706
	7	0.7302	0.6732	0.6824
	8	0.8090	0.7779	0.7886
	9	0.6515	0.6433	0.6521
	10	0.5890	0.5684	0.5762
	11	0.5604	0.5386	0.5459
	12	0.5887	0.5684	0.5762
	13	0.9659	0.9275	0.9402
	14	0.7608	0.7300	0.7400
	15	0.6035	0.5805	0.5884
	16	0.8544	0.8258	0.8371
	17	0.6181	0.5984	0.6066
	18	0.8863	0.8527	0.8644
	19	0.6676	0.6433	0.6521
	20	0.6495	0.5684	0.5762
	21	0.8377	0.8078	0.8189
	22	0.6803	0.6552	0.6642
	23	0.9323	0.8976	0.9099
	24	0.6799	0.6582	0.6672
	25	0.6355	0.6133	0.6217

Table 31: Results for the flexible transfer line

The comparison of the analytically calculated results with those of the simulation indicates again a high degree of agreement. This is especially surprising since the processing times at the stations can take on only two values (depending on the product variation mounted on a pallet), whereas the processing times must be exponentially distributed in the classical CQN model. Note that the analytical procedures provide a pessimistic estimate of the performance of the production system. It should be noted, that a single run of the simulation model required about *five minutes* of computation time, while both variations of the MVA procedure are completed after less than two seconds. Since in order to assure the statistical accuracy of the results the simulation program must be run repeatedly, the computational effort for the analytical performance evaluation is an order of magnitude less than that of the simulation approach.

The flexible production systems which have been investigated up to now were chosen so that important characteristics relevant in industrial FMS practice (product dependent pallets, groups of identical machines) could be observed. One characteristic is true for all the FMSs, however. *They all have a relatively low utilization of the transportation system and sufficient capacity in the central buffer.* Thus blocking and starving due to limited local buffer areas, as will be described in section 3.1.2., are not likely to be problems for these systems. The classical CQN model for the analysis of these FMSs can, therefore, provide satisfactory results. Furthermore, it has been assumed here that all the system components operate without technical problems and that machine breakdowns are excluded. This aspect will be discussed later in section 3.1.3.

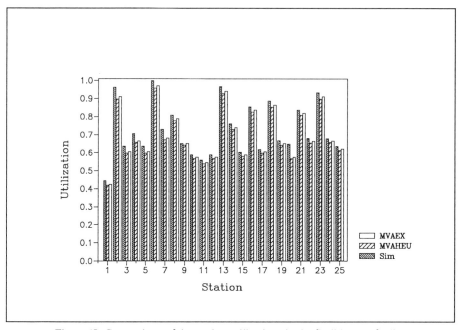

Figure 65: Comparison of the station utilizations in the flexible transfer line

In recent years the classical CQN model has been used as part of comprehensive performance evaluation approaches.

- *Co, Wu and Reisman*[180]

as well as

- *Kouvelis and Kiran*[181]

have suggested that the classical CQN model could be used in determining the layout of an FMS to measure the influence of the location of the machines on the production rate of the system.

- *Avonts and Van Wassenhove*[182]

use the classical CQN model as part of an approach to pre-release planning and routing optimization to compute the utilizations of the stations depending on the decision variables considered.

---

180 **Co/Wu/Reisman** (1989)
181 **Kouvelis/Kiran** (1990)
182 **Avonts/Van Wassenhove** (1988); for a similar approach see **Menga/Bruno/Conterno/Dato** (1984)

- *Kuhn*[183]

assumes *generally distributed processing times* and uses a CQN model to estimate the makespan of a batch of orders and thus the expected tardiness of the orders.

Further reading for section 3.1.1.2.:

Akyildiz/Bolch (1988)
Bard (1981)
Bruell/Balbo (1980)
Bruell/Balbo/Afshari (1984)
Buzacott/Shanthikumar (1992), (1993)
Lazowska/Zahorjan/Graham/Sevcik (1984)
Reiser/Lavenberg (1980)
Seidmann/Schweitzer/Shalev-Oren (1987)
Shalev-Oren/Seidmann/Schweitzer (1985)
Solot/Bastos (1988)
Suri/Hildebrant (1984)
Talavage/Hannam (1988)
Tempelmeier (1988)

3.1.2. Performance Evaluation of an FMS with Limited Local Buffers

It was shown in section 3.1.1. that extensive performance evaluations of an FMS can be carried out with the help of the classical closed queueing network model. Yet the usefulness of the procedures described above (partly implemented in the software systems CAN-Q[184], MVAQ[185], and FMS-Eval[186]) is generally limited to certain types of FMSs. These include primarily those in which *blocking*, resulting from limited local buffer space at the processing stations and the finite speed of the material flow system, plays little or no roll. In practice, however, FMSs with limited local buffers are the rule rather than the exception. Many FMS manufacturers offer machining centers with two local buffer areas as a basic module of their FMSs. One of these buffers is always kept free to support a pallet exchange. In most FMSs actually in use, however, at least one station (often the washing machine or the load/unload station) has no local buffer at all.

When only local buffers with limited capacity are present at the machines, or when the transportation vehicles must make a significant number of *idle trips* or trips to the *central buffer locations*, then significant errors may occur when the performance of an FMS alternative is estimated using one of the procedures based on the classical CQN model.

---

183 **Kuhn** (1990), pp. 121-146
184 **Stecke/Solberg** (1981a)
185 **Suri/Hildebrant** (1984)
186 see section 3.2.

The reason for this is that limited capacity local buffers at the stations can cause certain kinds of *blocking* which are totally unknown in the classical CQN model. This prevents a machine from operating and being productive although it has finished processing one workpiece and the next workpiece is already waiting at some other point in the FMS to be processed by this machine. Whereas the classical CQN model assumes that the machine is again working, in reality it is sitting idle.

Such errors result in an overestimation of the throughput of an FMS. It could be, for example, that an evaluation of the performance of a planned FMS configuration using the classical CQN model might estimate the average production rate to be 432 fully processed workpieces per shift. Due to the restrictions which arise from the limitations of the local buffer areas, the actual production rate is only 356 workpieces. The classical CQN model's overly optimistic judgment must be considered during the configuration planning so that the evaluation of the FMS according to economic criteria will be accurate.

In the first part of the following discussion the various types of blocking and the different techniques found in the literature for integrating this phenomenon into the closed queueing network model will be discussed. Thereafter some approaches developed by the authors themselves for taking blocking and starving in an FMS into consideration will be reviewed.

3.1.2.1. Types of blocking in an FMS with limited local buffers

Limited local buffer areas present difficult problems for the performance analysis of an FMS. Due to the possibility that blocking may occur at a machine (or a load/unload station) the *product form* necessary for the exact evaluation of the CQN model is generally destroyed. This is true because in a system with limited local buffer areas the stations are no longer independent of one another; instead an event at one node in a queueing network can directly influence what happens at another node.

The blocking problems at a machine in a closed queueing network due to a limited local buffer area have been dealt with relatively infrequently in the literature. That work which has been done is primarily related to the performance evaluation of computer and communication systems as well as to flow production systems (such as transfer lines)[187]. These are only of limited value for the analysis of a flexible manufacturing system. Before beginning a more detailed discussion of the difficulties in the performance evaluation of an FMS due to limited local buffers, the term itself as it is used in the literature will be explained.

In characterizing blocking phenomena in *computer and communication systems* as well as in *linear flow production systems* the terms *service blocking* and *transfer blocking* are used. These terms describe two particular situations that are distin-

---

187   For an overview see **Diehl** (1984); **Yao/Buzacott** (1985); **Altiok/Perros** (1986); **Suri/Diehl** (1986); **Yao/Buzacott** (1986); **Yao/Buzacott** (1987); **Akyildiz** (1988a); **Akyildiz** (1988b)

guished depending on the point in time at which they occur and the position of the workpiece at that time.

Transfer blocking (production blocking), as illustrated in figure (66), occurs when a workpiece is unable to leave a machine after being fully processed because access to the next station is prevented. In this situation, the machine is idle, despite the fact that its queue is not empty. Transfer blocking is particularly common in asynchronous flow lines with limited intermediate buffers.

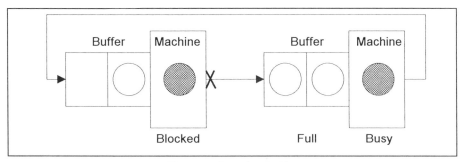

Figure 66: Transfer blocking

While transfer blocking occurs *after* a workpiece has been processed, *service blocking* (communication blocking) occurs *beforehand* [see figure (67)]. Here transfer blocking is prevented by checking *before processing begins* to see if a workpiece is going to be able to leave the machine after processing. If this is not expected to be possible, then processing is delayed. Service blocking is often found in communication networks in which one job is begun only when it is already clear that there will be space (or a server) available at the following station.

In both cases the workpiece is present at a station. When service blocking occurs, the workpiece is at the station where it was last processed (upstream station); and in the case of transfer blocking, it is at the station preceding that at which it will next be processed (downstream station).

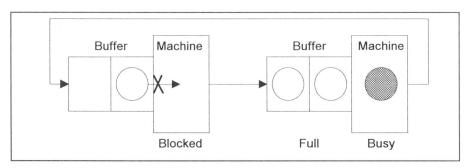

Figure 67: Service blocking

In the FMS literature the term blocking is often used to describe a situation in which a workpiece occupying the transportation system (i.e. a vehicle) is denied access to a station. Two possible reactions are available to the transportation vehicle in this case: it can wait with the workpiece in front of the station until the station is free (*block-and-wait*) or it can bring the workpiece back to the central buffer and attempt to get access to the station at a later time (*block-and-recirculate*)[188].

The *block-and-recirculate* strategy would suggest an FMS layout as illustrated in figure (68). The workpieces are transported to the machines on a circular conveyor belt on which the workpieces remain until they can gain access to a machine[189]. At the same time the conveyor belt acts as a central buffer. If a workpiece cannot be accepted at the next station because the local buffer there is full, then it must remain for another circulation on the conveyor belt. It is assumed here that the necessary transportation mechanism for removing a workpiece from a machine after processing is so fast that a machine is never blocked because the departure of an already processed workpiece is delayed.

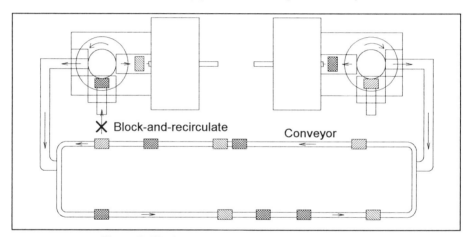

Figure 68: Block-and-recirculate strategy (MHS blocking)

A configuration like this will be rarely found in practice. It has been frequently discussed in the literature, however, because the associated closed queueing network exhibits a *product form* in this case[190].

The second strategy is called the *block-and-wait* strategy [see figure (69)]. Here the vehicle waits until the station is able to accept the workpiece. As in the case of the block-and-recirculate strategy, a separate transportation mechanism must be available to the machine that can remove processed workpieces from the machine without hindering the vehicle already waiting in front of the station with a

188 **Buzacott** (1989), pp. 129-130; **Zhuang/Hindi** (1990)

189 In place of a circular conveyor belt an FMS with an AGV might be considered.

190 **Yao/Buzacott** (1985); see also the following section 3.1.2.2.

new workpiece. This form of vehicle blocking will also rarely be found in practice due to intelligent vehicle control.

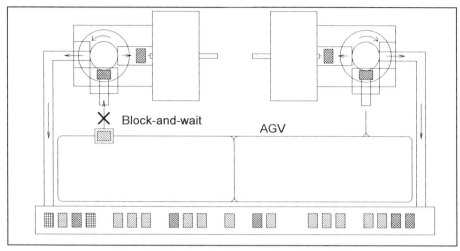

Figure 69: Block-and-wait strategy (MHS blocking)

It is clear that both concepts are based on the assumption that a workpiece has left a machine after processing and is currently being transported by a vehicle or other transportation device. This assumption makes it possible to prevent machines from being blocked by an already processed workpiece remaining on the machining table. The focus of the analysis is thus either the transportation system or the workpiece currently being transported.

Little attention has been paid in the literature, up to now, to the problems arising for the machines in an FMS when workpieces cannot leave the machining table due to limited local buffers. In this section these problems will be more closely analyzed.

Consider a typical FMS with several stations (machine groups, setup areas, etc.), a central buffer and a central transportation system. A station m includes one or several (S_m) identical machines (servers) as well as a local buffer with room for P_m pallets. This is shown in a simplified way in figure (70).

A *local buffer* is assumed to be located directly in front of the machine with an integrated material-handling mechanism performing the workpiece transfer between the buffer and the machining table. It is thus not possible for the transportation system to directly supply a machine. In this case, it is necessary to keep at least one buffer space free to provide handling room for preventing the station from getting totally blocked.

The *total blocking* of a station is impossible as long as one buffer place or one machine inside the station is kept free. If P_m denotes the number of buffers and S_m is the number of machines at the station m, then $N_{max(m)}$ pallets can be present at the station, if total blocking is to be avoided [see equation (98)].

$$N_{max(m)} = P_m + S_m - 1 \qquad\qquad\qquad m=1,2,\ldots,M-1; \; P_m > 0 \qquad (98)$$

     └ number of machines at station m

   └ number of local buffer spaces at station m

└ maximum number of pallets at station m

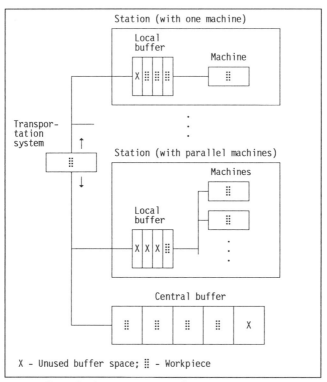

X - Unused buffer space; ⸬ - Workpiece

Figure 70: Logical structure of the FMS considered

If the FMS is properly controlled, the number of pallets at a station will not exceed this limit. As long as one buffer space always remains free, it can be used for the exchange of an unprocessed workpiece for one that is ready to leave a machine.

Stations such as setup areas or washing machines with no local buffers are often found in FMSs, however. At such a station the maximum number of pallets is limited by the number of machines at the station:

$$N_{max(m)} = S_m \qquad\qquad\qquad m=1,2,\ldots,M-1; \; P_m = 0 \qquad (99)$$

In what follows it is again assumed that a constant number of N *universal pallets* is circulating in the system. The workpieces are mounted on the pallets, and they move through the system in accordance with their process plans. The transportation system is responsible both for workpiece movements between the stations as well as between the stations and the central buffer. The total load on the transportation system is then made up of the following components:

- *Supply trips* (direct transportation of a workpiece between two workstations; transportation of a workpiece from the central buffer to a workstation),

- *Disposal trips* (workpiece transportation from a station to the central buffer),

- *Idle trips*.

It has already been pointed out that a clear functional distinction between the central buffer and the material flow system is often not practically possible. As in the case of the block-and-recirculate strategy, a transportation system may simultaneously serve as central buffer. In the following analysis, however, it will be assumed that the transportation system exercises only a transportation function, and that it does not systematically serve as a temporary storage area for workpieces.

The local buffer areas are only available to the particular station to which they are assigned. Temporarily shifting of pallets into local buffers dedicated to machines at which no machining operation occurs is prohibited. Local buffers can be used, however, to store unprocessed and processed workpieces before and after a particular operation, respectively. While an unprocessed workpiece waits for a machine to become free, a processed workpiece waits for a transportation vehicle to arrive so that it may be carried to the next machine or to the central buffer. A situation, often found in practice, in which the local buffer acts as both an input and an output buffer is thus included in this analysis.

It is furthermore assumed, as dictated by the classical CQN approaches to the performance analysis of FMSs, that the processing times at the stations are *exponentially distributed* and that the FCFS queueing discipline is followed at all stations. The transition times between a station and a transportation vehicle or inside a station itself are considered to be part of the transportation or processing time (e.g. pallet handling, positioning, tool exchange, transfer time of the NC-program for the next processing step).

In the following considerations it will be assumed that after a workpiece has been fully processed at a station, the strategy for controlling the material flow shown in figure (71) is followed.

1. First, it must be determined whether or not the workpiece can be transported to the downstream station at which the next operation will take place.
2. If the downstream station is not able to accept the pallet, then temporarily storing the workpiece in a central buffer, if present, is considered.

3. If both the local buffer of the downstream machine and the central buffer are full, then the available space of the *local output buffer* must be reviewed to see if the workpiece could be stored there.
4. If this is also not possible, then the workpiece must wait on the machining table (or the setup table) until one of the above alternatives becomes available.

During the time from the end of one operation to the time when the newly processed workpiece can leave the machining table the machine is unable to operate, i.e. the machine is *blocked*.

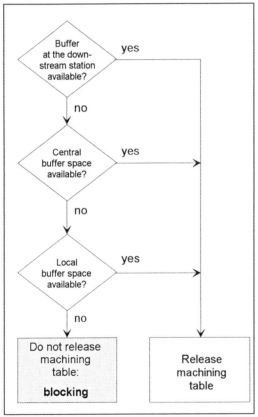

Figure 71: Material flow strategy considered

Blocking of a machine in a flexible manufacturing system can be defined as a state in which a machine stands still because it has finished processing one workpiece but cannot begin processing the next workpiece, though that piece is already waiting. This situation might emerge because the processed workpiece has not yet left the machine and is thus occupying the machining table, or because the new unprocessed workpiece has physically not yet arrived at the machine for processing. A further requirement for a machine's standstill to be considered to result from blocking is that the workpiece which should next be processed at the machine be present and awaiting processing at that machine somewhere in the FMS (e.g. in the central buffer area or the local output buffer of the upstream machine).

In the following it will be assumed that *total blocking of the FMS* (a standstill of unlimited length that can only be ended by manual intervention of the system operator; deadlock[191]) can be prevented by properly controlling of the FMS. Total blocking of an FMS occurs, for example, in a system with a full central

---

191 The deadlock problem is discussed by **Diehl** (1984).

buffer in which the only vehicle is occupied by a workpiece awaiting processing at a machine that in turn is occupied by another workpiece that cannot pass on to its next station without access to the transportation system. Such a situation is illustrated in figure (72). Here workpiece A has just finished processing at station k and is waiting for access to station m. Station m, however, is occupied by workpiece B which in turn is waiting to begin its next operation at machine k. All the spaces in the central buffer are taken up by workpieces whose down-stream station is either station k or station m. Such a total blocking can only be relieved through manual intervention, such as the "misuse" of the setup area for temporary storage. Another possibility would be to equip the transportation vehicle with two pallet spaces so that the pallet exchange could be effected without needing a temporary buffer at the station. In this case all the buffer places at a station could be occupied.

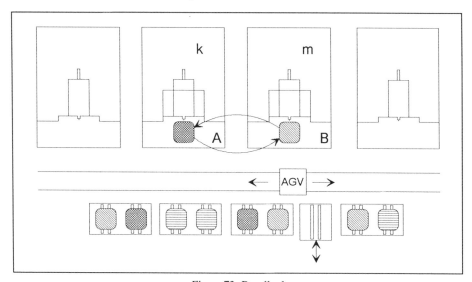

Figure 72: Deadlock

Excluding the possibility of a *deadlock*, which can only be relieved by a manual intervention from outside the system, a machine in an FMS with limited local buffers can suffer from either *blocking* or *starving* in addition to idleness. Both of these phenomena are found rarely if at all in FMSs with unlimited local buffers.

· **Blocking**

In the case of blocking, the machine m is blocked when no buffer space is available for storing the newly processed workpiece F. The next workpiece U, requiring processing at the downstream station m and waiting in the output buffer of another (upstream) station or in the central buffer, cannot gain access to the appropriate machine m. The machine m remains idle until the waiting workpiece U gains access to the machining table of the machine m [see figure (73)].

Blocking can be prevented in industrial practice by assuring adequate capacity of the central buffer. Since a central buffer place represents a relatively low capital investment, compared to that of the machines, the expansion of its capacity is generally limited only by the physical dimensions of the factory building in which the FMS is to be constructed. In contrast, starving is a much more serious problem.

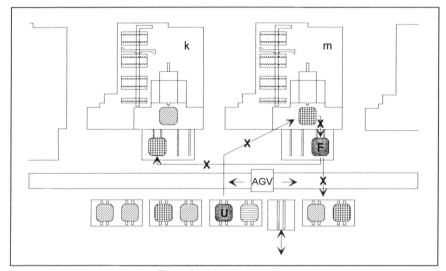

Figure 73: Machine blocking

- **Starving**

The term starving is used to describe idle times of a machine due to the *finite speed* of the transportation vehicles together with limited size of the local buffer at a station. When a station m with a limited local buffer is to be supplied with unprocessed workpieces from a central buffer, starving can occur if the waiting machine stands idle without a workpiece while the new workpiece is being transported. In figure (74) a situation is represented in which the workpiece U had just previously attempted to enter the input buffer of the station m. Since this was full, the workpiece was temporarily stored in a central buffer area. The machine m has processed the workpiece that had been in the input buffer and that piece is now in the output buffer. The control of the FMS dictates that the workpiece U should be the next workpiece to be processed at the machine m. It must, however, first be transported to machine m. Up to the point at which the workpiece U is ready for processing in the machining area, machine m is starved.

This kind of machine downtime due to the transportation system would not be possible if the local buffers had unlimited capacity. In that case all the workpieces next in line to be processed at each machine would be waiting in the buffer directly at that machine. Starving is equally unlikely in a system with an infinitely fast transportation system and a sufficiently large central buffer. In this case the central buffer acts as a virtual local buffer.

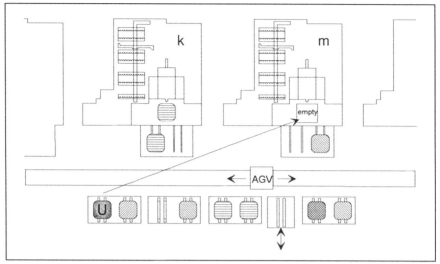

Figure 74: Starving

Considering all the different forms of utilization losses described above, four different possible *states* of a machine can be distinguished:

1. The machine is *operating*. It is *busy*.
2. The machine is *not* operating since no unprocessed workpiece is available for the machine in the FMS. It is *idle*.
3. The machine is not operating because it is *blocked*.
4. The machine is not operating because it is *starved*.

The relative significance of these different states is shown for a real-life FMS in figure (75). States 1 (machine is *working*) and 2 (machine is *idle*) are considered in the classical CQN model, but states 3 (*blocking*) and 4 (*starving*) are not taken into consideration in that model. In the last two states, though a machine has completed processing of a workpiece and another workpiece awaits processing at that machine - perhaps in the central buffer - the workpiece cannot be processed. Either the machining table cannot be released and is thus blocked, or the workpiece still has to be transported from the central buffer to the machine. The workpiece must wait until the machine is no longer blocked or starved and access to it is readily available.

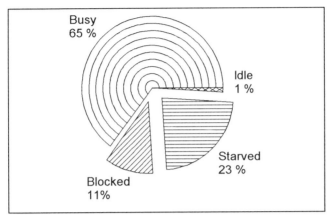

Figure 75: States of a machine

The total *flow time* of a workpiece at a machine is thus made up of the following components:

- The normal *queueing delay* of a workpiece while the other work-pieces are being processed by the machine.

- The *delay* while the machine is *blocked or starved*.

- The *processing time* of the workpiece.

A method based on the following ideas for including these different types of performance deterioration in the evaluation of an FMS is described at a later point in this analysis. If the queueing delay during the time a machine is blocked can be estimated with sufficient accuracy, then it must be possible *to increase the "normal" processing time at the machine by the amount of the queueing delay due to blocking and/or starving*. The system could then be treated like an FMS with unlimited local buffers. The key parameters (production rate, flow time, utilization, etc.) could then be determined with the help of the numerical procedures introduced above for the evaluation of the classical closed queueing network (CQN model).

At this point several of the methods for including blocking in a CQN model described in the literature will be presented.

3.1.2.2. An FMS operating with the "block-and-recirculate" strategy

One often cited method for including limited local buffers has been proposed by *Yao and Buzacott*[192]. They consider a CQN model of an FMS in which each

---

192 **Yao/Buzacott** (1985); **Yao/Buzacott** (1986); **Zhuang/Hindi** (1990)

machine is attached a return conveyor. This allows all processed workpieces to be carried directly to a central buffer with unlimited capacity, thus blocking at the machines can be prevented.

The *local buffers* at the stations are of limited size. It is possible then that a workpiece can be denied access to a station. It would remain in the central buffer, or, if a circular conveyor is present, circulate in the material flow system until it can access the appropriate station (*block-and-recirculate strategy*).

The state space $S'(N,M)$ (the distribution of the N pallets among the various stations) of the FMS is a *subset* of the state space $S(N,M)$ that is possible under the assumptions of the classical CQN model. At most $N_{max(m)}$ pallets can be present at a station, instead of N pallets as in the classical model. This is graphically illustrated in figure (76). It is assumed that five pallets are circulating in the FMS. Each possible state can be represented by a sequence of squares ("filled-in" from left to right). One possible state might be that all 5 pallets are present at station 1, while all the other stations are empty. Another possibility might be for station 1 to have four pallets and station 2 one pallet, etc.

The number of different states is equal to the number of different combinations of filled-in squares in the four rows, the total length of which is equal to the number of pallets N in the system. Obviously, the longer the rows the larger is the number of possible states. In the case described here it is assumed that the number of pallets at the stations 1,2,3, and 4 is limited to 5,2,4 and 3 pallets, respectively. As a consequence, the number of different states of the FMS is reduced. Thus the state depicted on the left in figure (76) is no longer possible, as the buffer at station 2 has only a capacity of two pallets.

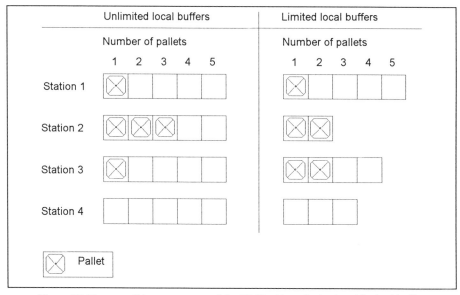

Figure 76: Two possible state spaces of the FMS with unlimited and limited buffers

The state space of such an FMS with limited buffers can be described as follows[193]:

$$S'(N,M) = \{(n_1,n_2,\ldots,n_M) \in S(N,M) \mid 0 \leq n_m \leq N_{max}(m) \ (m=1,\ldots,M-1);$$

$$\max \left[0, \ N - \sum_{m=1}^{M-1} N_{max}(m)\right] \leq N_M \leq N\} \tag{100}$$

The number of different states is limited by the buffer capacity available at the individual stations. The pallet surplus that cannot be accommodated at a machining station must be stored in the local buffer of the transportation station. This can also be interpreted to be a central buffer. *Yao and Buzacott* prove that the solution of this CQN model with a state space limited in this way also exhibits a *product form*. They describe a procedure for the computation of the normalization constant for the closed queueing network with this limited state space[194].

In the model considered a workpiece is rejected at a station if all the buffers at that station are full. With respect to the externally fixed arrival probabilities, a new downstream station for the workpiece is determined. As a consequence, in such an FMS there will be a difference between the externally fixed *arrival probabilities* (routing)[195] *and the actual arrival frequencies* (loading) of the workpieces at the stations. Obviously, the arrival frequency at a station with a *local buffer that is often full* will be smaller than the arrival probability derived from the process plans of the products.

Assume, for example, that in an FMS with 5 machining stations the stationary arrival probabilities are equally distributed with $p_m = 0.2$ $(m = 1,\ldots,5)$. If, however, access to station 1 is denied 50% of the time, then the actual arrival frequency (loading) at this station will be equal to 0.1. Since the workpieces denied access to station 1 will be moved on to one of the other four stations, the loadings of the other stations are increased from 0.2 to 0.225.

In contrast, in the classical CQN model the arrival probabilities predetermined outside the system with respect to the process plans, p_m $(m = 1,2,\ldots,M-1)$, are identical to the real arrival frequencies of the stations.

Yao and Buzacott have studied several variations of such an FMS in which a "block-and-recirculate" strategy is followed.

- **Fixed-Probability-Routing (FPR)**

  It is assumed in the first case that, due to the limited local buffers, the arrival frequencies (loadings) vary. The external arrival probabilities (routing) at the stations that are used to determine the next downstream station in case of a workpiece rejection remain constant, however. This model is called a *fixed-probability-routing* model (FPR). A workpiece that is denied access to a sta-

---

193   The index M again denotes the transportation station.
194   **Yao/Buzacott** (1985)
195   These are the quantities p_m $(m = 1,2,\ldots,M)$ derived from the process plans; see section 3.1.1.1.1.

tion due to its limited buffer remains in the central buffer (or on the circular conveyor belt). The next station at which the workpiece is to be processed is again determined on the basis of the same probability distribution. Obviously, this could be a station other than the one to which the workpiece had just been denied access. It is thus not guaranteed in this setting that the predetermined distribution of arrival probabilities at the stations will be mirrored in the arrival frequencies. Instead, the stations that have larger buffers, and are relatively less utilized, are supplied more frequently with workpieces because they will less frequently reject an incoming workpiece.

Since the arrival probabilities are derived from the process plans, as described in section 3.1.1.1.1., one can conclude that changes in the actual arrival frequencies at the stations must be associated with a *qualitatively different production program*. This seems to make the model rather unrealistic for practical applications because the relationship between the machining operations must be quantitatively constant. If that were not true, a situation could arise, for example, in which many "lathe" operations could have been completed, but the number of "drill" operations would be much smaller due to the limited local buffer capacity at the drilling station. This would result in many partially completed workpieces waiting for the drilling machine either inside or outside the FMS.

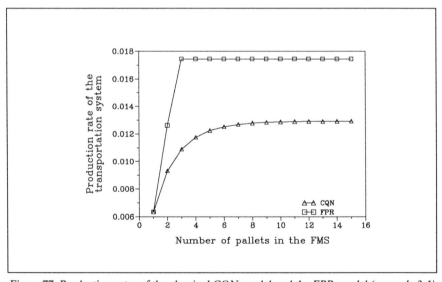

Figure 77: Production rates of the classical CQN model and the FPR model (example 3-1)

Consider figure (77), where the development of the production rate from example 3-1 is illustrated under the assumption that there is no buffer space available at the three stations L/UL, M1 and M2. Hence, $N_{max(m)} = 1$ (1,2,3). The curve labeled "CQN" represents the production rate for the case of unlimited buffers as calculated using the procedure described in section

3.1.1.1.2. based on the classical CQN model. The curve labeled "FPR" was calculated using the procedure from *Yao and Buzacott*[196]. The results for the same example, assuming $N = 4$ universal pallets, are shown in detail in table (32).

Input data			FPR			CQN	
m	b_m	p_m	X_m	U_m	p^*_m	X_m	U_m
1	90.00	0.5	0.009823	0.8841	0.5630	0.005881	0.5293
2	295.67	0.1	0.002819	0.8337	0.1616	0.001176	0.3478
3	193.33	0.4	0.004806	0.9291	0.2754	0.004705	0.9095
4	5.90	1.0	0.017449	0.1029	1.0000	0.011762	0.0694

Table 32: Comparison of the classical CQN model with the FPR model (example 3-1)

It can be clearly seen that *limiting* the local buffers at the stations results in a significant *increase in the production rate*. This is obviously due to the redistribution of workpieces from the full, and fully utilized, stations to the less frequented, and generally less utilized, stations. Under these circumstances workpieces can be processed that would otherwise be waiting in a local buffer of a station for a machine to become free. As indicated above, however, this redistribution of the workload is associated with a change in the qualitative characteristics of the processed workpieces. The resulting *arrival frequencies* p^*_m show the rearrangement of the workpiece flow. The real arrival of workpieces at the bottleneck machine 3 is reduced to 0.2754, as compared to a stationary arrival frequency of $p_m = 0.4$. This machine will often reject incoming workpieces due to its high utilization and limited buffer capacity. The rejected workpieces are redistributed among the other stations. This results in higher arrival frequencies and therefore leads to *higher utilizations* at these stations.

The *Yao and Buzacott* concept does not seem well suited to an FMS in which several consecutive operations are to be carried out on the workpieces (multi-stage process plans). Its usefulness is rather in the analysis of an *FMS*, in which one complex operation is carried out on a workpiece during a single visit to a single processing station (single-stage process plans). The analysis could be extended to cover the role of the FMS in a larger production environment. Figure (78) shows a possible layout for such a single-stage FMS supplied with workpieces by a conveyor. The unprocessed workpieces are kept in a storage area near the entrance to the system.

After a processed workpiece has been unloaded from one of the pallets circulating in the FMS, the next workpiece is taken out of the storage area. A check is then made to see if the appropriate machine is able to accept the workpiece. The distribution of the workpieces to the machines is made in accordance with the arrival probabilities p_m (m = 1,2,...,M-1).

---

196 **Yao/Buzacott** (1985)

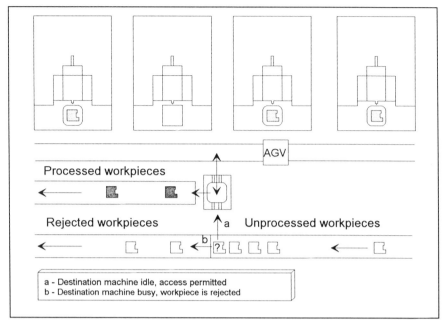

Figure 78: Hypothetical layout of an FMS with "fixed probability routing"

If the downstream machine is free, then the workpiece is loaded onto the pallet and processed normally in the FMS (case a). If the machine is busy, then the workpiece is rejected and transferred to another manufacturing segment, such as a conventional job shop (case b). The material flow on the conveyor system must be large enough to always be able to provide the FMS with the raw material required.

It is assumed here that only one machining operation takes place and that the time for loading and unloading is included in the transportation time.

- **Fixed-Probability-Loading (FPL)**

Yao and Buzacott attempt to circumvent the problems described above regarding the change in the qualitative characteristics of the production by assuming, in a further variation of the "block-and-recirculate" strategy, that through the control of the FMS it can be assured that the predetermined arrival probabilities at the stations will be retained for the case of limited local buffers as well. This approach is called *fixed-probability-loading* (FPL).

In order to ensure that the real arrival frequencies (loading) are equal to the arrival frequencies derived from the process plans, the probability distribution of arrivals (routing) at the stations must be appropriately modified. *Yao and Buzacott*[197] suggest an iterative procedure. Here the arrival probabi-

---

197 **Yao/Buzacott** (1985)

lities at the stations, which provide the basis for the workpiece flow in the FMS, are modified. This continues until the desired distribution of the actual arrival frequencies at the stations, and thus the desired relationship among the station dependent production rates, has been reached.

The production rates of the transportation system in example 3-1, with varying numbers of pallets, are shown in table (33) and figure (79).

N	CQN	FPL
1	0.006337	0.006337
2	0.009333	0.011936
3	0.010898	0.012546
4	0.011762	0.012546
5	0.012252	0.012546
6	0.012536	0.012546
7	0.012700	0.012546
8	0.012797	0.012546
9	0.012853	0.012546
10	0.012885	0.012546
11	0.012905	0.012546
12	0.012916	0.012546
13	0.012922	0.012546
14	0.012926	0.012546
15	0.012928	0.012546

*Table 33: Production rates of the classical CQN model
and the FPL model (example 3-1)*

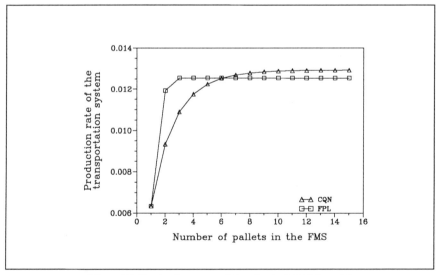

*Figure 79: Production rates of the classical CQN model
and the FPL model (example 3-1)*

It is interesting to note that between two and five pallets the production rate of the FPL model is actually higher than that of the classical CQN model.

The "limited" model estimates a higher production rate than the "unlimited" model. Also noteworthy is that the production rate increases more rapidly as the number of pallets increases than under the classical CQN model. After a certain point, increases in the number of pallets no longer affect the production rate.

In contrast to the FPR model, in the FPL model the routing is equal to the loading derived from the process plans. The results for $N=4$ pallets, for example, are given in table (34). It is easy to show that the production rates of the stations are in a relationship of 5:1:4:10. The modified arrival probabilities, however, can vary quite significantly from the original p_m values. The shift in the workpiece flow to the bottleneck station 3 (M1) is particularly noticeable.

Input data			FPL (N=4)			CQN	
m	b_m	p_m	x_m	U_m	$p_m^{\star}$	x_m	U_m
1	90.00	0.5	0.006290	0.5661	0.0855	0.005881	0.5293
2	295.67	0.1	0.001254	0.3703	0.0117	0.001176	0.3478
3	193.33	0.4	0.005003	0.9673	0.9027	0.004705	0.9095
4	5.90	1.0	0.012546	0.0740	1.0000	0.011762	0.0694

Table 34: Production rates, utilizations and modified arrival probabilities of the FPL model (example 3-1)

In interpreting the results of the FPL model for the example under consideration, *several different cases* must be distinguished. Here the number of pallets N and the spatial distribution of the buffers among the stations are of central importance.

Case 1:   *The number of pallets is not greater than the receptive capacity of the smallest station.*

$$N=1; \ N \leq \min_{m \leq M-1} \{N_{max}(m)\} = 1$$

If the number of pallets is not greater than the smallest receptive capacity of the three processing stations in the FMS, then the assumptions underlying the classical CQN model are satisfied: buffer limits do not affect the system and the results are consistent with those of the classical CQN model.

Case 2:   *The number of pallets is not greater than the total receptive capacity of all the stations but is greater than the receptive capacity of the smallest station.*

$$N=2,3; \ 3 = \sum_{m=1}^{M-1} N_{max}(m) \geq N > \min_{m \leq M-1} \{N_{max}(m)\} = 1$$

Here the number of pallets is small enough that the total amount of space available at all stations is sufficient to accept all the pallets. There is, however, at least one station whose receptive capacity is *not* sufficient to accept all the pallets. The limited buffer at this station can thus have an affect on the performance of the FMS. The reduction in the state space of the queueing network results in the sum of all the probabilities (always equal to one) being distributed among fewer states. In example 3-1, at most one work-piece can be found at any given station - except the transportation station. When $N=2$ workpieces are circulating in the system, the following states could develop:

$$S'(2,4) = \begin{cases} (1,1,0,0) \\ (1,0,1,0) \\ (1,0,0,1) \\ (0,1,1,0) \\ (0,1,0,1) \\ (0,0,1,1) \\ (0,0,0,2) \end{cases}$$

number of pallets at station AGV (unlimited)
number of pallets at station L/UL
number of pallets at station M1
number of pallets at station M2

The states $(2,0,0,0)$, $(0,2,0,0)$ and $(0,0,2,0)$ *cannot* occur because there is no local buffer at the load/unload station or at either machine. Therefore, only one pallet, the one which is currently being processed, can find space at that station.

The reduced state space includes only those in which no queues develop at the machining stations due to the buffer limits. Such states obviously tend to be "more productive" than those in which a pallet must wait at one station while another station is idle. In the infeasible state $(2,0,0,0)$, for example, only one of the two pallets present at station 1 is being processed, while in the feasible state $(1,0,1,0)$ two machines at stations 1 and 3 are operating. Thus it makes sense to limit the state space of an FMS to those states in which the heavily utilized bottleneck station has preference in the supply of pallets. This results in shorter queueing delays for pallets at stations which are relatively less utilized and improves the production rate compared to an FMS in which it is allowed that pallets may join a queue instead of being pro-cessed at an available station. This is the reason why a "limited" FMS exhibits a higher production rate than the classical CQN model FMS.

Case 3:   *The number of pallets is greater than the total receptive capacity of all the stations: a central buffer is necessary or some pallets will not be able to find space in the FMS.*

$$N>3; \; N > \sum_{m=1}^{M-1} N_{max}(m) = 3$$

In this case the total space available at all stations has been used up. If the number of pallets circulating in the system is increased further the pro-duction rate no longer follows suit. The additional pallets will be stored in the (unlimited) queue of the transportation system, in accordance with the assumptions of the FPL model. The production rate in this last case can, there-fore, not be further increased by increasing the number of pallets beyond three.

In contrast to the FPR model, the production rates computed under the FPL model assumptions are qualitatively equivalent. This is so because the sta-tionary arrival probabilities of the closed queueing network model are modi-fied so that the actual loadings of the stations are equal to the desired load-ings, as derived from the process plans in example 3-1.

Thus a preliminary conclusion can be drawn from the development of the production rate as illustrated in the example. Under the assumptions of the FPL model, the number of pallets circulating in the FMS should never be greater than the total space available at all the processing stations (excluding the transportation station) ($\Sigma_{m=1,...,M-1}N_{max(m)}$), since successive pallets do not lead to an increase in the productivity of the FMS.

As shown in figure (79), it is better, under the given assumptions and for a small number of pallets, to limit the queues at the stations either *physically* (by eliminating buffer space) or *logically* (using a release strategy). The rela-tionships described above can be used to systematically optimize the pro-duction rate when each machining station is assigned a *logical buffer capacity*, independent of its physical buffer capacity, that then provides the basis for workpiece release into the FMS. A station's logical buffer capacity is the ma-ximum number of workpieces allowed in the FMS at any one point in time (in the local buffers or the central buffer) that will be processed at that sta-tion.

Assume that it is assured in the release of the workpieces into the FMS that at most $N_{max(m)}$ (m = 1,2,...,M-1) workpieces having to be processed at the sta-tion m will circulate in the FMS at any one time. As has been shown, the re-sulting distribution of the pallets among the various stations leads to a higher production rate, for cases with few pallets, than in the classical case with un-limited buffers. Only for larger numbers of pallets can benefits be drawn from eliminating the limit on the number of pallets (i.e. under the assump-tions of the classical CQN model).

The superiority of the classical CQN model (elimination of the limits on the logical buffers) for large numbers of pallets is more obvious with a more heavily utilized transportation system. Queueing processes become then more likely. In the FPL model these lead to a shortage of workpieces and an associated decrease in the load on the machining stations. The $[N-\Sigma_{m=1,...,M-1}N_{max(m)}]$ pallets, which exceed the total receptive capacity of the local buffers of the FMS, cannot all be used. They do not contribute to an improved utilization of the stations, as would be the case with unlimited local buffers.

To make this effect more clear, the average transportation time in example 3-1 has been increased from 5.9 to 20 minutes. The development of the pro-duction rate of the transportation system as a function of the number of pal-lets for the classical CQN model (CQN) and the FPL model (FPL) is sum-marized in table (35) and figure (80). It can be seen even more clearly here than in figure (79) that the classical CQN model procedure - where a systematic release of the workpieces into the FMS is absent - allows a higher production rate for the transportation system (and thereby for the entire FMS) for larger numbers of pallets.

N	CQN	FPL
1	0.005818	0.005818
2	0.008855	0.010442
3	0.010552	0.011348
4	0.011533	0.011348
5	0.012108	0.011348
6	0.012447	0.011348
7	0.012647	0.011348
8	0.012765	0.011348
9	0.012835	0.011348
10	0.012875	0.011348
11	0.012899	0.011348
12	0.012913	0.011348
13	0.012921	0.011348
14	0.012926	0.011348
15	0.012929	0.011348

Table 35: Production rates of the transportation system with a mean transportation time of 20 minutes (example 3-1)

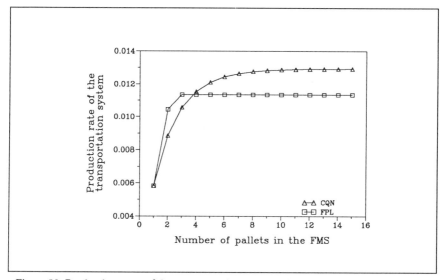

Figure 80: Production rates of the transportation system with a mean transportation time of 20 minutes (example 3-1)

It is possible, however, to exploit the effects which increase productivity in cases with few pallets (due to the limited logical buffers at the stations) for cases with many pallets as well. This can be achieved by distributing the given number of pallets N circulating in the system in such a way as to maximize the production rate of the FMS (as calculated using the FPL model). The distribution of the pallets among the stations then defines the logical buffer capacities that must be observed during the release of the workpieces.

Since N pallets can be distributed in a variety of ways to the stations with different production rates, the following *optimization problem* arises:

$$\max \; X(\underline{N}_{max}) \tag{101}$$

subject to

$$\sum_{m=1}^{M-1} N_{max}(m) \leq N \tag{102}$$

$$N_{max}(m) \geq 1 \qquad\qquad m=1,2,\ldots,M-1 \tag{103}$$

The set of feasible solutions for this decision model consists of the possible combinations of N objects into M-1 groups, where each group must contain at least one element. Each solution is described by a vector $\underline{N}_{max}$. The *optimal solution* can be determined, for example, with total enumeration, where each feasible solution can be evaluated with the FPL model. For small FMSs with few pallets this approach may be practical but not for large FMSs with many pallets.

The stations' optimal logical buffer capacities (including the one space available at each machine) for the modified example 3-1 (transportation time 20 minutes) are given in table (36) and figure (81) for increasing numbers of pallets, N. When N is less than 3 the sum of the logical buffer capacities is greater than N since $N_{max(m)}=0$ would mean that the station m would not be operated at all.

N	L/UL $N_{max}(1)$	M2 $N_{max}(2)$	M1 $N_{max}(3)$	AGV X_M
1	1	1	1	0.005818
2	1	1	1	0.010442
3	1	1	1	0.011348
4	1	1	2	0.012688
5	1	1	3	0.012910
6	1	1	4	0.012942
7	1	1	5	0.012949
8	2	1	5	0.012951
9	2	1	6	0.012952
10	2	1	7	0.012952
11	2	1	8	0.012952

Table 36: Distribution of pallets among three stations (logical buffer spaces)

If the optimal solution for this example is more closely examined, it becomes clear that the optimal production rate can be found when the logical buffer at the bottleneck station M1 ($N_{max(3)}$) is first increased. At the point N=7, a further increase in the production rate is only possible when the logical buffer at the station L/UL ($N_{max(1)}$), the station with the second highest workload, is increased. When the number of pallets is increased further, then the logical buffer of the bottleneck machine M1 must again be enlarged.

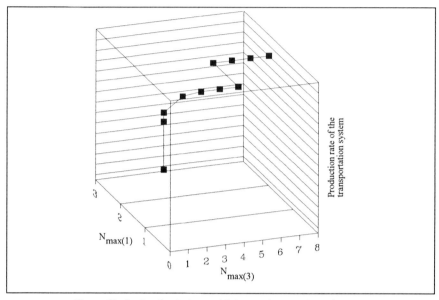

Figure 81: Optimal solutions with increasing number of pallets

In table (37) and figure (82) the production rates calculated by using the approach with variable logical buffers are compared with the equivalent values derived from the classical CQN model and the FPL model with constant (physical) buffers. Figure (83) shows a close-up view on the graph in figure (82).

N	CQN	FPL Constant local buffers	FPL Variable buffers
1	0.005818	0.005818	0.005818
2	0.008855	0.010442	0.010442
3	0.010552	0.011348	0.011348
4	0.011533	0.011348	0.012688
5	0.012108	0.011348	0.012910
6	0.012447	0.011348	0.012942
7	0.012647	0.011348	0.012949
8	0.012765	0.011348	0.012951
9	0.012835	0.011348	0.012952
10	0.012875	0.011348	0.012952
11	0.012899	0.011348	0.012952
12	0.012913	0.011348	0.012952
13	0.012921	0.011348	0.012952
14	0.012926	0.011348	0.012952
15	0.012929	0.011348	0.012952

Table 37: Production rate of the transportation system

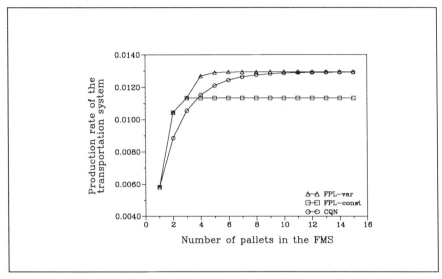

Figure 82: Production rate of the transportation system with a mean transportation time of 20 minutes and limited local buffers

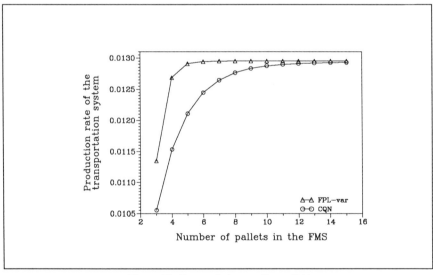

Figure 83: Zoomed view on figure (82)

Figure (84) illustrates the development of the objective function for the above optimization model (production rate of the transportation system) for $N = 7$ pallets in the FMS, as a function of $N_{max(3)}$, and for different values of

$N_{max(1)}$. The efficient solutions, in which no pallets wait inactive in the central buffer, are connected with a double line.

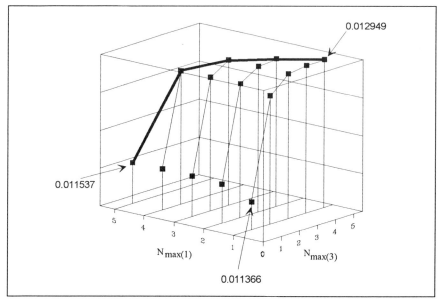

Figure 84: Objective function with $N = 7$ and $N_{max(2)} = 1$

These results make plain the superiority of the release strategy considered as compared to an unsystematic release of workpieces into the FMS. By using the FPL strategy combined with the concept of logical buffers, production rates can be reached with low numbers of pallets that could only be reached with significantly more pallets in the classical CQN model. Considering the costs of the capital associated with the pallets circulating in an FMS (for pallets, physical storage space, and work-in-process), the importance of the release strategy for the economic viability of an FMS is obvious.

- **Dynamic Routing (DR)**

In another model *Yao and Buzacott*[198] considered an FMS control strategy in which the station having the most unused buffer space is always supplied with a workpiece. To do this the station with the most available buffer space must first be found. A workpiece that needs to be processed at this station is then chosen from the central buffer, mounted on a pallet and transported to the station. Under this strategy the actual arrival frequencies (loading) are functions of the interaction between the externally predetermined arrival probabilities (routing) and the limited local buffer sizes at the stations.

198   **Yao/Buzacott** (1986)

3.1.2.3. The Akyildiz approach

Although *Akyildiz*[199] did not directly consider FMSs, the essence of his work can easily be extended to an FMS. He proposed a modified version of the exact MVA procedure for a closed queueing network with *universal pallets*. In the recursive calculations of the key parameters of the system, each situation in which a workpiece's downstream station is full and thus blocks the upstream station is considered explicitly.

Akyildiz introduces two modifications in order to account for blocking (transfer blocking):

- Increase of the flow time by the blocking time of a machine

  When a *pallet's upstream station is blocked* it means that the pallet spends a correspondingly longer time at that station. The average flow time is thus increased by the amount of time lost by the workpiece waiting for space to become free at the downstream station. This time period is the residual service time of the next finished workpiece at the downstream station.

  For an FMS with universal pallets the average flow time at station m can be described with equation (104).

$$D_m(n) = b_m \cdot Q_m(n-1) + b_m + bl_m(n) \qquad\qquad m=1,2,\ldots,M; \ n=1,2,\ldots,N \qquad (104)$$

  $\uparrow$ mean blocking time of the upstream station m

  The problem now is to determine the average blocking time $bl_m(n)$ of the upstream station m. Since, as usual, it has been assumed that the processing times are exponentially distributed, the residual service time of the workpiece currently being processed at the downstream station j is also exponentially distributed[200]. In order to find the average blocking time of the station m, *Akyildiz* multiplies the average residual service time at the downstream station j by the transition probability from m to j, r_{mj}. This, in turn, is multiplied by the ratio of the relative arrival frequencies of the two stations for those cases when the average number of pallets at station j is greater than its maximum receptive capacity [see equation (105)].

$$bl_m(n) = \sum_{\substack{j=1 \\ j\neq m;\ Q_j(n)>N_{max}(j)}}^{M} b_j \cdot r_{mj} \cdot \frac{p_m}{p_j} \qquad m=1,2,\ldots,M; \ n=1,2,\ldots,N \qquad (105)$$

  $\uparrow$ mean residual service time of a workpiece at the downstream station

---

199　**Akyildiz** (1988a)
200　see section 3.1.1.2.2.

The ratio of the relative arrival frequencies should take account of the work-piece flow to both stations. The blocking time is cumulated in a repeat-until loop that is performed several times, if necessary [see figure (85)].

Procedure MVABLO	
Initialize	
$Q_m(0)=0$	$m=1,2,\ldots,M$
$bl_m(1)=0$	$m=1,2,\ldots,M$
$z_m(1)=1$	$m=1,2,\ldots,M$
for n=1 to N do	
repeat	
$D_m(n) = b_m \cdot Q_m(n-1)+b_m \cdot z_m(n)+bl_m(n)$	$m=1,2,\ldots,M$
$X_m(n) = [p_m \cdot n]/\left(\sum_{j=1}^{M} p_j \cdot D_j(n)\right)$	$m=1,2,\ldots,M$
$Q_m(n) = X_m(n) \cdot D_m(n)$	$m=1,2,\ldots,M$
for m=1 to M do	
if $Q_m(n)>N_{max(m)}$ then	
$z_m(n)=0$	
$bl_j(n)=bl_j(n)+b_m \cdot r_{jm} \cdot p_j/p_m$	$j=1,2,\ldots,M$ $j\neq m$
else	
$z_m(n+1)=z_m(n)$	
$bl_m(n+1)=bl_m(n)$	
endif	
endfor	
until $Q_m(n)<N_{max(m)}$	$m=1,2,\ldots,M$
endfor	

Figure 85: Procedure MVABLO of Akyildiz[201]

- Flow time at a station that is full

When a *station is full* it cannot accept any more pallets. The average flow time of such a station is made up of the sum of the processing times of all the pallets already waiting at that station. This is described in equation (106) by means of the binary auxiliary variables z_m.

---

201 The procedure may run into a endless loop between *repeat* and *until*, if - following the case when $Q_m(n)>N_{max(m)}$ and the queue length has been corrected - no solution is found in which the condition $Q_m(n)\leq N_{max(m)}$ holds for all stations. This situation may arise, although the number of pallets, N, is smaller than the total space at all stations.

$$D_m(n) = b_m \cdot A_m(n) + z_m(n) \cdot b_m \qquad\qquad m=1,2,\ldots,M \qquad (106)$$

$\uparrow$ mean number of pallets at station m *upon arrival of a pallet*

with

$$z_m(n) = \begin{cases} 0, & \text{if station m is full [i.e. } Q_m(n) > N_{max(m)}] \\ 1, & \text{else} \end{cases} \qquad m=1,2,\ldots,M \qquad (107)$$

Akyildiz accounts for both of these situations in the exact MVA procedure. In each recursion step (with respect to the number of pallets in the system) at every station it is tested as to whether the number of pallets exceeds the available space of the station. For stations at which this is true, the average flow time is modified in accordance with equation (106). Then the average weighted residual service time, according to equation (105), is shifted back onto all the other stations as the blocking time. This procedure is summarized in figure (85), where the symbol $Q_m(n)$ indicates the number of pallets at station m when n pallets are circulating in the FMS.

Akyildiz' model considers only the *average values* of the quantities under study, just as does the exact variation of the MVA for the classical CQN model. Therefore, blocking is assumed to develop when the *average* number of pallets at a station is greater than the station's receptive capacity. In this approach, however, those states in which more than the average number of pallets are present at a station are not considered. In these situations blocking can obviously be a problem, although they are not considered in the *Akyildiz* approach. As a consequence, this approach will be less precise as the variance of the probability distribution of the number of pallets at a station with limited buffer space increases.

This model does not take the specific processes occurring in an FMS into consideration and therefore needs to be developed further. The assumption that the pallets remain always at their upstream station whenever their downstream station is full (transfer blocking) is particularly unrealistic for FMSs. In most real FMSs the pallets are stored in a *central buffer*, if possible, or they are exchanged for unprocessed workpieces from a station's local buffer.

3.1.2.4. A new method for the approximation of blocking

A method for the approximation of blocking that has been especially designed for the situations found in an FMS will be described in this section. First, the situations and conditions under which blocking can occur will be characterized. Following that, the effects of these situations will be quantified and integrated into the CQN model.

3.1.2.4.1. Conditions and process of blocking

In order to characterize blocking it is first assumed that the transportation system is infinitely fast[202]. Starving and its effects on the processes of the FMS are thus excluded. Consider the following situation: a workpiece F_m is supposed to leave a machine (or the machining table) after its processing at station m has been completed. At the station m, however, at the next station j (according to the process plan), and in the central buffer all the buffer spaces are occupied. Also there is no unprocessed workpiece in the local buffer of station m against which the processed workpiece could be exchanged. Therefore the workpiece F_m is blocking the station m since the workpiece U_m, waiting at the station k or in the central buffer to be processed at the station m, cannot gain access to station m: a typical case of *blocking*. Figure (86) illustrates the blockage situation of a machine. Due to blocking at the machine, the workpiece U_m must wait for access to station m.

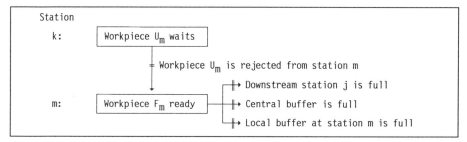

Figure 86: Blocking at station m

The machine at station m remains blocked until the workpiece U_m can enter the station m and occupy the machining table. In a system with an infinitely large local buffer space (or with an infinitely large central buffer and an infinitely fast material flow system) such a situation cannot arise.

Figure (87) presents simulation results showing the relationship between the *amount of local buffer space* and the share of blocking in the total amount of time a station is in operation. It can easily be observed that as the amount of local storage space at the station decreases, the station's average non-productive time increases due to blocking.

---

202 For this section see also **Tempelmeier/Kuhn/Tetzlaff** (1989)

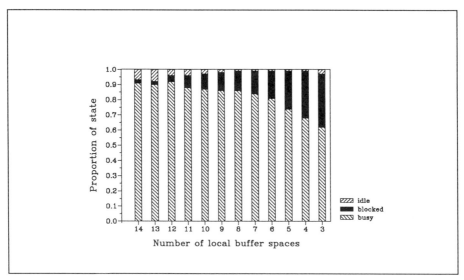

Figure 87: States of a station vs. number of local buffer spaces

The following conditions must be met for *blocking* to occur at a station m (the quantities n_m and n_{CB} represent the number of pallets at the station m and in the central buffer, respectively):

Condition 1: Workpiece exchange at station m

Processing of the workpiece F_m at the station m has been completed. A further unprocessed workpiece U_m is ready for processing at station m and waiting in another station k or in the central buffer. If the conditions mentioned below are satisfied, this workpiece will be temporarily denied access to the blocked station m.

Condition 2: Central buffer is full

The *central buffer is fully occupied*. That means there is no room available for the workpiece F_m: $n_{CB} = N_{max(CB)}$.

Condition 3: Current station m is full

All local buffers at the *station m* at which the workpiece has just finished being processed are *full*. Therefore, the machine under consideration here cannot be unloaded. All the other machines at the station m are full as well[203]: $n_m = N_{max(m)}$.

---

203 The unprocessed workpiece can, therefore, not proceed to any parallel machines there may be at that same station.

Condition 4: No unprocessed workpieces available in the local buffer

In the local buffers of the current station m there are *no unprocessed work-pieces* U_m that must be processed next at this station. Otherwise, a workpiece U_m could be exchanged for the just finished workpiece F_m[204].

Condition 5: Downstream stations of the processed workpieces F_m are full

It is impossible to remove the processed workpieces F_m from the station m because both their downstream stations j ($n_j = N_{max(j)}$) and the central buffer are full.

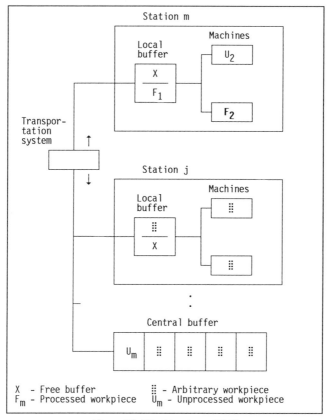

Figure 88: Blocking in an FMS

An example can serve to make these conditions somewhat more concrete [see figure (88)]. The workpiece F_2 has just been processed at the station m. This

---

204 A workpiece exchange would be technically possible, since one buffer space is always kept free for this pur-
    pose.

workpiece remains on the machine's machining table. The workpiece U_m in the central buffer is supposed to be processed next at the station m and requires access to this station (condition 1). The central buffer is fully occupied with five pallets (condition 2). The station m is at maximum capacity ($N_{max(m)}$) with three pallets (condition 3). There is no unprocessed workpiece in the local buffer at station m, therefore, a workpiece exchange is impossible (condition 4). This means that the next workpiece U_m processed at a machine in station m must come from another station or from the central buffer, as in the previous example. If there were any unprocessed workpieces waiting in the local buffer of the station m, these could be channeled to the free machine, and blocking at station m could be avoided. Another workpiece U_2 is being processed at the other machine in station m. The two workpieces F_1 and F_2 must be processed next at station j. This station is also occupied at its maximum level ($N_{max(j)}$) with three pallets (condition 5).

The workpiece U_m has to wait now until either the workpiece F_1 or F_2 has been removed. This would follow from space in the central buffer or in the buffer at the downstream station j becoming free, thus allowing access to station m. Blockage at the machine m exists from the time processing of the workpiece F_2 is finished and the unprocessed waiting workpiece U_m has demanded access to the station m to the time when workpiece U_m gains access to the station. To simplify the analysis, it is assumed that the transportation system is infinitely fast. In reality, delays due to transportation processes can also play a role.

Let us now consider the question of how many pallets are necessary to cause blocking. The conditions described above can only be satisfied when the central buffer is full, and when the two stations having together the smallest receptive capacity are full as well. Looking more closely at the above example reveals the fact that blocking in this FMS can occur (though it must not) when at least 11 pallets (five in the central buffer, three at station m and three at station j) are circulating in the FMS. This is true as long as there is no other station in the FMS which has a lower receptive capacity than either station m or j. If the capacity of the central buffer is denoted by $N_{max(CB)}$, then the minimum total number of pallets N_{SB} necessary for blocking to occur is given by equation (108).

$$N_{SB} \geq \min_{\substack{m, j \leq M-1 \\ m \neq j}} \{N_{max(m)} + N_{max(j)}\} + N_{max(CB)} \qquad (108)$$

This is a necessary but not a sufficient condition for the occurrence of blocking in an FMS. Whether the system becomes blocked or not depends on the process plans of the products and the resulting pallet flow through the FMS.

3.1.2.4.2. Accounting for blocking times in the CQN model

After having analyzed the process of blocking in the previous section, the relevant conditions now have to be quantified. This can be done as follows. First the FMS under study must be modelled and evaluated with the help of the classical CQN model. The principal objective of this step is the determination of the *stationary probability distributions of the number of pallets at the stations* in the FMS, $P\{\underline{n}_m\}$ (m = 1,.2,...,M). These probability distributions will be used to quantify the blocking conditions and to estimate the *blocking times*. The blocking times are then added to the "normal" average processing times at the stations. The revised average processing times are now introduced into the solution procedure for the classical CQN model. This procedure is repeated until the results vary only slightly. Its basic structure is depicted in figure (89).

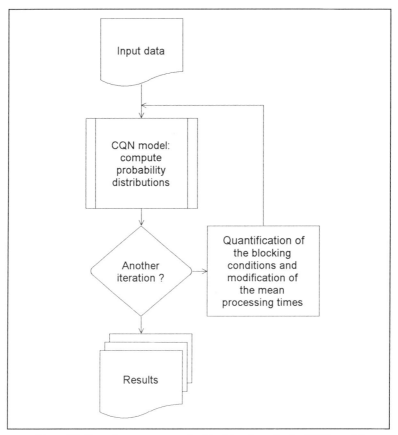

Figure 89: Procedure to account for blocking times in the CQN model

Assume that six pallets are circulating in the system described in example 3-1. The receptive capacity of the central buffer is limited to three pallets, and both machines and the setup area can each accept a maximum of $N_{max(m)} = 1$ pallets. Blocking could therefore occur. The stationary probability distributions of the pallets in this FMS are summarized in table (38).

m \ n_m	0	1	2	3	4	5	6	$P\{n_m \geq 0\}$
1 (L/UL)	0.4358	0.2531	0.1464	0.0839	0.0468	0.0242	0.0097	1.0000
2 (M2)	0.6293	0.2364	0.0876	0.0317	0.0109	0.0034	0.0008	1.0000
3 (M1)	0.0306	0.0509	0.0831	0.1314	0.1959	0.2591	0.2490	1.0000
4 (AGV)	0.9260	0.0686	0.0050	0.0003	0.0000	0.0000	0.0000	1.0000

Table 38: Stationary probability distributions of the number of pallets at the stations
(example 3-1)

These probability distributions provide the preliminary starting point for the estimation of the blocking times. It is also necessary to know the probability that the transportation system will transport a workpiece directly to station j after it leaves station m. These transition probabilities r_{mj} (m,j = 1,...,M-1) result from the process plans, as described in section 3.1.1.1.1. The values shown in table (39) apply to example 3-1.

To From	1 (L/UL)	2 (M2)	3 (M1)
1 (L/UL)	0.0	0.2	0.8
2 (M2)	1.0	0.0	0.0
3 (M1)	1.0	0.0	0.0

Table 39: Transition probabilities
(example 3-1)

80% of the workpieces that leave the setup area in the current example are transported to machine M1, while 20% continue their processing at machine M2. All workpieces return to the setup area after processing at either station so that they may be unloaded or that their setup may be changed.

3.1.2.4.2.1. Quantification of the blocking conditions

Some of the above formulated blocking conditions can be directly quantified using the classical CQN model. These include conditions 1, 3 and 5.

Condition 1: Workpiece exchange at station m

The processing of workpiece F_m at station m is completed, and a planned transition from station m to station j takes place. This process is represented by the transition probability r_{mj}.

Condition 3: Current station m is full

There are at least $N_{max(m)}$ workpieces at the station. The probability $P\{n_m \geq N_{max(m)}\}$ can be used to describe this situation.

Condition 5: Downstream stations of the processed workpieces F_m are full

The downstream stations j of all the workpieces being processed in station m are full; at least $N_{max(j)}$ workpieces can be found at each of these stations. After evaluating the CQN model, this situation can be described with the probability $N_{max(j)}$.

The *blocking conditions* 2 (central buffer full) and 4 (only processed workpieces at station m) cannot be quantified using corresponding elements from the CQN model because neither a central buffer nor processed workpieces are known in this model. There is no *central buffer* in the classical CQN model because it is assumed that all the stations have unlimited local buffers. No *processed workpieces* are found at a station, since after processing at a station every workpiece immediately becomes an unprocessed workpiece in the transportation system (i.e. a transportation job).

Two problems can arise here. First, the blocking conditions 2 and 4 themselves have to be quantified, and second their effects on the quantification of the blocking conditions 3 and 5 have to be considered. The influence of blocking condition 2 on conditions 3 and 5 is introduced into the analysis as follows. Since the central buffer is full when blocking occurs (blocking condition 2) the pallets which have been stored there can no longer circulate in the FMS. For that reason, when calculating the stationary probability distribution of the pallets among the stations, the total number of pallets circulating in the FMS is reduced by the capacity of the central buffer. The probabilities given in table (38) can thus be replaced by those in table (40).

m \ n_m	0	1	2	3	P$\{n_m \geq 1\}$
1 (L/UL)	0.5096	0.2844	0.1472	0.0587	0.2844+0.1472+0.0587=0.4904
2 (M2)	0.6777	0.2333	0.0723	0.0167	0.2333+0.0723+0.0167=0.3223
3 (M1)	0.1573	0.2345	0.3102	0.2980	0.2345+0.3102+0.2980=0.8427

Table 40: Probability distributions of the number of pallets at the stations with reduced workpiece flow (N = 3)

Observe that the probabilities have shifted to the left because fewer pallets circulate in the FMS when the central buffer is excluded.

In order to actually quantify the blocking conditions 2 and 4, only those states of the FMS are considered in which the stations are so heavily congested that some of the pallets in the system are not given access to their downstream stations. These "surplus" pallets must be stored in the central buffer. If the capacity of the central buffer is limited, a precondition for blocking to occur, then it is possible that the space in the central buffer could be exhausted. Workpieces which have been processed at a station and which, according to the control strategy of the FMS, should be stored in the central buffer are rejected by the central buffer and remain in the local buffer of their current station. Those workpieces which have been rejected by the central buffer can be interpreted to be *processed* workpieces which are waiting at one station for access to the next machine at which they are to be processed.

The probability that *both the central buffer will be full and that only processed workpieces will be present at the station m* is approximated by the *correction factor* given in equation (109).

$$
KF_m = \min \left[\frac{\overset{M}{\underset{\substack{j=1 \\ j \neq m}}{\Sigma}} \left\{ \overset{N}{\underset{n=1}{\Sigma}} P\{n_j = n\} \cdot \max \left[0, [n - (N_{max(j)} + N_{max(CB)} \cdot p_j)] \right] \right\} \cdot r_{mj}}{N_{max(m)}}, \ 1 \right] \quad m=1,2,\ldots,M \quad (109)
$$

"share" of station j in the central buffer

with

n_j	-	number of pallets at station j (waiting or in process)
p_j	-	stationary arrival probability of a pallet at station j
r_{mj}	-	probability that a pallet, upon leaving station m must next be transported to station j
$m = M$	-	index of the transportation system
$m < M$	-	index of a processing station
M	-	number of stations in the FMS
$N_{max(m)}$	-	space for pallets at station m
$N_{max(CB)}$	-	central buffer size

The expression enclosed in the large curved brackets describes the number of pallets expected to be at station j for which there is room neither at the downstream station nor in the central buffer. If the space available in the central buffer is distributed in proportion to the average arrival frequency p_j of pallets at the stations (relative workpiece flow to the stations), then the quantity $N_{max(CB)} \cdot p_j$ represents the share of the central buffer planned for station j - assuming all the stations use the central buffer to a degree which corresponds to their share of the workpiece flow. This quantity can also be interpreted as the storage space in the central buffer that should be reserved for the station j. By adding to this the maximum pallet space of station j, $N_{max(j)}$, the total buffer space in the FMS that may be interpreted as being reserved for pallets assigned to station j, $(N_{max(j)} + N_{max(CB)} \cdot p_j)$, can be found.

To the degree that the number of pallets (n) at station j exceeds the available buffer space, there develops a *pallet surplus* that has to be stored at another station. If it is assumed that these pallets had been previously at the station m, they can then be redistributed to station m through multiplication with the transition probability r_{mj} and designated as *processed workpieces of the station m*. Next, the surpluses at all the downstream stations (with respect to workpieces located at station j) are added together, and the total surplus is divided by the maximum number of pallets at station m, $N_{max(m)}$. This quotient serves as an approximation of the probability that the central buffer is full (otherwise there would be no surpluses) *and* that only processed workpieces are present at station m.

As indicated, *blocking increases the queueing time of a workpiece at a station*. The length of this additional waiting time depends largely on the specific conditions at a workpiece's upstream station m and its downstream station j. It is influenced by the residual service time of the workpiece currently being processed at the station j. This workpiece must free station j before the workpiece at station m can leave the machining area where it resides. The *expected duration of the blockage at station m due to the workpiece transition from station m to station j*, $E\{BZ_{mj}\}$ can be quantified with reference to the above-mentioned blocking conditions, as shown in equation (110)].

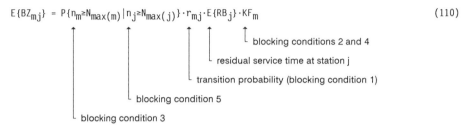

$$E\{BZ_{mj}\} = P\{n_m{\geq}N_{max(m)}|n_j{\geq}N_{max(j)}\}\cdot r_{mj}\cdot E\{RB_j\}\cdot KF_m \tag{110}$$

blocking conditions 2 and 4

residual service time at station j

transition probability (blocking condition 1)

blocking condition 5

blocking condition 3

The *conditional probability* $P\{n_m{\geq}N_{max(m)}|n_j{\geq}N_{max(j)}\}$, used in equation (110), that station m will be full and that station j is full as well, is given by equation (111).

$$P\{n_m{\geq}N_{max(m)}|n_j{\geq}N_{max(j)}\} = \frac{P\{n_m{\geq}N_{max(m)},n_j{\geq}N_{max(j)}\}}{P\{n_j{\geq}N_{max(j)}\}} \tag{111}$$

The following procedure can be carried out to calculate the *joint probability* that both stations will be full [the numerator of equation (111)]. First, the probability that of all the N pallets circulating in the FMS at least n pallets will be present at station m must be determined. With reference to the state space of the FMS, this can be described with equation (112)[205].

$$P\{n_m{\geq}n,N\} = \sum_{\substack{\underline{n}\in S(N,M) \\ n_m{\geq}n}} P\{n_1,\ldots,n_m{\geq}n,\ldots,n_M\}$$

$$= \frac{1}{g(N,M)}\cdot\sum_{\substack{\underline{n}\in S(N,M) \\ n_m{\geq}n}}\prod_{i=1}^{M}f_i(n_i) \qquad\qquad \begin{matrix} m=1,2,\ldots,M \\ n=0,1,\ldots,N \end{matrix} \tag{112}$$

To determine this probability, look first at the breakdown of all the different states of the FMS with $n_m{\geq}n$ shown in figure (90). Here the subset of states is considered in which exactly n pallets are present at station m ($n_m{=}n$) and the complementary set of those states with the rest of the N-n pallets distributed among the other stations (including the $n_m{-}n$ pallets at station m).

205   see also section 3.1.1.1.2., equation (30)

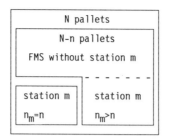

Figure 90: Partition of the state space

Equation (112) is then rewritten so that the factors dependent on station m $f_m(n_m)$ are taken out of the product and written down separately:

$$P\{n_m \geq n, N\} = \frac{1}{g(N,M)} \cdot \sum_{\substack{n \in S(N,M) \\ n_m \geq n}} \left[\prod_{\substack{i=1 \\ i \neq m}}^{M} f_i(n_i) \right] \cdot f_m(n_m) \qquad \begin{array}{l} m=1,2,\ldots,M \\ n=0,1,\ldots,N \end{array} \qquad (113)$$

Now look at the state space depicted in figure (90) with respect to the number of pallets at station m ($n_m = n$ and $n_m > n$). To develop this further it is useful to break down the factor $f_m(n_m)$ into two components and to introduce the auxiliary variable $\bar{n}_m = n_m - n$ [see equation (114)].

$$f_m(n_m) = f_m(n) \cdot h_m(\bar{n}_m, n) \qquad m=1,2,\ldots,M; \; n_m \geq n \qquad (114)$$

At a station with $S_m = 2$ machines in a state with $n_m = 5$ pallets, the following breakdown for $n=2$ of the product $f_m(n_m)$ results. This is due to the definition given in equation (19):

$$f_m(n_m) = \underbrace{\frac{w_m}{1} \cdot \frac{w_m}{2}}_{f_m(n_m=n)} \cdot \underbrace{\frac{w_m}{2} \cdot \frac{w_m}{2} \cdot \frac{w_m}{\underset{\min(S_m, \bar{n}_m + n)}{2}}}_{h_m(\bar{n}_m, n)}$$

$$= \frac{w_m^2}{1 \cdot 2} \cdot \frac{w_m^3}{2 \cdot 2 \cdot 2} \qquad m=1,2,\ldots,M; \; n_m \geq n \qquad (115)$$

with

$$\bar{n}_m = n_m - n \qquad m=1,2,\ldots,M; \; n_m \geq n \qquad (116)$$

The auxiliary function $h_m(\bar{n}_m, n)$ is equivalent to the function $f_m(n_m)$[206]. However, the multiplication is begun with the $(n+1)^{th}$ quotient $w(.)/A(.)$. The multiplica-

---

206 see equation (19)

tion for every number of pallets up to and including n is already included in the factor $f_m(n)$. In general, therefore, the auxiliary function $h_m(\tilde{n}_m,n)$ can be written as follows:

$$
h_m(\tilde{n}_m,n) = \begin{cases} \dfrac{w_m^{\tilde{n}_m}}{\prod\limits_{l=n+1}^{\tilde{n}_m+n} a_m(l)} & \tilde{n}_m \geq 1 \\[2em] 1, & \tilde{n}_m = 0 \end{cases} \qquad m=1,2,\ldots,M; \; n \geq 0 \qquad (117)
$$

with

$$
a_m(l) = \begin{cases} 1, & l \leq S_m \\ S_m, & l > S_m \end{cases} \qquad m=1,2,\ldots,M \qquad (118)
$$

After breaking down the quantity $f_m(n_m)$ equation (119) shows how those states can be investigated in which exactly n pallets are present at station m ($n_m=n$). This is done by pulling out the factor $f_m(n)$ and placing it before the sum thus reducing the remaining state space to $S(N-n,M)$. The n pallets then present at station m can no longer circulate in the queueing network.

$$
P\{n_m \geq n, N\} = \frac{f_m(n)}{g(N,M)} \cdot \sum_{\underline{n} \in S(N-n,M)} \left[\prod_{\substack{i=1 \\ i \neq m}}^{M} f_i(n_i) \right] \cdot h_m(\tilde{n}_m,n) \qquad \begin{array}{l} m=1,2,\ldots,M \\ n=0,1,\ldots,N \end{array} \qquad (119)
$$

A single vector of the reduced state space $S(N-n,M)$ can take the form $(n_1,\ldots,\tilde{n}_m,\ldots,n_M)$, where $\tilde{n}_m$ can take on values between 0 and N-n. Similarly, equation (120) can be used to find the probabilities that the previously determined minimum number of pallets n and k will be present at the stations m and j respectively.

$$
\begin{aligned}
P\{n_m \geq n, n_j \geq k, N\} &= \sum_{\substack{\underline{n} \in S(N,M) \\ n_m \geq n \\ n_j \geq k}} P\{n_1,\ldots,n_m \geq n,\ldots,n_j \geq k,\ldots,n_M\} \\[1em]
&= \sum_{\substack{\underline{n} \in S(N,M) \\ n_m \geq n \\ n_j \geq k}} \frac{1}{G(N,M)} \cdot \prod_{i=1}^{M} f_i(n_i) \\[1em]
&= \frac{f_m(n) \cdot f_j(k)}{g(N,M)} \cdot \sum_{\underline{n} \in S(N-n-k,M)} \prod_{\substack{i=1 \\ i \neq m \\ i \neq j}}^{M} \left[f_i(n_i) \right] \cdot h_m(\tilde{n}_m,n) \cdot h_j(\tilde{n}_j,k)
\end{aligned}
$$
$$
\begin{array}{l} m,j=1,2,\ldots,M; \; m \neq j \\ n=0,1,\ldots,N-k \\ k=0,1,\ldots,N-n \end{array} \qquad (120)
$$

For the single server case (*one machine per station*) equations (119) and (120) can be significantly simplified. Then the following is true:

$$h_m(\tilde{n}_m, n) = w_m^{\tilde{n}_m}$$

$$= f_m(\tilde{n}_m) \qquad\qquad m=1,2,\ldots,M;\ \tilde{n}_m \geq 0 \qquad (121)$$

Since the functions $h_m(\tilde{n}_m, n)$ and $f_m(\tilde{n}_m)$ are identical in this case, the states in which more than n pallets are present at station m can remain directly in the equation via the factor $f_m(n_m)$. The following then results[207]:

$$P\{n_m \geq n, N\} = \frac{f_m(n)}{g(N,M)} \cdot \underbrace{\sum_{\underline{n} \in S(N-n,M)} \prod_{i=1}^{M} f_i(n_i)}_{= g(N-n,M)}$$

$$= \frac{f_m(n) \cdot g(N-n,M)}{g(N,M)}$$

$$= w_m^n \cdot \frac{g(N-n,M)}{g(N,M)} \qquad\qquad \begin{array}{l} m=1,2,\ldots,M \\ n=0,1,\ldots,N \end{array} \qquad (122)$$

$$P\{n_m \geq n, n_j \geq k, N\} = \frac{f_m(n) \cdot f_j(k)}{g(N,M)} \cdot \underbrace{\sum_{\underline{n} \in S(N-n-k,M)} \prod_{i=1}^{M} f_i(n_i)}_{= g(N-n-k,M)}$$

$$= \frac{f_m(n) \cdot f_j(k) \cdot g(N-n-k,M)}{g(N,M)}$$

$$= w_m^n \cdot w_j^k \cdot \frac{g(N-n-k,M)}{g(N,M)} \qquad\qquad \begin{array}{l} m,j=1,2,\ldots,M;\ m \neq j \\ n=0,1,\ldots,N-k \\ k=0,1,\ldots,N-n \end{array} \qquad (123)$$

The conditional probabilities given in equation (111) can also be simplified for the case of a *single server station*:

$$P\{n_m \geq n \mid n_j \geq k, N\} = f_m(n) \cdot \frac{g(N-n-k,M)}{g(N-k,M)} \qquad\qquad \begin{array}{l} m,j=1,2,\ldots,M;\ m \neq j \\ n=0,1,\ldots,N-k \\ k=0,1,\ldots,N-n \end{array} \qquad (124)$$

For the example considered here (with single server stations), the following joint probabilities, $P\{n_m \geq N_{max(m)} = 1, n_j \geq N_{max(j)} = 1\}$, result according to equation (123).

---

207   **Buzen** (1973), p. 528 and p. 530

m \ j	1 (L/UL)	2 (M2)	3 (M1)
1 (L/UL)	–	.1354	.3540
2 (M2)	.1354	–	.2326
3 (M1)	.3540	.2326	–

Table 41: Joint probabilities

With the help of these joint probabilities, the *conditional probabilities* can be calculated using equation (124). They are summarized in table (42).

m \ j	1 (L/UL)	2 (M2)	3 (M1)
1 (L/UL)	–	.4200	.4200
2 (M2)	.2760	–	.2760
3 (M1)	.7217	.7217	–

Table 42: Conditional probabilities

Observe that the conditional probabilities in the previous example are independent of the downstream station, since the stations have identical buffer capacities.

The *expected value of the residual service time* $E\{RB_j\}$ of the workpiece currently being processed at station j, i.e. the workpiece that will be released next from station j, is equal to the average processing time of the station j (assuming exponentially distributed processing times)[208].

The expected blocking times are now added to the "normal" processing times. The new processing times b_m^s, as modified by the blocking times, can be described as shown in equation (125).

$$\underset{\text{mean blocking time between stations m and j}}{\big\lceil}$$

$$b_m^s = b_m + \sum_{\substack{j=1 \\ j \neq m}}^{M-1} E\{BZ_{mj}\} \qquad\qquad m=1,2,\dots,M-1 \qquad (125)$$

$\mathrel{\llcorner}$ mean increase of processing time of a workpiece at station m due to blocking at station m

$\mathrel{\llcorner}$ mean "normal" processing time of a workpiece at station m

$\mathrel{\llcorner}$ modified processing time of a workpiece at station m including blocking time

When equation (110) and equation (125) are solved simultaneously, the resulting equation system (126) can be used to solve for the modified processing times $\underline{B}^s$:

---

208 see section 3.1.1.2.2.

$$\underline{B} = \underline{D} \cdot \underline{B}^S \tag{126}$$

where $\underline{D}$ is a matrix with the following elements:

$$d_{mj} = -P\{n_m \geq N_{max(m)} | n_j \geq N_{max(j)}\} \cdot r_{mj} \cdot KF_m \qquad\qquad m \neq j \tag{127}$$

and

$$d_{mm} = 1 \tag{128}$$

3.1.2.4.2.2. Implementation in the CQN model

In the last section it was described how to compute the average processing times and how to correct them for the blocking times after a preliminary evaluation of a classical CQN approximation of the FMS under consideration. Using the modified average processing times of the workpieces, the classical CQN model can then be reevaluated. The stationary probability distributions of the pallets among the stations, taking blocking into consideration, can be found with the help of equation (129)[209].

$$P\{\underline{n}\} = \frac{1}{g(N,M)} \cdot \prod_{m=1}^{M} f_m(n_m) \tag{129}$$

with

$$f_m(n_m) = \frac{w_m(n_m)^{n_m}}{A_m(n_m)} \tag{130}$$

$$A_m(n_m) = \begin{cases} n_m! & n_m \leq S_m \\ S_m! \cdot S_m^{(n_m - S_m)} & n_m > S_m \end{cases} \tag{131}$$

$$w_m(n_m) = \begin{cases} P_m \cdot b_m & n_m < N_{max(m)} \\ P_m \cdot b_m^S & n_m \geq N_{max(m)} \end{cases} \tag{132}$$

In contrast to the usual calculation of the probability distribution in the classical CQN model, the workload of a station is differentiated here *depending on the number of pallets at the station*. The key parameters of the FMS (utilization, queue lengths, flow times) can be determined with-the help of these stationary probability distributions and the associated normalization constant g(N,M).

---

[209]   see also section 3.1.1.1.2.

3.1.2.4.3. Numerical results for the case of blocking

The quality of the above described method for the integration of blocking into the CQN model will be demonstrated using numerical examples. Several FMS configurations with different loads on the machines will be studied. For each system alternative the results of a detailed simulation (SIM) will be compared with the results obtained by the proposed procedure (CQNBLK) as well as by the classical CQN model (CQN). For space reasons, the *production quantity of only the first station 1* (M1) over a simulated time of 10,000 minutes for each FMS variation will be shown. The following specific FMS variations will be studied:

- FMS 4:   FMS with 4 machines
- FMS 5:   FMS with 5 machines
- FMS 12:   FMS with 12 machines
- FMS FL: FMS with 4 machines (flow shop structure)

■ **FMS 4:** FMS with 4 machines

The structure of the material flow in this FMS is depicted in figure (91). Table (43) shows the matrix of the transition probabilities, the stationary arrival probabilities derived from them, and the average processing times at the stations. The transition probabilities have been standardized so that their sum is equal to one. The processing times are assumed to be exponentially distributed, thus the assumptions of the classical CQN model are largely satisfied. Station M1 has a central function (e.g. a station where the position of a workpiece on a pallet is changed). From here the workpieces are directed through the transportation system (not shown in this illustration) to the other machining stations, in accordance with the predetermined transition probabilities. In order to prevent a total blockage in those FMS variations having no central buffer, the station M1 is provided with sufficient buffer capacity.

r_{jm} to from	M1	M2	M3	M4
M1	–	0.188	0.124	0.063
M2	0.062	–	0.126	–
M3	0.125	–	–	0.125
M4	0.188	–	–	–
p_m	0.375	0.188	0.250	0.188
b_m^{210}	1.00	3.00	2.25	2.50

Table 43: Description of the FMS 4

---

210 minutes

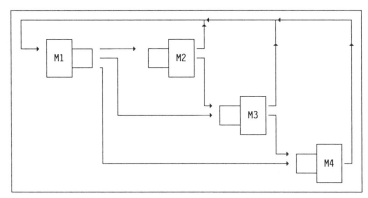

Figure 91: Material flow in the FMS 4

In order to investigate the effects of certain critical factors that have an influence on the performance of a given FMS variation, local and central buffers of various sizes will be considered.

The first two variations of FMS 4 have *no central buffer*. The figures (92) and (93) compare the *production rates of station M1* calculated with the simulation with the analytically determined values for different buffer sizes at stations M2 and M3. Since there are no local buffers known in the classical CQN model, the use of this model results in the same values in both FMS variations.

Since no central buffer is planned for this case, blocking can occur in the first variation ($N_{max(2)} = 1$; $N_{max(3)} = 1$) when there are at least two pallets in the system. According to equation (108) the minimum number of pallets at which blocking could occur is derived from the sum of the maximum receptive capacities of the stations M2 and M3 ($N_{max(2)} = 1$, $N_{max(3)} = 1$). Since at most one pallet can be present at each of these stations, blocking could occur at station M2 when a finished workpiece at this station is denied access to station M3 because that station is occupied. In the second variation blocking can only occur when there are at least 4 pallets in the FMS. This is also illustrated in figures (92) and (93). Obviously the CQNBLK procedure generates the same results for $N < 2$ (or $N < 4$) as the CQN model. When the number of pallets increases, and thereby also the probability that blocking might occur, significant differences between the two procedures can arise. It is particularly interesting to note that the classical CQN model can sometimes overestimate the performance of the FMS considered by more than 40%.

The results given in figure (93), for which the local buffers of the stations M2 and M3 have been expanded ($N_{max(2)} = 2$; $N_{max(3)} = 2$), make clear the influence of the size of the local buffers on the quality of the classical CQN approximation - especially for increasing numbers of pallets in the FMS.

$N_{max}(CB)=0$, $N_{max}(1)=20$, $N_{max}(2)=1$, $N_{max}(3)=1$, $N_{max}(4)=2$					
N	SIM	CQNBLK	Diff[211]	CQN	Diff[212]
1	1881	1858	1.22	1858	1.22
2	2970	2969	0.03	2986	-0.54
3	3690	3658	0.87	3733	-1.17
4	4062	4076	-0.34	4260	-4.87
5	4322	4317	0.12	4648	-7.54
6	4369	4444	-1.72	4943	-13.14
7	4477	4499	-0.49	5174	-15.57
8	4384	4513	-2.94	5359	-22.24
9	4310	4502	-4.45	5509	-27.82
10	4274	4501	-5.31	5633	-31.80
11	4325	4541	-4.99	5737	-32.65
12	4412	4584	-3.90	5824	-32.00
13	4183	4614	-10.30	5899	-41.02
14	4319	4636	-7.34	5963	-38.06
15	4318	4664	-8.01	6019	-39.39
16	4368	4683	-7.21	6067	-38.90
17	4381	4692	-7.10	6110	-39.47
18	4308	4713	-9.40	6147	-42.69
19	4317	4716	-9.24	6181	-43.18
20	4322	4727	-9.37	6210	-43.68

Figure 92: Results for FMS 4, variation 1

211 Diff = 100*(SIM-CQNBLK)/SIM
212 Diff = 100*(SIM-CQN)/SIM

$N_{max}(CB)=0$, $N_{max}(1)=20$, $N_{max}(2)=2$, $N_{max}(3)=2$, $N_{max}(4)=2$					
N	SIM	CQNBLK	Diff	CQN	Diff
1	1881	1858	1.22	1858	1.22
2	2979	2986	-0.23	2986	-0.23
3	3711	3733	-0.59	3733	-0.59
4	4239	4248	-0.21	4260	-0.50
5	4633	4606	0.58	4648	-0.32
6	5024	4844	3.58	4943	1.61
7	5090	4993	1.91	5174	-1.65
8	5271	5079	3.64	5359	-1.67
9	5176	5122	1.04	5509	-6.43
10	5195	5140	1.06	5633	-8.43
11	5220	5140	1.53	5737	-9.90
12	5067	5138	-1.40	5824	-14.94
13	5129	5118	0.21	5899	-15.01
14	5333	5111	4.16	5963	-11.81
15	5271	5092	3.40	6019	-14.19
16	5178	5075	1.99	6067	-17.17
17	5182	5066	2.24	6110	-17.91
18	5163	5039	2.40	6147	-19.06
19	5266	5040	4.29	6181	-17.38
20	5302	5034	5.05	6210	-17.13

Figure 93: Results for FMS 4, variation 2

The following results show the *influence of the size of the central buffer* on the production rate of machine M1. Since altogether 10 central buffer spaces are available, blocking can occur beginning at 12 (14) pallets. When these critical numbers of pallets are exceeded, the *production quantity begins to sink* again, as the proportion of time when the machines cannot be productively used due to blocking increases.

$N_{max}(CB)$=10, $N_{max}(1)$=20, $N_{max}(2)$=1, $N_{max}(3)$=1, $N_{max}(4)$=2					
N	SIM	CQNBLK	Diff	CQN	Diff
1	1881	1858	1.22	1857	1.28
2	2970	2986	-0.54	2986	-0.54
3	3743	3733	0.27	3733	0.27
4	4258	4260	-0.05	4260	-0.05
5	4673	4648	0.53	4648	0.53
6	5047	4944	2.04	4943	2.06
7	5086	5175	-1.75	5174	-1.73
8	5268	5360	-1.75	5359	-1.73
9	5304	5510	-3.88	5509	-3.87
10	5544	5634	-1.62	5633	-1.61
11	5655	5737	-1.45	5737	-1.45
12	5403	5341	1.15	5824	-7.79
13	5310	5202	2.03	5899	-11.09
14	4963	5126	-3.28	5963	-20.15
15	4389	5064	-15.38	6019	-37.14
16	4320	5006	-15.88	6067	-40.44
17	4344	4955	-14.07	6110	-40.65
18	4342	4940	-13.77	6147	-41.57
19	4216	4921	-16.72	6181	-46.61
20	4369	4883	-11.76	6210	-42.14

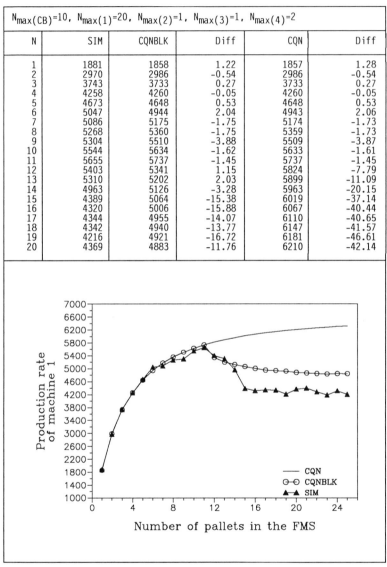

Figure 94: Results for FMS 4, variation 3

$N_{max}(CB)=10$, $N_{max}(1)=20$, $N_{max}(2)=2$, $N_{max}(3)=2$, $N_{max}(4)=2$					
N	SIM	CQNBLK	Diff	CQN	Diff
1	1874	1858	0.85	1857	0.91
2	3024	2986	1.26	2986	1.26
3	3735	3733	0.05	3733	0.05
4	4216	4260	-1.04	4260	-1.04
5	4687	4648	0.83	4648	0.83
6	5103	4944	3.12	4943	3.14
7	5127	5175	-0.94	5174	-0.92
8	5299	5360	-1.15	5359	-1.13
9	5473	5510	-0.68	5509	-0.66
10	5747	5634	1.97	5633	1.98
11	5523	5737	-3.87	5737	-3.87
12	5876	5825	0.87	5824	0.88
13	5994	5899	1.58	5899	1.58
14	5909	5741	2.84	5963	-0.91
15	5955	5661	4.94	6019	-1.07
16	5852	5585	4.56	6067	-3.67
17	5622	5521	1.80	6110	-8.68
18	5434	5470	-0.66	6147	-13.12
19	5327	5434	-2.01	6181	-16.03
20	5128	5397	-5.25	6210	-21.10

Figure 95: Results for FMS 4, variation 4

- **FMS 5: FMS with 5 machines**

The material flow in this FMS is depicted in figure (96) and table (44). In this system blocking can only occur at stations M3 and M5. There is no central buffer. In the variations studied here the size of the local buffer at station M3 is varied.

r_{jm}	to from	M1	M2	M3	M4	M5
	M1	–	0.172	0.073	–	–
	M2	0.139	–	0.139	–	–
	M3	–	–	–	0.106	0.106
	M4	0.0795	0.0795	–	–	–
	M5	0.0265	0.0265	–	0.053	–
p_m		0.245	0.278	0.212	0.159	0.106
b_m		1.00	1.00	2.00	3.00	5.00

Table 44: Description of the FMS 5

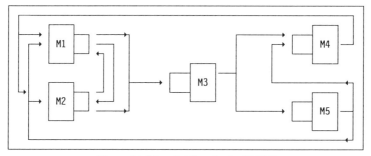

Figure 96: Material flow in the FMS 5

Figures (97) and (98) compare the results of the detailed simulation and the analytically determined results in graphic and tabular form. As can be seen here as well, approximating the performance of an FMS with the classical CQN model can generate significant errors, whereas the proposed CQNBLK procedure produces satisfactory estimates of the production rate of the machine M1.

$N_{max(CB)}=0$, $N_{max(1)}=25$, $N_{max(2)}=25$, $N_{max(3)}=1$, $N_{max(4)}=2$, $N_{max(5)}=2$					
N	SIM	CQNBLK	Diff	CQN	Diff
1	1172	1223	-4.35	1223	-4.35
2	2051	2027	1.17	2027	1.17
3	2660	2572	3.31	2586	2.78
4	2943	2914	0.99	2991	-1.63
5	3077	3095	-0.58	3293	-7.02
6	3320	3170	4.52	3525	-6.17
7	3215	3187	0.87	3705	-15.24
8	3312	3186	3.80	3849	-16.21
9	3210	3153	1.78	3965	-23.52
10	3292	3150	4.31	4060	-23.33
11	3314	3122	5.79	4138	-24.86
12	3090	3117	-0.87	4203	-36.02
13	3141	3092	1.56	4258	-35.56
14	3102	3095	0.23	4305	-38.78
15	3101	3072	0.94	4344	-40.08
16	3270	3082	5.75	4378	-33.88
17	3128	3060	2.17	4407	-40.89
18	3260	3074	5.71	4432	-35.95
19	3132	3053	2.52	4454	-42.21
20	3161	3068	2.94	4474	-41.54
21	3289	3069	6.69	4490	-36.52
22	3175	3047	4.03	4505	-41.89
23	3231	3045	5.76	4518	-39.83
24	3168	3065	3.25	4529	-42.96
25	3227	3065	5.02	4540	-40.69

Figure 97: Results for FMS 5, variation 1

$N_{max}(CB)=0$, $N_{max}(1)=25$, $N_{max}(2)=25$, $N_{max}(3)=2$, $N_{max}(4)=2$, $N_{max}(5)=2$					
N	SIM	CQNBLK	Diff	CQN	Diff
1	1172	1223	-4.35	1223	-4.35
2	2089	2027	2.97	2027	2.97
3	2723	2586	5.03	2586	5.03
4	3027	2973	1.78	2991	1.19
5	3238	3227	0.34	3293	-1.70
6	3566	3376	5.33	3525	1.15
7	3585	3452	3.71	3705	-3.35
8	3529	3485	1.25	3849	-9.07
9	3655	3488	4.57	3965	-8.48
10	3412	3487	-2.20	4060	-18.99
11	3568	3472	2.69	4138	-15.98
12	3519	3462	1.62	4203	-19.44
13	3437	3451	-0.41	4258	-23.89
14	3674	3437	6.45	4305	-17.17
15	3624	3429	5.38	4344	-19.87
16	3625	3412	5.88	4378	-20.77
17	3633	3402	6.36	4407	-21.30
18	3565	3391	4.88	4432	-24.32
19	3590	3404	5.18	4454	-24.07
20	3642	3403	6.56	4474	-22.84
21	3673	3379	8.00	4490	-22.24
22	3648	3391	7.04	4505	-23.49
23	3680	3388	7.93	4518	-22.77
24	3436	3386	1.46	4529	-31.81
25	3495	3384	3.18	4540	-29.90

Figure 98: Results for FMS 5, variation 2

■ **FMS 12:** FMS with 12 machines

The material flow of FMS 12 is illustrated in figure (99) and table (45). In this system the stations M1 and M2 have central functions for the material flow.

r_{jm} ⟍ to / from	M1	M2	M3	M4	M5	M6	M7	M8	M9	M10	M11	M12
M1	-	0.02	0.02	0.02	0.02	0.02	0.02	0.02	0.02	0.02	0.02	-
M2	-	-	-	-	-	-	-	-	-	-	-	0.04
M3	-	-	-	-	-	-	-	-	-	-	-	0.04
M4	-	-	-	-	-	-	-	-	-	-	-	0.04
M5	-	-	-	-	-	-	-	-	-	-	-	0.04
M6	-	-	-	-	-	-	-	-	-	-	-	0.04
M7	-	-	-	-	-	-	-	-	-	-	-	0.04
M8	-	-	-	-	-	-	-	-	-	-	-	0.04
M9	-	-	-	-	-	-	-	-	-	-	-	0.04
M10	-	-	-	-	-	-	-	-	-	-	-	0.04
M11	-	-	-	-	-	-	-	-	-	-	-	0.04
M12	0.2	0.02	0.02	0.02	0.02	0.02	0.02	0.02	0.02	0.02	0.02	0.04
p_m	0.2	0.04	0.04	0.04	0.04	0.04	0.04	0.04	0.04	0.04	0.04	0.40
b_m	2.00	10.0	10.0	10.0	10.0	10.0	10.0	10.0	10.0	10.0	10.0	10.0

Table 45: Description of the FMS 12

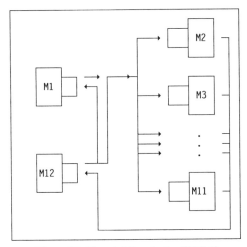

Figure 99: Material flow in the FMS 12

As can be seen in figure (100), the maximum error in the estimation of the classical CQN model is ca. 80%. When the results of variation 1 are compared with those of variation 2, the influence of increasing local buffer space at the stations on the performance of the FMS becomes clear.

$N_{max}(CB)=0$, $N_{max}(m)=1$ $(m=1,\ldots,11)$, $N_{max}(12)=40$					
N	SIM	CQNBLK	Diff	CQN	Diff
2	766	768	-0.26	768	-0.26
4	1334	1300	2.55	1332	0.15
6	1688	1680	0.47	1763	-4.44
8	2038	1944	4.61	2104	-3.24
10	2062	2120	-2.81	2379	-15.37
12	2221	2230	-0.41	2607	-17.38
14	2263	2293	-1.33	2799	-23.69
16	2251	2328	-3.42	2962	-31.59
18	2063	2346	-13.72	3102	-50.36
20	2198	2357	-7.23	3225	-46.72
22	2276	2361	-3.73	3332	-46.40
24	2182	2362	-8.25	3428	-57.10
26	2252	2363	-4.93	3513	-55.99
28	2119	2364	-11.56	3589	-69.37
30	2224	2365	-6.34	3658	-64.48
32	2242	2362	-5.35	3720	-65.92
34	2190	2362	-7.85	3777	-72.47
36	2217	2362	-6.54	3829	-72.71
38	2222	2362	-6.30	3877	-74.48
40	2185	2362	-8.10	3921	-79.45

Figure 100: Results for FMS 12, variation 1

$N_{max(CB)}=0$, $N_{max(m)}=3$ $(m=1,\ldots,11)$, $N_{max(12)}=40$

N	SIM	CQNBLK	Diff	CQN	Diff
2	783	768	1.92	768	1.92
4	1354	1332	1.62	1332	1.62
6	1784	1763	1.18	1763	1.18
8	2069	2104	-1.64	2104	-1.69
10	2333	2379	-1.97	2379	-1.97
12	2698	2606	3.41	2606	3.37
14	2809	2795	0.50	2799	0.36
16	2924	2953	-0.99	2962	-1.30
18	2961	3086	-4.22	3102	-4.76
20	3078	3195	-3.80	3225	-4.78
22	3228	3282	-1.67	3332	-3.22
24	3154	3347	-6.12	3428	-8.69
26	3145	3391	-7.82	3513	-11.70
28	3222	3414	-5.96	3589	-11.39
30	3327	3416	-2.68	3658	-9.95
32	3035	3415	-12.52	3720	-22.57
34	3215	3400	-5.75	3777	-17.48
36	3272	3385	-3.45	3829	-17.02
38	3088	3370	-9.13	3877	-25.55
40	3100	3353	-8.16	3921	-26.48

Figure 101: Results for FMS 12, variation 2

- **FMS FL: FMS with 4 machines (flow shop structure)**

The FMS FL allows the performance capability of the proposed procedure to be tested in FMS variations that exhibit a regularity rather untypical of the material flow in the FMS concept. This FMS has a flow shop structure in which all the workpieces move through the machines in the order M1-M2-M3-M4 [see figure (102)].

r_{jm} to from	M1	M2	M3	M4
M1	–	0.25	–	–
M2	–	–	0.25	–
M3	–	–	–	0.25
M4	0.25	–	–	–
p_m	0.25	0.25	0.25	0.25
b_m	1.00	3.00	2.25	2.50

Table 46: Description of the FMS FL

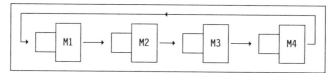

Figure 102: Material flow in the FMS FL

The results for this FMS [see figure (103)] indicate that here too a good approximation of the production quantity of machine 1 can be made.

When the results for all the different FMSs presented here are examined in detail, one must come to a single conclusion: the proposed method for including blocking in an analytical model for the estimation of the performance of an FMS makes significantly more precise estimates of the system's performance indicators than the classical CQN approach, where the blocking phenomenon does not emerge and thus cannot be accounted for.

$N_{max(CB)}=10$, $N_{max(1)}=3$, $N_{max(4)}=3$, $N_{max(4)}=3$, $N_{max(4)}=3$					
N	SIM	CQNBLK	Diff	CQN	Diff
1	1113	1117	-0.36	1117	-0.36
2	1773	1764	0.51	1764	0.51
3	2154	2174	-0.93	2174	-0.93
4	2501	2449	2.08	2449	2.08
5	2699	2645	2.00	2645	2.00
6	2803	2787	0.57	2787	0.57
7	2903	2895	0.28	2895	0.28
8	2988	2978	0.33	2978	0.33
9	3018	3043	-0.83	3043	-0.83
10	3102	3095	0.23	3095	0.23
11	3238	3137	3.12	3137	3.12
12	3180	3171	0.28	3171	0.28
13	3151	3198	-1.49	3198	-1.49
14	3166	3221	-1.74	3221	-1.74
15	3213	3240	-0.84	3240	-0.84
16	3204	3215	-0.34	3255	-1.59
17	3238	3200	1.17	3268	-0.93
18	3180	3180	0.00	3279	-3.11
19	3149	3158	-0.29	3288	-4.41
20	3088	3137	-1.59	3295	-6.70
21	3023	3111	-2.91	3301	-9.20

Figure 103: Results for FMS FL, variation 1

3.1.2.5. A new method for the approximation of starving

The negative effects of blocking at a station on the performance of an FMS can be avoided through the use of a sufficiently large central buffer. Additional pallet storage capacity is relatively inexpensive in comparison to the machines themselves. Starving, the other phenomenon that can lead to a deterioration in the performance of an FMS, is not as easily prevented[213].

Starving occurs when a free machine waits for a workpiece which had previously attempted to gain access to that machine but was rejected due to insufficient local buffer space. The workpiece is located either at the upstream machine at which it has just been processed, in the central buffer, or it is in transit on its way to the machine under consideration. As the machine is already waiting, the workpiece could be processed at the machine, but it is physically not yet in a position that would make that possible. The machine suffers from a raw material supply shortage.

The period of time during which starving can occur includes the transportation times (for loaded trips between the processing stations). These time elements can also arise with unlimited local buffers and have already been described in the context of the classical CQN model. The process of starving will be more closely investigated in this section.

3.1.2.5.1. General description of the starving phenomenon

For the analysis of starving it will be assumed that blocking does not occur[214]. This holds true when the central buffer is so large that every pallet which cannot be stored in a station's local buffer can find space in the central buffer.

Starving begins at the moment when one workpiece has completed processing at a machine, and at the same time a new workpiece which is required to be processed at that machine is still located somewhere else in the FMS (workpiece exchange). There are thus *two different forms of idle times at a machine*: the starving delay of a machine with *unlimited local buffers* and the delay at a machine with *limited local buffers* (starving in the narrow sense).

- **Starving delay of a machine with unlimited buffers**

    Starving delays in FMS with unlimited local buffers occur when a machine has finished processing a workpiece and is ready to begin the next one, but this next workpiece has not yet been transported to the machine. From the point of view of the workpiece, this means that the processing time at the machine is delayed by the *transportation time*, and possibly also by the time it has to *wait* for transportation (because the transportation vehicle is currently transporting another workpiece, for example). The starving delay of a machine through the end of a transportation process is already included in the

---

213 For this section see also **Tempelmeier/Kuhn/Tetzlaff** (1991)
214 In section 3.1.2.6. blocking and starving will be considered together.

classical *CQN model*, in that the material flow system is modelled as a central station whose processing time is equal to the transportation time during a loaded trip (supply trip)[215]. The machine is considered to be *idle* during this time as long as it is not able to begin work on another workpiece.

- **Starving with limited local buffers**

Starving can occur in an FMS with limited local buffers when the next work-piece to be processed on a machine has *not yet arrived at the machine*. Instead it is either in a central buffer, a local output buffer of another station or in transit to this particular machine. This situation must have arisen because the workpiece was denied access to its downstream station when its proces-sing was finished at its last (upstream) station.

Figure (104) depicts a machine m without a local buffer and with a logical *queue* whose members are *physically* present at other points in the FMS: ei-ther the central buffer or the local (output-) buffer of another machine.

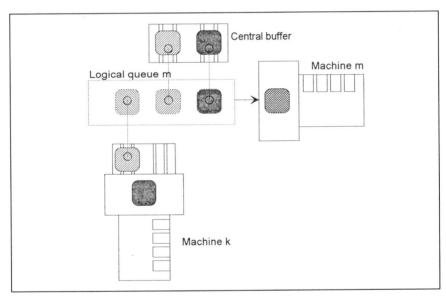

Figure 104: Queue in front of a starved machine

The workpiece positioned at the top of the queue at machine m was, at some point in the past, picked up by a transportation vehicle, and it attempted to gain access to machine m. Access was denied, however, and the workpiece was temporarily stored in the central buffer to wait for its destination ma-chine to become free. The transportation process as described by the classi-

---

215 That is why in the literature this form is *not* called *blocking*.

cal CQN model has thus already been completed[216]. If this workpiece is to be transported to the machine m, however, it must first be brought to the machine. During this time the machine is *starved*.

Two other factors in an FMS that directly influence the workload of the transportation system, and thus indirectly the degree of starving, have to be included. These are,

- **Idle trips** of the transportation vehicles

and

- **Trips to the central buffer** (disposal trips).

Neither of these components of the load on the transportation system is accounted for in the classical CQN model. The effects of starving and of the extra trips to the central buffer caused by the limited local buffers at the machines will be discussed using a sample FMS whose descriptive data are summarized in table (47). The FMS considered here comprises four machines, each of which has two local buffers, a transportation vehicle and a central buffer.

r_{jm}	to from	M1	M2	M3	M4
	M1	–	0.119	0.119	0.119
	M2	0.119	–	0.095	–
	M3	0.119	–	–	0.095
	M4	0.119	0.095	–	–
p_m		0.357	0.214	0.214	0.214
b_m		2.00	3.83	4.17	2.67
Transportation time		0.1			
Central buffer travel time		2.0			

Table 47: Characteristics of an FMS exhibiting starving

Figure (105) shows the simulated production rate of machine M1 (based on 10,000 minutes simulation time) as a function of the number of pallets in the FMS. As can be seen, the *production rate of the machine being studied here increases as the number of pallets increases up to a certain point, but then it decreases*[217]. When there are many pallets circulating in the FMS, workpieces must be temporarily stored in the central buffer more frequently, since the local

---

216   If it had been possible for the workpiece to wait in the local output buffer of the upstream machine, then no
        transportation would have been performed.
217   In the classical CQN model the production rate of the FMS increases continuously with the number of
        pallets and approximates an upper bound. See section 3.1.1.1.3.

buffers at the workpieces' downstream stations are often full. The load on the transportation system is increased by these "unproductive" disposal trips to the central buffer. This then causes the transportation system to be less able to carry out its productive function and to supply the machines with workpieces for processing. The machines have to wait longer for the arrival of a new workpiece due to the high degree of starving in comparison with their total load. This causes a reduction in the production quantity of the FMS.

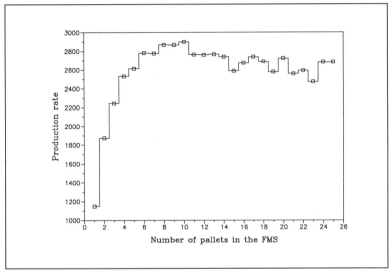

Figure 105: Production rate of machine M1 as a function of the number of pallets in an FMS exhibiting starving and with trips to the central buffer

3.1.2.5.1.1. Waiting for the transportation system with unlimited local buffers

A station with unlimited local buffers may also have to wait for the completion of a transportation process. This would occur when the processing at another station of a workpiece that is to be processed next at the machine is completed and a transportation order is released. The length of the waiting time depends on whether the station is *already idle* when the processing of the incoming workpiece is completed at the previous station (case 1), or if the station has a *local backlog* on which it can work in the mean time (case 2).

• *Case 1:* The next station is *idle* at the beginning of the transportation process.

If a workpiece's downstream machine is already idle at the time when the transportation order is released, then its waiting time is equal to the period

of time from the moment the transportation vehicle is requested by the
processed workpiece at the previous station up to the moment when the
workpiece arrives at the machine. Figure (106) illustrates this for a workpiece which has been processed at machine 1 and is supposed to be processed next at machine 2.

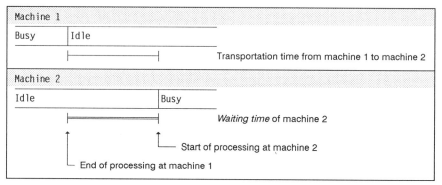

Figure 106: Waiting time of machine 2 (case 1)

- *Case 2:* The next station has a *local backlog* at the moment the transportation order is released

A different situation arises if, when the workpiece completes processing at
the previous station, the next machine is either *busy* with another workpiece,
or if it has a backlog of unprocessed workpieces in its local buffer. In this
case, the waiting time is equal to the residual transportation time between
the moment the current backlog at the machine is used up and the moment
when the new workpiece arrives. This is depicted in figure (107).

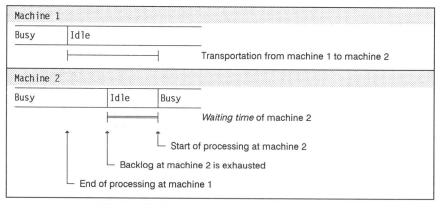

Figure 107: Waiting time of machine 2 (case 2)

Both of these cases are described in the classical CQN model by modelling the transportation system as a central server station. Any delay at a machine before a workpiece arrives is registered as *idle time*.

3.1.2.5.1.2. Starving of a station with limited local buffers

The previous section described circumstances under which delays associated with the transportation system could arise in FMSs with unlimited buffers and how these are included in the classical CQN model.

If the local buffer space at a station is limited, then it is possible that a workpiece that needs to be processed next at this station could be denied access because the local storage space of the station is full. It would then have to be stored in the central buffer or wait in the local output buffer of the previous station. The state of starving may arise when the downstream station is ready to process the workpiece. It must be distinguished, however, between stations with no local buffer space (case 1) and those with space for one or several pallets (case 2).

- Case 1: *No local buffer space available*

  If a station has *no local buffer space at all*[218], then starving begins immediately when the machine becomes free. Due to the lack of space, an unprocessed workpiece can never be waiting at the station. The next workpiece to be processed at the machine can only be transported there when the machine is already waiting[219]. The period of starving here is equal to the time from the moment the new workpiece requests a transportation vehicle to the moment that workpiece arrives at its downstream station for processing. Figure (108) illustrates this sequence of events for a workpiece B that is waiting in the central buffer (CB) for processing at machine 1.

  It is clear from the example that machine 1 cannot operate, *despite the fact that there is an unprocessed workpiece in the FMS* that must next be processed on this machine. In contrast to the classical CQN model, the *machine is idle*, although the logical *queue of workpieces dedicated to that station is not empty*.

  The term *transportation delay* will be used in the following to describe the time period between the completion of one workpiece's processing at a machine and the physical arrival of a new workpiece which is waiting to be processed next at that machine. In contrast, the term *transportation time* indicates the time a transportation vehicle is in use for the transportation of a particular workpiece, including both relevant idle trips and supply trips.

---

218   In this case there is only one space available which is used for workpiece exchange.

219   The FMS control system could initiate the next workpiece's transportation process such that it would arrive at the machine exactly at the point in time when the machine becomes idle. However, the just finished workpiece still occupying the machine would have to leave the station first. In this case, therefore, in order to prevent starving in the FMS at least two carts must be available whose transportation processes precisely match the instances when the machines become idle. As an alternative, instead of two carts it would be possible to use a double-cart with a space for pallet manoeuvring.

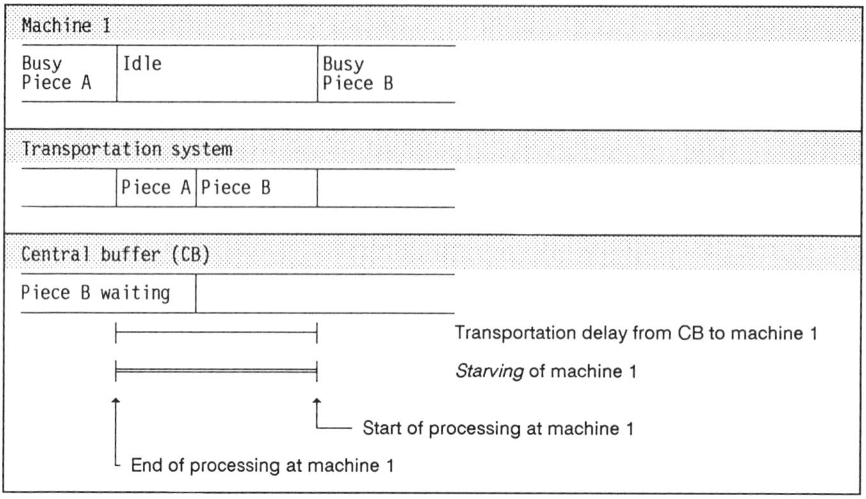

```
┌─────────────────────────────────────────────────────────────────────┐
│ Machine 1                                                             │
│ ┌─────────┬──────────────┬───────────────┐                          │
│ │ Busy    │ Idle         │ Busy          │                          │
│ │ Piece A │              │ Piece B       │                          │
│ └─────────┴──────────────┴───────────────┘                          │
│                                                                       │
│ Transportation system                                                 │
│ ┌──────────────┬─────────┬──────────────┐                           │
│ │              │ Piece A │ Piece B │    │                           │
│ └──────────────┴─────────┴──────────────┘                           │
│                                                                       │
│ Central buffer (CB)                                                   │
│ ┌────────────────┬───────┐                                          │
│ │ Piece B waiting │      │                                          │
│ └────────────────┴───────┘                                          │
└─────────────────────────────────────────────────────────────────────┘
```

|———————————————————| Transportation delay from CB to machine 1

|═══════════════════| *Starving* of machine 1

↑   └── Start of processing at machine 1

└ End of processing at machine 1

Figure 108: Idle times of machine 1 caused by starving (no local buffer)

- Case 2: *Local buffer space available*

  If one or more local buffer spaces are available at a station, then this station could have a backlog of workpieces that could be processed until the new workpiece arrives from the central buffer or the local buffer of the upstream station. Figure (109) illustrates this situation with respect to a workpiece C which is waiting in the central buffer to be processed at machine 1. When workpiece A completes processing, workpiece B is in the backlog in the local buffer of the station. Obviously, *starving can only occur* when the processing time of the workpieces already at the station (*backlog processing time*) is smaller than the transportation delay of the new workpiece between the central buffer and the downstream station.

The analysis makes it quite clear that the duration of starving is significantly influenced by the speed and the utilization of the *transportation system*[220] as well as by the availability of local buffers. In the case of unlimited buffers, only the transportation delay is important, whereas when local buffers are limited, the transportation delay and the number of local buffers are both critical.

When the average transportation time is relatively short in comparison to the processing times at the stations, then starving is comparatively rare. Starving becomes significant when the utilization of the material flow system and/or the transportation times increase in comparison to the processing times at the machines.

---

220 The velocity and the utilization of the transportation system have an influence on the time interval between the release of a transportation order and the arrival of the workpiece at its destination station. If the transportation system is heavily utilized, a queueing delay will often occur.

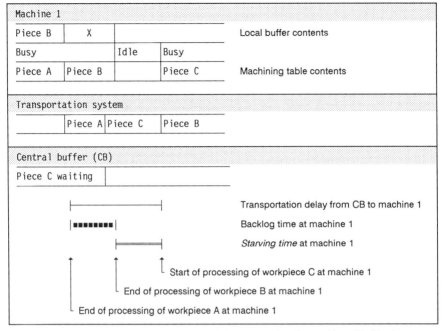

Figure 109: Idle times at machine 1 due to starving (several local buffers)

The simulation results shown in figure (110) describe the change in the *starving of a washing machine* (without local buffers) resulting from variations in the transportation time. These results apply to a real-life FMS with eight setup tables, twelve machines (some identical), four MHS carts and twenty pallets. As can be seen, starving almost disappears when the transportation times are short, but for extremely slow vehicles starving can be so severe as to reduce the productive utilization of the machines by more than half.

The more buffer spaces are added to the above-mentioned washing machine, the less the danger that starving may occur. The inverse relationship between the number of local buffer spaces and the degree of starving is shown in figure (111). Here the proportions of the washing machine's starving time and busy time are given for various numbers of pallets in the FMS ($N = 10,20,30$) as a function of the size of the machine's local buffer.

Providing this FMS with a local buffer at the machine being analyzed here results in a dramatic reduction in the utilization loss due to starving. At the same time, it is clear from the analysis that installing more than two local buffers would be largely pointless since starving is already insignificant with two local buffer spaces. Since there were no local buffer spaces planned for the washing machine in the construction of this FMS, fundamental *constructive measures* at the washing machine are necessary in order to achieve an improvement in the system.

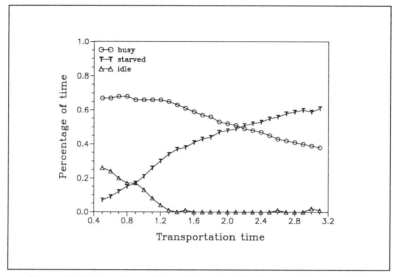

Figure 110: States of a machine without local buffers as a function of the mean transportation time

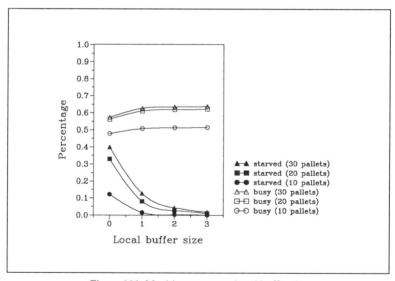

Figure 111: Machine states vs. local buffer size

3.1.2.5.2. Idle trips

A vehicle makes an *idle trip* when it moves from one place to another without carrying a workpiece. An idle trip is necessary whenever a vehicle which is assigned to a particular workpiece and the workpiece itself are not at the same location in the FMS. If a vehicle can load a new workpiece immediately after unloading one it has just transported[221], then there will be no idle trip associated with that transportation process. There is also no idle trip when a vehicle is already located at the station (idle) at the moment it is requested by a pallet. The latter is most often true in FMSs with only one vehicle. The fraction of idle trips of the total transportation workload is dependent on the *number of pallets, the number of machines, and the number of vehicles in the FMS*.

Idle trips occur in almost all FMSs, regardless of whether the local buffers are limited or not. Idle trips are treated here together with starving because, along with the trips between the processing stations and the central buffer (disposal trips), they make up the second component of the load on the transportation system that is not included in the classical CQN model. Idle trips can be roughly accounted for in the CQN model, however, by modifying the average transportation times.

3.1.2.5.3. Trips between the processing stations and the central buffer

If the FMS under consideration has a central buffer, then this places an *additional workload* on the transportation system. The extent of this workload depends on how often the central buffer is used as an outlet buffer for the workpieces. If there is enough space in the central buffer, then all workpieces rejected by the local buffers will be temporarily stored in the central buffer, according to the relevant material flow strategy[222]. A station m will always be supplied with unprocessed workpieces from the central buffer when the number of workpieces to be processed at that station exceeds its allowed maximum ($n_m > N_{max(m)}$).

In an FMS with a *limited* central buffer, it is possible, starting at a particular number of pallets, that a workpiece may have to wait in the local buffer of its current station for its downstream station to become free[223]. In this case, the workpiece does not need be transported to the central buffer. The load on the transportation system is reduced accordingly. The result is that the production rate of an FMS increases at first with the number of pallets, then it decreases due to the extra trips to the central buffer; finally it increases again when the central buffer is full and trips from the machines to the central buffer are no longer possible.

---

221 This is often possible at stations with two local buffers. However, a clever FMS control strategy is necessary in this case.
222 see section 3.1.2.1.
223 If in such a situation the local buffer of the upstream machine is full as well, blocking may occur.

3.1.2.5.4. Integration of starving into the CQN model

The factors described in the previous section which influence the performance of
an FMS and which can lead to starving of a machine will now be quantitatively
analyzed. They will then be integrated into an heuristic procedure for the analytical estimation of the performance of an FMS. This will be done in three stages,
as shown in figure (112).

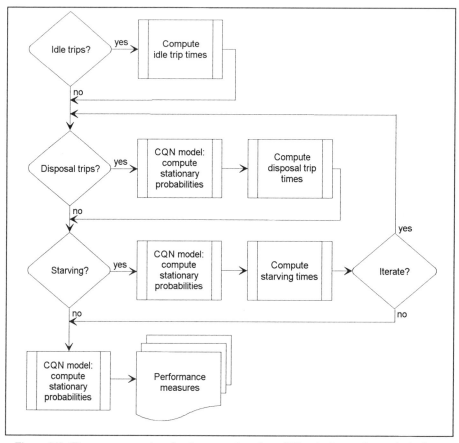

*Figure 112: Three-step procedure for the approximation of idle trip times, disposal trip times
and starving times*

First, the estimates of the average transportation time used in the classical CQN
model will be corrected for the influences of *idle trips* and *disposal trips to the
central buffer*. Simple approximations will be introduced to determine the idle
trip time. The trips between the processing stations and the central buffer are
approximated using the classical CQN model since the stationary probability

distributions of the numbers of pallets at the individual stations are employed here. Following that, the "normal" processing time of a workpiece at a machine will be increased by the mean starving times, just as was done for blocking. The classical CQN model and the new input data will then be used to iteratively evaluate the key performance parameters until a stable solution is found.

If all the queries in figure (112) are answered in the negative; i.e. if no estimates of the idle trip time, the trip time to the central buffer, and the starving time are necessary; then the analysis of this particular FMS can follow the lines of the classical CQN model. The approximation of the influence of starving on an FMS with *universal pallets* will be described in detail in section 3.1.2.5.4.1. An heuristically motivated extension of this approach for special pallets will then be presented immediately after that in section 3.1.2.5.4.2.

3.1.2.5.4.1. Universal pallets

3.1.2.5.4.1.1. Adjusting the average transportation time for idle trip and disposal trip times

As has already been discussed, the vehicles in the material flow system of an FMS carry out the following kinds of trips:

- *Supply trips* (transportation of workpieces directly from one processing station to the next; workpiece transportation from the central buffer to a processing station),

- *Disposal trips* (transportation of workpieces from a station to the central buffer), and

- *Idle trips*.

Each of these activities of the material flow system requires a certain amount of time, and this has to be taken into consideration when calculating the average transportation time. The average transportation time in the classical CQN model is based on the assumption that the transportation system executes only supply trips between machines. This assumption is only justified when idle trips and trips to the central buffer of an FMS are insignificantly small.

In the following, ways of estimating the idle trip time and the disposal trip time will be reviewed. These estimates provide the prerequisites for approximating the mean starving time of a machine. They can, however, also be used to improve estimates of the load on the transportation system in the classical CQN model.

- **Idle trips**

Before a vehicle can remove a workpiece from a station it must often travel without a workpiece to this station, i.e. it must execute an idle trip. In an FMS

with only one pallet idle trips do not occur because the vehicle usually stays at
the station where the single pallet is processed[224]. If there are two pallets circulating in an FMS, it is plausible to assume that for every other transportation
trip the vehicle will already be at the location of the workpiece requiring transportation, thus no idle trip will be necessary. At higher numbers of pallets the
share of idle trips rises accordingly. The number of idle trips will also be influenced by the number of independent stopping-places, such as machining
stations, central buffer spaces and parking stations. If the latter is less than the
number of pallets, then the frequency of idle trips will be determined by the
number of stopping-places in the FMS. The probability that an idle trip will be
necessary can, therefore, be roughly estimated as in equation (133).

$$F_L(N, M_M) = 1 - \max\left\{\frac{1}{N}, \frac{1}{M_M}\right\}$$ (133)

                                 ⌐ number of MHS stopping-places

⌐ proportion of idle trips depending on the number of pallets and stopping-places

The number of independent MHS stopping-places in the FMS (M_M) is given in
equation (134) as the total number of all the machines and the number of
central pallet storage locations, CB. A vehicle parking location (staging area)
could also be added to that.

$$M_M = CB + \sum_{m=1}^{M-1} S_m$$ (134)

If there are several (S_M) transportation vehicles in an FMS, then the probability
of an idle trip increases with the number of vehicles. This can be allowed for
through multiplication by the number of vehicles [equation (135)].

$$F_L(N, M_M, S_M) = \max\left\{1 - \max\left\{\frac{1}{N}, \frac{1}{M_M}\right\} \cdot S_M, 0\right\}$$ (135)

                                 ⌐ number of vehicles

⌐ idle trip proportion depending on the number of pallets, stopping-places, and vehicles

The quality of the approximation of the proportion of idle trips for different
numbers of pallets is shown in figure (113). These results where derived for an
FMS with 6 machines and 7 independent stopping-places. The idle trip proportion (F_L), calculated according to equation (135), and the proportion of idle trips
as measured by a simulation model (SIM) are compared for 1, 2, and 4 vehicles.

---

224 Trips to a battery charging station are not considered here.

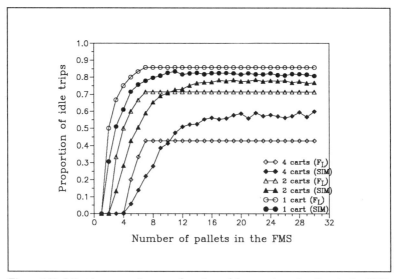

Figure 113: Idle trip proportion as a function of the number of pallets in the FMS: simulation vs. approximation according to equation (135)

The results show that the approximation for a single vehicle is very good, but for several vehicles better approximations may possibly exist. More work is necessary to reach a deeper understanding of the interactions among the various factors which influence the number of idle trips.

The *average transportation time*, including the expected idle trip time, can thus be described with equation (136).

$$T_L = b_M + [b_M \cdot F_L(N, M_M, S_M)] \tag{136}$$

with:
- mean idle trip time
- idle trip proportion
- mean transportation time (supply trips)
- mean transportation time (incl. idle trip time)

It is made up of the average transportation time b_M, as used in the classical CQN model to cover supply trips, and an *idle trip supplement*.

Similarly, the *average disposal trip time to the central buffer*, b_Z, handled in the next section, will also be increased by an idle trip supplement [see equation (137)].

$$B_{ZL} = b_Z + [b_Z \cdot F_L(N, M_M, S_M)] \tag{137}$$

- idle trip proportion
- mean disposal trip time
- mean disposal trip time (incl. idle trip time)

- **Disposal trips to the central buffer**

Disposal trips to the central buffer are necessary when the local buffer capacity of a workpiece's downstream station is exhausted. The average *total demand for central buffer space* U can be described with equation (138).

$$U = \sum_{m=1}^{M-1} \left\{ \sum_{n=1}^{N} P\{n_m = n\} \cdot \max\left[0, [n - (N_{max(m)})]\right] \right\} \tag{138}$$

- maximum space at station m
- number of pallets at station m
- total central buffer space requirement

The average *number of disposal trips to the central buffer* necessary when the downstream station m is full can be found by multiplying the arrival frequency p_m of workpieces at station m by the probability that all the local buffer spaces at this station will be full $[P\{n_m > N_{max(m)}\}]$. The actual number of trips successfully made to the central buffer depends on whether the central buffer is able to accept every workpiece (unlimited capacity), or if some of the workpieces are rejected by the central buffer and must therefore be stored in the output buffers of their current stations. In such a case, obviously no trip to the central buffer would be necessary.

When a *sufficiently large central buffer capacity* CB is available, the proportion of disposal trips to the central buffer is determined only by the use of the processing stations, as indicated in equation (139).

$$F_{Z'} = \sum_{m=1}^{M-1} [p_m \cdot P\{n_m > N_{max(m)}\}] \qquad\qquad U \leq CB \tag{139}$$

- probability that the downstream station m is full
- arrival probability at station m
- disposal trip proportion in a system with an unlimited central buffer

Several simulation experiments have been carried out to test the accuracy of the estimations for the proportion of disposal trips assuming different numbers of vehicles and pallets. The results suggest that the approximation described here provides a sufficiently accurate picture of the proportion of disposal trips. Figure (114) presents relevant results for the FMS described above with eight setup areas, twelve machines and unlimited local buffers.

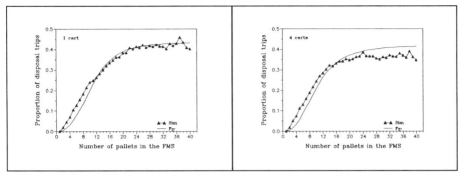

Figure 114: Disposal trip proportion vs. number of pallets in an FMS with one and four MHS carts

If the *capacity of the central buffer* $N_{max(CB)}$ is limited, however, then a disposal trip will not be necessary when it is full[225]. The proportion of disposal trips described in equation (139) must now be multiplied by the probability that the central buffer will be able to accept another workpiece. Since this probability is not known, however, the reduction in the number of disposal trips due to the limitations on the central buffer is represented by an availability factor P_Z [see equation (140)]. This factor assumes a value of one when the number of pallets in the FMS is so small that any limits on the capacity of the central buffer do not affect the frequency of disposal trips. As the number of pallets in the FMS increases, the availability factor decreases.

$$P_Z = \begin{cases} 1, & N \leq N_{max(CB)} + \min\{N_{max(m)}; \ m=1,\ldots,M-1\} \\ N_{max(CB)}/N & N > N_{max(CB)} + \min\{N_{max(m)}; \ m=1,\ldots,M-1\} \end{cases} \tag{140}$$

"availability" of the central buffer

The proportion of disposal trips can thus be described using equation (141).

$$F_Z = \sum_{m=1}^{M-1} [P_m \cdot P\{n_m > N_{max(m)}\}] \cdot P_Z \tag{141}$$

availability of the central buffer

probability, that the downstream station m is full

arrival probability at station m

disposal trip proportion

The average transportation time, as corrected for the influence of both disposal trips to the central buffer and idle trips, can then be approximated with equation (142).

---

225   In this case one of the five blocking conditions is met. See section 3.1.2.4.1.

$$T_{ZL} = T_L + F_Z \cdot B_{ZL} \qquad\qquad\qquad (142)$$

           ⌐ mean disposal trip time (incl. idle times)

     ⌐ disposal trip proportion

⌐ total transportation time (incl. idle and disposal trip times)

The procedure described here has been tested with numerous simulation experiments. Figure (115) shows the utilization of the transportation system for a configuration variation of FMS 4 in which every station has 2 local buffer spaces and the central buffer has only limited capacity ($N_{max(CB)} = 10$). The average trip time for supply trips between the machines is assumed to be 0.1 minutes, and 1.0 minutes for trips to the central buffer. Idle trips are explicitly included in the analysis. The curve labeled "CQN" shows the estimate of the utilization in the CQN model when only the supply trips to the machines are accounted for.

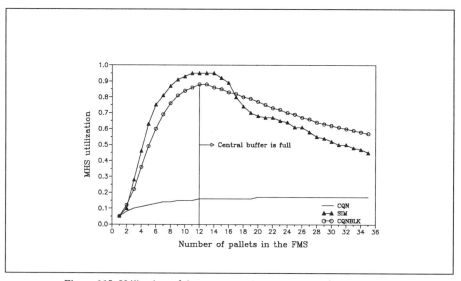

Figure 115: Utilization of the transportation system as a function of the number of pallets in the FMS

The graph illustrates quite well the influence of the limited central buffer on the load on the transportation system. As long as less than $N = 12$ pallets circulate in this FMS, the central buffer is able to provide room for the pallets, and the vehicle will make correspondingly more trips to the central buffer. If the receptive capacity of the central buffer is exhausted, then these trips become less frequent as the workpieces must be more frequently stored in the local (output) buffers of the machines where they have just been processed. The resulting decrease in the load on the transportation system means that it can be more effectively used for "productive" trips between machining stations. It will be shown in section 3.1.2.6.

that a machine's production quantity may also increase after some initial downward tendencies.

3.1.2.5.4.1.2. Quantifying starving and calculating starving times

The discussion in the previous section has been primarily of a preparatory character, in that it was working toward an improvement in the estimation of the average transportation time and thereby too the utilization of the transportation system. This was done by allowing for the effects of idle trips and disposal trips to the central buffer. At this point the processes leading to starving of a machine will be discussed in more detail. As has already been said, starving at a station occurs when the time period between the workpiece exchange and the arrival of the next workpiece is greater than the backlog processing time at the moment of the workpiece exchange, i.e. when the workpiece to be processed at a machine next is not yet available to that machine. Thus to find the length of the period of starving (the period in which a machine is already assigned to a workpiece but still cannot begin processing) the *backlog processing time* and the *transportation delay* must be determined and compared. It will be assumed in the following that the average duration of a supply trip (a trip to a station) is independent of its starting point (another processing station or the central buffer).

a) Backlog processing time at a station

The time period starting at a workpiece exchange and during which a station still has unprocessed workpieces waiting in its local buffer (*backlog processing time*) is influenced by the average processing time and by the *number of local buffer spaces* at that station. In a case with only one local buffer at a station, the backlog processing time is zero because this buffer space has to be kept free for workpiece exchange. The workpiece to be processed next can never be waiting in the buffer at such a station. As was described above, starving may occur when a workpiece's *downstream station is occupied* at the instant when the workpiece leaves the previous machine. The workpiece must then wait at another location in the FMS. The backlog processing time BV_m at station m can be described with equation (143).

$$BV_m = (P_m-1) \cdot b_m / S_m \qquad\qquad m=1\ldots,M-1 \qquad\qquad (143)$$

$\quad\quad$ └ number of machines at station m

$\quad\quad$ └ mean processing time at station m

$\quad\quad$ └ number of local buffers available for unprocessed workpieces at station m

$\quad\quad$ └ backlog processing time at station m

b) Time between a workpiece exchange and the arrival of the next unprocessed
   workpiece (transportation delay)

Immediately after a workpiece exchange at a station, a transportation order for
the removal of the processed workpiece (A) is initiated by the FMS control system. There must already exist a transportation order associated with the next unprocessed workpiece (B) in the transportation queue[226]. The order to remove
the processed workpiece (A) will be placed in the transportation queue immediately in front of the order for the transportation of the unprocessed workpiece
(B). The duration of the period from workpiece exchange to the arrival of the
next unprocessed workpiece (B) is influenced by the average *transportation time*
and by the queueing delay while the two workpieces (A and B) wait for a vehicle.
If the processed workpiece (A) is removed from the station and the unprocessed
workpiece (B) is brought to the station, then the following elements of the transportation delay can be distinguished:

- *The queueing delay* while the processed *workpiece* (A) waits at the station for
  a vehicle.

- *The transportation time of the processed workpiece* (A) to the next station
  (normal supply trip) or to the central buffer (disposal trip).

- *The transportation time of the workpiece* (B) that is next to be processed at the
  station (supply trip).

1. *Queueing delay*

The *queueing delay* while waiting for the transportation vehicle is the product
of the average transportation time and the average number of transportation
orders that are *in front of* the two workpieces (A and B) in the transportation
queue. If the transportation queue is relatively long, then it is possible that
several unprocessed workpieces (type B) all wishing to be transported to this
particular machine may be waiting for transportation. Since starving ends as
soon as the *first* unprocessed workpiece arrives at the machine, only the top
of the transportation queue (up to order A, which has been placed immediately in front of the highest ranking type B transportation order) is of interest. The form of the transportation queue shown in figure (116) results.
The average number of orders waiting for the transportation system is Q_M.
This includes both of the workpieces A and B. The goal of the following is to
determine the *length of the front of the queue*, excluding the transportation orders A and B. Assuming the load on the transportation system is shared
evenly among trips to all the stations in the FMS, the maximum length of the
relevant queue W_T (including orders A and B) can be approximated using
equation (144).

---

226 Otherwise the machine would be idle and starving would not occur.

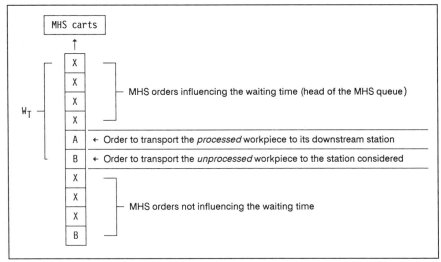

Figure 116: Composition of the MHS queue

$$W_T = min[Q_M, M_M]/2 \qquad\qquad (144)$$

⌐ number of processing stations and central buffer locations

⌐ length of the MHS queue

⌐ length of the relevant MHS queue (from the first order to order B)

In this part of the queue there are, in addition to workpieces A and B, also workpieces that will be transported to other stations in the FMS. The number of such workpieces can be estimated with equation (145).

⌐ stationary arrival probability of a workpiece at station m

$$W_{TAm} = W_T \cdot (1-\overline{p_m}) \qquad\qquad m=1,\ldots,M-1 \qquad (145)$$

⌐ proportion of orders *not* to be transported to station m (incl. order A)

⌐ length of the relevant MHS queue

⌐ number of workpieces in the MHS queue not to be transported to station m

The workpiece (A) which is set for removal from the station is also included in the quantity W_{TAm}. Since the transportation time of this workpiece is to be calculated directly, the length of the queue must be corrected for its presence. This is done with equation (146). The correction becomes increasingly smaller as the length of the queue increases.

$$W_{Tm} = W_{TAm} \cdot \frac{W_{TAm}}{W_{TAm}+1} = \frac{(W_{TAm})^2}{W_{TAm}+1} \qquad\qquad m=1,\ldots,M-1 \qquad (146)$$

The quantity W_{Tm} approximates the average number of workpieces present in the queue in addition to the two transportation orders already considered. The time the processed workpiece (A) has to wait for a transportation vehicle is now estimated with equation (147).

$$T_{Wm} = \frac{T_{ZL} \cdot W_{Tm}}{S_M} \tag{147}$$

2. Transportation time of the processed workpiece (A)

A processed workpiece is transported either directly to the downstream station or to the central buffer. The expected *transportation time of the processed workpiece A* is given by equation (148).

$$T_A = T_L \cdot (1-F_Z) + B_{ZL} \cdot F_Z \tag{148}$$

   └ mean disposal trip time to the central buffer (incl. idle trip time)

  └ mean transportation time to the downstream station (incl. idle trip time)

 └ mean transportation time of the processed workpiece

3. Transportation time of the unprocessed workpiece (B)

Equation (136) can be used to find the average *transportation time of the workpiece* B, the next workpiece to be processed at the station m.

The **average transportation delay** of a workpiece on the way to station m can be approximated with equation (149).

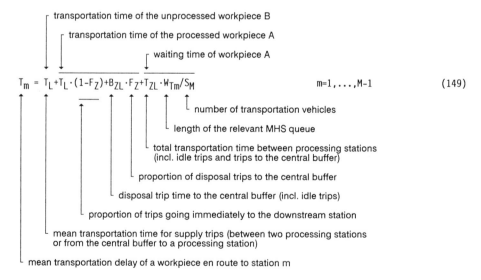

 ┌ transportation time of the unprocessed workpiece B

  ┌ transportation time of the processed workpiece A

   ┌ waiting time of workpiece A

$$T_m = T_L + T_L \cdot (1-F_Z) + B_{ZL} \cdot F_Z + T_{ZL} \cdot W_{Tm}/S_M \qquad m=1,\dots,M-1 \tag{149}$$

       └ number of transportation vehicles

      └ length of the relevant MHS queue

     └ total transportation time between processing stations (incl. idle trips and trips to the central buffer)

    └ proportion of disposal trips to the central buffer

   └ disposal trip time to the central buffer (incl. idle trips)

  └ proportion of trips going immediately to the downstream station

 └ mean transportation time for supply trips (between two processing stations or from the central buffer to a processing station)

└ mean transportation delay of a workpiece en route to station m

c) Starving time of the processing station

After having found the backlog processing time and the transportation delay, the next step is to calculate the average starving time of the processing station m. An observation of this random variable is described by equation (150).

$$l_m = \begin{cases} t_m - bv_m & t_m > bv_m \\ 0 & t_m \le bv_m \end{cases} \qquad m=1,\dots,M-1 \qquad (150)$$

The *average starving time*, assuming exponentially distributed processing and transportation times, is given by:

$$L_m = \frac{T_m^2}{T_m + BV_m} \qquad m=1,\dots,M-1 \qquad (151)$$

3.1.2.5.4.1.3. Implementation in the CQN model

The estimate for the mean transportation time, as corrected for idle trips and disposal trips to the central buffer, and the delays in the material flow in the FMS due to starving is used in the following procedure for the evaluation of the performance of an FMS [see figure (112)]. The stationary probability distributions of the pallets among the stations computed with the help of the classical CQN model provide the basis for these calculations. The procedure consists of three steps:

Step 1: Idle trip time

The idle trip times are dependent only on the parameters M_M, N and S_M of the FMS. They can, therefore, be calculated without having to evaluate the classical CQN model.

Step 2: Disposal trip time to the central buffer

The average disposal trip time to the central buffer depends on the degree to which the buffer spaces at the individual stations are occupied. This is described by the probability distribution of the pallets at the stations. For that reason, the classical CQN model is evaluated with the idle trip correction, but for now without consideration of the disposal trips. The resulting probability distributions of queue lengths are then used to determine the proportion of disposal trips.

Step 3: Machine idle time due to starving

The classical CQN model with the modified input data from steps 1 and 2 is used to calculate the average starving times of the processing stations. The average processing times at the stations are then increased by the average starving times [see equation (152)].

$$b_m^S = b_m + L_m \qquad\qquad\qquad m=1,\ldots,M-1 \qquad (152)$$

Starving can only affect those workpieces which were denied access to the local buffer of their downstream station. Therefore, the adjustment of the processing time applies only to those states of the FMS in which the local buffer capacity of a station is exhausted $(n_m > N_{max(m)})$. The average workload of station m can thus be found using equation (153).

$$w_m(n_m) = \begin{cases} p_m \cdot b_m & n_m \leq N_{max}(m) \\ p_m \cdot b_m^S & n_m > N_{max}(m) \end{cases} \quad m=1,\ldots,M-1 \qquad (153)$$

The stationary probability distribution of the number of pallets at the stations can be calculated in the same way as for the classical CQN model[227]. Since the modification of the average transportation time influences the probability distribution of the pallets $P\{\underline{n}\}$, the calculations in steps 2 and 3 are carried out iteratively until the maximum deviation in the successive determination of queue lengths does not exceed a given tolerance limit ϵ.

The performance parameters of the FMS (production rate, flow time, utilization) can be found, as described in section 3.1.1.1.2., using the stationary probability distribution of the number of pallets at the stations.

3.1.2.5.4.1.4. Numerical results for starving with universal pallets

The same FMS configurations which provided the basis for the numerical analysis of blocking will also be used here to test the performance of the approach described for starving[228]. When the number of pallets is varied, the number of spaces in the central buffer $N_{max(CB)}$ will be assumed to be equal to the number of pallets N in the system. It can thus be assured that only starving and not blocking could occur. The average transportation time b_M and the average time for disposal trips to the central buffer b_Z are equal to 0.333 minutes in FMSs 4, 5 and FL, while for FMS 12 0.2 minutes are assumed.

In all the cases the production quantity of the machine M1 in the FMS being considered is given for a simulated time period of 10,000 minutes. For different numbers of pallets in the FMS the results from the simulation will be compared to those of the approximation procedure suggested here and to the classical CQN model. The classical CQN model was applied without correcting for idle trips or for central buffer influences on the transportation time. The results presented are: simulation results (SIM), results calculated using the classical CQN model (CQN), and results of the approximation procedure described here (CQNBLK).

---

227   see also section 3.1.1.1.2.
228   see section 3.1.2.4.3.

- **FMS 4:** FMS with 4 machines

$N_{max}(CB)=N$, $N_{max}(1)=25$, $N_{max}(2)=1$, $N_{max}(3)=1$, $N_{max}(4)=2$					
N	SIM	CQNBLK	Diff[229]	CQN	Diff[230]
1	1660	1629	1.87	1629	1.87
3	2872	2723	5.19	3443	-19.88
5	3276	3111	5.04	4406	-34.49
7	3405	3326	2.32	4987	-46.46
9	3464	3400	1.85	5366	-54.91
11	3388	3452	-1.89	5627	-66.09
13	3485	3475	0.29	5814	-66.83
15	3533	3488	1.27	5952	-68.47
17	3491	3495	-0.11	6057	-73.50
19	3393	3499	-3.12	6138	-80.90
21	3516	3502	0.40	6203	-76.42
23	3429	3503	-2.16	6254	-82.39
25	3458	3503	-1.30	6297	-82.10

Figure 117: Results for FMS 4, variation 5

---

229 Diff = 100*(SIM-CQNBLK)/SIM
230 Diff = 100*(SIM-CQN)/SIM

$N_{max}(CB)=N$, $N_{max}(1)=25$, $N_{max}(2)=2$, $N_{max}(3)=2$, $N_{max}(4)=2$					
N	SIM	CQNBLK	Diff	CQN	Diff
1	1660	1629	1.87	1629	1.87
2	2554	2523	1.21	2696	-5.56
3	3243	3085	4.87	3443	-6.17
4	3686	3429	6.97	3991	-8.27
5	3971	3641	8.31	4406	-10.95
6	4047	3802	6.05	4730	-16.88
7	4229	3904	7.69	4987	-17.92
8	4176	3968	4.98	5195	-24.40
9	4148	4010	3.33	5366	-29.36
10	4130	4015	2.78	5508	-33.37
11	4118	4026	2.23	5627	-36.64
12	4121	4020	2.45	5728	-39.00
13	4057	4049	0.20	5814	-43.31
14	4066	4073	-0.17	5888	-44.81
15	4020	4094	-1.84	5952	-48.06
16	4072	4113	-1.01	6008	-47.54
17	4084	4128	-1.08	6057	-48.31
18	4133	4142	-0.22	6100	-47.59
19	4062	4154	-2.26	6138	-51.11
20	3991	4165	-4.36	6172	-54.65
21	4041	4175	-3.32	6203	-53.50
22	4072	4183	-2.73	6230	-53.00
23	4100	4191	-2.22	6254	-52.54
24	4062	4198	-3.35	6276	-54.51
25	4078	4205	-3.11	6297	-54.41

Figure 118: Results for FMS 4, variation 6

- **FMS 5: FMS with 5 machines**

$N_{max(CB)}=N$, $N_{max(1)}=25$, $N_{max(2)}=25$, $N_{max(3)}=1$, $N_{max(4)}=2$, $N_{max(5)}=2$					
N	SIM	CQNBLK	Diff	CQN	Diff
1	1024	1071	-4.59	1071	-4.59
3	2126	2008	5.55	2360	-11.01
5	2531	2384	5.81	3086	-21.93
7	2645	2544	3.82	3535	-33.65
9	2701	2610	3.37	3830	-41.80
11	2648	2639	0.34	4033	-52.30
13	2705	2650	2.03	4177	-54.42
15	2675	2655	0.75	4281	-60.04
17	2657	2644	0.49	4358	-64.02
19	2655	2643	0.45	4416	-66.33
21	2628	2588	1.52	4460	-69.71
23	2693	2581	4.16	4494	-66.88
25	2662	2585	2.89	4521	-69.83

Figure 119: Results for FMS 5, variation 3

$N_{max(CB)}=N$, $N_{max(1)}=25$, $N_{max(2)}=25$, $N_{max(3)}=2$, $N_{max(4)}=2$, $N_{max(5)}=2$					
N	SIM	CQNBLK	Diff	CQN	Diff
1	1024	1071	-4.59	1071	-4.59
3	2214	2118	4.34	2360	-6.59
5	2796	2580	7.73	3086	-10.37
7	3067	2782	9.29	3535	-15.26
9	3010	2866	4.78	3830	-27.24
11	2853	2887	-1.19	4033	-41.36
13	2885	2882	0.10	4177	-44.78
15	2821	2906	-3.01	4281	-51.75
17	2842	2921	-2.78	4358	-53.34
19	2837	2928	-3.21	4416	-55.66
21	2869	2931	-2.16	4460	-55.45
23	2832	2931	-3.50	4494	-58.69
25	2860	2929	-2.41	4521	-58.08

Figure 120: Results for FMS 5, variation 4

- **FMS 12:** FMS with 12 machines

$N_{max}(CB)=N$, $N_{max}(1)=1$, $N_{max}(m)=2$ $(m=2,\dots,11)$, $N_{max}(12)=40$					
N	SIM	CQNBLK	Diff	CQN	Diff
2	716	725	-1.26	742	-3.63
4	1265	1247	1.42	1295	-2.37
6	1678	1644	2.03	1723	-2.68
8	2054	1954	4.87	2063	-0.44
10	2161	2201	-1.85	2341	-8.33
12	2507	2400	4.27	2571	-2.55
14	2677	2561	4.33	2764	-3.25
16	2709	2692	0.63	2930	-8.16
18	2802	2797	0.18	3073	-9.67
20	2883	2881	0.07	3197	-10.89
22	2986	2944	1.41	3307	-10.75
24	3010	2992	0.60	3404	-13.09
26	3016	3030	-0.46	3491	-15.75
28	2969	3040	-2.39	3569	-20.21
30	3038	3060	-0.72	3639	-19.78
32	2996	3073	-2.57	3703	-23.60
34	2967	3085	-3.98	3761	-26.76
36	3027	3066	-1.29	3814	-26.00
38	3080	3083	-0.10	3863	-25.42
40	3018	3074	-1.86	3907	-29.46

Figure 121: Results for FMS 12, variation 3

$N_{max(CB)}=N$, $N_{max(m)}=3$ $(m=1,....,11)$, $N_{max(12)}=40$					
N	SIM	CQNBLK	Diff	CQN	Diff
2	727	728	-0.14	742	-2.06
4	1254	1262	-0.64	1295	-3.27
6	1678	1676	0.12	1723	-2.68
8	2081	2006	3.60	2063	0.86
10	2265	2275	-0.44	2341	-3.36
12	2513	2497	0.64	2571	-2.31
14	2807	2683	4.42	2764	1.53
16	2897	2842	1.90	2930	-1.14
18	3072	2978	3.06	3073	-0.03
20	3084	3095	-0.36	3197	-3.66
22	3301	3197	3.15	3307	-0.18
24	3210	3285	-2.34	3404	-6.04
26	3434	3361	2.13	3491	-1.66
28	3492	3427	1.86	3569	-2.21
30	3472	3484	-0.35	3639	-4.81
32	3545	3531	0.39	3703	-4.46
34	3640	3569	1.95	3761	-3.32
36	3814	3598	5.66	3814	0.00
38	3703	3616	2.35	3863	-4.32
40	3670	3624	1.25	3907	-6.46

Figure 122: Results for FMS 12, variation 4

- **FMS FL: FMS with flow shop structure**

$N_{max}(CB)=N$, $N_{max}(1)=3$, $N_{max}(2)=3$, $N_{max}(3)=3$, $N_{max}(4)=3$					
N	SIM	CQNBLK	Diff	CQN	Diff
1	984	992	-0.81	992	-0.81
2	1574	1526	3.05	1616	-2.67
3	1936	1899	1.91	2036	-5.17
4	2265	2135	5.74	2331	-2.91
5	2448	2282	6.78	2545	-3.96
6	2574	2388	7.23	2705	-5.09
7	2678	2459	8.18	2828	-5.60
8	2720	2509	7.76	2923	-7.46
9	2705	2542	6.03	2998	-10.83
10	2680	2565	4.29	3058	-14.10
11	2671	2580	3.41	3106	-16.29
12	2671	2587	3.14	3145	-17.75
13	2713	2587	4.64	3177	-17.10
14	2668	2589	2.96	3203	-20.05
15	2626	2602	0.91	3225	-22.81
16	2645	2614	1.17	3243	-22.61
17	2625	2624	0.04	3258	-24.11
18	2662	2633	1.09	3270	-22.84
19	2619	2642	-0.88	3280	-25.24
20	2646	2649	-0.11	3289	-24.30
21	2619	2656	-1.41	3296	-25.85
22	2593	2662	-2.66	3302	-27.34
23	2603	2668	-2.50	3307	-27.05
24	2630	2673	-1.63	3312	-25.93
25	2657	2678	-0.79	3315	-24.76

Figure 123: Results for FMS FL, variation 2

3.1.2.5.4.2. Special pallets

In the previous section, an approach allowing for the effects of starving on the performance of an FMS with exclusively universal pallets was described. The procedure was essentially to calculate the machines' expected starving times and then add these to the average "normal" processing times. These modified processing times were then used in the classical CQN model (for universal pallets) to estimate the key performance parameters of the FMS under consideration.

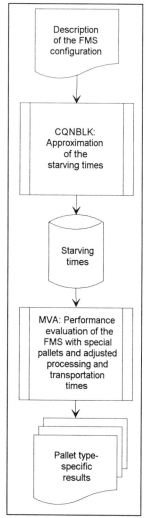

Figure 124: Structure of the procedure

The same basic idea can also be applied to FMSs with special pallets, following the procedure presented in figure (124). The first step is to find the average starving times using the CQNBLK procedure - assuming only universal pallets. This step then yields the average transportation times (including idle trip times and the times for disposal trips to the central buffer). The approximation of the transportation times for universal pallets is justified because it can be assumed that the average duration of the transportation processes - in contrast to the duration of the machining processes - is in the most real-life FMSs independent of the type of pallet and the type of workpiece being transported.

The modified transportation times are then input directly into the MVAHEU procedure, and the starving times are added to the average processing times of the pallets at the individual machining stations of the FMS. The MVAHEU procedure is then executed using the modified input data. The results provide an estimation of the performance characteristics of an FMS with special pallets in which starving due to limited local buffers can occur.

This approach was tested on several real-life FMSs with deterministic processing times by using detailed simulation models written in the SIMAN IV simulation language. It was found that the estimations of the starving times under the simplifying assumption of universal pallets is relatively accurate. A few examples will serve for purposes of illustration.

■ **FMS D: FMS with 3 pallet types**

The first FMS comprises five machines and two load/unload stations. Two of the machines (4a and 4b) are identical. Three different pallet types are circulating in the FMS with deterministic processing times and according to predetermined process plans. Since a specific product type is dedicated to each pallet type, it is no longer necessary to perform a random selection of the next workpiece to be mounted on a pallet. All processes in the FMS proceed deterministically. The size of the FMS's central buffer is fixed such that *only starving* could occur. The average transportation time is 2 minutes. This FMS is illustrated in figure (125).

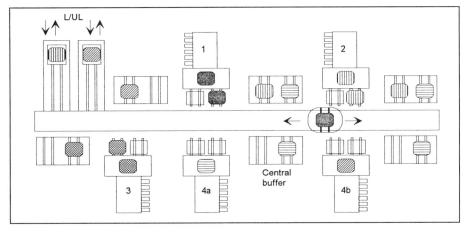

Figure 125: Layout of an FMS with starving and special pallets

Since the load/unload stations do not have any local buffers, it can be expected that starving will occur here. Two different configurations for this particular FMS will be studied. They are characterized by differing numbers of pallets and numbers of vehicles. The following three approaches for the analytical evalua- tion of the performance indicators of the FMS will be applied:

- The classical CQN model for special pallets *without* accounting for *starving* (MVAHEU-O).

- The classical CQN model for special pallets without accounting for starving, yet accounting for *idle and disposal trips* (MVAHEU-Z). The idle and disposal trip times are determined as described in section 3.1.2.5.4.1.1.[231].

- The classical CQN model for special pallets including the pre- vious approximation of the *starving times*, as shown in figure (124) (CQNBLK-MVAHEU).

---

231 This variation will give satisfactory results when starving times are negligible.

In table (48) the pallet type specific production rates, flow times and utilizations of the stations in the FMS are compared to the results from a detailed simulation model. It is assumed here that the FMS includes $N_1=8$, $N_2=2$ and $N_3=4$ pallets and one vehicle.

8/2/4 pallets (1 MHS cart)				
	Simulation	CQNBLK-MVAHEU	MVAHEU-O	MVAHEU-Z
Production rates:				
RATE1	0.02754	0.02822	0.03755	0.03325
RATE2	0.00779	0.00750	0.01075	0.00907
RATE3	0.00964	0.01034	0.01453	0.01258
Flow times:				
TIME1	289	283	213	240
TIME2	255	266	186	220
TIME3	414	386	275	317
Utilizations:				
UTIL-M1	0.48	0.49	0.67	0.59
UTIL-M2	0.23	0.23	0.32	0.27
UTIL-M3	0.18	0.19	0.27	0.23
UTIL-M4	0.44	0.45	0.60	0.53
UTIL-L/UL	0.69	0.69	0.94	0.82
UTIL-MHS	0.76	0.78	0.70	0.93

Table 48: Comparison of results for FMS D, variant A

The analysis of the utilizations shows that the vehicle is the bottleneck in this FMS configuration, and the machines are relatively low utilized. It is to be expected that an increase in the number of pallets, assuming a corresponding increase in the transportation capacity, can improve the production rate of the FMS. Therefore, in the second FMS configuration, the results of which are summarized in table (49), there are now $N_1=10$, $N_2=4$ and $N_3=6$ pallets and two vehicles.

In both cases, the production quantities and utilizations found using the combined CQNBLK-MVAHEU procedure agree quite closely with those from the simulation. The quality of the results is even more surprising considering that in the simulation model all processes of the FMS under study run deterministically, while in both the CQNBLK and the MVAHEU procedures exponentially distributed processing times are assumed. In both FMS variants it is also clear that neither the MVAHEU-O procedure (no accounting for starving or idle and disposal trips) nor the MVAHEU-Z (accounting for idle and disposal trips but not for starving) offered more than a relatively inexact estimate of the performance characteristics of the studied FMS.

10/4/6 pallets (2 MHS carts)				
	Simulation	CQNBLK-MVAHEU	MVAHEU-O	MVAHEU-Z
Production rates:				
RATE1	0.02908	0.02937	0.03513	0.03502
RATE2	0.01195	0.01212	0.01487	0.01481
RATE3	0.01231	0.01266	0.01556	0.01551
Flow times:				
TIME1	343	340	284	285
TIME2	335	330	269	270
TIME3	487	473	385	386
Utilizations:				
UTIL-M1	0.53	0.54	0.66	0.65
UTIL-M2	0.36	0.36	0.45	0.44
UTIL-M3	0.24	0.25	0.31	0.31
UTIL-M4	0.47	0.47	0.57	0.57
UTIL-L/UL	0.81	0.81	0.98	0.98
UTIL-MHS	0.51	0.46	0.37	0.56

Table 49: Comparison of results for FMS D, variant B

- **FMS E:** FMS with 24 pallet types

The second FMS is made up of six identical machines with two local buffers each, one complementary washing machine without a local buffer, and one setup station also without a local buffer. Twenty-four different pallet types represented by two pallets, each, circulate in the FMS, and all are transported by a single rail-guided vehicle. The central buffer is large enough to be able to accept all the pallets in the system, if necessary. Figure (126) is a graphic representation of the layout of this FMS. All workpieces follow the same machine sequence: *(load)-(machine)-(wash)-(reload)-(machine)-(wash)-(unload)*.

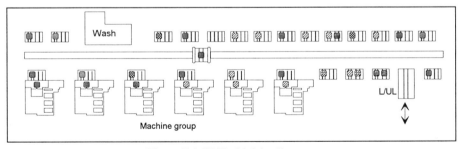

Figure 126: FMS with 24 pallet types

In table (50) and figure (127) the production quantities for each product estimated with the various analytical procedures are compared to the simulation results.

Product	Simulation	CQNBLK-MVAHEU	MVAHEU-O	MVAHEU-Z
1	0.002180	0.002120	0.002638	0.002626
2	0.002130	0.002102	0.002610	0.002599
3	0.002100	0.002102	0.002610	0.002599
4	0.001990	0.001941	0.002370	0.002360
5	0.002180	0.002115	0.002631	0.002619
6	0.002130	0.002041	0.002519	0.002508
7	0.002230	0.002080	0.002577	0.002565
8	0.002100	0.002154	0.002691	0.002678
9	0.002130	0.002178	0.002727	0.002714
10	0.002100	0.002173	0.002720	0.002707
11	0.002130	0.002136	0.002662	0.002650
12	0.002230	0.002113	0.002627	0.002615
13	0.002190	0.002171	0.002716	0.002704
14	0.002170	0.002102	0.002610	0.002599
15	0.002110	0.002041	0.002519	0.002508
16	0.002080	0.001992	0.002445	0.002435
17	0.002030	0.002133	0.002659	0.002647
18	0.002110	0.002127	0.002648	0.002636
19	0.002090	0.001884	0.002286	0.002277
20	0.001970	0.002008	0.002469	0.002458
21	0.002060	0.001986	0.002436	0.002426
22	0.002000	0.001928	0.002350	0.002341
23	0.002120	0.001986	0.002436	0.002426
24	0.001940	0.001928	0.002350	0.002341

Table 50: Production rates

It is clear from this example as well that even a very precise estimate of the average transportation time (MVAHEU-Z) alone *without* taking starving into consideration leads to unsatisfactory results. In this case the production quantities found using MVAHEU-Z differ only slightly from those found using the MVAHEU-O procedure. The reason for this lies in the utilization of the transportation system [see table (51)]. It is so low that an increase in the average transportation time to account for idle trips and trips to the central buffer significantly increases the utilization of the vehicle, yet this has little effect on the other stations.

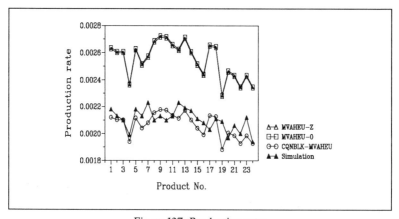

Figure 127: Production rates

	Simulation	CQNBLK/MVAHEU	MVAHEU-O	MVAHEU-Z
UTIL-MC	0.73	0.68	0.84	0.83
UTIL-WASH	0.73	0.80	0.98	0.98
UTIL-L/UL	0.86	0.80	0.98	0.98
UTIL-MHS	0.39	0.41	0.17	0.51

Table 51: Utilizations

On the whole, the results show that when the machines have limited local buffers - and starving is a potential problem - even when the utilization of the transportation system is low, a precise estimation of the average trip times is not sufficient (MVAHEU-Z). It is more important to explicitly consider the development of starving at the individual stations.

Addendum: A special production policy

In evaluating this specific FMS it had been assumed that a particular production policy would be followed. At the beginning of a planning period (a month) the required production quantities for the various products in the FMS would be determined. The system would then begin production with all 24 pallet types. As soon as the desired quantity of one product had been reached, the *two pallets used for that product would be removed from the system* and stored in the central buffer to be re-activated at the beginning of the next planning period. The FMS would then continue processing only the remaining active products whose planned production quantity had not yet been reached. Note that under this policy the number of pallets circulating in the FMS is not constant over time but on the contrary it decreases. This production policy can be analyzed with the help of the CQNBLK-MVAHEU procedure [see figure (128)]. *Kuhn*[232] has successfully applied a similar procedure for the approximation of batch cycle times in connection with release planning.

The considered production policy and the associated analytical approximation were studied using a detailed simulation model. All the input parameters (production quantities, process plans) assumed deterministic values, and the results are shown in figure (129). The completion time of each product type or pallet type in the simulation is marked with a vertical line. The little "flags" at the top of the "flag poles" represent the degree and direction of the deviation of the approximated values from the simulation results. A flag pointing to the left (right) indicates that the approximation found an earlier (later) completion time for that particular pallet type than did the simulation.

232 **Kuhn** (1990), pp. 140-142, p. 146

Procedure COMPLTIME
Iteration 0 (start):

Set of active product types $K=\{1,2,\ldots,24\}$
Initialize the time TNOW=0
Initialize the remaining production quantities: $q_k^1 = q_k$ $k \in K$

Iteration i:

Use procedure CQNBLK-MVAHEU to compute the performance criteria of the FMS with the set **K** of active product types (pallet types). Divide the remaining production quantities by the actual mean production rates to determine the product type that next will have completed its production quantity:

$$j = \arg\min_{k \in K} \{q_k^i / X_k\}$$

Eliminate product j from the set of active product types $K := K - \{j\}$. Compute the completion time of product type j:

$$T_j = TNOW + q_j^i / X_j$$

Update the time, $TNOW = T_j$, and the remaining production quantities:

$$q_k^{i+1} = q_k^i - X_k \cdot q_j^i / X_j \qquad k \in K$$

If $K=\{\}$, STOP; otherwise perform the next iteration.

Figure 128: Procedure for the computation of the expected lot completion times

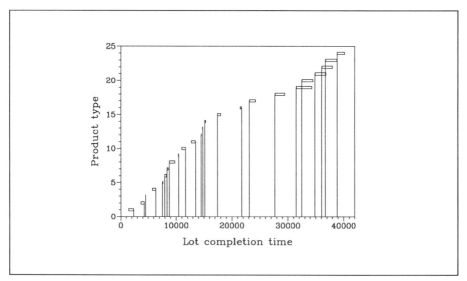

Figure 129: Computed vs. simulated lot completion times

Obviously, such a production policy is not optimal since the number of active pallets sinks over time. It is known, however, from the above discussion of sensitivity analysis that the performance of an FMS is to a large degree dependent on the number of pallets. Yet, this production policy would result in many machines standing idle for lack of work at the end of the planning cycle. This is expressed in figure (130) in which the *utilizations* of the individual system components over time are given.

Every kink in the utilization curves marks a moment when the planned production quantity for a product was reached and the relevant pallets were set aside. As can be seen, the utilization of the six identical machines (MC) tends to sink, but it does also rise at times. This is caused by the fact that the various product types affect the load on the machines in different ways. The rearrangement of the load resulting from a change in the product mix can, in some cases, lead to a more efficient utilization of the machines.

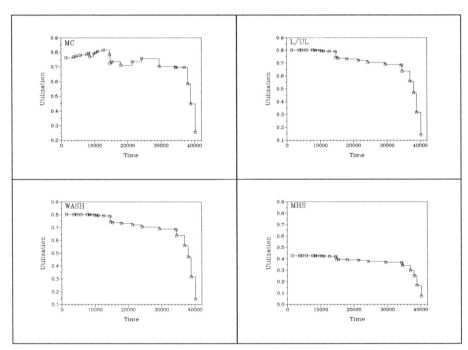

Figure 130: Development of the utilizations over time with a decreasing number of active pallets types

3.1.2.6. Integrating blocking and starving

The approximations for blocking and starving in an FMS described in the previous sections can also be combined. This is necessary when the central buffer is limited, when only limited local buffers are available at the stations, and when - as is usually the case - the speed of the material flow system is finite.

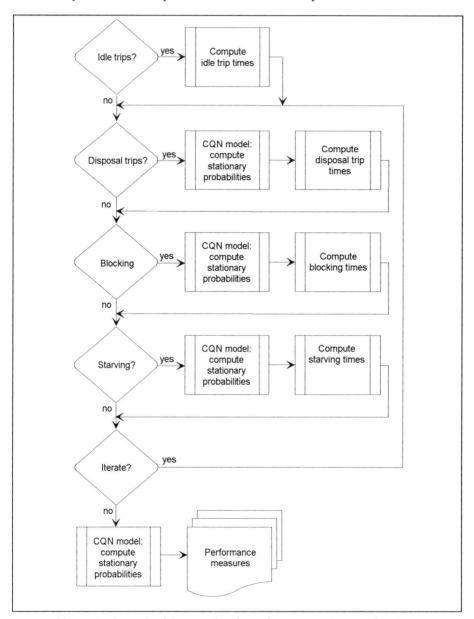

Figure 131: Synopsis of the procedure for performance evaluation of an FMS with limited local buffers

The development of the procedure for estimating all factors affecting both phenomena is depicted in figure (131). The procedure moves through four stages. First, the extent of the *idle trips* must be estimated, then an approximation of the disposal trips between the processing stations and the central buffer must be made. Since the number of disposal trips to be performed depends on how heavily the stations are populated with workpieces, the classical CQN model of the FMS is used to compute the probability distributions of the numbers of pallets at the stations. After completing these two preparatory steps, the extent of blocking and then that of starving are calculated. Since the input data for the CQN model are changed by modifying the average processing times; the results of which (probabilities) are used to estimate disposal trip, blocking and starving times; steps 2 to 4 are repeated iteratively until a stable solution is reached. Finally, all the performance measures (utilizations, flow times, starving times, etc.) are computed.

The quality of this method of accounting for both blocking and starving is demonstrated by using one of the configuration variants of the FMS 4[233]. The transportation times were changed so drastically that some interesting effects can be observed. The average transportation time for supply trips and the disposal trip time to the central buffer are assumed to be $b_M = 0.1$ and $b_Z = 1.0$, respectively. The capacity of the central buffer is $N_{max(CB)} = 10$. Figure (132) illustrates the production rate of the machine M1 for different numbers of pallets in the FMS.

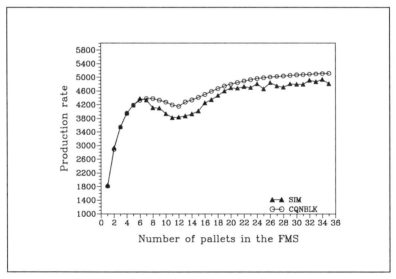

Figure 132: FMS 4 - Production rates of machine M1
(under blocking and starving)

---

233 This FMS is described in detail in section 3.1.2.4.3.

When the number of pallets is small, the production rate tends to increase because blocking does not occur. When the number of pallets rises, a reduction in the production quantity of the machine M1 can be observed. This is attributable to the need for the transportation system to be increasingly concerned with carrying pallets to the central buffer rather than with "productive" activities like keeping the machines supplied with workpieces. Delays in supplying the machines with unprocessed workpieces become more frequent because the transportation vehicle is busy moving between the processing stations and the central buffer. In the extreme, beginning at a certain number of pallets, the major part of the material flow passes through the central buffer since the local buffers tend to be full.

If the number of pallets in the FMS surpasses a certain critical limit - the limit depends on the size of the central buffer - then the central buffer capacity may be exhausted and thus may not be available for the storage of pallets. This, in turn, reduces the demands on the transportation system so that it can be again used for "productive" supply trips to the machines. Blocking might occur in this phase, but the counterproductive effects of starving are outweighed by the productivity enhancing effects of freeing up the transportation system. The changes in the utilization of the transportation system have already been graphically illustrated in figure (115)[234].

This extreme constellation of FMS data is rarely to be found in practice. For example, the central buffer would have to be located far outside the FMS to achieve the indicated relationship between the duration of disposal trips and that of the supply trips between the processing stations. The comparison between the simulation results and the analytical approximation in figure (132) shows, however, that such situations can also be analyzed using the approach described here.

Further reading for section 3.1.2.:

Akyildiz (1988a), (1988b)
Diehl (1984)
Suri/Diehl (1986)
Tempelmeier/Kuhn (1990)
Tempelmeier/Kuhn/Tetzlaff (1989), (1991)
Yao/Buzacott (1985), (1986)
Zhuang/Hindi (1990)

---

234   see section 3.1.2.5.4.1.1.

3.1.3. Performance Evaluation of an FMS under Consideration of Machine Failures

Up to now, it has been assumed that all the components in the FMSs being analyzed are always working with a technical availability of 100%. In practice, however, significant efficiency losses in an FMS may sometimes arise from *technical failures* in *single or several system components*. Due to the high complexity of an FMS, technical failures tend to be more common in FMS than in conventional job shop production systems. It can be assumed, however, that the service personnel can repair the majority of all failures within a couple of minutes, while only a few failures require specialized maintenance personnel and are associated with downtimes longer than several hours.

Two separate approaches have been proposed in the literature to account for the influence of failures or break-downs of machines on the performance characteristics of an FMS[235]:

- Modification of the workpieces' average processing times by the repair times

- Introduction of repair orders that are processed with the highest priorities at the stations

Both approaches are based on a classical CQN model, but additional assumptions must be made: all stations at which machine failures occur consist only of one machine (single server). Only one failure can occur at a time. An accumulation of causes for the failure and the associated extension of the repair time is not possible. Repairs on a machine which has failed must begin immediately without delay. The processing of the workpiece currently on the machining table is interrupted at the moment of the failure and is restarted when the repairs are complete. The repair times (including the actual working time, delays, etc.) of station m are exponentially distributed with a known mean value of $MTTR_m$[236]. The time during which a machine operates without failure, i.e. the time between the completion of a repair and the next failure (time to failure) is also assumed to be exponentially distributed with a mean value of $MTTF_m$[237].

The different modelling approaches proposed in the literature can also be distinguished according to when a failure occurs: only during a machining operation, or also during a period in which the machine is not busy. In the former case, the time to failure depends on the use of the machine (operation-dependent), whereas in the latter case it is influenced only by the total amount of time passed since the last repair (time-dependent).

---

235 A fundamental analysis of failures in the context of *open* queueing systems is given by **Kistner** (1974). **Hopp/Spearman** (1991) present an approach to account for machine failures in a flow shop environment modelled as a closed queueing network. A survey over the problems in the analysis of flow lines and transfer lines with respect to machine failures is provided by **Dallery/Gershwin** (1992).

236 Mean Time To Repair

237 Mean Time To Failure

The technical availability of the machine m, θ_m, can be derived from the mean time to failure and the mean time to repair, as described in equation (154).

$$\theta_m = \frac{MTTF_m}{MTTF_m + MTTR_m} \qquad\qquad m=1,2,\ldots,M \qquad\qquad (154)$$

mean time to repair

mean time to failure

The technical availability of machine m represents the average fraction of time that this machine would be operational if it were operated in isolation.

3.1.3.1. Modification of the processing times

A failure of a machine and the associated repair represent a special kind of capacity loss in which the machine is not available for workpiece processing, yet it can also not be considered idle. Since a workpiece must remain at the machine during a failure until its processing has been completed, failures directly affect the flow times of the workpieces and the production rate of a machine. It is thus possible to account for the influence of a failure on the capacity of a machine by adjusting the processing time.

- *Vinod and Altiok*[238]

developed an approach for the case of machine failures only during the processing of a workpiece (operation-dependent time to failure). As the processing time and the time to failure are random variables, a machine fails when the time to failure is less than the processing time of a workpiece. It is possible that after a repair a machine may break down again before it has finished processing the current workpiece. Indeed, it is theoretically possible that an infinite number of failures may occur during a single machining operation - though the probability of this is negligible. The length of time a machine is occupied is thus made up of a "processing" (uptime) part and a "machine failure" (downtime) part which may include several repair events. This is illustrated with figure (133).

If the probability that a specific number of failures will occur during the processing of one workpiece is known, then (under given probability distributions of the downtimes and the processing times) the completion time of a workpiece at a machine can be found.

---

238   **Vinod/Altiok** (1986)

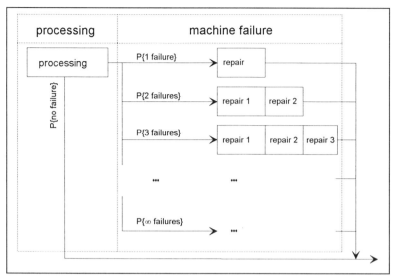

Figure 133: Representation of a station subject to failures

Altiok and *Stidham*[239] show that when all times are exponentially distributed, a workpiece's average completion time at a machine can be determined using equation (155).

$$b_m^a = b_m + \frac{MTTR_m}{MTTF_m} \cdot b_m \qquad\qquad m=1,2,\ldots,M \qquad\qquad (155)$$

with:
- mean repair time → $MTTR_m$
- mean time to failure → $MTTF_m$
- mean processing time → b_m

The relationship between the mean time to repair and the mean time to failure expresses the degree to which each unit of usable productive time must be adjusted for repair time. The mean time to repair for a workpiece during processing can be found through multiplication of this quotient by the average processing time. Adding both quantities gives the average completion time at a machine, b^a_m.

The completion time can now be interpreted as a modified processing time in a queueing model. It is no longer exponentially distributed, however. Therefore the M/M/1 queueing model is no longer an appropriate representation of a machine. Instead the M/G/1 model can be used, since it allows for arbitrary probability distributions of the processing times.

239   **Altiok/Stidham** (1983), p. 294; **Vinod/Altiok** (1986), p. 311

The squared coefficient of variation[240] of the above described completion time is given by equation (156)[241].

$$CV_m^{a^2} = \frac{2 \cdot MTTF_m}{b_m \cdot \left[1 + \frac{MTTF_m}{MTTR_m}\right]^2} + 1 \qquad\qquad m=1,2,\dots,M \qquad\qquad (156)$$

Altiok and *Stidham*[242] have shown that under the above-mentioned assumptions, the length of a workpiece's completion time at a station follows a two-stage Coxian distribution with the parameters {length of phase 1: Ω_{1m}, length of phase 2: Ω_{2m}, probability of reaching phase 2: α_m}. These are described by equations (157)-(159).

$$\Omega_{1m} = b_m \cdot (1-\alpha_m) \qquad\qquad m=1,2,\dots,M \qquad\qquad (157)$$
$\uparrow$ mean length of phase 1

$$\Omega_{2m} = \frac{MTTR_m}{1-\alpha_m} \qquad\qquad m=1,2,\dots,M \qquad\qquad (158)$$
$\uparrow$ mean length of phase 2

$$\alpha_m = \frac{1}{2} - \frac{MTTR_m}{2 \cdot MTTF_m} - \frac{MTTR_m}{2 \cdot b_m} + \frac{1}{2} \cdot \sqrt{\left[1 + \frac{MTTR_m}{MTTF_m} + \frac{MTTR_m}{b_m}\right]^2 - \frac{4 \cdot MTTR_m}{b_m}} \qquad m=1,2,\dots,M \qquad (159)$$
$\uparrow$ probability of the occurrence of phase 2

The mean value of a two-stage Coxian distributed random variable is:

$$b_m^a = \Omega_{1m} + \alpha_m \cdot \Omega_{2m} \qquad\qquad m=1,2,\dots,M \qquad\qquad (160)$$

The completion time of a workpiece at a machine can thus be determined by adding two exponentially distributed random variables, Ω_{1m} and Ω_{2m}, with the second variable only appearing with a probability of α_m [see figure (134)].

If the described transformation of the completion time is performed for all stations at which failures could occur, then the result is an equivalent closed queueing network of the FMS whose nodes have the structure depicted in figure (134). This equivalent queueing network is shown in figure (135). The average (modified) processing time is given by equation (155) or (160). Since the modified processing times at the stations are *not exponentially distributed*, the closed queueing network no longer has a product form. The *exact* calculation of the key performance characteristics of the closed queueing network is, therefore, not possible.

---

240 The coefficient of variation of a random variable is defined as the standard deviation divided by the mean.
241 **Vinod/Altiok** (1986), p. 311
242 **Altiok/Stidham** (1983), p. 294

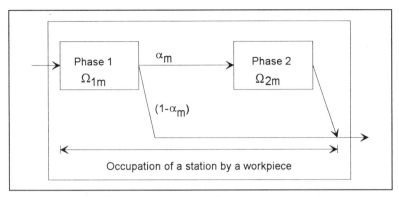

*Figure 134: Completion time of a workpiece at a station
described by a two-stage Coxian distribution*

Vinod and Altiok propose, as an approximation, to evaluate with one of the algorithms described in section 3.1.1.1.2. the CQN model shown in figure (135) with
the average processing times modified according to equation (155)[243]. Such an
approach certainly has the advantage that the extra work involved in accounting
for machine failures is restricted to the adjustment of the input data. The results
of numerical investigations provided by *Vinod and Altiok* agree quite well with
the corresponding simulation results.

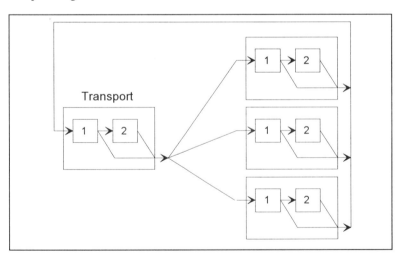

Figure 135: CQN model with machine failures

For purposes of illustration, consider the FMS from example 3-1. The aggregate
description of this system is again summarized in table (52).

---

243 **Vinod/Altiok** (1986)

m	p_m	b_m	
1	0.5	90.00	L/UL
2	0.1	295.67	M2
3	0.4	193.33	M1
4	1.0	5.90	AGV
Number of pallets (N): 4			

Table 52: Data for the FMS of example 3-1

It is assumed that the machines M1 and M2 exhibit two different failure and re-pair patterns. The first pattern is characterized by the fact that the machines fail in exponentially distributed intervals (time to failure) averaging MTTF = $MTTF_2 = MTTF_3 = 60$ minutes. Varying exponentially distributed repair times averaging $MTTR = MTTR_2 = MTTR_3$ between 5 and 240 minutes are also assumed, though these are identical for both machines. The technical availability is thus *identical for both machines* and lies between 20% and 92%. The completion times, modified according to equation (155) for both machines, and the squared coefficients of variation are compiled in table (53). The assumed values cover a wide range of possible (and occasionally extremely inconvenient) failure scenarios. It may be pointed out, however, that the squared coefficient of variation is relatively small for this failure and repair pattern.

			M2	M1	M2	M1
MTTR	MTTF	Availa-bility	b_2^a	b_3^a	cv_2^{a2}	cv_3^{a2}
5	60	0.92	320.31	209.44	1.00	1.00
10	60	0.86	344.95	225.55	1.01	1.01
15	60	0.80	369.59	241.66	1.02	1.02
20	60	0.75	394.23	257.77	1.03	1.04
25	60	0.71	418.87	273.88	1.04	1.05
30	60	0.67	443.51	290.00	1.05	1.07
60	60	0.50	591.34	386.66	1.10	1.16
90	60	0.40	739.18	483.33	1.15	1.22
120	60	0.33	887.01	579.99	1.18	1.28
180	60	0.25	1182.68	773.32	1.23	1.35
240	60	0.20	1478.35	966.65	1.26	1.40

Table 53: Completion times at the stations M2 and M1 with varying downtimes (failure and repair pattern 1)

In order to test the quality of the *Vinod and Altiok* approach, a simulation model of the FMS will be used in which the *random failures* of both stations are considered in addition to the *deterministic machining operations*. For every value of the mean time to repair $MTTR = MTTR_2 = MTTR_3$ ten independent simulation runs are carried out covering 1,000,000 minutes of simulated time. The results for the failure data given in table (53) are presented in figure (136). The line connects the average values from the simulation runs. The rectangles indicate the 95% confidence interval, and the vertical lines represent the range of the simulated production quantities of the FMS.

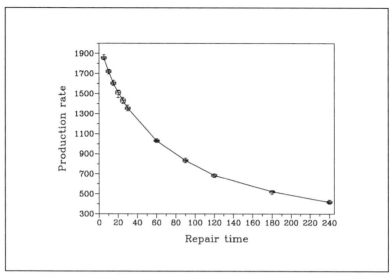

*Figure 136: Simulation results for example 3-1 with failures at the
stations M2 and M1 (failure and repair pattern 1)*

The *production quantities* of the FMS calculated with the *Vinod/Altiok* approach
(CQN-V/A) are compared to the simulation results (SIM) in table (54) and figure (137). All the production quantities are based on a period of 1,000,000 minutes. As was to be expected, the production rate of the FMS with machine failures is less than that calculated without accounting for failures[244].

MTTR	CQN-V/A	SIM	Diff (%)
5	1834	1854	1.11
10	1720	1719	-0.06
15	1618	1603	-0.94
20	1527	1510	-1.14
25	1445	1430	-1.03
30	1371	1353	-1.30
60	1043	1031	-1.23
90	840	832	-0.95
120	702	683	-2.83
180	528	522	-1.24
240	423	418	-1.31

*Table 54: Comparison of simulated production rates for example 3-1 with the values computed
with the Vinod and Altiok approach
(failure and repair pattern 1)*

The results show a high degree of agreement. This is even true for the extremely
low availabilities of the two machines, something that would be rare in practice.

---

244 See table (12), section 3.1.1.1.2.

It should be noted, however, that the squared coefficient of variation deviated only slightly from 1, the value for exponential distributions.

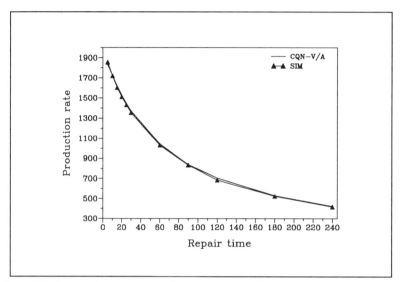

Figure 137: Comparison of simulated production rates for example 3-1 with the values computed using the Vinod and Altiok approach (failure and repair pattern 1)

In order to test the robustness of the *Vinod and Altiok* approach, a *second failure and repair pattern* for the FMS from example 3-1 will be considered. This pattern has significantly higher values for the squared coefficient of variation. The relevant data are combined in table (55).

			M2	M1	M2	M1
MTTR	MTTF	Availa-bility	b_2^a	b_3^a	CV_2^{a2}	CV_3^{a2}
100	1200	0.92	320.31	209.44	1.05	1.07
200	1200	0.86	344.95	225.55	1.17	1.25
300	1200	0.80	369.59	241.66	1.33	1.50
400	1200	0.75	394.23	257.77	1.51	1.78
500	1200	0.71	418.87	273.88	1.70	2.07
600	1200	0.67	443.51	290.00	1.90	2.38
1200	1200	0.50	591.34	386.66	3.03	4.10
1800	1200	0.40	739.18	483.33	3.92	5.47
2400	1200	0.33	887.01	579.99	4.61	6.52
3600	1200	0.25	1182.68	773.32	5.57	7.98
4800	1200	0.20	1478.35	966.65	6.20	8.95

Table 55: Completion times at the stations M2 and M1 with varying downtimes (failure and repair pattern 2)

Significantly longer times to failure and repair times will be assumed in this failure and repair pattern. The machine failures occur less frequently, but when they do occur they last much longer. The relationship between the two quantities is such that the same availability θ_m applies here as did to the first failure and repair pattern. In an extreme case, the mean time to repair is 4800 minutes (= 80 hours). Since the repair times are exponentially distributed, a real machine failure could last significantly longer.

The values taken in the second failure and repair pattern for this example with relatively long completion times are not likely to be very common in industrial practice. They were chosen in order to test the quality of the *Vinod and Altiok* approach for FMSs in which the repair times are long relative to the processing times. This can be true for FMSs with relatively short average processing times. Serious doubts about the economic advantages of an automated production system would arise for an FMS with data constellations having the low availabilities exhibited in the example FMS - including those in the first failure and repair pattern.

The simulation results are shown in figure (138). For each mean time to repair between 100 and 500 minutes 10 simulation runs were executed for 1,000,000 simulated minutes. For the remaining repair times (≥ 600 minutes) the lengths of the runs were increased to 5,000,000 minutes to enhance the statistical validity of the simulation results.

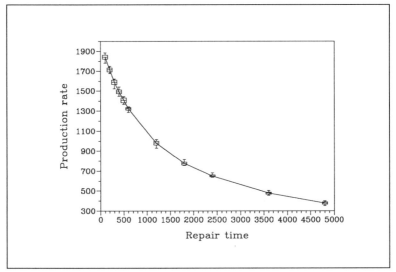

Figure 138: Simulation results for example 3-1 with failures at the stations M2 and M1 (failure and repair pattern 2)

Table (56) and figure (139) compare the analytically calculated results with those of the simulation.

MTTR	CQN-V/A	SIM	Diff (%)
100	1834	1841	0.38
200	1720	1714	-0.35
300	1618	1590	-1.76
400	1527	1492	-2.35
500	1445	1408	-2.63
600	1371	1323	-3.62
1200	1043	980	-6.43
1800	840	776	-8.25
2400	702	651	-7.83
3600	528	477	-10.69
4800	423	378	-11.90

Table 56: Comparison of simulated production rates for example 3-1 with the values computed by the Vinod and Altiok approach (failure and repair pattern 2)

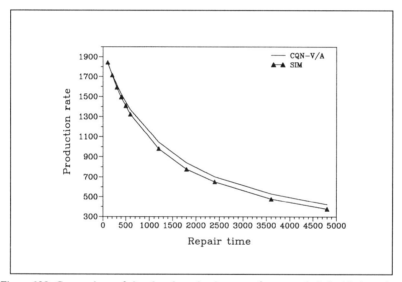

Figure 139: Comparison of simulated production rates for example 3-1 with the values computed by the Vinod and Altiok approach (failure and repair pattern 2)

The analytical results are the same for both failure and repair patterns since in the *Vinod and Altiok* method (CQN-V/A) the coefficients of variation are not considered. The quality of the approximation is good for the first failure and repair pattern, even for extremely low availabilities at both machines. In the second failure and repair pattern, however, the values deviate significantly at availabilities under 50%.

The quality of the approximation depends primarily on the coefficient of variation of the completion times. While a coefficient of variation of 1 is assumed in the analytical model, according to the exponential distribution assumption, the actual coefficients of variation deviate significantly from 1. The deviations increase with the ratio of the mean repair time to the average processing time.

This becomes clear when the equation for the squared coefficient of variation is rewritten [see equation (161)].

$$CV_m^{a^2} = \frac{2}{\dfrac{b_m}{MTTF_m} + \dfrac{2 \cdot b_m}{MTTR_m} + \dfrac{b_m \cdot MTTF_m}{MTTR_m^2}} + 1 \qquad\qquad m=1,2,\ldots,M \qquad (161)$$

The coefficient of variation is significantly greater than 1 when the mean time to repair is large relative to the average processing time and/or to the mean time to failure. In such cases, significant errors - overestimates - can be made in assessing the performance of an FMS using the *Vinod and Altiok* method.

One way of including *generally distributed service times* (completion times) and explicitly considering their coefficients of variation in a node of a closed queueing network may be found in the approach suggested by

• *Agrawal, Buzen and Shum*[245].

This method can be combined with the *Vinod and Altiok* approach and be applied to FMSs with machine failures.

Vinod and Altiok approximate the two-stage Coxian-distributed completion time of a workpiece at machine m via an exponential distribution with a mean value according to equation (155). *Agrawal, Buzen and Shum*, on the other hand, suggest fixing the average service time at a machine with reference to an M/G/1 queueing model in such a way that the average flow time that would result from an analysis of the machine with the M/M/1 queueing model is identical to that resulting from an analysis of the machine as an M/G/1 queueing system.

A station with generally distributed service times is thus replaced by an equivalent station, with respect to the flow time, having exponentially distributed and modified service times. The average flow time of a customer (workpiece) in an M/G/1 queueing system can be found using the Pollaczek-Khintchine formula[246] [see equation (162)].

$$D_{(M/G/1)m} = b_m^a + \frac{(1+CV_m^{a^2}) \cdot b_m^a \cdot U_m}{2 \cdot (1-U_m)} \qquad\qquad m=1,2,\ldots,M \qquad (162)$$

The utilization U_m of station m, according to the *Agrawal, Buzen and Shum* proposal, is calculated after evaluating the entire closed queueing network under the assumption of exponentially distributed service times (classical CQN model).

The average flow time of a station with exponentially distributed service times (M/M/1 queueing system) is given by equation (163)[247].

---

245 **Agrawal/Buzen/Shum** (1984), pp. 64-65
246 **Kleinrock** (1975), p. 191
247 **Kleinrock** (1975), p. 190

$$D_{(M/M/1)m} = \frac{b_m^a}{1-X_m \cdot b_m^a} \qquad\qquad m=1,2,\ldots,M \qquad\qquad (163)$$

To prevent distortions in the mean flow times, the average flow time of the M/M/1 station must be equal to that of the M/G/1 station, according to equation (164).

$$D_{(M/G/1)m} = D_{(M/M/1)m}$$

$$= \frac{b_m^{a*}}{1-X_m \cdot b_m^{a*}} \qquad\qquad m=1,2,\ldots,M \qquad\qquad (164)$$

After rewriting equation (164), equation (165) can be used to find the desired *modified service time* of the M/M/1 node. This can then be used in the classical CQN model as the average service time of a workpiece at a machine under conditions of generally distributed service times.

$$b_m^{a*} = \frac{D_{(M/G/1)m}}{1+X_m \cdot D_{(M/G/1)m}} \qquad\qquad m=1,2,\ldots,M \qquad\qquad (165)$$

Since the utilizations of the stations change along with the modification of the service times in accordance to equation (165), and since the flow times computed with the Pollaczek-Khintchine formula [equation (162)] change, both equations and the production rates X_m of all the stations will be iteratively calculated until the production rates differ only insignificantly from one iteration to the next. The utilization of the stations must then be calculated using the completion times from equation (155), as shown in equation (166).

$$U_m = \frac{X_m}{b_m^a} \qquad\qquad m=1,2,\ldots,M \qquad\qquad (166)$$

In this way the *Vinod and Altiok* approach, as modified according to the *Agrawal, Buzen and Shum* proposal, can be described as follows [see figure (140)].

Procedure V/A-ABS
Iteration 0:
Compute the mean completion times of workpieces at the stations with equation (155) and the squared coefficients of variation according to equation (156). Compute utilizations and production rates of the FMS using the classical CQN model.
Iteration 1:
For each station subject to failures (resulting in a coefficient of variation that differs significantly from 1), compute the mean flow time $D_{(M/G/1)m}$ according to equation (162). Adjust the completion times at the stations according to equation (165). Compute the FMS performance indicators based on the classical CQN model. If the FMS production rate changed by less than ϵ, STOP; otherwise perform another iteration.

Figure 140: Integration of the approaches proposed by Agrawal, Buzen and Shum and by Vinod and Altiok

To test the suitability of integrating the *Agrawal, Buzen and Shum* concept into the *Vinod and Altiok* approach, the FMS from example 3-1 will be revisited. In table (57) the results for both repair and failure patterns are summarized.

Availa-bility	CQN-V/A pattern 1 and 2	Pattern 1			Pattern 2		
		V/A-ABS	SIM	Diff (%)	V/A-ABS	SIM	Diff (%)
0.92	1834	1833	1854	1.13	1829	1841	0.65
0.86	1720	1720	1719	-0.06	1707	1714	0.41
0.80	1618	1618	1603	-0.94	1596	1590	-0.38
0.75	1527	1526	1510	-1.06	1497	1492	-0.34
0.71	1445	1443	1430	-0.91	1407	1408	0.07
0.67	1371	1369	1353	-1.18	1327	1326	-0.08
0.50	1043	1041	1031	-0.97	981	974	-0.72
0.40	840	837	832	-0.60	774	770	-0.52
0.33	702	700	683	-2.49	637	661	3.63
0.25	528	526	522	-0.77	469	469	0.00
0.20	423	421	418	-0.72	370	356	-3.93

Table 57: Comparison of simulated production rates for example 3-1 with the values computed with the procedure V/A-ABS

A portion of the results is shown in figure (141). Obviously the combination of the two proposals from *Agrawal, Buzen and Shum* and from *Vinod and Altiok* produces far better estimates of the production quantities in the second repair and failure pattern (the one associated with relatively high coefficients of variation[248]) than the *Vinod and Altiok* proposal in its original form in which the variation of the completion times is neglected. The two procedures can be considered nearly equivalent for the first failure and repair pattern.

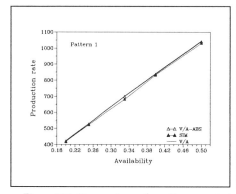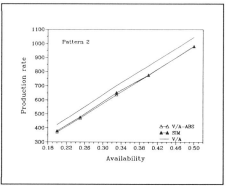

Figure 141: Comparison of results computed with the Agrawal, Buzen and Shum approach (example 3-1)

Another way to model an FMS with machine failures as a closed queueing network with generally distributed service times that can also be applied in combination with the *Vinod and Altiok* procedure has been proposed by

- *Reiser*[249].

Here equation (87) is used to find a workpiece's *residual processing time*.

When the processing times are exponentially distributed, the average residual processing time upon arrival of a type c pallet at station m, br_{cm}, is equal to the mean processing time b_{cm}. If the squared coefficient of variation is no longer equal to one, then the estimate of the average residual processing time used in equation (88), as seen by the arriving type c pallet, must be modified as follows:

$$WO^a_{cm} \approx \sum_{j=1}^{C}\left[U_{jm}\cdot b^a_{jm}\cdot\frac{1+CV^{a^2}_{jm}}{2}\right] - U_{cm}\cdot b^a_{cm}\cdot\frac{1+CV^{a^2}_{cm}}{2\cdot N_c} \qquad \begin{array}{l} c=1,2,\ldots,C; \\ m=1,2,\ldots,M\,|\,S_m=1 \end{array} \qquad (167)$$

The estimate of the residual processing time upon arrival of a type c pallet at station m, as revised according to equation (167), can be exchanged for the approximation of the average residual processing time described in section 3.1.1.2.2. [see equation (87)].

Kuhn tested the described modification of the heuristic mean value analysis in a simulation experiment and found that it provides satisfactory results for coeffi-

248 With the failure and repair patterns considered here, high coefficients of variation coincide mainly with low technical availabilities. However, high coefficients of variation may also exist with high technical availabilities.

249 **Reiser** (1979), p. 1204

cients of variation of $CV_{jm} < 2^{250}$. As can be seen in the example considered here, however, *Reiser*'s proposal yields inadequate approximations of the production quantity for the second failure and repair pattern [see table (58)]. This may be partially due to the fact that the processing times during the simulation were set according to deterministic process plans in order to model the operations performed in an FMS as realistically as possible.

Availa-bility	CQN-V/A pattern 1 and 2	Pattern 1			Pattern 2		
		SIM	V/A-REIS	Diff (%)	SIM	V/A-REIS	Diff (%)
0.92	1834	1854	1780	3.99	1841	1768	3.97
0.86	1720	1719	1665	3.14	1714	1629	4.96
0.80	1618	1603	1563	2.50	1590	1499	5.72
0.75	1527	1510	1471	2.58	1492	1381	7.44
0.71	1445	1430	1389	2.87	1408	1277	9.30
0.67	1371	1353	1315	2.81	1326	1184	10.71
0.50	1043	1031	993	3.69	974	813	16.53
0.40	840	832	795	4.45	770	613	20.39
0.33	702	683	663	2.93	661	492	25.57
0.25	528	522	496	4.98	469	351	25.16
0.20	423	418	397	5.02	356	273	23.31

Table 58: Comparison of the simulated production rates with the values computed with the Vinod and Altiok procedure supplemented according to Reiser (example 3-1)

The *Vinod and Altiok* approach, as supplemented according to *Reiser*, provides worse estimates for this particular FMS than either the original *Vinod and Altiok* procedure or its revision in line with the *Agrawal, Buzen and Shum* concept. It must be pointed out, however, that the *Reiser* revision may also be applied to the study of *FMSs with special pallets*, and that the results for the first failure and repair pattern - even for extremely unfavorable availabilities - are relatively accurate.

If the results presented here are considered in addition to the discussion found in the literature on the achievable quality of a performance approximation of an FMS with machine failures, then it can be assumed that the *Vinod and Altiok* procedure will yield good estimates for most realistic failure and repair patterns. For extremely high coefficients of variation, the relatively easy to implement modification of the completion times according to *Agrawal, Buzen and Shum* may be used. The *Reiser* modification to the *Vinod and Altiok* approach is the most appropriate for FMSs with special pallets.

Both the concepts from *Agrawal, Buzen and Shum* and from *Reiser* are not exclusively applicable to cases of machine failures, as described in this section. They can also be used when the squared coefficient of variation of the processing times at a station deviates from 1. This is the case, for example, under constant processing times.

---

250 **Kuhn** (1990), p. 144

3.1.3.2. Introduction of repair orders

The second possible way to account for machine failures in the analysis of an FMS is to interpret a failure and the associated repair as a special form of a production order, and to model the machines' failures with machine-specific repair orders.

• *Vinod and Solberg*[251]

have proposed such a concept. The closed queueing network of the FMS can, in this case, be presented as in figure (142).

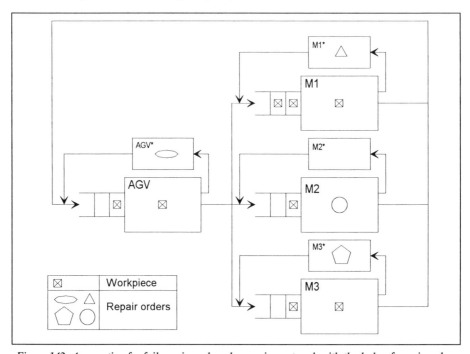

Figure 142: Accounting for failures in a closed queueing network with the help of repair orders

Every station m of the closed queueing network is assigned a delay server m*, i.e. a server where no queueing occurs. A station-specific repair order, represented in figure (142) by circles, polygons, etc., circulates between station m and its associated delay server. The repair order represents the machine failure and the repair. The repair order is kept at the delay server m* between two consecutive failures of station m. The "processing time" at the station m* is thus equal to the time to failure of the station m. The "processing time" of the repair order at the machining station m is equal to the time to repair beginning from a failure at station m. Thus, for every station m there is a separate repair order which is

---

251 **Vinod/Solberg** (1984); see also **Widmer/Solot** (1990)

modelled as a special pallet type. In an FMS with C different "real" pallet types, there would be C+M "real" and "artificial" pallet types. Each "artificial" pallet type circulates with one pallet between the stations m and m*.

One special problem that arises in this type of modelling is that when a failure occurs (i.e. when a delay period at station m* ends) a station generally fails immediately[252]. This means that the workpiece currently being processed at station m is displaced by the repair order. Processing can restart when the station has been brought back into its original working condition. The queueing discipline is no longer first come first served (FCFS), but rather a discipline with preemption in favor of the repair order. Such a closed queueing network model has no product form, however, so the exact performance indicators of the CQN model can no longer be determined.

For the heuristic determination of the key performance parameters of the FMS it is assumed that a machine's time to failure (the time period between completing a repair on a machine and its next failure) is relatively long compared to the processing time of a workpiece. In this case, it can be assumed that a machine breaks down only *once* during a particular operation[253]. It is thus no longer necessary to include the preemption of a workpiece currently being processed into the failure model. Instead, it is sufficient to assume that the repair order is carried out directly after a workpiece's processing has been completed. A repair order can thus be interpreted as an order with the highest priority that will be processed before all other waiting workpieces. An heuristic procedure for evaluating a CQN model with other than FCFS queueing disciplines has been proposed by *Shalev-Oren, Seidmann, and Schweitzer*. It is a variation of the mean value analysis, called PMVA[254] in which differing priorities of the waiting workpieces can be considered.

Aside from excluding the possibility of more than one machine failure during the processing of a workpiece, the model according to the *Vinod and Solberg* proposal also excludes consideration of the fact that the time to failure is also influenced by the utilization (busy time) of a station. In the model shown in figure (142) the possibility that a machine may fail is independent of when the machine is actually used, i.e. the timing of the next machine failure depends only on how much time has past since the last repair (time-dependent failures).

If the time to failure is indeed dependent on the *completion time* at a processing station (operation-dependent failures), this can then be accounted for in the iterative PMVA procedure by modifying the service time of the repair order at the artificial station m* (time to failure) with the utilization of station m according to equation (168).

---

252 Some failures may allow completion of the processing of the current workpiece, however (delayed failures). **Kistner** (1974), p. 19

253 In the model presented in section 3.1.3.1. this was not assumed. In the simulation model used for the example considered here, it is possible that a machine may fail several times during the processing of a particular workpiece.

254 Priority-Mean-Value-Analysis; **Shalev-Oren/Seidmann/Schweitzer** (1985), pp. 126-128

$$MTTF_m^{\star} = \frac{MTTF_m}{\sum\limits_{c=1}^{C} U_{cm}} \qquad\qquad m=1,2,\ldots,M \qquad\qquad (168)$$

In table (59) the results from the *Vinod and Solberg* approach for the example from section 3.1.3.1., where the time to failure is operation-dependent (MVA-V/S), are compared to the simulation results for the failure and repair patterns 1 and 2.

Availa- bility	Pattern 1			Pattern 2		
	MVA-V/S	SIM	Diff (%)	MVA-V/S	SIM	Diff (%)
0.92	1879	1854	-1.34	1809	1841	1.74
0.86	1849	1719	-7.56	1697	1714	0.99
0.80	1820	1603	-13.54	1583	1590	0.44
0.75	1790	1510	-18.54	1473	1492	1.27
0.71	1760	1430	-23.08	1371	1408	2.62
0.67	1729	1353	-27.79	1278	1326	3.62
0.50	1548	1031	-50.15	886	974	9.03
0.40	1374	832	-65.14	669	770	13.12
0.33	1218	683	-78.33	537	661	18.76
0.25	968	522	-85.44	382	469	18.55
0.20	795	418	-90.19	297	356	16.57

Table 59: Comparison of the simulated production rates with the values computed with the Vinod and Solberg approach

Observe that the production quantity is systematically overestimated for the first failure and repair pattern. The quality of the approximation is significantly better for the second pattern. Here, the mean time to failure is, in most cases, much longer than the average processing time. It therefore becomes less important to include multiple machine failures during workpiece processing.

Figure (143) provides an overview of all the approaches discussed here that can account for machine failures by changing the processing times of the workpieces at the stations or by adding repair orders to the system.

It must be kept in mind that all the procedures described here have been designed for *stations with only a single machine*. The authors believe, however, that the discussed approaches should be transferable, at least approximately, to stations with several machines (multiple server stations).

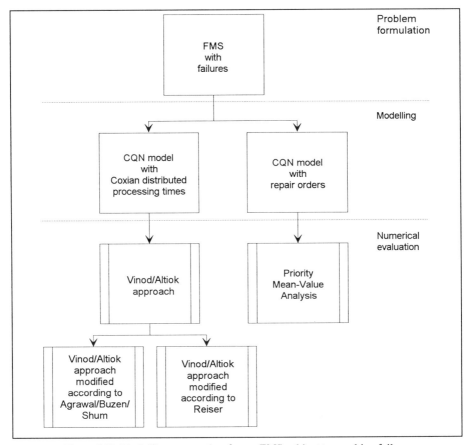

Figure 143: Modelling approaches for an FMS subject to machine failures

Further reading for section 3.1.3.:

Agrawal/Buzen/Shum (1984)
Hopp/Spearman(1991)
Kistner (1974)
Kuhn (1990)
Reiser (1979)
Vinod/Altiok (1986)
Vinod/Solberg (1984)
Widmer/Solot (1990)

3.2. FMS-EVAL - A SOFTWARE SYSTEM FOR RAPID MODELLING OF FLEXIBLE MANUFACTURING SYSTEMS

Obviously, the procedures for evaluating the performance of FMSs described in the previous sections are only of practical value to an industrial FMS planner if they are available on the planner's desktop as a ready-to-use performance evaluation tool.

Each of the algorithms presented has been, therefore, implemented in a software package named *FMS-Eval* running on an industrial standard personal computer under MS-Windows. This software package is designed to support the system planner's iterative procedure of incrementally changing the configuration of an FMS until the desired performance criteria are met. It supports primarily two tasks:

- *Definition of an FMS configuration.* Here the input data for the analytical performance evaluation procedures are defined (process plans, components of the FMS, number of pallets, etc.).

- *Numerical performance evaluation.* Here an appropriate numerical algorithm for the FMS under study is applied. This produces the key performance parameters required for the evaluation of the FMS design alternative considered.

The structure of the *FMS-Eval* software system is shown in figure (144). Aside from the numerical performance analysis of an FMS design alternative using one of the procedures described in the previous sections, an MS-Windows-based user interface is provided to input and edit the description of an FMS configuration, to start the numerical evaluation procedures and to graph the results in a user-friendly manner. The description of an FMS is saved in a file from which the algorithm-specific input data are generated.

In addition to the procedures specifically designed for the analysis of FMSs, another computational method based on the exact mean value analysis approach for the performance evaluation of *flexible transfer lines*[255] is implemented as well.

The structure of the *FMS-Eval* software system is modular so that future developments of algorithms for the computation of FMS performance measures may easily be implemented under the common user interface.

---

255 This procedure is applicable to flexible production lines with universal pallets and a transportation system with infinite capacity (delay server).

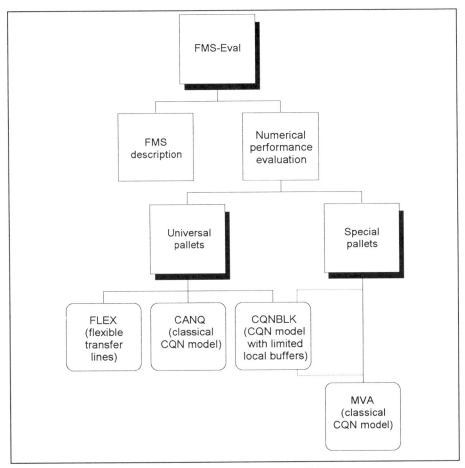

Figure 144: Software structure of FMS-Eval

Figure (145) shows how various FMS configurations can be generated in an iterative process and evaluated using an approximation procedure. Starting with a given FMS design alternative, the input data needed for the procedure to be used for the approximation of the key performance parameters must be generated. After applying the procedure and interpreting the results, it is decided whether or not the performance parameters of the observed FMS configuration alternative are satisfactory. If they are not, then the configuration is modified, e.g. the number of machines, the number of pallets or some other design variables may be changed, and the performance parameters are calculated anew. This is repeated until a satisfactory configuration is found, or until it can be determined that this type of FMS would be basically inappropriate for the particular application under consideration. In such a situation, it may be necessary to

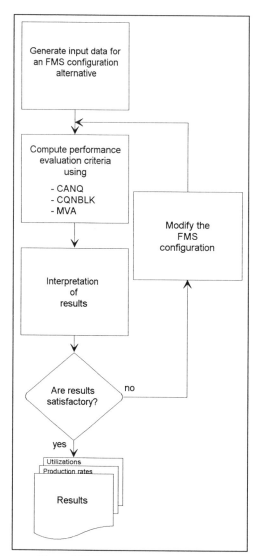

Figure 145: Evaluation process of FMS
configurations

return to the technological planning phase in which the technical framework of the planned FMS is modified.

The work with the software system *FMS-Eval* will be explained below using several *screen* snapshots. The user interface is designed such that even the occasional operator can use the software system without difficulty.

The functionality can be logically divided into a *description (data input) component* and an *analysis (computation of performance indicators) component*. The first step is to provide a description of the FMS under consideration and store it in an FMS definition file that may be edited later on. The FMS definition file includes information about the machines, load/unload area, pallet types, product types, process plans and the transportation system.

Before an appropriate algorithm for the performance evaluation of the FMS is started, in addition to the characteristics of the FMS configuration under consideration several options for the current computational experiment can be set. These options refers to the generation of an experimental log file and to the extent of the output to be generated, depending on the performance algorithm applied.

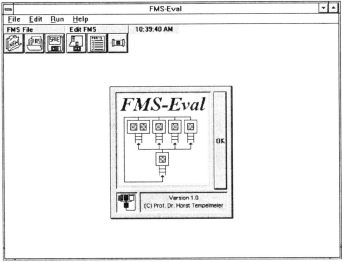

Figure 146: Main screen of FMS-Eval

3.2.1. Data Input - Description of a Flexible Manufacturing System

The definition of an FMS configuration alternative may start either with an existing FMS description file or with a template providing the basis for a *new FMS description*. The following quantities, among others, must be entered or changed in order to describe the FMS alternative under consideration:

· *Type and number of processing stations.*
· *Characteristics of the transportation system (number of vehicles) and possibly distances between stations.*
· *Product types, production ratios, pallet types.*
· *Process plans.*
· *Number of pallet types and number of pallets per pallet type.*

In the following some of the screens that are displayed during the FMS definition are shown. The easiest way to start defining an FMS alternative is to click on a button located in the file group on the tool bar. First, the different types of *stations* to be included in the FMS[256] are defined. The description of the processing stations is shown in figure (147).

A station (machine type) in the FMS is characterized primarily by the number of identical machines and the size of the local buffer. Information may also be provided about the machine's *failure and repair pattern*. This is used to correct the

---

256 This file contains the description of the FMS (**T**urbolader-**Ge**häuse-**Fa**brik) owned by BBC, Baden, published by Solot and Bastos. **Solot/Bastos** (1988)

average processing times at the machines for the effects of any breakdowns. The *Vinod and Altiok* approach described in section 3.1.3.1. is implemented.

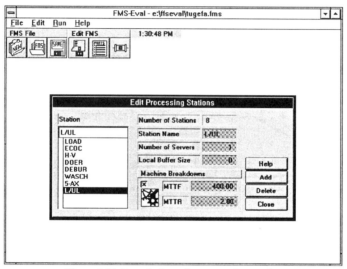

Figure 147: Description of a processing station

Next the *product types* that will be processed in the FMS are described. Upon selection of the product edit window [see figure (148)], the actual FMS description file is scanned for definitions of products.

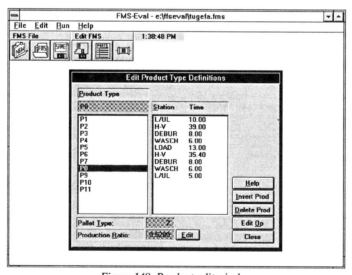

Figure 148: Product edit window

Whenever the cursor is scrolled through the product type list box, the associated process plan is shown in the list box on the right-hand side of the window and the desired *production ratio* and the *pallet type* used for this product are indicated. The user may click on an operation and edit the data of the selected operation, delete it or insert a new operation into the process plan [see figure (149)]. In another window not depicted the user is presented a simultaneous graphical view on the production ratios for all the product types assigned to a given pallet type.

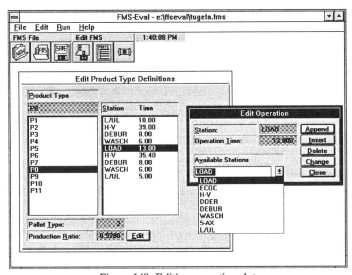

Figure 149: Editing operation data

The next step is the description of the transportation system. Here, the *number of vehicles* and the average transportation time are most important. The mean transportation time may be entered by the user or computed with reference to the distances between the stations and the process plans which are used to provide a rough estimation of the workload of the transportation system.

In addition to the transportation time, the mean pallet shifting time between a vehicle and a workstation may be specified. A check box may be set to include idle trip times. For an FMS with limited local buffers the mean disposal trip time (transportation between a workstation and the central buffer) may be entered. These components of the total transportation time can then be taken into consideration in the *CQNBLK* procedure.

After inputting the complete description of the FMS under study the data are stored in an FMS description file. This file provides the basis for the computation of the performance parameters of the FMS configuration alternative considered.

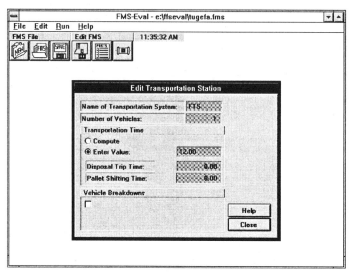

Figure 150: Description of the transportation system

3.2.2. Evaluation - Calculation of the Performance Parameters of a Flexible Manufacturing System

Once a specific FMS configuration to be evaluated has been defined, the performance criteria can be computed with the help of one of the applicable *analytical procedures*. Among the algorithmic options available are the exact evaluation of the classical CQN model for universal pallets (CANQ) and the heuristic evaluation of the classical CQN model for special pallets (MVA[257]); the heuristic procedure described in section 3.1.2., which accounts for blocking and starving, and estimates the effects of idle trips and disposal trips to the central buffer on the performance of an FMS (CQNBLK).

If, for example, the local buffers at the machining stations are small and the material handling system is comparatively slow or heavily loaded, then use of the CQNBLK procedure is advisable since it explicitly takes these factors into consideration. If, on the other hand, special emphasis is laid on results broken down by product groups or pallet types, then the MVA procedure would be preferred. For the purpose of evaluating an FMS with special pallets *and* limited local buffers, the combination of CQNBLK and MVA as described in section 3.1.2.5.4.2. is supported.

Furthermore, a procedure specially devised for the analysis of *flexible transfer lines* (FLEX) is also implemented. Here the exact version of the mean value analysis for single-machine stations connected by a transportation system modelled as a delay server is used. In the current example, the MVA procedure will

---

257   The heuristic mean value approach described in section 3.1.1.2. was implemented.

be chosen. After selecting the MVA algorithm, some options specific to this algorithm first must be set.

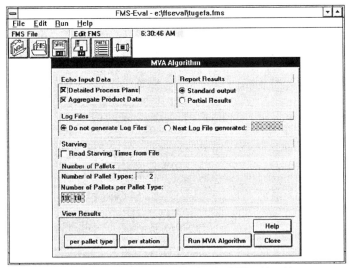

Figure 151: Options available for the MVA Algorithm

The algorithm itself is started by a simple click on the "Run MVA Algorithm" button. If the "Log File" option button is activated, then the results are stored in an ASCII file for documentation purposes.

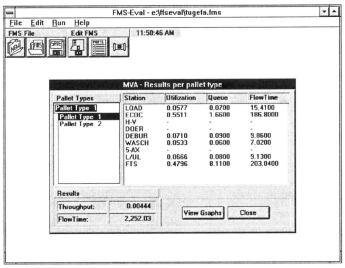

Figure 152: Numerical results per pallet type

The results can be shown graphically [see figure (153)]. If required, pictures may be saved in a file for documentation purposes.

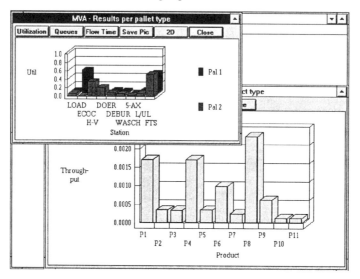

Figure 153: Graphic results

After analyzing the results for the relevant FMS configuration the operator will usually switch back into the edit mode and change some system parameters. This hopefully results in a modified FMS configuration variant with a higher perfor-mance than the previous one. Since a new evaluation run generally lasts only a few seconds or minutes - depending on the algorithm applied and on the size of the FMS - an FMS planner can calculate the critical values of an appropriate FMS configuration alternative quite quickly.

Aside from the interactive evaluation of a given FMS configuration, predefined sensitivity analyses[258] for FMSs with *universal pallets* can also be executed. This can be helpful in establishing an upper limit for the production rate and circum-scribe the range of the possible number of pallets. The results of a sensitivity analysis for an example are shown in figure (154).

---

258   see section 3.1.1.1.3.

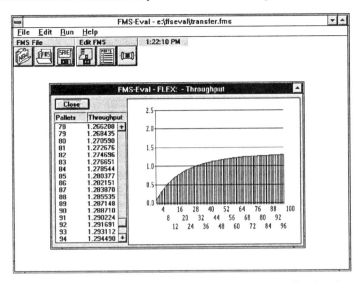

Figure 154: Sensitivity analysis with respect to the number of pallets in a flow line

3.3. SIMULATION MODELS FOR THE EVALUATION OF THE PERFORMANCE OF AN FMS CONFIGURATION

3.3.1. Basic Simulation Terminology

Simulation[259] involves the representation of a real problem (real system) by a formal model as well as the observation of the (usually dynamic) behavior of the model when external factors affecting the model are experimentally varied. Typical *characteristics* of a simulation include the following:

- *Quantitative models* are used which represent the system under study in such a way as to allow its evaluation to be performed by means of a computer.

- The simulation model is used to execute *computational experiments* with the help of numerical techniques. In contrast to a mathematical optimization model, a simulation model is not able to determine the optimal combination of the decision variables considered. Instead, a function with a large number of variables is only *evaluated*. Thus, a simulation model does not generate alternative decision proposals as does an optimization model, rather it evaluates *decision alternatives which have been explicitly defined by the user.*

- Simulation models have a special *problem orientation*, i.e. a concrete problem or system is modelled and investigated[260].

---

259 **Law/Kelton** (1982); **Banks/Carson** (1984); **Pritsker** (1986); **Carrie** (1988), p. 1; **Pegden/Shannon/Sadowski** (1990), p. 3

260 A high degree of similarity between a simulation model and the real-life system being modelled is in general only achievable at a considerable cost. A way of escaping from this dilemma is to use *simulators*. These are

Simulation models are generally used when analytical methods would not provide a sufficiently detailed analysis of a real system. It is possible, as has been shown in the previous sections, to calculate a product type's average flow time through an FMS assuming a set of given conditions with the help of analytical procedures from queueing theory. If the assumptions do not hold, or if certain problem aspects are to be investigated which can be only poorly if at all included in the concept of the analytical model, then the relevant performance parameters of a real system may often only be determined using a detailed simulation model.

In section 3.1. some different ways of representing an FMS analytically were illustrated. It became clear that certain aspects of real FMSs had to be excluded since they presented awkward problems for the currently available analytical methods. The problems associated with the *supply of tools* to the machines in an FMS, for example, could not be included in the analytical performance estimation. This is also true for *transition phenomena* before a system reaches its steady state, since their effects on the performance of an FMS cannot be adequately approximated using analytical methods. Some *production policies* which depend on a deterministic release of batches into an FMS cannot be covered by the stochastic approaches to modelling in which the long term stationary behavior of an FMS is observed. In all of these cases simulation can be a useful method for estimating the performance of an FMS.

The computational experiments with a simulation model are generally carried out using a computer. Nowadays workstations as well as personal computers are used. Simulation is thus often defined as a *numerical technique for the performance of computational experiments with computers*.

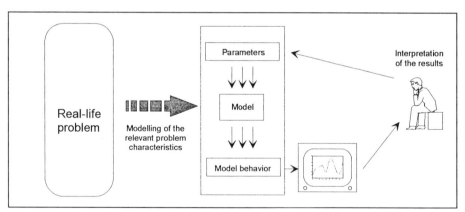

Figure 155: Structure of a simulation study

In a *simulation experiment* [see figure (155)] the relevant components of a real system are depicted using a (often stochastic) *simulation model*. The system

---

predefined simulation models for a particular problem domain that are adapted to a specific system type to be simulated by use of several model parameters.

components which will act as variable *parameters* in a simulation experiment must be determined. When building a simulation model of an FMS it is necessary, for example, to decide if the number of machines of a particular type is to be fixed in advance, or if it - and possibly the machines' characteristics, such as breakdown and repair patterns - should be considered as variables throughout the simulation experiment. All the other design variables discussed in section 2.1.2. could be treated as variables in a simulation model as well.

One or more simulation runs are performed for each of the combinations of these parameters, depending on whether or not the simulation model includes stochastic components. The evaluation and interpretation of the results of the simulation runs provide clues both as to how the parameters need to be changed in order to reach the desired simulation results and how to find a solution for the real problem depicted by the simulation model.

Simulation is often seen as the last resort for the analysis of complex systems. Analysts can be forced to use a simulation model for several important *reasons*[261].

- The structure of a problem (system) may be too complex to be solved by means of an analytical procedure, because of nonlinear relationships or stochastic components of the system, for example.

- A sufficiently detailed model of a real system and the observation of the dynamic behavior of the model over time can lead to a more in-depth understanding of the system. Ideas for the development of new analytical approaches to problem solving can thus be gained.

- Analytically determined values can be verified by comparing them to simulation results[262].

- A simulation model can be used to investigate the effects of a deliberate change in a parameter on the relevant quantities in a real system. For example, it is possible to determine the influence on the utilization of the machines of changes in the structure of the process plans to be used in an FMS.

Simulation models are most often used in *FMS* planning when it is necessary to mimic in detail the dynamic behavior of an FMS over time. Simulation is often the last phase in the configuration of an FMS. It frequently serves to remove any lingering doubts about the performance capability of an FMS configuration alternative. The demands on the accuracy of the simulation model's representation of the FMS are correspondingly high.

In practice, simulation models are often used directly, without first applying an analytical procedure. The danger associated with this procedure, however, is that excessive computing time may be wasted only to find out that certain FMS configuration alternatives cannot provide satisfactory results. The considerable

---

261 **Law/Kelton** (1982), pp. 8-9; **Bratley/Fox/Schrage** (1983), pp. 1-7; **Banks/Carson** (1984), pp. 3-5; **Watson/Blackstone** (1989), pp. 15-16; **Pegden/Shannon/Sadowski** (1990), pp. 12-23
262 see sections 3.1.2.4.3. and 3.1.2.5.4.1.4.

modelling effort and comparatively long computation times often force an FMS planner to limit his analysis to just a few configuration alternatives in which essentially variable quantities have been randomly fixed. This may result in a sub-optimal FMS alternative being proposed for actual implementation.

3.3.2. Carrying out a Simulation Experiment

The steps which have to be carried out in a simulation experiment basically correspond to those in a model analysis (OR process)[263]. They include the following steps:

- Formulation of the problem.

- Collection of the problem relevant data.

- Development of a quantitative model of the system to be simulated, including verification (checking if the simulation model works according to the expectations of the model's developer) and validation of the model (checking if the real system has been depicted in the model with sufficient accuracy).

- Programming the simulation model, i.e. translating the quantitative model into a computer program.

- Planning the simulation experiment, i.e. determining which combinations of values of the model's parameters will be studied (factorial design).

- Experimentation, i.e. carrying out the simulation experiment.

- Processing, interpreting and documenting the simulation results.

The *problem formulation* phase includes the specification of the *goals* which are to be achieved by the simulation and determination of the *model parameters* which shall be manipulated in the experiment (decision variables and non-controllable external factors influencing the real system). Problem formulation has a great affect on the required degree of agreement between the real system and the simulation model. The most detailed model is not always the most useful one, because too much detail can cloud the view of the most important factors[264].

During the problem formulation phase special requirements for the data will arise. *Data gathering* can cover either *quantitative* or *qualitative* data. The following possibilities may be important for data input into a simulation model:

- *Raw data*

  Raw data are generally uncondensed empirical information about one portion of the real system being simulated. It is possible, for example, to feed the

---

263 **Banks/Carson** (1984), pp. 11-16; **Pegden/Shannon/Sadowski** (1990), pp. 3-28
264 **Law/McComas** (1989)

entire set of orders received in a given past period into the simulation model and mimic the processing of all these orders by the simulation model. The advantage of such a *data-driven* (trace-driven) simulation is that it is possible to precisely check the simulation model using knowledge available from actual experience with the behavior of the system in the past.

A disadvantage of a data-driven simulation is its high input intensity. Furthermore, it is often doubtful whether raw data based on past experience are also capable of achieving a high degree of detail in predicting the *future* development of the real system.

Since for an FMS which does not yet exist clearly no raw data are available, data-driven simulations are generally precluded in the design phase.

- *Aggregated data*

  Raw data can be aggregated by building empirical frequency distributions for the relevant quantities of the system to be simulated. The advantage of a distribution-driven simulation model is that data input in the simulation model is simplified significantly. It can also often be assumed that such a frequency distribution provides a good approximation of the studied variables in some future period. A data aggregation of this kind regarding the structure of the production program is generally performed. Prognoses about the future composition of the production program can be made based on empirical experience. These are then used to define the empirical probability distributions that will be applied in the simulation model.

- *Theoretical probability distributions*

  Further aggregation of the data can be achieved when the empirical frequency distribution is approximated with a *theoretical probability distribution*. This is a method often used in simulation models. The advantage is that the generation of observations of a random variable requires less computer time due to the theoretical probability distribution than searching through an empirical frequency table.

  A simulation based on theoretical probability distributions is particularly useful when the structure of the stochastic process on which the relevant random variables are based is known. It can, for example, be assumed that the arrival rates of telephone calls to a firm's central switchboard follow a Poisson distribution under certain circumstances.

  A variety of different *theoretical probability distributions* can be used to describe empirical situations. The selection of an appropriate distribution type and of the values for the distribution parameters is generally made based on a frequency distribution of the observed values of the variables which are to be approximated with the help of a theoretical probability distribution[265]. Several different test procedures may be applied in the evaluation of the quality of the adjustment of an empirical frequency distribution with a theoretical

---

265 **Banks/Carson** (1984), pp. 122-171

probability distribution. These include the Chi-square test or the Kolmogo-rov-Smirnov test.

When modelling a real system with a simulation model it is necessary to choose the fundamental *orientation* of the simulation model (world view). The model's orientation defines the way in which the state of the model changes over (simulation) time. Simulation orientations may be distinguished as follows[266]:

- *Event orientation*

  Here the course of the simulation is represented as a series of discrete events which influence the state of the components in the system being simulated. The individual events are defined and placed in chronological order by the model developer or the simulation model programmer. A purely event-oriented simulation system simply provides the user with a library of functions performing specific simulation tasks and a general control mechanism for the simulation process.

- *Process orientation*

  Process-oriented simulation models reflect the dynamic behavior of the system in a series of *processes. Processes are often repeating sequences of events.* The user defines processes made up of several events rather than the individual events themselves. A purely process-oriented simulation system can thus only be applied to those aspects of a real system for which processes in the simulation system are defined.

- *Activity scanning orientation*

  In an activity-oriented simulation model, the user defines the possible changes in state of the system components and formulates conditions under which these changes may occur. Since the conditions have to be reviewed after every change in the system's state, activity-oriented simulation concepts are associated with a relatively large amount of computing time.

- *Continuous simulation*

  The variables in a continuous simulation model are continuous functions of the simulation time. Continuous simulation models are especially good for simulating control processes. This modelling philosophy is usually not adequate for simulations of FMSs.

Some simulation software systems can also *combine* the different orientations or world views described here. A real system is first modelled using a process-oriented simulation model. Here process types are used which are made available by the simulation system with the help of a special syntax (simulation language). Such a process type can include a workpiece's request for a vehicle,

---

266 **Pritsker** (1986), pp. 52-65; **Pidd** (1988), pp. 51-78

the associated waiting process and the vehicle's idle trip to the workpiece. If certain elements or processes in the real system cannot be modelled with the process types supported by the simulation software, they may be accounted for in an event-oriented part of the simulation model. The programmer of the simulation model would define his own problem-specific events and process types and link them with the process-oriented simulation model via a well-defined programming interface. Such a problem-specific process type could, for example, be used in a special logic for the control of the idle vehicles in an FMS.

As computers have become increasingly common in the last decades, a whole series of dedicated *simulation software systems* has been developed. They take over many of the routine aspects of a simulation (including scheduling of new events, updating the calendar of events, updating the state of the system, etc.) and allow the user to concentrate on the modelling problems in the simulation. Two opposing categories of simulation software can be identified based on their special uses: *general-purpose simulation languages* and problem-specific *simulators* restricted to particular types of real systems. The various types of *program generators* are located between these two categories.

- *General-purpose simulation languages*

  General-purpose simulation languages include syntactical constructs (elements of the programming language) that may be used to model a real system. Among the many universal simulation languages are[267]: SIMULA, SIMSCRIPT, GPSS, SLAM II and SIMAN IV, but also AUTOMOD II. The performance of a simulation language is largely dependent on the number of implemented language elements and their functional specification. While a language element for the definition and management of a queue may be standard usage in all simulation languages, in some languages the set of "universal" language elements has been expanded through certain constructs especially designed for the simulation of *material flow systems*[268]. This allows a considerable reduction in the required modelling and programming time in comparison to other simulation languages.

- *Simulators*

  While general-purpose simulation languages can be used for almost any real system, *problem-specific simulators* are designed for use in one specific area. A large number of simulators has been developed in the last few years for simulating *production processes* (e.g. GRAFSIM[269], MAP/1[270], FMSSIM[271],

---

267 An overview is provided by **Banks/Carson** (1985). A list of simulation software vendors is annually compiled in the **Simulation** journal.

268 This is the case with SIMAN IV and SLAM II; **Pritsker** (1986); **Tempelmeier** (1991). A somewhat unique position among the simulation languages is held by AUTOMOD II. This simulation system combines a process-oriented PASCAL-like simulation language with an animation-based model design. AUTOMOD II offers the user a graphical interface where pictorial templates of several elements of material flow systems are positioned on the screen by use of CAD-techniques. These elements are assigned appropriate portions of the simulation program code describing the simulation model.

269 see section 3.3.3.

270 **Rolston/Miner** (1985)

SIMBED[272]). They can be divided according to both the diversity of problem variations considered and their user interface. Some production or material flow simulators[273] offer the user a set of objects which he can then position on the screen. After the user has chosen all the necessary objects for the model (e.g. machines, storage spaces) and determined the relevant parameters, the simulator generates the data structure of the simulation model and executes the simulation. A simulator allows the user to carry out extensive simulation projects without previous programming experience. One problem can arise, however, when the user wants to simulate system variations which the developers of the simulator did not have in mind when they built the simulator. In such a case, the user can either not carry out the analysis or he must begin again using a universal language.

- *Application-specific program generators*

  In order to find a compromise between the extremes of universality and low model development time, *program generators* are being increasingly developed which combine the advantages of a simulator (quick model development) with those of the universal programming languages (transparency and extendibility of the simulation model)[274]. It must be distinguished here between application-specific and application-independent program generators. An application-specific generator is able to generate directly executable simulation programs for certain application areas (problem domains) in a target language, such as GPSS or SIMAN IV. The program generator makes use of a predefined set of program building blocks which, after being provided with data from the user as to the characteristics of the real system to be simulated, are compiled in a ready-to-run simulation program.

- *The SIMAN module processor as an application-independent program generator*

  Normally the range of functions of simulation programs that can be generated by an application-specific program generator is limited by the model building blocks implemented during the development of the program generator. The concept implemented in the *SIMAN module processor*[275], on the other hand, is based on a complete separation of the model building blocks from the task of program generation. The SIMAN module processor is an MS-DOS based program which helps to interactively generate executable SIMAN IV simulation models based on a extendable set of SIMAN IV model building blocks (modules) predefined by the user. Contrary to the concept providing the basis for the program generators, the modules must be defined by the user and arranged in a problem-specific library. It is thus possible for the user to expand step-by-step the range of pre-programmed and

271   ElMaraghy (1982)
272   Ketcham/Watt (1989)
273   Law/Haider (1989); O'Keefe/Haddock (1991)
274   Co/Chen (1988); Schroer/Tseng/Zhang/Wolfsberger (1988)
275   Tempelmeier/Endesfelder (1987); Tempelmeier (1990)

recallable simulation program code and thereby to make adjustments for developments in the real system being simulated.

Simulation as a method for the evaluation of a decision alternative is generally part of a larger optimization process. In this case, the simulation model is evaluated repeatedly with different values for the decision variables. Preparations for an actual *computation experiment* include the determination of the number and duration of the simulation runs and of the parameters to be changed during the simulation experiment.

After the simulation has been carried out the *simulation output* has to be analyzed. This is possible both with graphic or statistical procedures[276]. A graphic representation of the simulation output is a good way to provide an overview of even complex interactions between components of the simulation model. One frequently used form of graphic data processing is to present different time series simultaneously in one diagram (e.g. lengths of several queues or machine utilization). It is also possible to analyze the results of simulation runs in some simulation systems with an ex post animation (after completion of the simulation run).

Finally, a graphic real-time animation (during the course of a simulation run) can be used to support the various phases of a simulation experiment. A graphic representation of a system can help to identify errors in the model formulation, and the search for the optimal combination of decision variables is made easier - or even inspired - through the consideration of the dynamic progress in the model.

3.3.3. The FMS Simulator GRAFSIM

Simulation requires programming knowledge that is time-consuming both to acquire and to update. For that reason, in the last few years simulators have been developed which make model building easier for the user[277]. The simulator *GRAFSIM* will be described here as a representative of the large number of simulators currently available[278]. The interactive work with this simulator is organized into several levels [see figure (156)]. First, the layout of the FMS to be simulated is defined with a graphic *layout editor*. Different objects are offered to the user (machines, storage spaces, etc.), and he must organize them on the screen and connect them with transportation paths.

Such a layout could look on a screen as shown in figure (157). The menu driven input of the process plans, supported by numerous data input screens, and data for tools and the NC programs (if required) are linked to the definition of the FMS components.

---

276   The statistical aspects of simulation are treated by **Law/Kelton** (1982); **Banks/Carson** (1984).
277   **Lenz** (1983); **Steudel** (1986); **Carrie** (1988)
278   **SIEMENS AG** (1988); **Neupert** (1988)

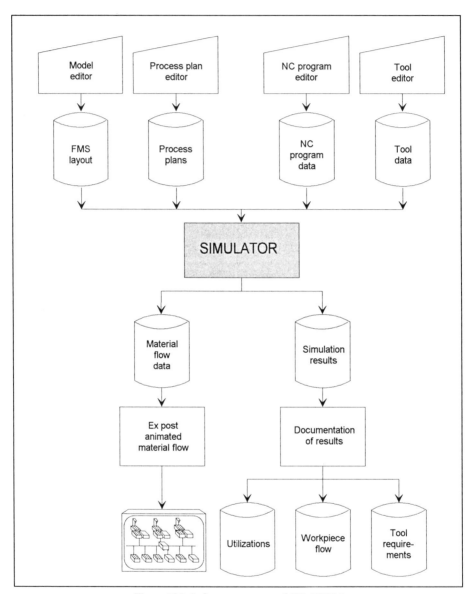

Figure 156: Software structure of GRAFSIM

When the FMS has been fully defined, GRAFSIM generates the internal representation (model and data structure) of the simulation model and executes the
simulation. The output is stored in a file and remains available for analysis and
ex post animation of workpiece and tool movements.

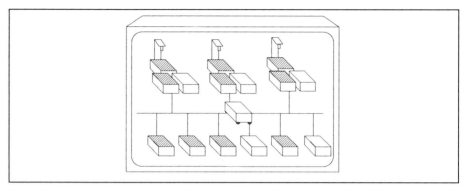

Figure 157: Animated GRAFSIM screen layout of an FMS (close-up view)

The advantage of this kind of a simulator is the speed with which even a user not familiar with a simulation language can put together an executable simulation model. Using simulators can be impossible when the analysis must be refined and strategies and model variations are to be simulated that the simulator cannot support. It is impossible to make generalizations on this subject, however, since experience has shown that the range of supported processes follows the ever changing development process of the simulation software.

3.3.4. Simulation of an FMS with the Simulation Language SIMAN IV

The simulation language SIMAN IV[279] is a general-purpose simulation language integrating the concepts of process-oriented, event-oriented and continuous simulation systems. In addition to the usual language elements necessary for the process-oriented simulation, SIMAN IV also has special extensions for the simulation of *material flow systems*. SIMAN IV is based on the host language FORTRAN. Since discrete event-oriented simulation is supported, SIMAN IV could be considered a *simulation package*. SIMAN IV offers a library of FORTRAN subroutines (or C-functions) which can make it easier for the user to plan and realize an event-oriented simulation.

The process-oriented simulation is realized through an integrated language compiler. It can thus be said that SIMAN IV offers a simulation language as well. The development of a SIMAN IV simulation model is supported through the use of graphical block symbols.

Lastly, a *continuous simulation* is also possible with SIMAN IV, in which the relevant system variables are continuous functions of the simulation time. The three modelling philosophies can be used together in one simulation model. Normally, a real system is first modelled with a process-oriented modelling approach. It is possible, however, that in the course of the simulation experiment it may become clear that certain system components could be better simulated

---

279 **Pegden/Shannon/Sadowski** (1990); **Tempelmeier** (1991)

with an event-orientated model or with the help of continuous concepts. In that case, these concepts can be integrated into the primarily process-oriented simulation model without having to change the simulation system used and without the time-consuming development of a new simulation model.

A SIMAN IV simulation model is made up of the following parts:

- *Model definition*
- *Definition of the experimental frame*

In the model definition the structure of the processes in the system to be simulated are modelled, such as seizing of machines, machining processes, release of the machines, requesting a vehicle, transportation processes, etc.

The experimental frame, on the other hand, includes information that might be varied during the investigation, such as the number and length of the simulation runs, parameters of the probability distributions, capacities of the resources (i.e. number of parallel machines), speed of the transportation vehicles, definition of the transportation paths, etc.

Both components of a simulation model, the model description and the definition of the experimental frame, are written in a special syntax (SIMAN IV language) and saved in text files (ASCII files). The model definition is interpreted with the SIMAN IV module *MODEL*, and the description of the experimental frame is translated by the SIMAN IV module *EXPMT*. Both SIMAN IV modules generate output files which are linked into a loadable simulation model by the SIMAN IV module *LINKER*. This model can then be processed and executed by the SIMAN IV executive program *SIMAN*. When the simulation is complete, the simulation output can be evaluated by the SIMAN IV module *OUTPT* - as long as the individual observations of variables have been stored in files (statistical analysis; graphic representation). In the following, two examples for the simulation of FMSs with SIMAN IV will be discussed.

3.3.4.1. "On-the-fly" simulation of an FMS

The first SIMAN IV simulation model [see figures (158) and (159)] is an *"on-the-fly" simulation* of an FMS modelled in the form of a closed queueing network. The structure of the FMS and the input data correspond to the *example 3-1* introduced in section 3.1.1.1.1. Three machining stations (STATIONS 1-3) and one "transportation station" (STATION 4) are simulated in the model. STATION 5 is the system exit. There are NPAL=4 pallets circulating in the system. The process plans of the workpieces, including the sequences of stations visited, are defined in the SEQUENCES element of the experimental frame. The (deterministic) operation time of a workpiece at a station is stored in the entity attribute with the symbolic name "OpTime". The relative frequency of the product types is defined in parameter set 1. The individual product types are assigned in the block labeled START according to this distribution.

Model definition:

```
BEGIN;
           CREATE,1:0,NPAL;                       Generate NPAL pallets
START      ASSIGN:NS=DP(1,1):MARK(ArrTime);       Assign product type number
           ASSIGN:IS=0;                           Initialize operation counter
GOON       ROUTE:0,SEQ;
;
           STATION,1-4;                           Stations (incl. transportation station)
           QUEUE,M;
           SEIZE:Mach(M);                         Seize a machine
           DELAY:OpTime;                          Operation time
           RELEASE:Mach(M):NEXT(GOON);            Free the machine
;
           STATION,5;                             Workpiece exchange
           TALLY:5,INT(ArrTime);                  Flow time (all product types)
           TALLY:NS,INT(ArrTime):NEXT(START);     Flow time per product type
END;
```

Figure 158: Model definition ("on-the-fly" simulation)

First, the CREATE block generates NPAL=4 entities (pallets). Since the product type is only used to select the correct SEQUENCE set, the number of the product type is stored in the special entity attribute NS. Since the pallets in the system circulate within a loop, the index for the pointer to the current station number in the sequence set, IS (operation counter) is reset. These two ASSIGN blocks located at the beginning of the model correspond to the exchange of a processed workpiece for a new unprocessed workpiece. The ROUTE block then follows, in which the pallet is passed on to the next station (machine) according to the sequence set which applies to the particular workpiece.

The machines and the transportation vehicle are represented in a *macro model* in which the following processes are simulated: entering a queue (QUEUE), seizing of a machine or the transportation vehicle (SEIZE), processing or transportation (DELAY), release of the machine or the transportation vehicle (RELEASE), and transfer to the next STATION [block modifier NEXT(GOON) and ROUTE].

In station 5 the flow time is first calculated for all product types together and then for each one separately (TALLY). Following that, the pallet (now empty) returns to the system entrance [block modifier NEXT(START)].

In the experimental frame, primarily the process plans (SEQUENCES) are defined. In the current example *deterministic processing sequences and processing times* are modelled. It is also possible, however, to precisely duplicate the assumptions of the classical CQN model. In this case for the processing times an exponential distribution could be used, and the workpiece movements between stations could be set with the help of the stationary arrival probabilities.

Experimental frame:

```
BEGIN;
PROJECT,FMS,HT,1/1/91;
DISCRETE,100,2,4,5;
 :           │    │ │ └ number of stations
 :           │    │ └ number of queues
 :           │    └ number of attributes
 :           └ number of concurrent entities (pallets) allowed
 :
RESOURCES:Mach(4);

VARIABLES:NPAL,4;                            number of pallets

ATTRIBUTES:OpTime:
          ArrTime;

SEQUENCES:1,3,60.&4,5.9&1,428.&4,5.9&3,90.&4,5.9&1,57.&4,5.9&
 !          │    │ │ └ contents of attribute OpTime at a transition between stations
 !          │    │ └ next station
 !          │    └ number of sequence set (here for product type 1)
 !

          3,90.&4,5.9&1,57.&4,5.9&3,90.&4,5.9&1,57.&4,5.9&
          3,90.&4,5.9&1,351.&4,5.9&3,90.&4,5.9&2,229.&4,5.9&
          3,30.&5:
        2,3,60.&4,5.9&1,470.&4,5.9&3,90.&4,5.9&2,639.&4,5.9&
          3,30.&5:
        3,3,60.&4,5.9&1,185.&4,5.9&3,90.&4,5.9&1,130.&4,5.9&
          3,30.&5:
        4,3,60.&4,5.9&1,47.&4,5.9&3,90.&4,5.9&1,223.&4,5.9&
          3,90.&4,5.9&2,19.&4,5.9&3,30.&5;

PARAMETERS:1,,2,1,.4,2,.8,3,1.,4;              distribution of product types
 :          │     │ └ product type number
 :          │     └ cumulative frequency: P{product type number≤1}
 :          └ number of parameter set
 :

TALLIES:FLTIM 1:
        FLTIM 2:
        FLTIM 3:
        FLTIM 4:
        FLTIM total;

DSTATS:NR(3),Util L/UL:
       NR(2),Util Mach 2:
       NR(1),Util Mach 1:
       NR(4),Util AGV;

REPLICATE,1,0,1000000;
           │      └ length of simulation run
           │
           └ one simulation run
END;
```

Figure 159: Definition of the experimental frame ("on-the-fly" simulation)

This simple simulation model can be expanded by additional stations due to the macro modelling capabilities provided by SIMAN IV. It is then only necessary to increase the range of station numbers and to integrate the stations as part of the process plans into the sequence sets of the product types.

Simulation results (1 run):

Replication ended at time   : .100000E+07

TALLY VARIABLES

Identifier	Average	Variation	Minimum	Maximum	Observations
FLTIM 1	3704.4	.10278	2756.5	4861.5	406
FLTIM 2	1757.1	.15231	1312.6	2757.8	445
FLTIM 3	1291.9	.24137	551.81	2379.8	885
FLTIM 4	1385.6	.24957	766.63	2642.8	409
FLTIM total	1862.9	.51699	551.81	4861.5	2145

DISCRETE-CHANGE VARIABLES

Identifier	Average	Variation	Minimum	Maximum	Final Value
Util L/UL	.56949	.86946	.00000	1.0000	.00000
Util Mach 2	.38510	1.2636	.00000	1.0000	.00000
Util Mach 1	.98502	.12331	.00000	1.0000	1.0000
Util AGV	.07454	3.5237	.00000	1.0000	.00000

Figure 160: Results of the "on-the-fly" simulation

The results of a simulation run for the above example are summarized in figure (160). A run over 1,000,000 minutes (=2083 shifts) of simulated production time lasted about 32 seconds on a PC with a 80486 processor with 25Mhz. From a statistical point of view, however, a single simulation run is not sufficient[280]. It is generally necessary to carry out several independent runs in order to assure that the observed simulation results reflect the "true" values of the performance measures of the FMS with sufficient precision (here: flow times and utilizations). The apparently relatively low computer time in this case increases greatly.

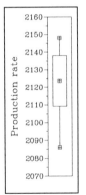

Figure 161: Simulation results (10 runs)

The results shown in figure (160) agree fairly well with those found using the classical CQN model for universal pallets[281]. This is largely due to the fact that the simulation model - aside from the deterministic processing times and workpiece flow through the system - represents de facto the classical CQN model. It must be remembered when interpreting the simulation output, however, that this is the result of *a single* simulation run. When *ten* statistically independent simulation runs are carried out, the results shift a bit, as shown in figure (161). The 95% confidence interval of the production quantity is indicated by the upper and lower edges of the rectangle[282].

---

280 **Bratley/Fox/Schrage** (1983), pp. 73-113; **Pegden/Shannon/Sadowski** (1990), pp. 165-216

281 section 3.1.1.3.

282 Results for 10 simulation runs: mean = 2123; minimum = 2086; maximum = 2148; width of the 95% confidence interval: 12.786. Problems associated with the statistical analysis of simulation results with respect to FMSs are discussed by **Fishman** (1989).

3.3.4.2. Detailed simulation of an FMS with automatic guided vehicles

In this last rough-cut simulation the activities of the material flow system were significantly simplified by modelling it as a *central server station* (station 4). In this way it was possible to analyze the queueing processes quite precisely while only roughly looking at the *spatial aspects* of the problem. Using the following example, the inclusion of a wire-guided transportation system will now be demonstrated. An FMS with a layout as depicted in figure (162) will be the subject of this analysis.

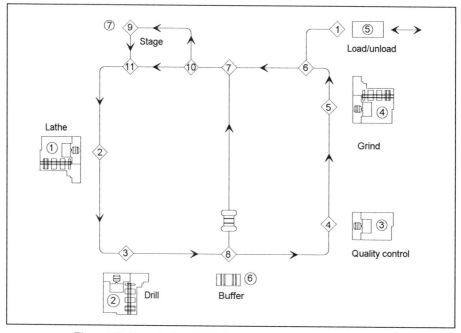

Figure 162: Layout of an FMS with automatic wire-guided vehicles

An automatic guided transportation system (AGV) (with one or more vehicles) supplies 4 stations with workpieces. The workpieces are fixed on their pallets and also exit the FMS at a L/UL station. Two product types are produced according to two different process plans. There are *no local buffers* at the stations. If a pallet with a workpiece arrives at a busy machine, it is re-routed to the *central buffer* where it waits to be called by its downstream machine when that has been set free.

Vehicles which are temporarily not needed are taken to a stage where they can wait for the next transportation job. This stage is necessary to prevent blocking of tracks by idle vehicles in a simulation model with several vehicles. The path layout is arranged in a *circular traffic* form. Only the entrance to the loading station is a *dead end*. This means that if a vehicle is at the L/UL station, no other vehicle can enter the track which leads to the L/UL station.

The SIMAN IV simulation model for this example is made up of several sections which can also be interpreted as modules. Workpieces are generated in the first section. The second section is for the modelling of the machining stations. The third section represents the L/UL station (system entrance and exit). Workpiece exchanges, including counting a workpiece's flow time, are carried out here. A further section models the central pallet storage areas (central buffer); for simplicity it is assumed that they are all accessible via a single loading point represented by a single station. In order to exactly mimic the material flow to and from the central buffer, one could include a station for each individual central buffer location. The last part of the simulation model includes the logic according to which a newly freed vehicle is either directed to the stage or to a workpiece. In the following, the individual sections of the model definition are presented with some more explanatory detail.

Model definition:

BEGIN;

Generate pallets and assign a workpiece (product type):

(1) NPAL entities (pallets) are generated;
(2) To each pallet a process plan number (product type number) is randomly assigned: 40% of all workpieces are of product type 1 and 60% are of product type 2;
(3) Initialize entity attribute IS with the number of the current operation; the attribute named "ArrTime" assumes the actual simulation time TNOW;
(4) Request a vehicle to come to the L/UL station; if necessary, wait for the vehicle in the queue with the symbolic name "Entrance";
(5) The vehicle transports the pallet to the next station according to the SEQUENCE set (process plan, defined in the experimental frame) assigned to the workpiece.

```
        CREATE:    0,NPAL;                              (1)
        ASSIGN:    NS=DISC(0.4,1,1.0,2);                (2)
        ASSIGN:    IS=0:                                (3)
                   MARK(ArrTime);
        QUEUE,     Entrance;
        REQUEST:   AGV(SDS),,Load_unload:              (4)
                   MARK(AGVWait);
        TRANSPORT: AGV,SEQ;                             (5)
```

Figure 163-1: Model definition

Processing stations: Lathe, Drill, Grind, QContr:

---

(1) Save the current station number in the attribute "Dest"; this is necessary because the workpiece may be transported to the central buffer for intermediate storage and its current destination must be known;
(2) The queue in front of a machine has zero capacity; i.e. all pallets that are not allowed to seize the machine immediately after their arrival at the station are rejected and sent to the block labeled MCCB;
(3) Seize the machine;
(4) A copy of the entity (this may be interpreted as an AGV order) is sent to the block labeled AGVChk, where the further scheduling of the vehicle will be initiated;
(5) Start processing the workpiece;
(6) Request a vehicle; the machine remains blocked until the arrival of the vehicle; in order to record the machine blocking time the workpiece is assigned to the STORAGE with the number M;
(7) After releasing the machine
(8) The workpiece searches in the central buffer queue for a pallet whose current destination "Dest" is this station;
(9) If such a pallet is found, remove it from the queue and send it to the block labeled BegCB, where it requests a vehicle;
(10) Send the workpiece just processed to the next station according to its process plan;
(11) Rejected pallets are transported to the central buffer;

```
          STATION,    Lathe-Grind;
          ASSIGN:     Dest=M;                            (1)
          QUEUE,      LatheQ+(M-Lathe),0,MCCB;           (2)
          SEIZE:      MC(M-Lathe+1);                     (3)
          DUPLICATE: 1,Process:
                      NEXT(AGVChk);                      (4)
 Process  DELAY:      OpTime;                            (5)
          QUEUE,      AGV MCQ;
          REQUEST,,M:AGV(SDS):
                      MARK(AGVWait);                     (6)
          RELEASE:    MC(M-Lathe+1);                     (7)
          ASSIGN:     Help=M;
          SEARCH,CBQ:Dest.EQ.Help;                       (8)
          BRANCH,1:
            IF,J.EQ.0,TranMC:
            ELSE,RemMC;
 RemMC    REMOVE:1,CBQ,BegCB;                            (9)
 TranMC   TRANSPORT: AGV,SEQ;                            (10)
 ;
 MCCB     TRANSPORT: AGV,Central;                        (11)
```

Figure 163-2: Model definition (continued)

Workpiece exchange: it is assumed that the workpiece exchange is always the last operation within a process plan; except for the start of the simulation, the process simulated equals the processes in the machining stations:

(1) If a pallet was created at the start of a simulation run by the CREATE-block - in this case IS = 0 - the assignment of a new product type number is skipped;
(2) In the normal case the pallet is assigned a new product type number (i.e. a new workpiece) after leaving the setup area; the new identity is stored in the attribute NS; the workpiece is forwarded on its way through the FMS.

```
          STATION,    Load_unload;
          ASSIGN:     Dest=M;
          QUEUE,      SetupQ,0,SetupCB;
          SEIZE:      Setup;
          DUPLICATE:  1,Exchange:
                      NEXT(AGVChk);
Exchange  DELAY:      ExchangeTime;
          QUEUE,      AGV InpQ;
          REQUEST:    AGV(SDS):MARK(AGVWait);
          RELEASE:    Setup;
          BRANCH,1:                                  (1)
             IF,IS.EQ.0,Setup0:
             ELSE,Setup1;
Setup1    TALLY:      FlowTime,INTERVAL(ArrTime);    (2)
          ASSIGN:     NS=DISC(0.4,1,1.0,2);
          ASSIGN:     IS=0:MARK(ArrTime);
Setup0    ASSIGN:     Help=M;
          SEARCH,CBQ:Dest.EQ.Help;
          BRANCH,1:
             IF,J.EQ.0,TranSP:
             ELSE,RemSP;
RemSP     REMOVE:1,CBQ,BegCB;
TranSP    TRANSPORT: AGV,SEQ;
;
SetupCB   TRANSPORT: AGV,Central;
```

Central buffer:

(1) The pallet is inserted into a queue assigned to the central buffer; it waits there until it is removed by another pallet and is sent to the block labeled BegCB;
(2) Request a vehicle;
(3) Reset the number of the current operation, so that we can find the station the pallet tried to enter before its was sent to the central buffer.

```
CentBuf   STATION,    Central;
          DUPLICATE:  1,Waitlb:
                      NEXT(AGVChk);
Waitlb    QUEUE,      CBQ:DETACH;                     (1)
BegCB     QUEUE,      CBAGV;
          REQUEST:    AGV(SDS):MARK(AGVWait);         (2)
          ASSIGN:     IS=IS-1;                        (3)
          TRANSPORT: AGV,SEQ;
```

Figure 163-3: Model definition (continued)

Check, whether the vehicle has been requested somewhere in the FMS: try to find a pallet waiting for a vehicle in a queue in front of a REQUEST-block;

(1) If a pallet is found, jump to the block labeled NoPark and release the vehicle at its current position; the vehicle starts its idle trip to the pallet that requested it; (2) Otherwise send the vehicle to the stage and then release it

```
AGVChk    BRANCH,    1:
                     IF,(NQ(AGV InpQ)+
                        NQ(AGV MCQ)+
                        NQ(CBAGV))==0,ParkAGV:
                     ELSE,NoPark;                         (1)
ParkAGV   TRANSPORT: AGV,Park;                            (2)
```

Stage:

(1) Record the time a vehicle was occupied by a pallet (incl. the trip time to the stage); (2) Release the vehicle and delete the copy of the workpiece.

```
          STATION,   Park;
NoPark    TALLY:     TripTime,INTERVAL(AGVWait);          (1)
          FREE:      AGV:DISPOSE;                         (2)
END;
```

Figure 163-4: Model definition (continued)

Although the processes in the material flow system are fairly complex, in the current example vehicle control can be largely left to SIMAN IV. Since the vehicles move in a circular traffic pattern, deadlock situations cannot arise (i.e. two vehicles on the same track moving in opposite directions and blocking each other's path). The occupation of the dead end (the entrance to the L/UL station) is also automatically managed by SIMAN IV. A deadlock situation would be possible if the vehicles could move in either direction along the tracks. This is not automatically prevented by SIMAN IV (e.g. by finding a detour in advance). Instead the developer of the simulation model must prevent deadlock situations with a forward-looking concept for vehicle control. SIMAN IV provides the appropriate supporting functions for this.

The definition of the *experimental frame* [see figure (164)] for the current example includes not only the usual information necessary for other (non-material-flow) simulation models but also the description of the material flow system. This is based on the following considerations. Track driven *vehicles* (TRANSPORTER) move in a *network* (NETWORK) that is made up of *intersections* (INTERSECTIONS) as well as *tracks* (LINKS). The locations of the machines (STATIONS) are assigned to individual intersections (INTERSECTIONS). The transfer of a pallet between the material flow system and the machining system takes place at these points. The central characteristics of an AGV network are described by the *tracks* (LINKS). A track connects two INTERSECTIONS. It is made up of one or several *zones* of specific length. A vehicle occupies the zone which lies immediately in front of it and releases the zone it has just left. The vehicle movements are described in this way, though the length of the vehicle, i.e. the amount of space it occupies on the track, is also included.

Experimental frame:

General declarations

```
BEGIN;
PROJECT,      FMS with AGV and CB,SMC_HT;

REPLICATE,    1,0,10000;

; Workpiece description

ATTRIBUTES:   ArrTime:
              OpTime:
              ExchangeTime:
              AGVWait:
              Dest;

; Global auxiliary variables

VARIABLES:    NPAL,5:
              Help;

; Queues

QUEUES:       AGV_InpQ:
              AGV_MCQ,LVF(ArrTime):
              LatheQ:
              DrillQ:
              QContrQ:
              GrindQ:
              SetupQ:
              CBQ:
              CBAGV:
              Entrance;

; Processing and L/UL stations

RESOURCES:    MC(4):
              Setup;

; Stations (incl. assignment of intersections)

STATIONS:     Lathe,2:
              Drill,3:
              QContr,4:
              Grind,5:
              Load_unload,1:
              Central,8:
              Park,9;

; Process plans per product type

SEQUENCES:    1, Lathe,      OpTime= 10.0 &
              Drill,         OpTime=  3.0 &
              Grind,         OpTime=  5.0 &
              QContr,        OpTime=  1.25 &
              Load_unload, ExchangeTime=2.5:

              2, Drill,      OpTime=  9.0 &
              Lathe,         OpTime=  3.5 &
              QContr,        OpTime=  1.25 &
              Load_unload, ExchangeTime=2.5;
```

Figure 164-1: Definition of the experimental frame

Definition of the material flow system

```
; Intersections (stopping-places in the network)

INTERSECTIONS: 1,, 1:
               2,, 1:
               3,, 1:
               4,, 1:
               5,, 1:
               6,, 1:
               7,, 1:
               8,, 1:
               9,, 1:
              10,, 1:
              11,, 1;
;                 └ length of an intersection transfer
;
; Tracks

LINKS:        1,, 6, 1,  1,10,Spur:
              2,, 6, 7,  6, 1:
              3,, 7,10,  1, 1:
              4,,10,11,  4, 1:
              5,,11, 2,  8, 1:
              6,, 2, 3,  8, 1:
              7,, 3, 8,  5, 1:
              8,, 8, 4, 10, 1:
              9,, 4, 5,  7, 1:
             10,, 5, 6,  3, 1:
             11,, 8, 7, 12, 1:
             12,,10, 9,  6, 1:
             13,, 9,11,  1, 1;
;                        └ length of a track
;                      └ number of tracks
;                   └ destination intersection
;              └ starting intersection
;
; Network

NETWORKS:     1,AGV tracks,1-13;

; Vehicles

TRANSPORTERS: 1,AGV,1,NETWORK(AGV tracks),50.0,LINK(12);
;                                           └ velocity
;                └ number of vehicles
```

Figure 164-2: Definition of the experimental frame (continued)

```
 ┌────────────────────────────────────────────────────────────────────────┐
 │ Data gathering                                                           │
 ├────────────────────────────────────────────────────────────────────────┤
 │ STORAGES:       1,BlockLathe:                                            │
 │                 2,BlockDrill:                                            │
 │                 3,BlockQContr:                                           │
 │                 4,BlockGrind;                                            │
 │                                                                          │
 │ TALLIES:        FlowTime:                                                │
 │                 TripTime;                                                │
 │                                                                          │
 │ DSTATS:                                                                  │
 │                                                                          │
 │ ! Queue lengths                                                          │
 │                                                                          │
 │                 NQ(AGV_MCQ)+NQ(AGV_InpQ)+NQ(CBAGV),Wait for AGV:         │
 │                 NQ(CBQ),Central buffer:                                  │
 │                                                                          │
 │ ! Utilizations                                                           │
 │                                                                          │
 │                 IT(AGV,1),AGV Cart 1 Utilization:                        │
 │                 NR(Setup),Setup Utilization:                             │
 │                 NR(1)-NSTO(1),Lathe Utilization:                         │
 │                 NR(2)-NSTO(2),Drill Utilization:                         │
 │                 NR(3)-NSTO(3),QContr Utilization:                        │
 │                 NR(4)-NSTO(4),Grind Utilization:                         │
 │                                                                          │
 │ ! Blocking                                                               │
 │                                                                          │
 │                 NSTO(1),BlockLathe:                                      │
 │                 NSTO(2),BlockDrill:                                      │
 │                 NSTO(3),BlockQContr:                                     │
 │                 NSTO(4),BlockGrind;                                      │
 │                                                                          │
 │ END;                                                                     │
 └────────────────────────────────────────────────────────────────────────┘
```

Figure 164-3: Definition of the experimental frame (continued)

The simulation output for one simulation run is shown in figure (165). 816 workpieces were manufactured in the simulated time period of 10,000 minutes. The utilization of the vehicle is relatively high, and the workpieces must, therefore, often wait for transportation. The degree of blocking at the machines while processed workpieces wait for transportation is between 2.375% (BlockGrind) and 4.454% (BlockLathe). The indicated travel time is based on a workpiece's one-time request for a vehicle. It includes the idle trip from the vehicle's current position, the supply trip to the downstream station, and the trip to the central buffer or the vehicle's idle trip to the parking position, if necessary.

By distinguishing between the description of the processing logic of the model and the definition of the experimental frame it is easy to change the structure of the network layout without having to redesign the logic in the model definition. The number of vehicles or the number of products to be processed (including the structure of the process plans) can also be increased without interfering with the model structure. Instead, only adjustments in the experimental frame are necessary.

Simulation results:

Replication ended at time   : 10000.0

TALLY VARIABLES

Identifier	Average	Variation	Minimum	Maximum	Observations
FlowTime	61.129	.49547	21.245	202.54	816
TripTime	2.1693	.50701	.39063	12.680	5326

DISCRETE-CHANGE VARIABLES

Identifier	Average	Variation	Minimum	Maximum	Final Value
Wait for AGV	.40868	1.6441	.00000	4.0000	.00000
Central buffer	2.4239	.34699	.00000	4.0000	3.0000
AGV Cart 1 Utilization	.74408	.58647	.00000	1.0000	.00000
Setup Utilization	.34192	1.3873	.00000	1.0000	.00000
Lathe Utilization	.54360	.91628	.00000	1.0000	.00000
Drill Utilization	.59552	.82414	.00000	1.0000	1.0000
QContr Utilization	.17142	2.1986	.00000	1.0000	1.0000
Grind Utilization	.18580	2.0933	.00000	1.0000	.00000
BlockLathe	.02957	5.7289	.00000	1.0000	.00000
BlockDrill	.04454	4.6314	.00000	1.0000	.00000
BlockQContr	.03981	4.9112	.00000	1.0000	.00000
BlockGrind	.02375	6.4117	.00000	1.0000	.00000

Figure 165: Simulation results (1 run)

One of the most important properties of simulation models is that it is possible to study the *dynamic behavior* of a system over time. This can be done in different ways. One simple possibility would be to store the observed values of a relevant parameter in a file and then to summarize the contents of the file with the help of a graphic program after the simulation is completed. The development over time of the occupation of the central buffer for the above FMS with 5 pallets is depicted in figure (166).

Animation offers another way to analyze the dynamic behavior of a simulation model. With SIMAN IV several animation concepts are available. In the text-oriented animation add-on *SIMANIM*[283] the state of the simulation model is shown on the screen in a largely standardized form. It is necessary only that some parameters be established to define the layout of the animation screen. Figure (167) shows a SIMANIM screen for a variation of the above FMS (2 vehicles, 10 pallets)

Each station is represented by a rectangle. On the bottom side of each rectangle the content of a particular attribute (animation attribute) of the workpiece just leaving or arriving at the station is indicated. In this way the path of the workpiece through the FMS can be roughly reconstructed. In the bottom right-hand corner of the screen all the attributes of the currently active workpiece are summarized. In another box (with the marking "MHS") the downstream intersections of the vehicles are shown.

---

283 Tempelmeier (1991)

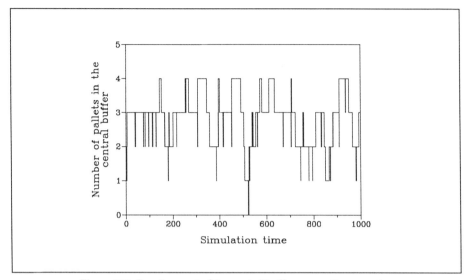

Figure 166: Development of the central buffer occupation over time

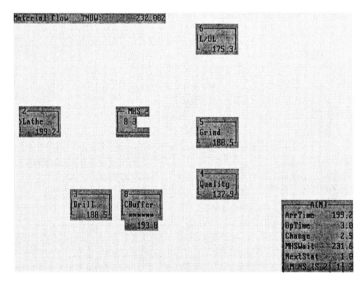

Figure 167: SIMANIM-Screen

Two vehicles are simulated in this example. The first is either at or on the way to
intersection 8 (in front of the central buffer), while the second is at or on the way
to intersection 3. The animation attribute of the workpiece at the head of the

queue at the central buffer is shown below the box representing the central buffer. If desired, the entire contents of any queue can be shown on the screen. This has been done for queue 8 (central buffer) [see figure (168)].

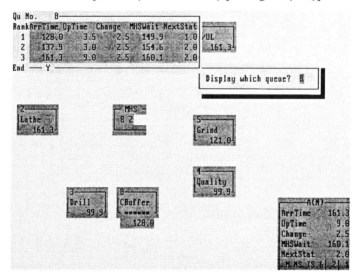

Figure 168: SIMANIM-Screen

As indicated in the contents of attribute 5 (NextStat), there is one workpiece waiting for access to station 1 (L/UL), and another two workpieces are waiting in the central buffer for access to station 2 (lathe). The animation with *SIMANIM* is especially useful during the model development phase. The animation layout is created very easily and provides, without significant time-loss, an overview of all the relevant system components in which the model-builder is interested.

The software system *CINEMA IV* offers a graphic-oriented user interface for a very realistic representation and animation of a simulation model. Figure (169) gives an example for a CINEMA layout[284] that has been designed for the FMS simulation model considered in this section.

A snapshot of the FMS is illustrated here in which the first of two AGVs included in the FMS has just delivered a workpiece to the drill machine which is now busy (this is indicated by the black machining table). The AGV is currently performing an idle trip. The second AGV is carrying a workpiece and is currently moving on the track between intersections 10 and 11. The other machines included in the FMS are idle. The central buffer holds two workpieces.

---

284   For further examples see **Pegden/Shannon/Sadowski** (1990), pp. 326-332

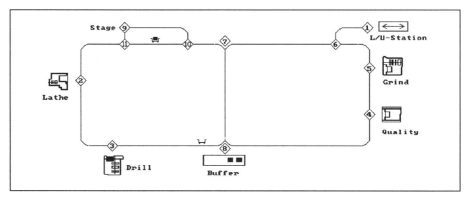

Figure 169: CINEMA-Screen

A CINEMA layout has to be drawn by the user himself with an arbitrary level of detail with the help of a special drawing program available for this purpose. First the animation background is painted, and then the various components of the simulation model (stations, machines, tracks, queues, etc.) are placed on the background.

Further reading for section 3.3.:

Banks/Carson (1984)
Bratley/Fox/Schrage (1983)
Carrie (1988)
Co/Jaw/Chen (1988)
Law/Haider (1989)
Law/Kelton (1982)
Pegden/Shannon/Sadowski (1990)
Rathmill/Cornwell (1986)
Tempelmeier (1991)

4. DECISION MODELS FOR THE DESIGN OF A FLEXIBLE MANUFACTURING SYSTEM

Whereas section 3. was dedicated to methods for *evaluating a given FMS configuration* with respect to specific performance indicators, in this section the problems associated with the selection of the *optimal* FMS configuration will be reviewed. Numerous model formulations and solution procedures have been suggested in the literature. In this chapter these approaches will be classified, and then selected decision models will be discussed in detail.

4.1. CLASSIFICATION OF DECISION PROBLEMS AND MODELS IN THE SELECTION OF THE OPTIMAL FMS CONFIGURATION

4.1.1. The Characteristics of Configuration Problems and Models

A large number of decision models have been proposed in the literature which can support a planner's search for the optimal FMS configuration alternative. These models may have a variety of different characteristics depending on which aspects of the configuration of an FMS are considered. These include the following:

- *Modelling of the FMS behavior*
- *Consideration of flexibility aspects (expansion flexibility)*
- *Decision variables considered*
- *Degree of uncertainty of the planning data*

- **Modelling of the FMS behavior**

Static models can be distinguished from dynamic models depending on how the model depicts the behavior of the FMS. *Dynamic models* result from the analysis of an FMS over time. They are especially well-suited to describe the random nature of the queueing processes at the machines, load/unload stations and transportation system as well as the characteristics of the material flow through the FMS. This is accomplished by using approaches from queueing theory which make it possible to calculate the relevant performance measures of an FMS as a function of the decision variables[285].

In a *static model* neither the queueing processes at the stations nor the characteristics of the material flow are included in the analysis. The production rate of a station is found by comparing the available capacity of a station per unit time

---

285 see also section 3.1.

with the total workload per unit time resulting from the number of workpieces to be processed. The production rate of the whole FMS is then determined by the production rate of the bottleneck machine, i.e. the machine with the highest workload per server (machine, setup area, transportation vehicle)[286].

The fact that the production quantity of the entire FMS is determined by the bottleneck machine allows simple and comprehensible linear programming models (LP models) to be formulated. These can be solved much more easily and efficiently with available standard algorithms than can models based on nonlinear queueing relationships.

This advantage of static approaches is generally balanced, however, by a loss in the precision of modelling detail with respect to the behavior of the FMS. As described in section 3.1.1.1.3., in the classical CQN model with universal pallets the production rate of the FMS approaches an upper bound asymptotically as the number of pallets increases. If the number of pallets continues to increase beyond a saturation point it will not result in an increase in the production rate, rather it will only cause the queue at the bottleneck machine to lengthen. Due to the flow-balance relationships among the individual nodes of the queueing network the production rate of a station cannot exceed the (maximum) service rate of the bottleneck machine. In the dynamic model as well, assuming an unlimited (or very large) number of pallets is circulating in the FMS, the system's production rate is also determined by the service rate of the bottleneck station. Therefore, the production rate at the saturation point in the dynamic model is identical to that of the bottleneck machine in a static model.

This relationship between the estimates of the performance of an FMS based on static and dynamic models is particularly important for solving mathematical programming models when the dynamic behavior of the FMS is of particular interest. Static models can in such cases be used to provide rough estimates in the first phase of a solution procedure. This makes it possible to significantly reduce the planning effort.

- **Consideration of flexibility aspects**

Various aspects of the flexibility of an FMS were discussed in section 1.3. It was pointed out then that in the long-term planning of an FMS the desired *product type spectrum* of the FMS can be considered constant. However, the *production quantities* of the different product types can be only considered constant in the medium and short-term. Variations in the planned production quantities will be caused by the integration of the FMS in the planning context of an overall production planning and control system. They can also be caused by the finite life cycles of the product types leading to changing production requirements. One well-known advantage of an FMS is that it is relatively easily reset to produce a new product type.

---

286   see also the discussion of the asymptotic model behavior for large numbers of pallets in section 3.1.1.1.3.

The different approaches for modelling FMSs can also be classified with respect to the expansion flexibility of an FMS. This describes whether and to what degree a given FMS configuration can be expanded with further machines, setup areas, vehicles, etc. With respect to the development over time of the product spectrum to be processed in the FMS, two kinds of modelling approaches can be distinguished: *single-period* and *multi-period* approaches. Single-period models observe a product type mix whose composition is constant over the entire life of the FMS. They concentrate their analysis on a "representative" period for which an appropriate FMS configuration must be designed.

If the composition of the product spectrum changes over time either in the make-up of its product types or in the production quantities, and if these changes can be predicted with sufficient accuracy, then a multi-period approach might be more appropriate. Here the entire life-time of the FMS is divided into a sequence of subperiods, each having its own period-specific production program. An optimal solution of the multi-period problem often includes the step-by-step expansion or adjustment of the FMS configuration according to the new production requirements. It is then possible to define a *development path* for an FMS along which the system is enlarged step-by-step and adjusted in conformance with changes in production requirements.

One aspect of the decision process is thus to determine if at the beginning of an investment period the FMS should be installed with excess capacity, or if an FMS configuration just sufficient for the current production requirements but allowing for expansion later would be more appropriate. Such questions can only be answered using a multi-period approach.

• Decision variables

All the factors influencing the performance of an FMS alternative described in section 3. can be considered as variables in the configuration phase. This is true not only for the number of machines, vehicles and pallets, but also for the quantities which had been assumed to be given in the evaluation of an FMS configuration, e.g. the composition of the product type spectrum, the structure of the process plans (routes), the production ratios of the product types or the lengths of the processing times.

It is assumed here that the principal decisions about the selection of the product type spectrum for processing in the FMS have been made, since this question is addressed in the technological planning phase[287] under consideration of engineering aspects. Thus the decisions which must be made in selecting the appropriate configuration of an FMS refer to three *basic types of decision variables*.

---

287 The structure of the FMS planning process is treated in section 2.1.1. Sometimes it will be necessary to return to the technological planning phase, for example if for a given product-mix even the best FMS design yields unsatisfactory results.

- *Assignment of products to routes and assignment of operations to machines*
  The focus of this type of problem is the determination of the operation sequences (routes) according to which a product is to be manufactured in an FMS. This is a result of the operation flexibility and the routing flexibility[288] of an FMS. The determination of the routes is particularly important in terms of its effects on the balanced utilization of resources and the subsequent consequences for the production rate of the FMS. With the help of variables reflecting the assignment of products to routes it can be determined whether or not a particular workpiece type should be processed in the given FMS.

- *Selection of the equipment to be integrated into the FMS*
  The amount of different equipment, i.e. machines, setup areas, vehicles, etc., to be installed in the FMS is determined with this set of decisions. Fixing these decision variables to a large degree defines the capacity of the FMS and thereby also the maximum possible production quantity.

- *Type and number of pallets or workpiece-carriers*
  As long as the number of pallets is not assumed to be unlimited, the optimum number of pallets must be determined. The number of pallets (workpieces) circulating in an FMS determines the degree to which the available capacity is used. If too few pallets are circulating in the FMS, then it is possible that individual machines may not be sufficiently supplied with unprocessed workpieces. If the number of pallets is too large, this will cause an unnecessary and unproductive increase of work-in-process inventory inside the FMS. Furthermore, it is necessary in many FMSs to distinguish among several pallet types.

Based on the scope of the decisions in the models described in the literature and on the decision variables used, it is possible to identify the following different *problem types*.

- *Routing optimization*
  The routing optimization controls the flow of workpieces through the FMS by either distributing the entire production quantity of a product type among alternative but equivalent routes, or by assigning the operations to alternative but equivalent station types. Since to do this the FMS must already exist, this problem will not arise directly during the configuration phase. Routing optimization is nevertheless considered to be a subproblem in many long-term decision models. Its solution is a prerequisite for the solution of a master problem. It is, for example, necessary to consider the routes according to which the workpieces move through the FMS when determining the number of identical machines to be installed in an FMS. A change in the routes gen-

---

288   see section 1.3.

erally leads to changes in the workloads of the machine groups (stations), and this then effects the optimal number of machines.

A *typical question* at this stage in the decision process might be if all workpieces of a given product type A should be exclusively processed according to a single route A_1, or would it be more practical to distribute the total production quantity of product type A between the routes A_1 and A_2 such that the proportions q_1 and q_2 of the workpieces would be produced according to routes A_1 and A_2 respectively.

- *Capacity optimization*

  A capacity optimization is necessary when the different types of equipment to be integrated into the FMS have already been determined (e.g. lathes, washing machines, setup areas, etc.). The next step is to determine how many units of each resource should be installed. The routes according to which the product types are to be produced have already been set, as has the question of which machine types (equipment types) should carry out which operations. The job of the capacity optimization model in this situation is to determine the necessary amount of equipment of each type, e.g. the number of machines per station or the number of vehicles for the transportation system. Capacity optimization models include equipment variables and often pallet variables as well.

  A *typical question* at this stage in the decision process could be if three or four AGVs should be included in the FMS.

- *Equipment optimization*

  Models for the optimization of equipment aid in the basic decision about which *types* of equipment (resources) to include in the FMS. Such models determine the type, number and use (via different routes) of the machines to be included in the FMS. The decision variables may be variables for the assignment of routes to products, as well as equipment and pallet variables. The equipment optimization problem includes the determination of routes and capacities (number of servers per station). If, for example, a particular machine type is not included in the FMS, then a route which requires this machine type will not be selected.

  A *typical question* at this stage of the decision process might be if a certain type of flexible machining center or a multiple-spindle drill should be integrated into the FMS.

- *Product type and equipment optimization*

  Aside from the equipment optimization, the workpiece spectrum intended for processing in the FMS must also be determined, though the results of the technological planning must be coordinated into this decision. The same decision variables are used here as for the equipment optimization. The alternatives for assigning workpieces to routes are defined in such a way as to make it possible to determine the product types to be processed in the FMS.

A *typical question* at this stage of the decision process might be if product type A should be processed in the planned FMS design. If not, would it make sense not to install machine X?

- *Production system and equipment optimization*

  FMSs are installed in many factories along side conventional job shops or transfer lines. The decision maker then faces the problem of whether or not and to what degree each of these different types of production systems could be combined with one another. Models for supporting this decision take several alternative types of production systems with different costs and performance characteristics into consideration and make it possible to choose the optimal combination of the available production system types. Decisions regarding the equipment to be included in an FMS could also be made in this context.

  A *question* at this stage in the decision process might be if an FMS should be installed instead of a conventional job shop, or if both types of production systems should process the workpiece spectrum in parallel.

- *Product type, production system, and equipment optimization*

  It is essentially possible to consider as variables the structure and capacity of the alternative production systems as well as the assignment of the desired products to these production systems. In such a model all the decisions which need to be made in the configuration planning of FMSs would be combined. A formal decision model of this type does not currently exist, however.

A summary of the problem types with respect to the decision variables discussed so far is presented in figure (170).

- **Degree of uncertainty of the planning data**

The choice of a particular configuration alternative is based on externally given information about the output to be achieved by the FMS. The desired output (production program, specified by type, quantity and time of requirements as well as by the point in time of the declaration of a requirement[289] or the available delivery lead time) is the result of a forecasting process which is, in many cases, subject to a high degree of uncertainty. Indeed the intrinsic flexibility of an FMS is supposed to deal with even unpredictable variations in the production requirements of an FMS. The consequence of this for the configuration phase is that deterministic output requirements cannot be counted upon, instead various scenarios under different assumptions about the future development of the company's environment and its corresponding needs have to be investigated.

---

289 This criterion defines the maximum lead time available for a given production order. The necessary reduction of this time span demanded by the marketplace is a main reason for the investment in FMS technology as an alternative to the large inventory that would otherwise be necessary.

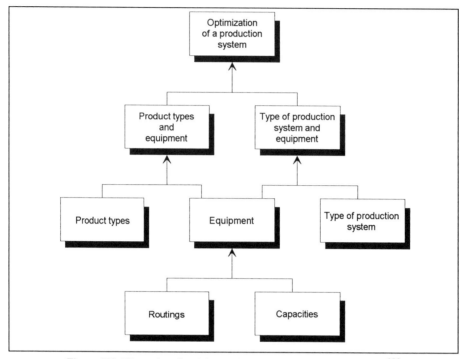

Figure 170: Hierarchy of problems arising in the configuration phase[290]

4.1.2. Quantifiable Goals of the Configuration Planning

A range of different goals may be sought with the installation of an FMS. They can be oriented around either the input side or the output side of the FMS, though in both cases there may be quantifiable and non-quantifiable elements. The quantifiable goals listed below will be considered in the decision models for the determination of an optimal FMS configuration in this section.

- *High production rate* while retaining flexibility, i.e. for arbitrary and simultaneous production of several product types.

- *Short flow times* of the jobs due to a reduction in setup times and lot sizes. At a given number of pallets, according to *Little's law*, the maximization of the production rate is equivalent to the minimization of the average flow time.

- *Low investment volume and low operating costs* for a given desired production program. If the planned output of an FMS is fixed, then its efficiency can only be increased via a reduction in the input necessary for production. Since

---

290   see also **Tetzlaff** (1990), p. 59

the type and quantity specifications in the production program are generally predetermined in a previous planning phase as givens, the system planner will attempt to find the FMS configuration that has the smallest investment

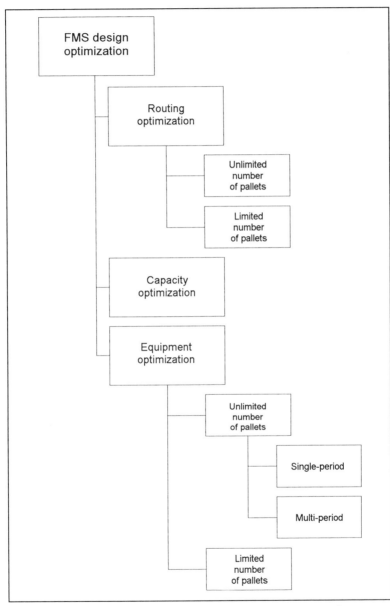

Figure 171: Overview of the configuration problems treated

volume and the lowest operating costs. It is necessary, however, to also consider the aspects of expansion flexibility, since from that point of view some deviations from the short-term optimum may be advisable in order to achieve a long-term optimum.

Selected decision models will be discussed in the following with which the search for the optimal FMS configuration can be supported. Primarily mathematical optimization models and solution procedures will be discussed. In contrast to the performance evaluation methods for FMSs described in section 3.1., these approaches reduce the number of different configuration alternatives without user interaction. They can, therefore, be used to exclude obviously suboptimal configuration alternatives from further analyzes at an early phase in the planning process. The term *configuration alternative* here stands for a set of decision variables considered with specified values.

In section 4.2. the effects arising from the capability of using several different process plans (routes) will be investigated. Following that, the discussion in section 4.3. will be dedicated to decision models which aid in the determination of the optimal number of machines, setup areas, vehicles (i.e. station capacities) and pallets in an FMS in which the machine types have already been selected. Finally, section 4.4. deals with the modelling and problem solving approaches for the determination of the machine types (equipment types) to be integrated into an FMS. Figure (171) provides an overview of the structure of the following discussion.

4.2. ROUTING OPTIMIZATION

The problem of routing optimization is to distribute the total production quantity of a product type which will be manufactured in an FMS among several alternative routes (process plans, operation sequences). This decision problem arises when there are several different routes that can be used alternatively and/or in parallel for the production of workpieces in the FMS for at least one product type. Each route is characterized by a specific flow of the workpieces through the FMS and a particular utilization of the equipment. Interesting for the following discussion is not the sequence of operations within a route, but rather the total processing time at a station needed for the complete processing of a workpiece in the FMS.

Route	L/UL	MC-1	MC-2	MC-3	Lath-1	Lath-2	AGV
1	15.00	10.00	5.00	5.00	10.00	-	15.00
2	15.00	-	10.00	30.00	-	5.00	12.00
3	10.00	-	30.00	30.00	-	-	9.00

Table 60: Alternative routes (mean workload per station) for a product type

Table (60) shows three routes according to which a given product type could be processed. Observe that station "Lath-2" is only used when route 2 is active. If this route is not used, then the machine "Lath-2" does not have to be included in the FMS configuration. It is possible to produce different workpieces of a single product type according to different routes, e.g. 20% according to route 1 and 80% according to route 2. This is reasonable when it leads to a more balanced utilization of the machines thus improving the overall production rate of the FMS. The analysis of several routes r ($r = 1,2,...,R_k$) for a product type k is on principle also possible with the representation of an FMS described in section 3.1.1.1.1. The only prerequisite is that the proportion of the total production quantity of product type k produced according to the various routes must be given. Instead of defining one single route for product type k, various routes for several dummy product types k' are defined. The sum of their production ratios $\alpha_{k'}$ must be equal to the production ratio of the product type k, α_k. In the following, the production ratio of a product type k processed according to route r will be designated as q_{kr}.

Routing optimization models take the route-dependent production ratios q_{kr} as variables. If there are R_k routes available for product type k, then equation (169) describes the relationship between the route-dependent production ratios q_{kr} and the total production ratio α_k of this product type.

$$\alpha_k = \sum_{r=1}^{R_k} q_{kr} \qquad\qquad k=1,2,\dots,K \qquad\qquad (169)$$

Decision models for routing optimization are designed to allocate the production ratios of the different product types to the routes defined for that product type. This is done by fixing the variables q_{kr} so as to optimize the performance indicator under consideration (production rate, flow time).

4.2.1. Routing Optimization with an Unlimited Number of Pallets

If the number of pallets in the FMS is unlimited, this means that the station with the heaviest load will be fully utilized. Since this machine is the bottleneck of the FMS, it never has to wait for the next workpiece it is going to process. There is always an unprocessed workpiece waiting for this machine to become free[291].

- *Secco-Suardo*[292]

suggested a linear optimization model for the determination of the optimal distribution of the products' production rates among the individual routes. Considering an FMS operating with a very large number of pallets, the goal of the optimization model is to *maximize* the *production rate* as a function of the assignment of the products to the routes. Each product type k can be processed according to R_k routes. The workload of the station m, w_{kmr}, for each of these

---

[291] see section 3.1.1.1.3.
[292] **Secco-Suardo** (1978), (1979)

routes r is known. It can be found by analyzing the product specific routes as follows [see equation (170)].

$$w_{kmr} = v_{kmr} \cdot b_{kmr} \qquad\qquad \begin{array}{l} m=1,2,\ldots,M; \\ r=1,2,\ldots,R_k; \ k=1,2,\ldots,K \end{array} \qquad (170)$$

     mean processing time of a workpiece of product type k at station m using route r

   average number of operations at station m for a workpiece of product type k that is manufactured according to route r

The quantities v_{kmr} and b_{kmr} differ from the variables v_{km} and b_{km} defined in section 3.1.1.1.1. only in their reference to r. The decision variables in the model proposed by *Secco-Suardo* are the route-dependent production rates of the product types.

Model AO-SE

$$\max \ X(\underline{x}) = \sum_{k=1}^{K} \sum_{r=1}^{R_k} x_{kr} \qquad\qquad\qquad\qquad (171)$$

subject to

$$\sum_{r=1}^{R_k} x_{kr} = \alpha_k \cdot \sum_{l=1}^{K} \sum_{r=1}^{R_l} x_{lr} \qquad\qquad k=1,2,\ldots,K \qquad (172)$$

     production rate of the FMS

$$\sum_{k=1}^{K} \sum_{r=1}^{R_k} x_{kr} \cdot w_{kmr} \le S_m \qquad\qquad m=1,2,\ldots,M \qquad (173)$$

     average number of machines used by route r of product type k at station m

$$x_{kr} \ge 0 \qquad\qquad\qquad k=1,2,\ldots,K; \ r=1,2,\ldots,R_k \qquad (174)$$

where

Data:

m	-	station index (m = 1,2,...,M)
k	-	product type index (k = 1,2,...,K)
r	-	route index (r = 1,2,...,R_k)
α_k	-	production ratio of product type k
R_k	-	number of routes defined for product type k
S_m	-	number of machines, load/unload stations, vehicles, etc. at station m
w_{kmr}	-	workload of station m with respect to route r of product type k

Variables:

$X(\underline{x})$	-	production rate of the FMS

x_{kr} -   production rate of product type k manufactured using route r

The objective function (171) describes the maximization of the production rate of the whole FMS, i.e. the sum of the production rates for all the products over all process plans. Equation (172) defines the quantitative relationships of the production rates of the different product types amongst each other. Here the sum of all the production rates of a product type k over all routes is equal to the product of the overall production rate of the FMS and the preset production ratio α_k of that product type. The constraints (173) describe the capacity limits at the stations. The average number of busy machines at station m[293], as derived from the product of the workloads w_{kmr} and the production rates, must not be greater than the number of available machines at the station.

The model AO-SE is a linear optimization model and may, therefore, be solved with the Simplex algorithm. The use of this model will be illustrated with a simple example with three product types. For each product type k there are R_k different routes. The possible routes are summarized in table (61). The information in the last column (AGV) is derived from the number of necessary transportation operations and the average trip time of 3 minutes in each case.

k	r	L/UL	MC-1	MC-2	MC-3	Lath-1	Lath-2	AGV
1	1	10.00	15.00	30.00	-	-	-	9.00
	2	15.00	20.00	-	-	20.00	-	9.00
2	1	5.00	-	-	10.00	5.00	16.00	12.00
	2	5.00	20.00	-	-	20.00	-	9.00
3	1	15.00	10.00	5.00	5.00	10.00	-	15.00
	2	15.00	-	10.00	30.00	-	5.00	12.00
	3	10.00	-	30.00	30.00	-	-	9.00

Table 61: Workloads (in minutes) at the stations with alternative routes (example 4-1)

The *configuration* of the FMS considered, for which the optimal distribution of the total production quantity among the available routes must be determined, is shown in table (62). It is made up of a transportation system with three vehicles, a setup station with three unloading or loading tables, various machining centers (MC-1, MC-2, MC-3) and two turning centers (Lath-1, Lath-2).

	L/UL	MC-1	MC-2	MC-3	Lath-1	Lath-2	AGV
S_m	3	2	2	1	2	2	3

Table 62: Configuration of the FMS (example 4-1)

The planned production ratios of the product types are given in table (63).

---

293   For single-server stations this quantity corresponds to the utilization.

k	1	2	3	Σ
α_k	0.289	0.395	0.316	1.0

Table 63: Planned production ratios (example 4-1)

Table (64) shows the LP tableau for the example 4-1 resulting from the AO-SE model.

	X11	X12	X21	X22	X31	X32	X33		
P-Rate	1	1	1	1	1	1	1		
Prod-1	.711	.711	-.289	-.289	-.289	-.289	-.289	=	0
Prod-2	-.395	-.395	.605	.605	-.395	-.395	-.395	=	0
Prod-3	-.316	-.316	-.316	-.316	.684	.684	.684	=	0
L/UL	10	15	5	5	15	15	10	<=	3
MC-1	15	20		20	10			<=	2
MC-2	30				5	10	30	<=	2
MC-3			10		5	30	30	<=	1
Lath-1		20	5	20	10			<=	2
Lath-2			16			5		<=	2
AGV	9	9	12	9	15	12	9	<=	3

Table 64: LP Tableau for example 4-1

The optimal solution is summarized in table (65). As can be seen, the production quantities for product types 1 and 2 are split between alternative routes, while only one route is used for product type 3.

Variable Status	Value	Comment
Structural variables:		q_{kr} $\qquad$ α_k
X11 BASIS	.0554039	product 1 - route 1 0.259 ⌐→ 0.289
X12 BASIS	.0063991	product 1 - route 2 0.030 ⌐
X21 BASIS	.0662116	product 2 - route 1 0.310 ⌐→ 0.395
X22 BASIS	.0182596	product 2 - route 2 0.085 ⌐
X31 BASIS	.0675769	product 3 - route 1 0.316 ⟶ 0.316
X32 NONBASIS	0	
X33 NONBASIS	0	
Slack variables:		
S.4 BASIS	.9139661	workload L/UL = 3-0.9139661 = 2.0860339
S.5 NONBASIS	0	MC-1 fully utilized
S.6 NONBASIS	0	MC-2 fully utilized
S.7 NONBASIS	0	MC-3 fully utilized
S.8 BASIS	.5	workload Lath-1 = 2-0.5 = 1.5
S.9 BASIS	.9406152	workload Lath-2 = 2-0.9406152 = 1.0593848
S.10 BASIS	.4712453	workload AGV = 3-0.4712453 = 2.5287547

Table 65: Optimal solution for example 4-1

The production rate of the FMS is $X(\underline{x}) = 0.213851$ workpieces per minute. This includes the sum of the values of all the structural variables. If the product-dependent production rates are divided by the production rate of the FMS, then the planned production ratios of the product types can be found. While the machines MC-1, MC-2 and MC-3 are fully utilized and thus represent the bottleneck of the FMS, unused capacity is still available at the other machines.

The model AO-SE describes a typical static allocation problem. It makes clear the influence of the use of alternative routes, i.e. the *operation flexibility*, on the performance of an FMS. This is primarily due to the improved distribution of the workload among the stations within the FMS allowed by the mix of different routes.

It must nevertheless be kept in mind that static modelling may only provide a rough approximation of the real behavior of an FMS. As has been pointed out, the route-dependent workload of a station influences the distribution of the pallets among the individual stations in the FMS and thus also the length of the queues[294]. These effects are not taken into consideration in the static approach described here. Since the queueing processes are completely ignored in the static approach, it is assumed that when the bottleneck machine becomes free there is always an unprocessed workpiece awaiting processing. This can result in a significant overestimation of the production quantity of the FMS when the number of pallets circulating is limited.

Other models have been presented in the literature which take a static point of view. For example,

- *Kimemia and Gershwin*[295]

formulate an LP model in which, in contrast to the AO-SE model, the analysis is based on the operations. The decision variables in this model refer to the *assignment of a product-specific operation to a station*. The routes can be put together after solution of the model through an inspection of the optimal values of the decision variables. This formulation has the advantage that not every possible route of a product has to be explicitly defined and represented with a decision variable. Yet the model must also include additional constraints which describe the set of feasible combinations of operations and routes and those which establish the coordination between the operation-dependent and the product type-dependent production quantities.

- *Avonts et al.*[296]

have formulated an LP model in which the products are assigned routes in such a way as to maximize the utilization of the FMS, i.e. the sum of the utilizations of all the stations. In this model both capacity limits and maximum production quantities for the individual product types must be observed. It is particularly useful for the decision of allocating a production quantity between the FMS and another *already existing conventional job shop*. The basic idea is to load the FMS as heavily as possible and to cover surplus capacity requirements with the conventional job shop. It is doubtful whether maximization of the utilization of the FMS stations at given capacities would be a useful objective for the configuration planning of an FMS. The primary objective is to achieve the maximum pro-

---

294   see section 3.1.1.1.2.
295   **Kimemia/Gershwin** (1979), (1985)
296   **Avonts/Gelders/Van Wassenhove** (1988)

duction rate possible for the FMS. In a case with differing processing times for the routing alternatives this goal will not be consistent with the goal of maximizing the machine utilization.

- *Leung and Tanchoco*[297]

have formulated a model for routing optimization whose objective is the maximization of the *contribution margin* over the direct operating costs. The latter is made up of the variable operating costs and the variable transportation costs. The decision variables are the product type and operation-dependent quantities which are transported between the machines. The assignment of the operations to the machines can be derived from these quantities. The model has a special structure which allows it to be broken down into several multi-commodity network flow models. These can then be solved with the Simplex algorithm. This model is only of limited use for configuration planning, however.

4.2.2. Routing Optimization with a Limited Number of Pallets

In contrast to the static modelling approaches described in the last section, the assumption that a limited number of pallets circulate in the FMS allows the stochastic behavior of an FMS - including any *queueing processes*, as described in the classical CQN model - to be included in the analysis. If the number of pallets is limited, it is possible that a *bottleneck machine* which has just become free may have to wait for a new workpiece because it is still being processed at another machine. This results directly in a loss of production.

Under the assumptions of the stochastic-stationary CQN modelling approach, the objective function is nonlinear. Therefore the linear programming solution approach is no longer applicable.

- *Tetzlaff*[298]

has formulated a model for the determination of the optimal route-dependent production ratios for an FMS with N *universal pallets* circulating. The product types can be produced according to various routes. The distribution of the production quantity for each product type among the different routes is to be accomplished in such a way as to *minimize* the *average flow time* D. If the number of pallets remains constant, then minimizing the flow time is equivalent to maximizing the production rate of the FMS. *Tetzlaff* takes the flow time as the key performance measure, since only with this variable can the convexity of the objective function be shown. The model reads as follows:

Model AO-TE

min D(q)   (175)

---

297   **Leung/Tanchoco** (1986)
298   **Tetzlaff** (1990), p. 77

subject to

$$\sum_{r=1}^{R_k} q_{kr} = \alpha_k \qquad\qquad k=1,2,\ldots,K \qquad\qquad (176)$$

$$q_{kr} \geq 0 \qquad\qquad k=1,2,\ldots,K; \; r=1,2,\ldots,R_k \qquad\qquad (177)$$

where

Data:

k	-	product type index ($k = 1,2,\ldots,K$)
r	-	route index ($r = 1,2,\ldots,R_k$)
α_k	-	production ratio of product type k
R_k	-	number of routes available for product type k

Variables:

q_{kr}	-	production ratio of product type k produced according to route r

The objective function (175) minimizes the average flow time $D(q)$ of a workpiece for an FMS with given capacities (machine types and the number of machines of each type) and in which N pallets circulate. The flow time is influenced by the distribution of the production ratios q among the various alternative routes r of the K product types. Constraints (176) guarantee that the planned production ratio α_k is achieved for each product type.

The objective function (average flow time) is a *nonlinear* function of the variables q_{kr}. The nonlinearity arises from the relationships underlying the *classical CQN model for universal pallets*: a change in q influences the average workload of station m, w_m. This then has a nonlinear effect on the average flow time of the pallets through the FMS. *Tetzlaff* developed a procedure for the solution of model AO-TE in which the relative marginal changes in the flow time are determined via their dependence on the routing variables q_{kr}. These values are defined in equation (178)[299].

$$l_{kr} = \frac{\left(\dfrac{\partial D(q)}{\partial q_{kr}}\right)}{D(q)} = \sum_{m=1}^{M} \frac{(Q_m(N)-Q_m(N-1))\cdot b_{kmr}\cdot v_{kmr}}{\displaystyle\sum_{l=1}^{K}\sum_{s=1}^{R_k} b_{lms}\cdot v_{lms}\cdot q_{ls}} \qquad k=1,2,\ldots,K; \; r=1,2,\ldots,R_k \qquad (178)$$

where

b_{kmr}	-	mean processing time at station m for a workpiece of product type k manufactured according to route r
$D(.)$	-	mean flow time of a workpiece through the FMS
l_{kr}	-	marginal relative flow time change for workpieces of product type k manufactured according to route r
q_{kr}	-	production ratio of product type k and route r

---

299 **Tetzlaff** (1990), p. 77

$Q_m(N)$ -   mean number of pallets at station m for N pallets circulating in the FMS
v_{kmr} -   mean number of operations at station m for a workpiece of product type k manufactured
according to route r

The procedure proposed by *Tetzlaff* modifies the route variables q_{kr} until the relative marginal changes in the average flow time for all of the routes used for one product type are the same.

Let us apply the AO-TE model to example 4-2. This example is essentially the same as example 4-1 as introduced with the AO-SE model except that $N = 20$ universal pallets circulate in this FMS[300]. As a *starting situation* assume that only the first route is used for a particular product type (the starting situation has been randomly chosen in this case). The feasible (though not optimal) solution illustrated in table (66) results.

k	1		2		3		
r	1	2	1	2	1	2	3
q_{kr}	0.289	0.0	0.395	0.0	0.316	0.0	0.0
x_{kr}	0.04835	0.0	0.06608	0.0	0.05286	0.0	0.0
					Production rate of the FMS: 0.16729		

Table 66: Route-dependent production ratios and production quantities
(example 4-2; arbitrary initial solution)

The overall production rate of the FMS is $X = 0.16729$ workpieces/minute. The average flow time is $D = 119.55$ minutes. The question is whether the flow time can be reduced by shifting the production ratios to routes not included in the current solution. For this reason the *relative marginal changes in the average flow time* with respect to the variables q_{kr} are calculated according to equation (178). These are summarized in table (67).

k	1		2		3		
r	1	2	1	2	1	2	3
l_{kr}	3.884	1.162	4.138	1.035	3.178	12.003	13.890

Table 67: Relative marginal flow time increases (initial solution; example 4-2)

If, for example, the routes of product type 1 are examined, it becomes clear that the average flow time of the workpieces of this product type can be reduced by shifting the production quantity from route 1 to route 2. The flow time is reduced by $3.884 \cdot \Delta q_1 \cdot D(\underline{q})$ units of time when the workload on route 1 is decreased by Δq_1, but it is only increased by $1.162 \cdot \Delta q_1 \cdot D(\underline{q})$ units of time when the use of route 2 is increased. With respect to the objective of minimizing the average flow time, a redistribution of the production quantities among the routes for

---

300   This example will be successively expanded by further details and marked with a unique number.

a given product type is only worthwhile until the flow time changes described by equation (178) with respect to all the q_{kr} variables are equal. This is only true for product types for which the entire production quantity is not already assigned to the best route. The average flow time for product 3, for example, cannot be reduced by shifting the production quantity to the two unused routes, because the relative marginal increase in the flow time for both routes (2 and 3) for product type 3 is greater than the relative marginal reduction in the flow time for route 1.

It is important to note that every shift of the production ratios among the routes for a particular product type in search of the optimal solution could affect the flow times of the other product types due to the interdependencies in a closed queueing network. The basis of the marginal analysis considerations is, therefore, constantly changing. *Tetzlaff* takes this fact into account in his analysis through an iterative procedure. The intermediate results found after further iterations are shown in table (68). The procedure is stopped after iteration 10, since the relative marginal changes in the flow time for all the active routes of a product type are almost the same.

k	1		2		3		
r	1	2	1	2	1	2	3
Iteration 0 (initial solution)							
q_{kr}	0.289	0.0	0.395	0.0	0.316	0.0	0.0
l_{kr}	3.884	1.162	4.138	1.035	3.178	12.003	13.890
Iteration 1							
q_{kr}	0.229	0.060	0.313	0.082	0.316	0.0	0.0
l_{kr}	4.305	3.854	3.309	3.637	3.933	8.296	9.345
Iteration 2							
q_{kr}	0.213	0.076	0.319	0.076	0.316	0.0	0.0
l_{kr}	3.867	3.935	3.522	3.714	3.997	8.691	9.453
Iteration 3							
q_{kr}	0.214	0.075	0.321	0.074	0.316	0.0	0.0
l_{kr}	3.832	3.838	3.596	3.617	3.990	8.927	9.701
...							
Iteration 10							
q_{kr}	0.214	0.075	0.322	0.073	0.316	0.0	0.0
l_{kr}	3.826	3.826	3.605	3.606	3.989	8.956	9.730

Table 68: Intermediate results (relative marginal flow time increases and production ratios; example 4-2)

Table (69) shows the optimal solution as determined with the AO-TE model and the corresponding route-dependent production rates for example 4-2. The *aver-*

age flow time sank from 119.55 to 111.58 minutes in comparison to the initial solution. The production rate increased from 0.16729 to 0.17925. The planned production ratios can be found by comparing the production rate for each product to that of the whole FMS.

For purposes of comparison, the optimal solution ($\underline{q}$) according to the AO-SE model was also evaluated with help of the classical CQN model for $N = 20$ universal pallets and included in table (69). The production rate of the FMS according to this solution is 0.17743. This is ca. 1% less than the optimal production rate. The average utilizations for the starting solution (iteration 0) and for the optimal solution (iteration 10) are given in figure (172). It can be seen that the relative load has been shifted from stations MC-2 and MC-3 to station MC-1, and from station Lath-2 to station Lath-1.

	k	1		2		3		
	r	1	2	1	2	1	2	3
AO-TE	x_{kr}	0.03836	0.01344	0.05772	0.01309	0.05664	-	-
	q_{kr}	0.214	0.075	0.322	0.073	0.316	-	-
					Production rate of the FMS: 0.17925			
AO-SE	x_{kr}	0.04597	0.00531	0.05493	0.01515	0.05607	-	-
	q_{kr}	0.259	0.030	0.310	0.085	0.316	-	-
					Production rate of the FMS: 0.17743			

Table 69: Production rates according to the optimal solution (example 4-2)

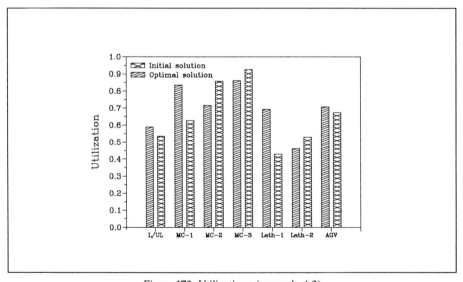

Figure 172: Utilizations (example 4-2)

The improvement in the solution associated with an increase in the average production rate (or with a reduction in the average flow time) corresponds with an all together higher utilization of the stations.

Figure (173) shows a vertical cut through the objective function at the optimal point parallel to the q_{11} axis (production ratio on route 1 of product type 1). The entire range of variation for this variable is limited by the planned production ratio of product 1, $\alpha_1 = 0.289$. When q_{11} is increased q_{12} is set to $q_{12} = 0.289 - q_{11}$.

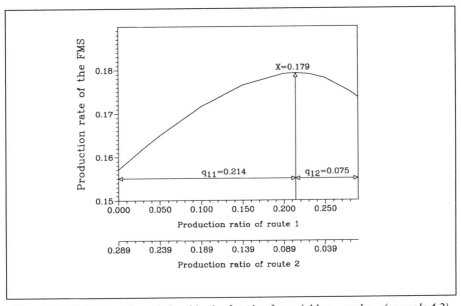

Figure 173: Vertical cut through the objective function for variable q_{11} and q_{12} (example 4-2)

When the production ratios of the routes for the product types 1 and 2 are varied simultaneously (q_{11}; $q_{12} = 0.289 - q_{11}$; q_{21}; $q_{22} = 0.395 - q_{21}$) and $q_{31} = 0.316$ remains constant, the production rate of the FMS develops as shown in figure (174). It can be clearly seen that the production rate of the FMS in this example is highly dependent on the distribution of the production quantities among the different routes. In the worst case ($q_{11} = 0$; $q_{12} = 0.289$; $q_{21} = 0$; $q_{22} = 0.395$) a production rate of only 0.111 can be reached. The lowest production rate resulting from a suboptimal selection of the routes is about 38% lower than the maximum possible production rate of the FMS.

When the results of the stationary-stochastic model AO-TE are compared with those of the static model AO-SE, significant differences can be noticed in the relative use of the routes for the products 1 and 2 - at least in the example 4-2. The two models agree only in the analysis of product 3 for which exclusively route 1 is used.

Nevertheless, the production rate of the optimal solution from model AO-SE lies just 1% under the maximum production rate. Here, neglecting the dynamic queueing processes in the static model AO-SE causes only limited losses in optimality. It is possible, however, that integrating the dynamic queueing processes into the analysis can become critical when the workload has to be distributed among machine types with significantly different numbers of machines.

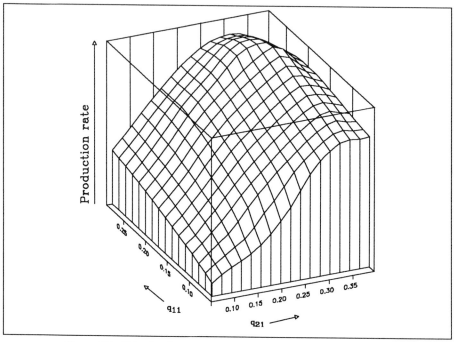

Figure 174: Objective function with varying q_{11} and q_{21} (example 4-2)

The static point of view of the AO-SE model tends to *overestimate* the production rate of an FMS, since in this approach at least one station is assumed to be always fully utilized. Possible idle times at the bottleneck machine due to the absence of unprocessed workpieces are excluded, since all stochastic interactions between the stations in the FMS are ruled out. This will particularly be a problem when model AO-SE leads to a solution in which several stations have almost the same high utilization. Other models, in which the distribution of production among various alternative routes is made under the assumption of a limited number of pallets in the FMS, have been proposed by

* *Kimemia and Gershwin*[301].

They consider an LP model whose objective function is the maximization of the production rate of the FMS, and they include some stochastic aspects. This is

---

301 **Kimemia/Gershwin** (1979), (1985)

done by adding a constraint which limits the number of pallets in the FMS to N. This constraint includes both the workpieces (pallets) under processing and the queues that might develop at the stations. *Kimemia and Gershwin* propose an approximation using the $M/M/1$ queueing model for the determination of the average queue lengths. A specialized solution procedure for the consideration of the nonlinear constraints thus introduced into the decision model is proposed.

- *Yao and Shanthikumar*[302]

consider a model of a specially structured FMS with several identical machine groups, each of which has several machines. The individual machine groups differ in their efficiency and in their corresponding processing times. The model determines the optimal distribution of the workpieces among the machine groups, i.e. that with maximum production rate. A workpiece is denied access to a machine group when all machines of that group are occupied, instead it is directed to an overflow area. Another constraint of the model assures that the production rate of the observed machine group is equal to the production rate of the previous production stage (which is not part of the model).

- *Tetzlaff*[303]

expands the approach of the AO-TE model by considering the case when the routes differ in their costs. He formulates a model to minimize the production costs which depend on the use of different routes, while still achieving a target production quantity. *Tetzlaff* suggests a Lagrangean optimization procedure for the solution of the model.

4.3. CAPACITY OPTIMIZATION

In the process of configuring an FMS questions arise about how many machines of a particular type and how many pallets should be integrated into the FMS. It has already been shown in section 3.1.1.1.3. that these design variables can significantly affect the performance of an FMS. Too few machines, setup areas, vehicles or pallets can prevent an FMS from reaching the desired production quantity per period.

If too much processing capacity (setup areas, machines, vehicles) is planned for a station, then this will not be fully utilized, and the investment expenses for the FMS will be higher than necessary. If too many pallets with workpieces circulate through the FMS, they will not contribute to an increase in the production rate, instead they will spend most of the time in queues at the stations. Since - aside from the capital costs of the pallet itself - every pallet is associated with work-in-process inventory (workpieces) and requires buffer space, it is generally preferable to have as few pallets circulating in the FMS as possible. Due to the interdependencies between the number of pallets and the capacity utilization of the individual stations it is necessary to consider these two configuration variables simultaneously.

302 **Yao/Shanthikumar** (1986), (1987)
303 **Tetzlaff** (1990), pp. 83-87

- *Vinod and Solberg*[304]

have proposed a decision model for the determination of the optimal capacity (system size) of an FMS. This model considers the simultaneous determination of the optimal numbers of machines, load/unload stations, transportation vehicles, and the number of *universal pallets* circulating in the FMS. The routes and the production ratios of the products are determined externally and not considered as decision variables - in contrast to the routing optimization model described in section 4.2. The objective function of the *Vinod and Solberg* model includes the costs per period depending on the investment volume per period (depreciation, capital costs) as well as the operating costs of the FMS. Both cost components are described as a function of the number of machines, setup areas, etc. and the number of universal pallets circulating in the FMS.

These fixed costs per time period are to be minimized by determining the number of machines of each type (station) and the number of setup areas and universal pallets under the constraint of achieving a desired minimum production rate X_{min}. This decision model reads as follows:

Model CA-VS

$$\min Z(\underline{S},N) = \sum_{m=1}^{M} (C_m \cdot S_m) + C_N \cdot N \qquad (179)$$

number of universal pallets

number of machines (load/unload stations, vehicles) at station m

subject to

$$X(\underline{S},N) \geq X_{min} \qquad (180)$$

production rate of the FMS

$$S_m, N \geq 1 \text{ and integer} \qquad m=1,2,\ldots,M \qquad (181)$$

where

Data:

m	-	station index $(m = 1,2,\ldots,M)$
C_m	-	fixed costs per period of a resource (machine, setup table, vehicle, etc.) at station m, i.e. of type m
C_N	-	fixed costs per period of a universal pallet
$X(\underline{S},N)$	-	production rate of the FMS
X_{min}	-	desired minimum production rate of the FMS

---

304 **Vinod/Solberg** (1985)

Variables:

N   -   number of universal pallets in the FMS
S_m -   number of machines, setup tables, vehicles, etc. at station m

The machine types which must be included in the model can be determined by inspecting the process plans of the product types to be manufactured in the FMS. The minimum size of a station is, therefore, equal to one. If an FMS configuration $(\underline{S},N)$ is given, then the classical CQN model for universal pallets[305] can be used to find the associated production rate $X(\underline{S},N)$.

Vinod and Solberg[306] suggested a multi-stage procedure for the solution of this decision model. It has been improved by *Dallery and Frein* and will be described in this form.

• *Dallery and Frein*[307]

assume that the production rate of the FMS and the value of the objective function (i.e. the fixed costs per period) are non-decreasing functions in the number of machines in the FMS. This means that an additional machine will not negatively affect the production rate of a station, and that all machines and pallets induce non-negative costs. *Dallery and Frein* develop a procedure that is executed in several steps [see figure (175)].

The procedure DALLERY-FREIN is explained in detail with the help of example 4-3, which results when the example 4-1 from section 4.2. is expanded by the cost parameters described in table (70). With respect to the route-dependent production ratios, the optimal solution for the AO-TE model shown in table (69) is assumed. The minimum production rate that must be achieved by the FMS configuration to be determined is $X_{min} = 0.17$ pieces/minute (10.2 pieces/hour).

Station	Costs
L/UL	500
MC-1	10000
MC-2	8000
MC-3	12000
Lath-1	15000
Lath-2	8000
AGV	200
Pallet	200

Table 70: Costs per equipment type and pallet (example 4-3)

---

305   see section 3.1.1.1.
306   **Vinod/Solberg** (1985)
307   **Dallery/Frein** (1986), (1988)

Procedure DALLERY-FREIN
Step 1: *Minimum configuration*
Determine a minimum configuration ($\underline{S}^b,N^b$); this configuration normally is infeasible, as it does not achieve the desired production rate.
Step 2: *Increase the number of pallets*
Increase the number of pallets in the minimum configuration until the desired production rate is achieved; name this first feasible solution ($\underline{S}^h,N^h$). The corresponding value of the objective function is Z^h.
Step 3: *Improve the current solution by increasing the size of one station*
Consider the solution ($\underline{S}^h,N^b$), i.e. start with the currently best station sizes and the minimum number of pallets. From the set of stations for which after the increase of the number of machines the costs are less than Z^h, select the station with the largest increase of the production rate per cost increase. If the set of stations is empty, go to step 5.
Step 4: *Increase the number of pallets*
For the current station sizes, increase the number of pallets until the desired production rate is achieved. If after the necessary increase in the number of pallets, the costs are less than the costs of the current best solution, update the current best solution with Z^h and ($\underline{S}^h,N^h$); go to step 3.
Step 5: *Find the optimal FMS configuration*
Starting with the minimum configuration ($\underline{S}^b,N^b$), find the optimal solution by implicit enumeration with Z^h as an upper bound for the objective function.

Figure 175: Procedure DALLERY-FREIN

Step 1: Determination of a minimum configuration

In the *first step*, *lower limits* for the capacities of the stations and the number of pallets, i.e. a minimum configuration ($\underline{S}^b,N^b$), are determined. This is done by using the so-called "asymptotic bound analysis" (ABA)[308], in which the desired production rate is related to the route-dependent workloads of the stations. A rough estimate of the minimum number of servers needed at station m, S_m, is provided by equation (182)[309].

---

308 **Denning/Buzen** (1978); **Lazowska/Zahorjan/Graham/Sevcik** (1984), pp. 70-97
309 The symbol "$[\ ]^+$" denotes rounding up to the next integer.

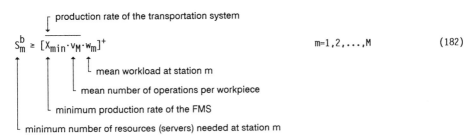

$$S_m^b \geq [X_{min} \cdot v_M \cdot w_m]^+ \qquad\qquad m=1,2,\ldots,M \qquad (182)$$

The *capacity* (number of machines) of station m must not be less than the product of the minimum production rate of the transportation system, $X_{min} \cdot v_M$, and the average workload w_m (per single operation) at the station according to equation (10). This estimate focuses on the bottleneck station of the system, as described in section 3.1.1.1.3.

The lower limit for the *number of pallets* is determined with the help of *Little's law*[310]. The total flow time D(.) of an average pallet through the FMS is approximated by the average total workload of the FMS, w_{FS} [equation (183)]. All queueing times are therefore neglected. The total workload of the FMS w_{FS} is found by summing up all the station-dependent workloads w_m [see equation (184)].

$$N^b \geq [X_{min} \cdot v_M \cdot w_{FS}]^+ \qquad\qquad\qquad (183)$$

$$\text{total workload of the FMS}$$

$$w_{FS} = \sum_{m=1}^{M} w_m \qquad\qquad\qquad (184)$$

The data necessary for the determination of the minimum FMS configuration for example 4-3 are summarized in table (71).

Station	Arrival probability p_m	Mean operation time b_m	Mean workload w_m
L/UL	0.25291	9.9800	2.52404
MC-1	0.17147	13.7611	2.35962
MC-2	0.13404	15.0943	2.02324
MC-3	0.16136	7.5235	1.21399
Lath-1	0.19879	9.8346	1.95502
Lath-2	0.08144	16.0000	1.30304
AGV	1.00000	3.0000	3.00000
Mean number of operations per workpiece (v_M):			3.59400
Mean production rate (X_{min}):			0.17000
Total workload of the FMS (w_{FS}):			14.78950

Table 71: Mean workloads (example 4-3)

---

310 **Little** (1961); see also equation (56)

When these data are introduced into equations (182) and (183), the following results:

Station	Mean work load w_m	$X_{min} \cdot v_M \cdot w_m$	S_m^b
L/UL	2.52404	$0.17 \cdot 3.594 \cdot 2.52404 = 1.69660$	2
MC-1	2.35962	$0.17 \cdot 3.594 \cdot 2.35962 = 1.58608$	2
MC-2	2.02324	$0.17 \cdot 3.594 \cdot 2.02324 = 1.35997$	2
MC-3	1.21399	$0.17 \cdot 3.594 \cdot 1.21399 = 0.81601$	1
Lath-1	1.95502	$0.17 \cdot 3.594 \cdot 1.95502 = 1.31412$	2
Lath-2	1.30304	$0.17 \cdot 3.594 \cdot 1.30304 = 0.87587$	1
AGV	3.00000	$0.17 \cdot 3.594 \cdot 3.00000 = 2.01653$	3
Minimum number of pallets (N^b):		$0.17 \cdot 3.954 \cdot 14.7895 = 9.66524$	10

Table 72: Determination of the minimum configuration (example 4-3)

Step 2: Isolated variation of the number of pallets

In this way the minimum configuration is determined. This does not yet represent a feasible solution, however, because the desired production rate $(X_{min} = 0.17)$ will not be reached under stochastic conditions. The above configuration (with $N = 10$ pallets) has a production rate of 0.1240178. This is obviously well under the desired production rate for the FMS (0.17).

Beginning with the minimum configuration $(\underline{S}^b, N^b)$, the number of pallets in the FMS is increased until the desired production rate is achieved. This procedure will always reach a feasible solution since the minimum configuration will achieve the desired production rate at least when $N = \infty$. Table (73) shows the development of the production rate of the FMS as a function of the number of pallets.

N	$X(\underline{S}^b, N)$
10	0.1241856
11	0.1301784
12	0.1354632
13	0.1401440
14	0.1443079
15	0.1480278
16	0.1513646
17	0.1543692
18	0.1570844
19	0.1595465
20	0.1617861
21	0.1638293
22	0.1656986
23	0.1674132
24	0.1689897
25	0.1704426

Table 73: Production rates vs. number of pallets (example 4-3)

The desired production rate is reached when $N = 25$ pallets. This first feasible solution is called $(\underline{S}^h, N^h)$. It induces costs of $Z^h = Z(\underline{S}^h, N^h) = Z(\underline{S}^b, N) = 92600$. These costs represent a temporary upper bound for the objective function.

Step 3: Isolated variation of the station capacities

In the third step the minimum number of pallets N^b ($=10$) is assumed, and a station is sought for which an increase in the capacity (number of machines, setup areas, vehicles) would induce lower costs than the current upper limit of the objective function, Z^h. For this purpose the quotient Δ_m, the growth in the production rate per increase in the objective function (relative production rate increase), is calculated with equation (185) when station m is expanded by one machine.

$$\Delta_m = \begin{cases} \dfrac{X(\underline{S}+\underline{1}_m, N^b)-X(\underline{S}, N^b)}{Z(\underline{S}+\underline{1}_m, N^b)-Z(\underline{S}, N^b)}, & \text{if} \quad Z(\underline{S}+\underline{1}_m, N^b) < Z^h \\ 0 & \text{if} \quad Z(\underline{S}+\underline{1}_m, N^b) \geq Z^h \end{cases} \qquad m=1,2,\ldots,M \qquad (185)$$

Here $\underline{1}_m$ represents a vector with a one in the mth place and all other elements zero. The value Δ_m represents an indicator for the station whose capacity could be increased by one unit. If the cost of this increase exceeds the cost of the current best solution, then increasing the capacity of this station is not worthwhile ($\Delta_m = 0$).

The intermediate results for the example considered are summarized in table (74).

m	Z_m	dZ_m	dX_m	Δ_m
1 (L/UL)	90100	500	0.0037346	0.000007469
2 (MC-1)	99600>92600			0
3 (MC-2)	97600>92600			0
4 (MC-3)	101600>92600			0
5 (Lath-1)	104600>92600			0
6 (Lath-2)	97600>92600			0
7 (AGV)	89800	200	0.0009984	0.000004992

$Z(\underline{S}^h, N^b)=89600$

Z_m – Costs with the size of station m increased by one machine ($)

dZ_m – Change of the value of the objective function ($)

dX_m – Change of the production rate (workpieces/minute)

Δ_m – Relative increase in the production rate [workpieces/(minute·$)]

Table 74: Intermediate results (example 4-3)

An increase in the capacity of station 1 (L/UL) is associated with the largest relative increase in the production rate.

Step 4: Changing the number of pallets

After the capacity of a station (station 1 in the example) has been increased by one unit, the number of pallets is increased (beginning from the minimum number of pallets $N^b = 10$). This continues until the desired minimum production rate

X_{min} has been achieved and thereby an feasible solution has been found, or until the costs exceed the best current value of the objective function. This is shown in table (75) for the example considered.

N	X(N)	Costs
10	0.1279800	90100
11	0.1343365	90300
12	0.1399823	90500
13	0.1449667	90700
14	0.1493825	90900
15	0.1533085	91100
16	0.1568113	91300
17	0.1599467	91500
18	0.1627623	91700
19	0.1652981	91900
20	0.1675883	92100
21	0.1696621	92300
22	0.1715445	92500

Table 75: Production rates vs. number of pallets after increasing the number of machines at station 1 (example 4-3)

After increasing the number of pallets the value of the objective function for the second feasible solution is compared to that of the current best solution $Z^h = Z(\underline{S}^h, N^h) = 92,600$. If the costs have been reduced ($Z = 92,500$), then the new solution will be stored as the new best current solution. This step 3 procedure is continued until no further reductions in the value of the objective function are possible.

The development of the various solutions is graphically represented in figure (176). The transition between the first feasible solution and the improved solution clearly shows that an exchange between a "pallet-dependent" and "station-dependent" portion of the production rate has taken place. This means it was possible to achieve a saving of three pallets, at $200 each, by expanding the setup station (station 1) by one unit at a cost increase of $500.

After completing the heuristic phase (steps 1 to 4) the optimal solution is determined by implicit enumeration. The costs of the best heuristic solution Z^h provide the upper bound Z^o of the value of the objective function. Beginning with the minimum configuration found in the first step, all feasible (i.e. larger) configuration vectors are enumerated. In each step the costs Z of each configuration alternative $(\underline{S}, N)$ are compared with the current upper bound Z^o. If they are lower than Z^o, it must be determined whether or not that configuration is feasible, i.e. if the minimum production rate X_{min} can be reached. If this is true, then the process is continued with a new best solution $(\underline{S}^o, N^o)$ and a new upper bound Z^o.

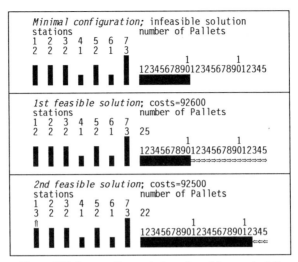

Figure 176: Intermediate solutions found (example 4-3)

If, however, the costs of the configuration $(\underline{S},N)$ exceed the upper bound Z°, then because of the monotone increase of the objective function it is impossible that an FMS configuration with an objective value better than Z° could exist which has larger stations or more pallets than the FMS configuration associated with Z°. Further branches of the solution tree can thus be closed. In the current example, the second feasible solution shown in figure (176) is optimal.

The CA-VS model and the associated solution procedure can be used for an FMS with universal pallets. It is possible to expand this approach to cover several pallet types. It would, however, then only be possible to find the number of machines per station and not the number of pallets from each type; i.e. only the quantity S_m could be used as a decision variable[311].

• *Solot*[312]

proposed a modelling approach whose goal is to determine the optimal number of pallets in an FMS with special pallets. He finds the number of pallets of each type with which the production rate will reach its maximum. Since the number of pallets according to this objective would approximate infinity, *Solot* introduces a correction factor into the objective function which makes increases in the production quantity become ever smaller as the number of pallets increases. This enforces a finite solution of the model.

• *Yao and Shanthikumar*[313]

propose other decision models for the determination of the optimal capacity of an FMS. In their analysis the guiding interest is the determination of the optimal

311   **Dallery/Frein** (1988)
312   **Solot** (1990a)
313   **Yao/Shanthikumar** (1986), (1987)

number of machines, the optimal allocation of a given number of machines among various machine groups, and the optimal sizing of the buffers.

* *Tetzlaff*[314]

has formulated a decision model for the determination of the number of machines and pallets which will yield the maximum production rate under a given capital budget constraint. He proposes a two-step procedure in which an heuristic solution is found, followed by an exact enumeration procedure.

* *Lee, Srinivasan and Yano*[315]

take the analysis a step further by treating, in addition to the number of machines and pallets, the distribution of the workload of the FMS among the machines as a decision variable. It is assumed that in an FMS with identical machines of *one machine type* several machine groups (stations) of possible different sizes will have to be installed. Upper and lower limits for the workload to be assigned to each machine group must be established. Furthermore, a total workload derived from the process plans of the product types is given which must be allocated among the individual machine groups with respect to their capacities (number of machines). *Lee, Srinivasan and Yano* propose an exact procedure for the solution of this problem.

4.4. EQUIPMENT OPTIMIZATION

Equipment optimization is concerned with determining not only the number of machines, but also the *types of machines* which are to be integrated into an FMS. Obviously, the operations to be carried out in the FMS play a significant role in the selection of the most appropriate machines. Such questions come up often in industrial practice. It might, for example, be asked if a complementary machine, such as a washing machine, should be planned as an integral part of the FMS and be connected to the other machines with the automatic transportation system, or if it would be better to install this machine outside the FMS. This would mean that the operation "wash" would have to be removed from the process plans for the product types in the FMS and would have to be carried out externally. Such situations can only be considered when it is technically possible to consider alternative routes. If, for technical reasons, there is only one possible route for each product, a machine which is needed for one of these routes cannot be removed from the FMS.

Equipment optimization also includes the problem of choosing between functionally almost identical machines with limited differences in performance offered by different FMS suppliers at different costs.

There are relatively few modelling approaches proposed in the literature for handling these types of problems. Here too it is possible to distinguish between static approaches (with an unlimited number of pallets) and stochastic-stationary

314 Tetzlaff (1990), pp. 105-109
315 Lee/Srinivasan/Yano (1989), (1991a), (1991b); see also Dallery/Stecke (1990)

models (with a limited number of pallets). There also exists a modelling approach in this field that explicitly considers the multiple-period structure of the decision problem and thus *flexibility aspects* and expansion flexibility[316] as well.

4.4.1. Equipment Optimization with an Unlimited Number of Pallets

The assumption of an unlimited number of pallets leads to the representation of the FMS in a deterministic LP model. There are both single-period and multi-period approaches to equipment optimization.

4.4.1.1. Single-period models

A decision model particularly aimed at designing flexible assembly systems has been proposed by

* *Graves and Whitney*[317]

They devised an LP model for the selection of machine types and the assignment to these machines of operations ordered according to a process plan. The basic assumptions of the model refer to a transfer line with machining stations that may be equipped in different ways. Every operation can be carried out on any of several alternative machines each with specific processing times and processing and investment costs. Thus the decision problem of which machines to include in the newly designed flow shop system configuration arises.

The objective function of this model includes annual fixed costs for the machines as well as operating costs which may be dependent on the assignment of an operation o (or an operation-dependent production quantity) to a station m. It must, however, be distinguished between production costs and loading and unloading costs. The latter are omitted when the operation immediately preceding the current one was carried out at the same machine. The decision variables of the models describe the assignment of the operations to the stations.

Model EQS-GW

$$\min Z = \sum_{m=1}^{M} C_m \cdot \gamma_m + \sum_{r=1}^{R} (CO_{om} \cdot x_{om} + CB_{om} \cdot y_{om}) \qquad (186)$$

└ variable loading and unloading costs for operation o at station m

└ variable production costs for operation o at station m

└ fixed costs of station m

---

316 see section 1.3.
317 **Graves/Whitney** (1979); see also **Graves/Lamar** (1983); **Graves/Redfield** (1988)

subject to

operation time

load and unload time

$$\sum_{o=1}^{0} b_{om} \cdot x_{om} + l_{om} \cdot y_{om} \leq g_m \cdot \gamma_m \qquad\qquad m=1,2,\ldots,M \qquad\qquad (187)$$

capacity of station m per period (hours)

$$\sum_{m=1}^{M} x_{om} = 1 \qquad\qquad o=1,2,\ldots,0 \qquad\qquad (188)$$

$$y_{om} \geq x_{om} - x_{0-1,m} \qquad\qquad m=1,2,\ldots,M; \ o=1,2,\ldots,0 \qquad (189)$$

$$x_{om}, \ y_{om} \geq 0 \qquad\qquad m=1,2,\ldots,M; \ o=1,2,\ldots,0 \qquad (190)$$

$$\gamma_m = \{0,1\} \qquad\qquad m=1,2,\ldots,M \qquad\qquad (191)$$

where

Data:

m	-	station index ($m = 1,2,\ldots,M$)
o	-	operation index ($o = 1,2,\ldots,O$)
b_{om}	-	processing time for operation o at station m
CB_{om}	-	variable loading and unloading costs for operation o at machine m (with respect to the total production rate per period)
CO_{om}	-	variable production costs for operation o at machine m (with respect to the total production rate per period)
C_m	-	fixed costs of station m
g_m	-	capacity of station m (hours/year)
l_{om}	-	load and unload time for operation o at station m

Variables:

x_{om}	-	production rate for operation o at station m
y_{om}	-	production rate for operation o to be loaded and unloaded at station m
γ_m	=	$\begin{cases} 1 \text{, if station is included in the production system} \\ 0 \text{, otherwise} \end{cases}$

The objective function (186) describes the fixed costs per period for all the stations in the FMS as well as the variable production, loading, and unloading costs. The constraints (188) guarantee that the *entire production quantity (= 1) will be manufactured for each operation.* It is not asked whether or not a particular operation will be executed by the new production system. The only concern is which machine type(s) should carry out this operation. The constraints (187) enforce that the workload of a station does not exceed its available capacity g_m. The loading and unloading quantities for the operations are defined by the inequalities (189). It is assumed that the operations to be performed are numbered according to the order of their execution (position in the process plan). If x_{om} is less than or equal to $x_{o-1,m}$, this means that the entire production quantity is already present at the station, as it has been loaded into the station for operation (o-1). An additional loading and unloading operation is no longer necessary. In this case y_{om} is equal to zero. If instead x_{om} is greater than $x_{o-1,m}$, then y_{om} loading and unloading operations must be carried out.

The model EQS-GW is a large mixed-binary linear program for which *Graves and Whitney* suggested a specialized branch-and-bound procedure. It has been expanded by

• *Graves and Lamar*[318]

on the basis of a reformulation as a network flow problem. It is also possible in this formulation to include tool exchange operations and the stations' associated idle times in the analysis. Both modelling approaches are of only limited value for the type of FMSs considered here, however, because of their orientation towards paced flow line systems.

A straight-forward extension of the model AO-SE[319] for equipment optimization (determining the type and number of machines, setup areas, and vehicles to be included in the FMS) leads to the following mixed-integer linear optimization model:

> ### Model EQS-MIP

$$\min Z = \sum_{m=1}^{M} \underbrace{C_m \cdot S_m}_{} + \sum_{k=1}^{K} \sum_{r=1}^{R_k} \underbrace{CO_{kr} \cdot x_{kr}}_{} \qquad (192)$$

↑ fixed costs of station m

↑ variable production costs for route r of product type k

subject to

$$\sum_{k=1}^{K} \sum_{r=1}^{R_k} x_{kr} \cdot w_{kmr} \leq S_m \qquad\qquad m=1,2,\ldots,M \qquad (193)$$

$$\sum_{r=1}^{R_k} x_{kr} = \alpha_k \cdot \underbrace{\sum_{l=1}^{K} \sum_{r=1}^{R_l} x_{lr}}_{} \qquad\qquad k=1,2,\ldots,K \qquad (194)$$

↑ production rate of the FMS

$$\sum_{r=1}^{R_k} x_{kr} \geq X_{min} \qquad\qquad k=1,2,\ldots,K \qquad (195)$$

$$x_{kr} \geq 0 \qquad\qquad k=1,2,\ldots,K;\ r=1,2,\ldots,R_k \qquad (196)$$

---

318 **Graves/Lamar** (1983)
319 see section 4.2.1.

$S_m \geq 0$ and integer $\qquad\qquad$ m=1,2,...,M $\qquad\qquad\qquad$ (197)

where

Data:

k	-	product type index (k = 1,2,...,K)
m	-	station index (m = 1,2,...,M)
r	-	route index (r = 1,2,...,R)
α_k	-	production ratio of product type k
C_m	-	fixed costs of a resource (machine, setup table, vehicle, etc.) at station m
CO_{kr}	-	variable production costs for product type k produced using route r
R_k	-	number of routes for product type k
w_{kmr}	-	workload of station m when route r of product type k is used
X_{min}	-	minimum desired production rate of the FMS

Variables:

S_m	-	number of machines, load/unload stations, vehicles, etc. at station m
x_{kr}	-	production rate of product type k produced using route r

The model EQS-MIP differs from the model AO-SE in that the number of machines per station (S_m) is viewed as a decision variable instead of a given. The objective function is also changed and there are additional constraints (195) which fix the minimum required production rate of the FMS. The objective function includes the station-specific fixed costs per resource C_m as well as the variable operating costs CO_{kr} for the routes of each product type.

To explain the model EQS-MIP example 4-1 will be modified and renamed example 4-4. It is assumed that the desired production rate of the FMS is $X_{min}=0.213851$ workpieces/minute and that the fixed costs per resource C_m are equal to those given in table (70). The costs of only one machine at station 6 (Lath-2) were set quite high ($30,000) in order to illustrate the relationship between the costs of the machine and the use of the routes. To keep the example simple, production costs CO_{kr} have been set to zero. The resultant LP tableau is shown in table (76).

	S1	S2	S3	S4	S5	S6	S7	X11	X12	X21	X22	X31	X32	X33	
Z	500	10000	8000	12000	15000	30000	200								
A1	-1							10	15	5	5	15	15	10	<= 0
A2		-1						15	20		20	10			<= 0
A3			-1					30				5	10	30	<= 0
A4				-1						10		5	30	30	<= 0
A5					-1				20	5	20	10			<= 0
A6						-1				16				5	<= 0
A7							-1	9	9	12	9	15	12	9	<= 0
B1								.711	.711	-.289	-.289	-.289	-.289	-.289	= 0
B2								-.395	-.395	.605	.605	-.395	-.395	-.395	= 0
B3								-.316	-.316	-.316	-.316	.684	.684	.684	= 0
C1								1	1	1	1	1	1	1	= .213851

Table 76: LP tableau for model EQS-MIP (example 4-4)

If the objective function of the model EQS-MIP is evaluated for the number of machines assumed in the example for the model AO-SE [$\underline{S}=(3,2,2,1,2,2,3)$], the total fixed costs per period will be found to be $140,100. As expected, the route-dependent production rates agree with the solution for model AO-SE.

If model EQS-MIP is solved for example 4-4, an entirely different solution comes out with costs of only $115,100. This is summarized in table (77).

Stations							
m	1	2	3	4	5	6	7
S_m	3	4	2	1	3	0	3
Routes							
k	1		2		3		
r	1	2	1	2	1	2	3
x_{kr}	0.033333	0.028468	0.0	0.084469	0.041090	0.0	0.026485
						$\Sigma\ x_{kr}$ =	0.213845

Table 77: Optimal solution of model EQS-MIP (example 4-4)

With the assumed cost parameters, station 6 (Lath-2) will not be included in the FMS. This means that all the routes that make use of this station (route 1 of the product type 2 and route 2 of the product type 3) can also not be used. The production rates of the other routes have been increased accordingly.

The model EQS-MIP shows clearly that decisions about the type of machines (stations) and the use of alternative routes for the product types must be considered together. An ex ante determination of one group of these variables can result in significant deviations from the optimum solution.

Model EQS-MIP can be solved with the help of a standard algorithm for mixed-integer linear optimization. Since the number of integer variables is dependent on the number of stations, the determination of the optimal solution is no problem. The above solution was calculated on a 80486/25MHz PC in about ten seconds.

- *Tetzlaff*[320]

proposed a generalized model in which the costs of a station are divided into a fixed part, independent of the number of machines at a station, and a variable part, dependent on the *size* of the station.

Tetzlaff considers various expansion levels for a station, and introduces a binary variable for each one. The number of integer variables will be increased significantly with this modelling technique. However, this makes it possible to allow for concave cost functions (unit costs declining with increasing station size). *Tetzlaff* has developed one heuristic and several exact procedures for solving the resulting large mixed-binary programming model.

---

320 **Tetzlaff** (1990), pp. 118-119

- *Irani, Leung and Snyder*[321]

suggested a very simple LP model to support the decision about whether some machines in an existing conventional job shop should be replaced by a more highly automated production system (e.g. a flexible manufacturing cell). They assume that the alternative production systems differ with respect to their performance (production rate) and their costs. The performance differences are due primarily to different processing times per workpiece and a smaller transportation demand.

4.4.1.2. A multi-period model

Expansion flexibility was described in section 1.3. as a special quality of an FMS. This includes the ability to replace components of an FMS after it has already been in use for some years, and the ability to expand an already existing FMS by adding new components. One important reason for expanding is to react to a change in the quantity or type structure of the production program. This is often due to developments in the life cycles of the product types. Changes in the production program may be so massive that they cannot be satisfactorily responded to within the *volume flexibility* of a given FMS configuration, i.e. the ability to change products without additional investments. It has been assumed up to now that the qualitative and quantitative demands on the performance of an FMS would remain the same over time. Therefore, the considerations during the selection of an FMS configuration could be restricted to an average period. This assumption will no longer hold true in the following discussion. It will instead be assumed that the production quantity to be delivered by the FMS may be subject to dynamic changes over time. The planning period is now divided into H ($h = 1, 2, ..., H$) separate subperiods for which the product type-dependent production quantities X_{kh} ($k = 1, 2, ..., K$; $h = 1, 2, ..., H$) are deterministically fixed in advance.

Variations in the production requirements derived from the production program can obviously also change the optimal configuration of an FMS. It may, therefore, make sense to install a "small" FMS when the production quantity is low. If it is expected that demand for the products being manufactured in the FMS will increase after a number of years, it would be possible to install additional FMS components and to enlarge the FMS. The planned expansion of an FMS as a result of a change in demand could not be included in the models presented up to now, since these describe FMS configurations that are only designed with "normal" production requirements in mind.

If the production quantity is expected to increase, a fundamental question must be asked. Should the additional capacity be built into the FMS when it is installed? This would require that the corresponding surplus capacity (resulting in low utilizations of individual stations) be accepted. On the other hand should instead a "small" FMS configuration be chosen that could later be adjusted in ac-

---

321 **Irani/Leung/Snyder** (1986)

cordance with any necessary change in production quantity through an additional investment.

An expansion at the time of demand has the advantage that the capital costs of the FMS components will be incurred only at this later time. Perhaps more important is that the decision about the final expansion of the FMS may be made when the relevant information is available with a greater degree of confidence. The disadvantage of this method is that the expansion of an existing facility is often more expensive than the integration of the relevant FMS components into the initial installation. It is also often true that an expansion investment can only be accomplished when the FMS is closed down, resulting in opportunity costs due to lost output. Furthermore, the supply and disposal systems can often be more easily made accessible during the initial installation than during an expansion at a later time.

Since various times of investment are explicitly included in the analysis, all of the payments associated with the investment will be discounted with respect to the reference time 0. Assuming a deterministically preset and dynamically changing demand, the decision problem consists of setting up the *installation and expansion plan* for an FMS such that it minimizes the present value of all outpayments. In the following a decision model will be formulated that focuses on the determination of the optimal sequence of initial and expansion investments as well as the optimal use of the FMS through alternative *routes* in the individual subperiods of a multi-period planning horizon. The multi-period decision model for equipment optimization reads as follows:

Model EQD-TE

$$\text{Min } Z = \sum_{h=0}^{H-1} \sum_{m=1}^{M} (1+i)^{-h} \cdot AI_{mh} \cdot z_{mh} + \sum_{h=0}^{H} \sum_{k=1}^{K} \sum_{r=1}^{R_k} (1+i)^{-h} \cdot AO_{krh} \cdot x_{krh} \tag{198}$$

- operating expenses in period h associated with production of product type k using route r
- number of machines installed at station m at the beginning of period h
- investment expenditure for a machine at station m installed in period h
- discount rate

subject to

$$\sum_{k=1}^{K} \sum_{r=1}^{R_k} x_{krh} \cdot w_{kmr} \leq \sum_{l=0}^{h-1} z_{ml} \qquad m=1,2,\dots,M; \ h=1,2,\dots,H \tag{199}$$

- number of machines at station m installed in period l
- utilization of station m with respect to product type k in period h

$$\sum_{r=1}^{R_k} x_{krh} = X_{kh} \qquad\qquad\qquad k=1,2,\ldots,K;\ h=1,2,\ldots,H \qquad (200)$$

       ⌐ planned production rate of product type k in period h

    ⌐ production rate for product type k using route r in period h

$$x_{krh} \geq 0 \qquad\qquad\qquad\qquad \begin{array}{l} k=1,2,\ldots,K;\ r=1,2,\ldots,R_k; \\ h=1,2,\ldots,H \end{array} \qquad (201)$$

$$z_{mh} \geq 0 \text{ and integer} \qquad\qquad m=1,2,\ldots,M;\ h=1,2,\ldots,H \qquad (202)$$

where

Data:

h	-	period index (h = 1,2,...,H)
k	-	product type index (k = 1,2,...,K)
m	-	station index (m = 1,2,...,M)
r	-	route index (r = 1,2,...,R_k)
AI_{mh}	-	investment expenditure for a resource of type (station) m in period h
AO_{krh}	-	operating expenses in period h associated with the production of a unit of product type k using route r
i	-	discount rate
R_k	-	number of routes available for product type k
w_{kmr}	-	mean workload of station m resulting from route r of product type k
X_{kh}	-	planned production rate of product type k in period h

Variables:

x_{krh}	-	production quantity of product type k produced in period h using route r
z_{mh}	-	number of resources installed at station m in period h

It is assumed that period-specific production quantities X_{kh} for each of the individual product types are given in advance, based on a planning horizon with H periods. Every product type can be manufactured according to one or more routes. An appropriate number of the necessary machine types (stations) must, therefore, be installed. If a machine (setup area, vehicle) is installed at station m in period h, it induces investment expenditures of AI_{mh}. If a machine at station m is used to produce x_{krh} units of product type k according to route r in period h, then operating expenses of $AO_{krh} \cdot x_{krh}$ are incurred. The objective function includes the sum of the investment expenditures and operating expenses over all the H periods in the planning horizon - both discounted to the reference time 0. Investments are possible up to time H-1, i.e. until the beginning of the period H.

The constraints (199) assure that sufficient capacity is made available in each period to produce the planned production quantity. Smoothing out production by building up or reducing inventory is not allowed in this model. The capacity of a station in period h is based on all the machines installed from the reference time 0 to the beginning of period h (time h-1). It is assumed, however, that only expansions are possible. The elimination of individual machines is not considered. Equation (200) assures that the production quantities of all the routes used for a product type agree with the planned production quantities in period t.

- *Tetzlaff[322]*

proposes an heuristic procedure for the solution of the EQD-TE model which is based on dynamic optimization. The procedure uses a representation of the multi-period investment and allocation problem as a network. The network's nodes are the points in time when a change in the FMS configuration is possible (the ends of periods), and its arcs represent the duration of the use of this configuration for production. Figure (177) illustrates such a network for four periods.

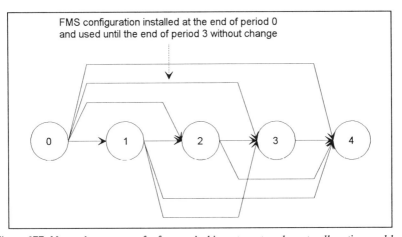

Figure 177: Network structure of a four period investment and route allocation problem

Each arc between the nodes τ and h ($\tau < h$) represents a particular configuration which was fixed at the end of period τ and remained unchanged until the end of period h. This configuration must possess sufficient capacity to be able to meet even the largest demand in a period since using inventory for production smoothing is not possible and backorders are not allowed. A change in an FMS configuration is associated with a node, i.e. it takes place at the end of a period.

A *cost* is assigned to each arc between the nodes τ and h. This is made up of the present value of the additional investment expenditures in period τ and the present value of the operating expenses attributable to production in the periods $\tau+1$ to h. The additional investment expenditures are due to changes in the optimal FMS configuration for the period from 0 to τ in comparison with the FMS configuration which is best able to produce the entire quantity required in the periods $\tau+1$ to h.

The *cost* assigned to an arc is only known when the problem of the simultaneous determination of the optimal FMS configuration and the optimal allocation of

---

322 **Tetzlaff** (1990), pp. 130-132

the production quantities of the individual periods has been solved. *Tetzlaff* suggests an heuristic procedure with which the optimal FMS configuration can be found that is able to produce the required production quantities for the time periods $\tau + 1$ to h associated with an arc. The production quantities are heuristically distributed among the alternative routes for each period separately.

Before discussing the procedure further, consider example 4-5, actually example 4-3 expanded to include multi-period demand quantities. It is based on a planning horizon of 4 periods for which product type and period-specific production quantities have already been fixed. The discount rate is assumed to be $i = 10\%$. Operating expenses are excluded for purposes of simplicity. Each period is 180,000 minutes long.

Station	Investment expenditure	Period	Production rates Product 1	Product 2	Product 3
L/UL	500	1	6000	8000	7000
MC-1	10000	2	9000	12000	8000
MC-2	8000	3	11000	12000	10000
MC-3	12000	4	12000	12000	12000
Lath-1	15000				
Lath-2	8000				
AGV	200				

Table 78: Costs per machine and planned production rates (example 4-5)

Figure (178) shows the costs associated to the network's arcs. The FMS configurations (S_1, S_2, etc.) corresponding to each arc are given in the rows marked "$\underline{S}$". The rows marked "$\underline{z}$" indicate the additional resources, as compared to their individual reference configuration, which have been included in the FMS configuration. Since this example is still a manageable size, an exact solution (amount of equipment and production quantity) can be found for each arc with the help of the EQS-MIP model. *Tetzlaff* suggests an heuristic procedure especially designed for larger problems[323].

The *expenses of the additionally installed equipment* are given in the rows labeled ΔI. For example, the valuation of the arc between the nodes 2 and 4 is 12,975. This value is based on the fact that the FMS configuration that is able to produce the planned production quantities in periods 3 and 4 is developed from the best FMS configuration found for the time from period 1 to period 2. This is configuration $\underline{S} = (2,2,2,1,1,1,2)$[324]. In addition to this configuration it is necessary to install one machine each at stations 1 and 5 as well as to integrate one additional vehicle into the FMS configuration. The present value of the additional investment expenditures at time 2 is thus $(500 + 15,000 + 200) \cdot (1 + 0.1)^{-2} = 12,975$.

---

[323] **Tetzlaff** (1990), pp. 130-132

[324] The best configuration alternative used as a basis for an FMS expansion is marked as the starting node of the corresponding arc.

		To node			
		1	2	3	4
From node 0	S	2 1 1 1 1 1 2	2 2 2 1 1 1 2	2 2 1 1 2 1 3	3 2 1 1 2 1 3
	Z	2 1 1 1 1 1 2	2 2 2 1 1 1 2	2 2 1 1 2 1 3	3 2 1 1 2 1 3
	ΔI	54400	72400	79600	80100
	ΣI	54400	72400	79600	80100
1	S		2 2 2 1 1 1 2	2 2 1 1 2 1 3	3 2 1 1 2 1 3
	Z		- 1 1 - - - -	- 1 - - 1 - 1	1 1 - - 1 - 1
	ΔI		16364	22909	23364
	ΣI		70764	77309	77764
2	S			2 2 3 1 1 1 3	3 2 2 1 2 1 3
	Z			- - 1 - - - 1	1 - - - 1 - 1
	ΔI			6777	12975
	ΣI			77541	83739
3	S				3 2 1 1 2 1 3
	Z				1 - - - - - -
	ΔI				376
	ΣI				77685

Figure 178: Arc costs (example 4-5)

If the valuations (arc lengths) of the all together $[H \cdot (H+1)]/2$ arcs have been computed, then the solution of model EQD-TE can be calculated by establishing the *shortest path through the network*. The cumulative lengths of the arcs, i.e. the present values of all the investment expenditures throughout a particular expansion path, is given in the rows marked with ΣI. The optimal strategy of expansion can now be found by following the path with the lowest sum of discounted expenditures. Figure (178) suggests that the best way to get from node 0 to node 4 is via nodes 1 and 3. This would then result in the development of the configuration of the FMS shown in table (79).

Period	L/UL	MC-1	MC-2	MC-3	Lath-1	Lath-2	AGV	Present value of the investment expenses
0	2	1	1	1	1	1	2	54400
1	2	1	1	1	1	1	2	
		↓			↓		↓	
2	2	2	1	1	2	1	3	22909
	↓							
3	3	2	1	1	2	1	3	376
							Total:	77685

Table 79: FMS configurations developed (example 4-5)

Figure (179) shows the network representation of the solution. The optimal route-dependent production quantities for the individual FMS configurations, found with help of the EQS-MIP model, are given in table (80).

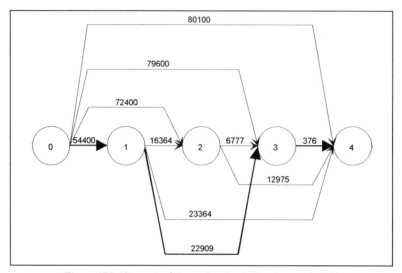

Figure 179: Network of the optimal solution (example 4-5)

k	1		2		3		
r	1	2	1	2	1	2	3
h=1	2113	3887	6340	1660	3736	0	3264
h=2	4667	4333	11250	750	8000	0	0
h=3	4000	7000	8000	4000	8000	2000	0
h=4	3918	8082	10780	1220	11511	489	0

Table 80: Production rates per route[325] (example 4-5)

The procedure used in example 4-5 for the solution of the EQD-TE model has in many ways an heuristic nature. Particularly the representation of the multi-station-problem as *one* network is heuristic. It would only be exact if the FMS was made up of only one machine type (station). In order to devise an exact network representation of the problem several networks would have to be built, and their paths would have to be optimized with respect to one another. Furthermore, in the approach suggested by *Tetzlaff* the allocation of the production quantity among the alternative routes and the determination of the

---

325 As opposed to the models discussed in section 3., the production rates refer to a time period of one year = 250·12·60 = 180,000 minutes.

FMS configuration are achieved with an heuristic procedure. Even large problems can be solved efficiently in this way, however.

• *Suresh and Sarkis*[326]

as well as

• *Suresh*[327]

have discussed other mixed-integer linear programming formulations that aim at the determination of the optimal development of the installation and expansion of an FMS over time. It is assumed that the components of the FMS can be expanded, if necessary, to satisfy an increase in production requirements. Predetermined capital budgets are accounted for in the individual periods of the planning horizon, though the funds required for financing an expansion investment are artificially reduced by using a so called reinvestment factor. The objective function of the models is made up of the present values of both the one-time and operating expenses associated with the investments. Standard mixed-integer optimization algorithms are used to solve the models.

4.4.2. Equipment Optimization with a Limited Number of Pallets

The influence of the assignment of an operation to a machine type on the dynamic system behavior, such as the development of queues, has been excluded from the models discussed up to now.

• *Tetzlaff*[328]

proposed a stochastic-stationary model in which these phenomena are explicitly integrated into the analysis. The objective function includes the fixed costs for the machines and the pallets as well as for the workpieces and other devices. Variable operating costs are not considered, though it is possible to expand the model to include them.

Model EQ-TE

$$\min Z = \sum_{m=1}^{M} \sum_{b=1}^{B_m} C_{bm} \cdot \gamma_{bm} + C_N \cdot N \tag{203}$$

↑ └ fixed costs of pallets (incl. costs for fixtures and inventory costs)

└ fixed costs of station m if assigned to size class b (with b machines)

---

326 **Suresh/Sarkis** (1989)
327 **Suresh** (1990), (1991)
328 **Tetzlaff** (1990), pp. 137-155

338 4. Decision models for the design of a flexible manufacturing system

subject to

$$\sum_{r=1}^{R_k} q_{kr} = \alpha_k \qquad\qquad k=1,2,\ldots,K \qquad\qquad (204)$$

production ratio of product type k

production ratio of route r of product type k

$$X(N,\underline{q},\underline{\gamma}) \geq X_{min} \qquad\qquad\qquad\qquad (205)$$

minimum production rate of the FMS

production rate of the FMS

$$N \leq N_{max} \qquad\qquad\qquad\qquad\qquad (206)$$

maximum number of pallets in the FMS

number of pallets

$$q_{kr} \geq 0 \qquad\qquad k=1,2,\ldots,K;\ r=1,2,\ldots,R_k \qquad (207)$$

$$\gamma_{bm} = \{0,1\} \qquad\qquad m=1,2,\ldots,M;\ b=1,2,\ldots,B_m \qquad (208)$$

$$N \geq 1 \text{ and integer} \qquad\qquad\qquad\qquad (209)$$

where

Data:

b	-	size class index (number of machines, setup tables, vehicles) of the stations ($b = 1,2,\ldots,B_m$)
k	-	product type index ($k = 1,2,\ldots,K$)
m	-	machine index ($m = 1,2,\ldots,M$)
r	-	route index ($r = 1,2,\ldots,R_k$)
α_k	-	production ratio of product type k
B_m	-	number of size classes defined for station m
C_{bm}	-	fixed costs at station m if assigned to size class b
C_N	-	fixed costs of a pallet (incl. costs for fixture and inventory)
N_{max}	-	maximum number of pallets in the FMS
R_k	-	number of routes for product type k
X_{min}	-	minimum production rate of the FMS
$X(.)$	-	production rate of the FMS

Variables:

N	-	number of universal pallets
q_{kr}	-	production ratio of product type k manufactured using route r
γ_{bm}	$= \begin{cases} 1 \text{, if station m is assigned to size class b} \\ 0 \text{, otherwise} \end{cases}$	

The objective function includes the fixed costs for the stations. The binary variable γ_{bm} determines the size of station m, i.e. if b type m machines, loading and unloading stations, or transportation vehicles (inducing costs of C_{bm}) are included in the FMS. This formulation also allows the consideration of concave costs functions (decreasing marginal costs). The fixed costs of the pallets are also included in the objective function. These are made up primarily of the costs of the capital tied up in the pallets and the clamping devices as well as in the work-in-process inventory which is directly dependent on the number of pallets circulating in the system.

The constraints (204) assure that the entire produced quantity of a product type k over all its routes is equal to the production ratio α_k of this product type. Furthermore, inequality (205) represents the requirement that a minimum production rate X_{min} for the FMS be met. The quantity $X(.)$ must be calculated by evaluating the classical CQN model for every combination of the variables N, q_{kr} and γ_{bm} considered in the search for the optimal solution. A maximum limit for the number of universal pallets circulating in the FMS is given in the inequality (206). *Tetzlaff* proposes an implicit enumeration procedure for the solution of this nonlinear model.

Modelling of the system behavior Decision variables	Unlimited number of pallets (static modelling of the system behavior)	Limited number of pallets (dynamic modelling of the system behavior)
Routing optimization	Secco-Suardo (1978) Secco-Suardo (1979) Kimemia/Gershwin (1979) Avonts et al. (1988) Leung/Tanchoco (1986)	Kimemia/Gershwin (1980) Yao/Shanthikumar (1986) Tetzlaff (1990)
Capacity optimization		Vinod/Solberg (1985) Yao/Shanthikumar (1986) Yao/Shanthikumar (1987) Dallery/Frein (1988) Dallery/Stecke (1990) Solot (1990a) Tetzlaff (1990) Lee/Srinivasan/Yano (1991b)
Equipment optimization	Graves/Whitney (1979) Graves/Lamar (1983) Graves/Redfield (1988) Tetzlaff (1990) Suresh/Sarkis (1989) Irani/Leung/Snyder (1986)	Tetzlaff (1990)
Product and equipment optimization	Whitney/Suri (1985)	
System and equipment optimization	Sarin/Chen (1986)	

Table 81: Synopsis of decision models for FMS optimization

All of the models discussed in this section are presented together in table (81). It can be seen that particularly the problem of the simultaneous determination of the product spectrum and the resources of a production system have received little attention in the literature up to now.

The models and solution methods described in this section make it quite clear that there are manifold interdependencies between the numerous decision variables. If these are neglected significant productivity losses in comparison to the optimal FMS configuration may result.

It must be pointed out, however, that the decision models described here cannot be directly used as the sole basis for the selection of an FMS configuration, due to the many restrictive assumptions required in order to get a well-behaved problem. They can nevertheless play an important role as part of an overall planning concept for the determination of the optimal configuration of an FMS. Optimization models can, though they are based on restrictive assumptions, help to reduce significantly the number of FMS configuration alternatives that have to be investigated with more realistic models. The pre-optimized configuration proposals must be studied more closely at a later planning stage, for example with simulation models.

Further reading for section 4.:

Buzacott/Shanthikumar (1993)
Dallery/Frein (1988)
Dallery/Stecke (1990)
Kimemia/Gershwin (1979), (1980), (1985)
Lee/Srinivasan/Yano (1989), (1991b)
Secco-Suardo (1978), (1979)
Shanthikumar/Yao (1988)
Solot (1990a)
Solot/van Vliet (1990)
Tetzlaff (1990), (1992)
Vinod/Solberg (1985)
Yao/Shanthikumar (1986), (1987)

5. DECISION MODELS FOR PRE-RELEASE PLANNING IN FLEXIBLE MANUFACTURING SYSTEMS

Sections 3. and 4. were concerned with decision problems and solution procedures that arise in the configuration phase and *before the installation* of an FMS. In the following this phase will be assumed to have been completed, and the discussion will instead be dedicated to questions which come up *during the operation* of an already installed FMS. In section 2.2.2. it was stated that of the short-term planning phases the *pre-release phase* is more critical to the successful operation of an FMS than the control phase because the former largely determines the degree of flexibility of the latter. It was also indicated that planning errors in the pre-release phase, such as the release of an unfavorable mix of orders, can only with difficulty be reversed in the control phase.

5.1. CLASSIFICATION OF DECISION PROBLEMS AND MODELS IN THE PRE-RELEASE PHASE

The decision models found in the literature to support the production planning of an FMS are in general oriented around the specific *characteristics* of the FMS under study and its integration into the firm's production environment. Aside from the characteristics of the FMS, the relevant objectives for production planning are critical in the formulation of decision models and in the development of appropriate solution procedures. Therefore, the central classification criteria of decision problems and models in the pre-release phase of an FMS will be presented, and the associated objectives will be described. Following that, the modelling and solution approaches which have been formulated in the literature will be discussed.

511. Characteristics of Pre-Release Problems

Two important groups of characteristics affecting the classification of decision problems and models in the pre-release phase can be identified. The technical and organizational characteristics of the FMS are of central importance in the first group. These include the *technical FMS structure*, the *structure of the machining processes*, the form of the *system setup* (largely dependent on the first two factors), and the type of *order release*. The second group describes the planning environment of the FMS, i.e. the *size* and the *temporal distribution* of the production orders as determined by the central production planning and control (PPC) system.

More specifically, the following criteria may be used for the classification of decision problems and models in the pre-release phase:

- Technical and organizational characteristics of the FMS

  - The *number of concurrent orders* in the FMS
  - The *process of releasing* orders into the FMS
  - The *technical structure of the FMS*, i.e. the availability of identical and/or complementary machines in the FMS
  - The *structure of the process plans* of the products, i.e. the degree to which alternative process plans are available for the products

- Planning environment of the FMS

  - The *order size* and
  - The *order arrival process*

The individual characteristics will be explained in more detail below.

- **Number of concurrent orders in the FMS**

The ability to simultaneously process workpieces of different types requiring different operations and tools and in random order without significant setup delays is one of the main advantages of an FMS (see section 1.1.).

This ability depends primarily on the supply of tools to the machines. The often mentioned goal "lot size 1" can only be reached if the following conditions are met. First, the FMS must have an efficient central tool supply system. It should be able either to promptly provide the tools required for an operation on an unlimited number of *part types or workpiece sequences*, or the local tool magazines must be sufficiently large that they are able to contain all the required tools. Second, the workpieces must be able to be mounted on the pallets in a random order.

This situation would imply that the number of concurrent orders for different product types in the FMS is not limited by technical restrictions at any one time. An FMS with these characteristics would have an unlimited *process flexibility* with respect to the short-term production program. Under such conditions grouping the orders in batches (batching) and planning the setup of the tool magazines (system setup planning) are not necessary.

These conditions are not met in many real-life FMSs, however. Indeed, the following factors often limit the number of concurrent orders in an FMS. The setup time required for preparing the *local tool magazines* to process a *new order* is often so high that all the workpieces of an order that is currently being processed are completed before the tools are replaced with those required for the next order. If only a few different workpiece types are being processed in the FMS simultaneously, then several machines can eventually be equipped with identical sets of tools. The *groups of identical machines* that result from such a strategy can, under certain circumstances, positively affect the production rate of the FMS[329].

The need to exchange *fixtures* along with new workpieces can also limit the number of orders of different product types that can be processed simultaneously in an FMS[330]. It may also be sensible to limit the number of concurrent workpiece types in the batching and system setup planning when the *machine workload capacities* are limited or when identical machines of different efficiencies are used in the FMS. The latter causes problems in the assignment of operations to the machines. Finally, if the planning efficiency of the FMS control software is insufficient it may be necessary to limit the number of orders being simultaneously processed in the FMS so as to make the planning tasks easier.

Since generally at least one of these influencing factors is present, it can be assumed that the number of orders of different product types to be processed simultaneously in an FMS must be *limited*. It will be assumed in the following that this is done during the pre-release planning phase.

- **Process of releasing orders**

The type of the process of releasing orders is closely associated with the number of orders that can simultaneously be processed in an FMS. If the number of concurrent orders in an FMS is unlimited, it is possible to release the orders into the system in an arbitrary sequence. In realistic situations (with limited number of different orders), however, the orders selected for simultaneous production in the FMS can be grouped in a *fixed batch* in a static release process or in an almost *continuously changing (flexible) batch* which is altered in a continuous release process.

A *fixed batch* is processed completely as determined at a specific planning point in time before the next batch is released into the FMS. This happens even in the situation when the central production planning system assigns new orders to the FMS for processing before the last order of the current batch has been completed. Since once a batch has been created it is never again changed, the determination of the batch size also fixes both the beginning and the duration of its production (makespan, batch cycle time). The intervals between the planning events are generally variable, because the batches will usually have different makespans [see figure (180)].

The manufacture of fixed batches can be necessary for technical reasons if the tool magazines of all the machines in the FMS can only be equipped with new tools in a common tool setup period, during which all of the equipment is shut down and the tools are changed. A major or total tool changeover would then be performed. All tools that are no longer required are taken out of the tool magazines and the new tools needed for the operations of all workpiece types of the next scheduled batch are loaded. Building fixed batches can also be useful when

---

329 **Stecke/Solberg** (1985); see also section 5.3.1.
330 **Co/Biermann/Chen** (1990)

coordinating production with the environment of the FMS's planning process, e.g. when time fences (planning periods, production shifts) must be observed.

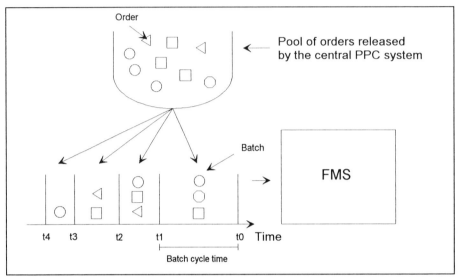

Figure 180: Batch release with fixed batches

If an FMS is completely emptied of workpieces before the simultaneous reloading of all the tool magazines is performed, the machines may experience significant idle times during the transition phases (end of one batch and beginning of a new batch)[331]. It is, therefore, generally better to arrange the local tool magazines and the FMS control so as to allow overlapping manufacture of successive batches. Here the first workpieces of a new batch are released into the system while the last workpieces of the previous batch are still under processing.

In *continuously changeable (flexible) batches* the batch being released can be adjusted according to orders newly released by the central PPC system. The changes in a batch are generally made during the manufacture of the orders.

In the example shown in figure (181) three orders were removed from the order pool at time t. These were grouped together in a batch and released for production in the FMS. The remaining orders will be considered for release during the next planning period. At time t+dt the order represented as a triangle is completed. This event is taken as a signal to look again at the planning of the batch currently being processed. All the orders which were at first put aside and all the orders of the current batch are considered. The new plan could result in a new batch in which an order that had been included into the batch at time t was returned to the order set, while orders which had not been a part of the batch are now released. This is illustrated in figure (181).

---

331 See also the special production policy described in section 3.1.2.5.4.2.

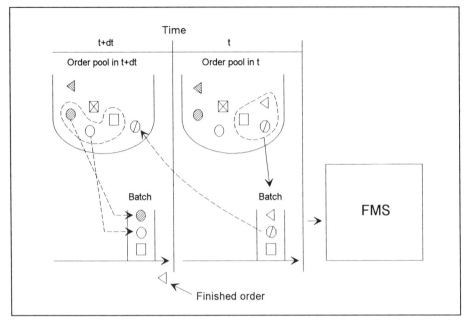

Figure 181: Batch release with flexible batches

Obviously, due to the frequent changes in the batch assignments of orders under continuous release a certain *nervousness* of the planning system can arise. An order which at time t has just been assigned to a batch can be removed from the batch at the next planning event t + dt if another order better matches the batch currently being processed. It is, therefore, possible that an order may be assigned to a number of different batches over time. Although such nervousness has no consequence in a planning system which runs automatically, there may be some negative effects if humans are engaged interactively in the control decisions in the FMS. The more frequently the control software proposes that the actual batch should be changed, the more likely it becomes that the operator will doubt the reasonableness of the planning system's proposals, and the greater the possibility that he will make improvised (and perhaps suboptimal) changes in the batch structure.

Stecke and Kim[332] compared the fixed and the flexible approach to order release in a numerical investigation. They concluded that the makespan tends to be shorter with a continuous release process. This is not surprising since the idle times at the machines are reduced due to the higher degree of freedom during the planning process. However, with respect to meeting due dates the opposite effects may be observed[333]. A decision for or against one of the two release approaches thus requires that several conflicting goals be considered (makespan,

---

332 **Stecke/Kim** (1986), (1988), (1989)
333 **Kuhn** (1992a); see also **Amoako-Gyampah/Meredith/Raturi** (1992)

order flow time, number of tool changes, tool requirements, planning complexity, etc.). A choice of one or the other release approach is often not possible, however, due to organizational or technical constraints.

• Technical FMS structure

An FMS can be made up of solely complementary machines[334]. This is called a multi-level FMS. An FMS may, however, instead include both identical and *complementary* machines. In a multi-level FMS the problem of assigning operations to machines does not arise. The lack of alternatives dictates that an operation must be performed by a particular machine. Batching is the dominant part of the pre-release planning under such conditions. On the other hand, an FMS with *identical* machines requires, in addition to the batching decisions, a decision about which machine will carry out a certain operation. In the most extreme case, this decision could be made for each individual workpiece of an order.

• Structure of the machining processes

The structure of the machining processes describes the degree of *routing flexibility*, i.e. the number of possible process plans according to which a workpiece can be processed. The process structure may be *fixed*; in this case the process plan for a workpiece is set in advance defining the visiting sequence at the various stations (load/unload stations, machines). The process structure may, however, also be *variable*. Here a particular operation can be performed by alternative machines and may involve varying costs or processing times. In this case a route selection[335] decision is required.

• Order size

The frequently praised advantage of an FMS that it can realize "lot size 1" is only rarely found under real production conditions. More often a variety of factors dictate that larger production orders be created. The lot size is generally set by the central PPC system. Under these conditions, the order size is a given for the FMS pre-release phase[336]. The order sizes determine how frequently releasing must be planned and how frequently production orders will be released into the FMS.

If the orders are sufficiently large, then in an FMS with identical machines it must be determined whether *identical tool sets* should be provided to the identi-

---

334 It must be pointed out that a machine's processing capability may change over time with the tool magazine setup.

335 Problems of this kind may also arise in a conventional job shop.

336 However, due to the flexibility of an FMS it may sometimes make sense to partition an order in the release planning phase; **Co/Biermann/Chen** (1990).

cal machines. This would improve the FMS's ability to process several work-pieces of an order at different machines simultaneously. It may even make sense under certain conditions to equip several machines with absolutely identical tool sets[337]. The order size, therefore, leads to the decision problem of whether to provide the identical machines with single or multiple tool sets. This has direct consequences for the system setup planning.

- **Order arrival process**

The order arrival process is either *static* or *dynamic*. In a *static arrival process* a set of orders is defined at the beginning of the planning period, which has to be processed within the given planning horizon. This set of orders may include workpieces which have already been released for the last planning period but have not yet been finished. A static order arrival process is given, for example, when the central PPC system releases a set of orders (order pool) at the beginning of each planning period (e.g. once a week). At this point in time, the FMS planning and control system takes responsibility for the orders and informs the central PPC system when their processing has been completed.

A *dynamic order arrival process* applies when the set of orders changes within a period. In this case it is assumed that the contents of the order pool changes continuously, and that these changes are to be considered within the current planning period. Changes can be caused when new orders are released (e.g. additional orders or high-priority orders) or when orders which have already been released are cancelled. Table (82) provides an overview of the characteristics of the pre-release problems and their instances.

Characteristic	Variation		
Number of orders	Unlimited	Limited	
Release procedure	Static	Continuous	
Structure of the FMS	Only complementary machines	Only identical machines	Complementary and identical machines
Process structure	Fixed	Variable	
Order size	Large	Small	
Order arrival process	Static	Dynamic	

Table 82: Characteristics of pre-release planning problems

---

337 **Stecke/Solberg** (1981a) pp. 35-36; **Stecke/Morin** (1985); **Stecke/Solberg** (1985); **Stecke** (1986); **Mazzola/Neebe/Dunn** (1989), p. 130. For an analysis of the effects of tool magazine duplication see **Chen/Chung** (1991); see also **Kuhn** (1990), pp. 244-297

The type of the order arrival process, together with the form of the release process, determine the type of batching to a large degree. With a static order arrival process and a release of fixed batches it may be logical to group all the orders in batches. On the other hand, under dynamic order arrival conditions it may be better to consider only the production batch to be processed next. In the case of a continuous release process, the approaches in the literature suggest creating only the next batch for both static and dynamic arrival processes. In addition, the latter offers the possibility to change the batch structure at any moment when a new order is released by the central PPC system. Table (83) provides an overview of all of these relationships.

Order release procedure		
	Fixed All orders in a batch are completed before the next batch is released.	**Flexible** A batch may be adjusted during manufacturing of the orders.
Order arrival process		
Static At the time of planning all orders are available for release.	At the time of planning orders are grouped into batches for simultaneous processing.	Upon completion of an order a new order may be removed from the order pool and released into the FMS.
Dynamic Orders arrive continuously over time.	Upon completion of *all orders assigned to a batch* a new batch is formed. The orders are taken from the current order pool.	Upon completion or arrival of a *single order* the currently processed batch may be adjusted.

Table 83: Relationship between the order release procedure and the order arrival process

5.1.2. Objectives of Pre-Release Planning

As described above, the different approaches to pre-release planning can be classified based on the technical and organizational characteristics of a particular FMS. These influence the number of decision alternatives. On the other hand, the approaches can be categorized according to the objectives they seek to achieve. The objectives can be divided into financial (economic) or technical objectives[338]. While financial objectives can be derived from a company's broader set of general income objectives, the technical objectives serve as surro-

---

338 **Kuhn** (1990), pp. 33-53. In the following human objectives are not considered.

gates for the original financial objectives since these may be difficult or impossible to quantify.

- **Financial objectives**

If financial objectives are dominant, then the costs and revenues influenced by a pre-release decision are the most important part of the analysis[339]. The goal then is to maximize the difference between revenues and costs, to the extent that this is dependent on the pre-release planning, as a kind of partial objective optimization.

The primary financial component of the pre-release planning are *costs*. The most important cost types are inventory costs for work-in-process inventory, idle time costs, setup costs, and penalty costs incurred when the planned completion time (due date) of an order is not met. Other types of costs include transportation costs, adjustment costs, procurement costs, distribution costs, and costs associated with the planning process. It may be quite difficult to quantify these costs. This is particularly true for idle time costs which are basically opportunity costs of the lost productive time of the FMS. Their extent depends on whether idle times in the FMS due to non-optimal production planning can be productively used in other ways.

The *revenue effects* of pre-release planning can generally be neglected. It can be assumed that revenue cannot be influenced since the production program is given. To the degree that revenue effects of production scheduling with a predetermined production program are present, they are primarily due to sales deductions resulting from penalties for delayed delivery.

Aside from the direct effects on revenues, indirect effects on future revenues must also be considered. The latter can be affected by either losses of goodwill when the due dates are not met or possible effects of the current pre-release planning on future production program planning. Such effects are very difficult to quantify.

- **Technical performance measures**

Determining the cost and revenue effects caused by pre-release planning is extremely difficult under real-life conditions. For this reason technical performance measures[340] are often used which are assumed to correlate positively with the primary financial objectives. The following technical optimization criteria are considered in short-term planning of FMSs:

---

339 **Kusiak** (1985b), (1985c); **Leung/Tanchoco** (1986), p. 58; **Sarin/Chen** (1987), p. 1083; **Jaikumar/Van Wassen-hove** (1989), p. 63

340 **Stecke** (1983), p. 279; **Hwang** (1986), p. 304; **Tang/Denardo** (1988a), p. 767; **Tang/Denardo** (1988b), p. 778; **Mazzola/Neebe/Dunn** (1989), p. 133. For an overview over multi-criteria decision models for short-term production planning for an FMS see **Gupta/Evans/Gupta** (1991).

- Minimization of the *makespan*
- Minimization of the *number of batches*
- Maximization of the *production rate*
- Maximization of the *machine utilizations*
- Minimization of the *tardiness of orders*
- Minimization of the *number of tool switches or the number of needed tools*

When the entire set of orders released by the PPC system is completed early within a short *makespan* it may be possible to process additional orders that would not have otherwise been possible. This may result in extra contribution margins. Furthermore, any gained slack time in the FMS might be used for maintenance or inspection. It would also be possible to begin earlier than originally planned with the production of the next set of orders.

The objectives of minimizing the number of batches and maximizing the production rate or the utilization of the machines can, under certain conditions, be derived from the objective of minimizing the makespan. Hence, the same motivations mentioned above may be applied for these objectives[341].

Efforts to minimize the orders' *tardiness* are motivated by the fact that when the due date agreed to with the customer is not met it may be that the customer denies acceptance of the delayed order. This would mean a loss of contribution margins. It is also possible that penalties may be due or that discounts must be granted. Some loss of goodwill always results when due dates are not met. If the due dates were determined internally by the PPC system, then adjustment activities or adjustment costs in downstream manufacturing stages may be incurred.

Minimizing tool exchanges or the *number of needed tools* is motivated by the following considerations. Tool exchange processes generate the workload for the tool exchange equipment. The problem here is that if the supply of tools is not perfectly coordinated, a workpiece may have to wait at a machine for the arrival of a tool it needs. This problem is particularly acute when the tools are still stored in a central tool magazine and are used to supplement the local tool set at the machines. In such a situation frequent tool exchanges between the local and central tool magazines can cause the tool supply system to be overloaded. The result could be called *tool blocking*[342], i.e. a machine with a workpiece loaded on its machining table cannot start processing because the required tool is not yet available. If only few tool exchanges are necessary, it is possible to save on extra capacity in tool preparation and tool supply. If savings in the number of copies of a tool are realized, this results in a direct cost reduction.

As has already been pointed out, due to the high complexity of pre-release planning it is generally suggested in the literature that pre-release planning should be divided into the subproblems *batching* and *system setup planning (loading)*. This structuring will be used in analyzing the planning problems in the discussion below. In section 5.2. different ways of grouping the orders released by the PPC system into batches will be illustrated. A discussion then follows in section 5.3.

---

341 **Kuhn** (1990), pp. 38-39, p. 42
342 **Tetzlaff** (1992a)

about decision models and solution procedures for the system setup (loading) problem, assuming that batches have already been created. Finally, section 5.4. is dedicated to different approaches to the simultaneous solution of the batching and loading problems. The structure of the following discussion of pre-release planning is shown in figure (182).

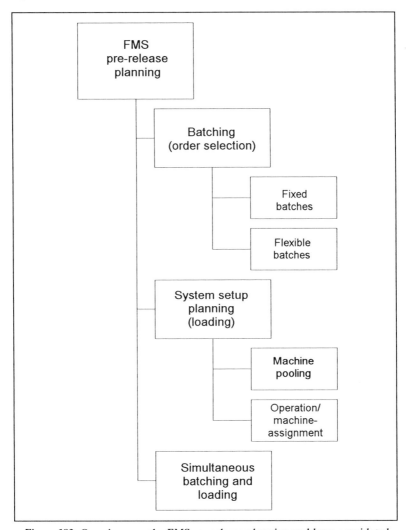

Figure 182: Overview over the FMS pre-release planning problems considered

5.2. BATCHING

Batching (order selection)[343] is the first stage in the successive approach of pre-release planning considered here. Starting from a pool of orders released by the central PPC system, the decision problem in this planning stage is to determine

- *which orders* (workpiece types) should be manufactured together, and
- *when this should happen.*

Figure (183) illustrates the structure of the batching problem.

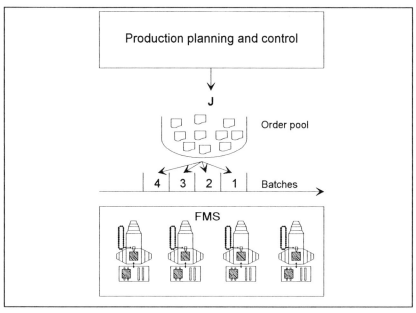

Figure 183: The batching problem

The different approaches to batching discussed in the literature are based on the following main assumptions:

- Planning begins with a given pool of orders of size J ($j = 1,2,...,J$) which has been released for processing in the FMS by the central PPC system.
- The order j is made up of n_j identical workpieces of a particular product type. Each workpiece is manufactured as a single identifiable unit in the FMS.
- The FMS consists of M different machines[344] ($m = 1,2,...,M$).

---

343 This phase is often called *part type selection.* **Stecke** (1985), p. 8; **Van Looveren/Gelders/Van Wassenhove** (1986), pp. 9-10; **Sawik** (1990), p. 179

344 In order to simplify the exposition single server stations (with one machine) are assumed. However, the data may be modified such that stations with multiple identically tooled machines can also be considered.

- Most workpieces are processed by more than one machine, depending on their process plans. One machine can, however, only process one workpiece at a time.
- The processing time of a workpiece in order j at the machine m is equal to b_{jm} (units of time). In contrast to sections 3. and 4., a deterministically known time span is considered here instead of an *average processing time* at a station, b_m.
- Several tools from the entire tool set including T tools must normally be made simultaneously available for processing a workpiece of type j at machine m.
- Every machine m has its own (local) tool magazine with a capacity of h_m tool slots.

5.2.1. Release of Fixed Batches

When fixed batching is applied, the order pool released by the PPC system for processing in the FMS is partitioned into distinct and separate batches which are processed one after the other. As all orders assigned to a batch will be completely processed without external supply of tools, the local tool magazines must be equipped with all the required tools. The number and types of orders which can be grouped together in one batch is thus either technically and/or temporally limited. The *technical constraint* on batch size is due to the limited tool magazine capacities, since all orders of a batch are supposed to be processed after setting up the tool magazine only once. This means that while producing a batch no tool exchange at the local tool magazines should be performed. The *temporal restrictions* associated with releasing in *fixed batches* can result from the planning horizon being divided into planning periods. In such a case the makespan of a batch should not be longer than a single planning period. Otherwise the remaining unprocessed workpieces of a batch would have to be transferred into the next planning period.

Figure (184) illustrates, in the form of an entity-relationship diagram[345], the structure of the relevant data which must be considered when releasing in fixed batches. A batch is made up of several orders, each consisting of individual workpieces of a certain type (in a relationship type with complexity 1:n). There exists an m:n complexity between the workpieces and the operations as well as between the operations and the tools. The result of batching is stored in the relationship type BATCH-ORDER.

A decision model (model SEF) is presented below which can be considered the *basic batching model*[346] since this model is extended in several ways. Various objective functions are formulated that can be used alternatively. In the following several different procedures for solving the model are discussed.

---

345 **Scheer** (1989), p. 18
346 **Kuhn** (1990), p. 148, pp. 168-169

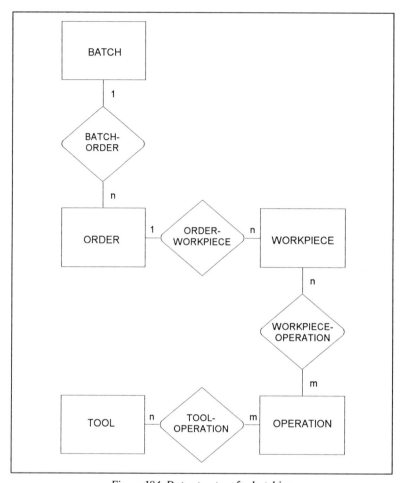

Figure 184: Data structure for batching

One way the models and solution procedures for batching presented in the literature differ is in their treatment of the number of batches as a fixed or variable quantity. They can also be distinguished based on whether all of the available orders are partitioned into batches (complete batching) or if only the next batch to be released is determined before the planning process is stopped. Basically, all the different approaches can be applied both to cases in which only the next batch is created and to cases in which all the available orders are completely grouped.

The decision model for batching when fixed batches are released can be described for three different objectives as follows:

Model SEF

$$\min Z_1 = L$$

  number of batches

(210)

or

$$\min Z_2 = \sum_{l=1}^{L} (H(J_l) + s)$$

  setup time between two consecutive batches

  makespan of batch l

(211)

or

$$\min \text{ or } \max Z_3 = f(x_{jl})$$

  general objective function, depending on the allocation of orders to batches

(212)

subject to

$$\sum_{l=1}^{L} x_{jl} = 1 \qquad\qquad j=1,2,\ldots,J \qquad\qquad (213)$$

$$\sum_{j=1}^{J} \sigma_{jtm} \cdot x_{jl} \leq J \cdot y_{tml} \qquad\qquad t=1,2,\ldots,T; \; m=1,2,\ldots,M; \qquad (214)$$
$$l=1,2,\ldots,L$$

$$\sum_{t=1}^{T} \sigma_t \cdot y_{tml} \leq h_m \qquad\qquad m=1,2,\ldots,M; \; l=1,2,\ldots,L \qquad (215)$$

$$x_{jl} \in \{0,1\} \qquad\qquad j=1,2,\ldots,J; \; l=1,2,\ldots,L \qquad (216)$$

$$y_{tml} \in \{0,1\} \qquad\qquad t=1,2,\ldots,T; \; m=1,2,\ldots,M; \qquad (217)$$
$$l=1,2,\ldots,L$$

where:

Data:

j -   order index ($j=1,2,\ldots,J$)
l -   batch index ($l=1,2,\ldots,L$)
m -   machine index ($m=1,2,\ldots,M$)
t -   tool index ($t=1,2,\ldots,T$)
h_m -   tool magazine capacity of machine m
s -   setup time between two batches (sequence independent)
σ_t -   number of tool magazine slots occupied by tool t
σ_{jtm} = $\begin{cases} 1 \text{ , if order j uses tool t at machine m} \\ 0 \text{ , otherwise} \end{cases}$

Variables:

$H(J_l)$	-	makespan of batch l
J_l	-	set of orders assigned to batch l
L	-	number of batches
x_{jl}	$= \begin{cases} 1 \text{ , if order j is assigned to batch l} \\ 0 \text{ , otherwise} \end{cases}$	
y_{tml}	$= \begin{cases} 1 \text{ , if tool t is assigned to machine m for processing batch l} \\ 0 \text{ , otherwise} \end{cases}$	

The equations (210) and (211) describe the objectives of minimizing the number of batches and minimizing the makespan of the entire set of orders, i.e. all those released for production in the FMS and available for planning during the planning period. The smaller the *number of batches*, the less frequently the tool magazines will have to be re-tooled. The shorter the makespan of the set of all orders, the sooner the FMS will be ready to begin processing the next set of orders. Equation (212) describes a general objective function the value of which is dependent on the partition of the orders. The constraints (213) force the assignment of each order j (j=1,2,...,J) to one and only one batch l (complete batching). The constraints (214) assure that all the necessary tools will be provided at the machines. The limited capacity of the tool magazines at the machines are represented by the constraints (215). Equations (216) and (217) define the ranges of the variables.

The models described in the literature for the solution of particular variations on the basic batching model SEF will be reviewed in the following sections.

5.2.1.1. Minimization of the number of batches

First, decision models and solution procedures for the minimization of the number of batches will be discussed. The number of orders which can be assigned to a batch is limited by the tool magazine capacity of the machines. The different workloads on the machines associated with different orders are not considered. Giving priority to the tool magazines in batching makes sense when the workloads can be balanced in a later planning phase and when the setup times of the batches are independent of the sequence in which they are processed. The minimization of the number of batches is identical to the minimization of the makespan, if a balanced workload can be achieved in the subsequent planning step. In this case the processing times of the orders can be neglected during the batching of the orders. The determination of the minimum number of batches may, however, be useful as it provides an initial solution in the search for the optimum number of batches[347].

---

347 section 5.4.4.

Considering the inverse relationship between the size of a batch and the number of batches (assuming a constant set of orders)

- *Hwang*[348]

suggests minimizing the number of batches by maximizing the number of orders or workpiece types included in one batch. He formulates the binary linear model shown below[349]. This is applied repeatedly in an iterative procedure to the diminishing set of remaining orders which at a given iteration have not yet been assigned to a batch (set J_0) until all orders are allocated.

> **Model SEF-HWANG**

$$\max Z_1 = \sum_{j \in J_0} x_{j1} \tag{218}$$

$\mathrel{\llcorner}$ number of orders assigned to the current batch l

subject to

$$\sum_{j \in J_0} \sigma_{jtm} \cdot x_{j1} \leq J \cdot y_{tm} \qquad t=1,2,\ldots,T; \ m=1,2,\ldots,M \tag{219}$$

$$\sum_{t=1}^{T} \sigma_{tm} \cdot y_{tm} \leq h_m \qquad m=1,2,\ldots,M \tag{220}$$

$$x_{j1} \in \{0,1\} \qquad j \in J_0 \tag{221}$$

$$y_{tm} \in \{0,1\} \qquad t=1,2,\ldots,T; \ m=1,2,\ldots,M \tag{222}$$

where:

Data:

j	-	order index ($j = 1,2,\ldots,J$)
l	-	batch index ($l = 1,2,\ldots,L$)
m	-	machine index ($m = 1,2,\ldots,M$)
t	-	tool index ($t = 1,2,\ldots,T$)
h_m	-	tool magazine capacity of machine m
J_0	-	set of orders not yet assigned to a batch
σ_{tm}	-	number of tool magazine slots required by tool t at machine m
σ_{jtm}	$= \begin{cases} 1, & \text{if order j requires tool t at machine m} \\ 0, & \text{otherwise} \end{cases}$	

Variables:

x_{j1}	$= \begin{cases} 1, & \text{if order j is assigned to batch l} \\ 0, & \text{otherwise} \end{cases}$	

---

348 **Hwang** (1986), p. 306; **Hwang/Shogan** (1989), p. 1354.
349 *Hwang* considers the FMS as one single machine (i.e. one global tool magazine). Here the discussion is extended to several machine types.

$$y_{tm} = \begin{cases} 1 \text{, if tool } t \text{ is assigned to machine } m \\ 0 \text{, otherwise} \end{cases}$$

The model SEF-HWANG is used to select a subset J_1 from the set J_0 of orders not yet assigned to a batch and combines these into a new batch. The objective function (218) maximizes the number of orders in the current batch l. The constraints (219) assure that all the necessary tools will be provided for the current batch. If an order j requiring the tool t at machine m is integrated into the batch, this tool must be available at the machine's tool magazine. The limited capacity tool magazines at the machines are represented in constraint (220). Model SEF-HWANG is applied repeatedly, according to the procedure shown in figure (185), until the set J_0 of orders not yet assigned to a batch is empty.

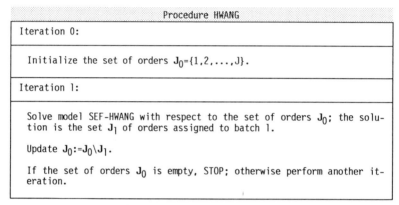

Figure 185: Procedure HWANG

The sequential character of the HWANG procedure may result in low quality solutions since orders with low tool requirements are assigned to a batch first, but orders with high tool requirements are only selected at the end of the procedure. If the order arrival process is dynamic, orders with large tool requirements will possibly never be assigned to a batch.

• *Stecke and Kim*[350]

have attempted to address this deficiency by slightly modifying the model. They weight an order/batch assignment (variable x_{jl}) in the objective function with the number of tool slots required at the *tool bottleneck machine* [see the modified objective function (223) and equation (224)]. The tool bottleneck machine is the machine at which the ratio between the tool slots required (for the remaining orders that are to be assigned) and the tool magazine capacity is the largest. This weighting scheme gives priority to orders with a greater demand for space in the tool magazine.

---

350 **Stecke/Kim** (1988), pp. 15-16

$$\max \sum_{j=1}^{J_0} [\sum_{t=1}^{T} \sigma_{jti} \cdot \sigma_{ti}] \cdot x_{j1} \qquad (223)$$

$\llcorner$ total number of tools required by order j at the tool bottleneck machine

$$i = \arg \max_{m} [(\sum_{j=1}^{J_0} \sum_{t=1}^{T} \sigma_{jtm} \cdot \sigma_{tm})/h_m] \qquad (224)$$

$\llcorner$ tool magazine capacity at machine m

$\llcorner$ total number of tools required at machine m

Both the SEF-HWANG model and the *Stecke and Kim* modified variation can be solved with standard algorithms for binary optimization[351]. It is guaranteed, however, in neither of the two approaches that the minimum number of batches will be found: in both cases the original problem is solved heuristically through a decomposition into several subproblems which are processed one after the next.

A model similar to model SEF-HWANG is presented by

* *Ohashi and Hitomi*[352].

In addition to the problem characteristics treated in model SEF-HWANG, these authors add constraints with respect to the maximum makespan of a batch and include tool wear that depends on the processing speed.

* *Tang and Denardo*[353]

proposed an exact branch-and-bound procedure for minimizing the number of batches (model SEF), even though it may be limited to small problems.

In order to compute strong lower bounds for the minimum number of batches

* *Oerlemans*[354]

developed a column generation approach based on the linear relaxation of the set covering formulation of the problem. In addition he suggested several local search procedures.

* *Kuhn*[355]

investigated several variations of an heuristic procedure to solve model SEF, assuming the objective of minimizing the number of batches, in which basically the procedure outlined in figure (186) is applied. An order is selected based on a specific criterion and assigned to the batch currently being created. This is repeated until no further orders can be assigned without exceeding the tool magazine capacity. After completing a batch, a new one is started. The procedure is continued until all orders have been assigned to a batch.

Kuhn uses, among other criteria, the set of *common tools* and the set of *additional tools* at the tool bottleneck machine as sorting criteria for the orders. Con-

---

351 **Hwang** (1986), p. 306; **Stecke/Kim** (1988), p. 15; **Sawik** (1990), p. 179
352 **Ohashi/Hitomi** (1991)
353 **Tang/Denardo** (1988b), pp. 780-783
354 **Oerlemans** (1992), pp. 49-123; **Crama/Oerlemans** (1993)
355 **Kuhn** (1990), pp. 147-166.

sidering two different orders, additional tools are those required by one order but not by the other one. This means that such tools could be removed or must be added to a tool magazine during an order exchange.

Procedure SEF-KUHN

Iteration 1:

Start of a new batch:

Choose as a *batch seed* from all orders not yet assigned to a batch that order requiring the greatest number of tools at the machine with the largest relative tool magazine occupation.

Increase the batch size:

Sort the remaining orders according to a *sorting criterion* and assign them to the batch seed until the tool magazine capacity is exhausted.
If all orders are assigned to a batch, STOP; otherwise perform another iteration.

Figure 186: Heuristic batching procedure

An experimental analysis of the SEF-KUHN procedure shows that it is advantageous if an order which is about to be assigned to a batch has as many *common tools* as possible with the orders assigned previously. The criterion "minimum number of additional tools" which is often used in industrial practice leads to inferior results. Furthermore, when using the "common tool" rule it is advantageous to look at the new order's tool requirements at the tool magazine with the smallest number of free tool slots.

Consider a *ten-order example* ($J = 10$) to compare the described approaches for a single machine problem. The example 5-1 is kept simple enough to allow even the *Tang and Denardo* branch-and-bound procedure to be used. A machine with a tool magazine capacity of $h_m = 8$ tools is considered. All together $T = 21$ tools are required to process the orders. Table (84) illustrates the tool requirements of the individual orders.

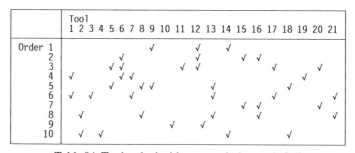

	Tool 1	2	3	4	5	6	7	8	9	10	11	12	13	14	15	16	17	18	19	20	21
Order 1							√				√		√								
2						√					√			√	√						
3				√	√					√	√					√		√			
4	√				√	√											√				
5					√			√	√				√			√					
6	√		√			√							√			√					√
7														√	√				√		
8	√					√						√				√					√
9									√		√										
10	√		√										√				√				

Table 84: Tool-order incidence matrix (example 5-1)

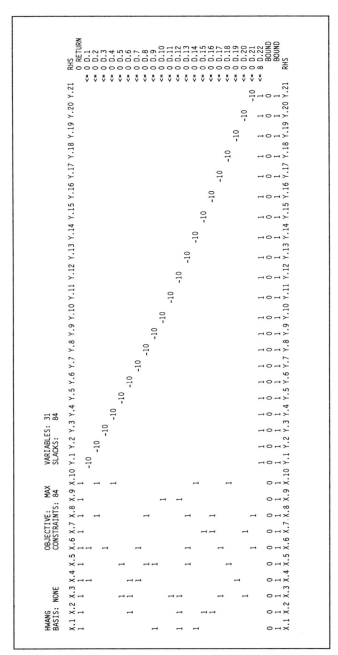

Table 85: LP tableau for the procedure HWANG (Iteration 1)

First, the application of procedure HWANG is illustrated. All orders are considered in model SEF-HWANG during the *first iteration*. The corresponding LP tableau is presented in table (85). The optimal solution of this binary linear optimization problem is $x_1 = 1$, $x_2 = 1$, $x_7 = 1$, $x_9 = 1$. All other x variables are equal to zero. Hence, the first batch consists of the orders 1, 2, 7 and 9.

Before performing the *second iteration* of the procedure, these orders will be removed from the set of orders J_0. In the tableau shown in table (85) this is accomplished simply by setting the upper bound of the corresponding x variables equal to zero. The optimal solution of the resulting optimization problem is $x_5 = 1$, $x_{10} = 1$. So the second batch includes orders 5 and 10. The batch created in the *third iteration* is made up of orders 4 and 6. The batches 4 and 5 have only one order each: 3 and 8 respectively.

The structure of the batches, the number of tools required by the orders in each batch, and the tool assignment to the tool magazine are all shown in table (86). The tools 6, 12, 15, 16, 20, 9, 14 and 10 are all needed by the first batch. An asterisk "*" indicates a tool required by an order which has already been integrated into the tool magazine for another order. Thus, it takes up no additional space in the tool magazine (tool commonality).

	Tool slot	1	2	3	4	5	6	7	8
Batch 1	Order 2	6	12	15	16				
	Order 7			*	*	20			
	Order 1		*				9	14	
	Order 9		*						10
Batch 2	Order 10	2	4	14	18				
	Order 5				*	5	9	8	13
Batch 3	Order 6	1	3	7	13	17	21		
	Order 4	*		*				6	19
Batch 4	Order 3	5	6	11	12	17	20		
Batch 5	Order 8	2	8	13	16	21			
* - Tool already available									

Table 86: Tool requirements of the batches (example 5-1)

The batch structures shown in table (87) result from the application of the SEF-KUHN procedure with the *sorting criteria* "maximum number of common tools" and "minimum number of additional tools" to example 5-1. The batches are quite different from the results of the HWANG approach.

The criterion "minimum number of *additional* tools" leads to a non-optimal number of batches. The optimal solution in this example is achieved by applying the criterion "maximum number of *common* tools". This conclusion is based on an analysis using the *Tang and Denardo* branch-and-bound procedure. The optimal solution for this example is also found by applying the modified objective function in model SEF-HWANG according to *Stecke and Kim*.

	Maximum number of common tools									Minimum number of additional tools								
Batch	Tool slot	1	2	3	4	5	6	7	8	Tool slot	1	2	3	4	5	6	7	8
1	Order 3 Order 2 Order 7	5	6 *	11	12 *	17	20	15 *	16 *	Order 3 Order 9	5	6	11	12 *	17	20		10
2	Order 6 Order 4	1 *	3	7 *	13	17	21	6	19	Order 6 Order 4	1 *	3	7 *	13	17	21	6	19
3	Order 8 Order 5	2	8 *	13 *	16	21	5	9	18	Order 5 Order 1	5	8	9 *	13	18	12	14	
4	Order 10 Order 1 Order 9	2	4	14 *	18	9	12 *	10		Order 8 Order 7	2	8	13	16 *	21	15	20	
5										Order 2 Order 10	6	12	15	16 2	4	14	18	

Table 87: Results for the procedure SEF-KUHN (example 5-1)

5.2.1.2. Minimization of the makespan

Processing times were neglected in the SEF-HWANG model described in the previous section. Therefore, large differences among the makespans of the batches may result. This depends both on the order size and on the specific processing times for the part type associated with an order. It is thus possible that the workloads on the different machines in an FMS can be very unbalanced. It makes sense, therefore, to create batches which are feasible with respect to their tool requirements, but which will also spread the workload relatively evenly among the different machines in the FMS. This is tried to achieve with the objective *"minimization of the makespan"*. Models which follow this objective partition orders into batches so as to minimize the time elapsed between the beginning of processing of the first order and the completion of the last order of the entire order pool.

- *Rajagopalan*[356]

has proposed creating batches such that the bottleneck machine of a considered batch is identical to the overall bottleneck machine.

The overall bottleneck machine is found by adding the processing time requirements of all the orders at the individual machines. In the example depicted in figure (187), machine 2 is the overall bottleneck machine. The sum of all the processing times of all the orders at this machine is 60 time units (regardless of their assignment to batches). Figure (187) shows two different batch constellations which require the same total processing time at the three machines. The heights of the rectangles represent the total processing times of all orders in a batch at a machine.

---

356 **Rajagopalan** (1985), pp. 22-23; (1986)

Machine	Constellation 1			Constellation 2		
	1	2	3	1	2	3
Batch 1						
Workload:	10	20	10	10	30	10
Batch 2						
Workload:	10	20	10	10	20	
Batch 3						
Workload:	10	20	10	10	10	20
Makespan:		60			70	

Figure 187: Example illustrating the approach of Rajagopalan[357]

A *lower bound for the makespan* can be found by adding the workloads at the overall bottleneck machine for all batches. In the example the *minimum make-span* is 60 time units. The *minimum makespan* is reached if the overall bottle-neck machine has the largest workload (batch bottleneck) in each batch. This is not the case in constellation 2 of the example. The batch bottleneck of the third batch (machine 3) is not identical with the overall bottleneck (machine 2). The makespan is thus equal to the theoretical lower bound (60) plus the difference between the processing time at the bottleneck of the third batch (machine 3) and the processing time of the overall bottleneck machine (machine 2). The make-span is thus equal to 70 instead of 60 time units.

Rajagopalan first determines the processing time requirements of all orders at the individual machines and then calculates the ratios between the workloads on each machine and the overall bottleneck machine. Following that, the orders in a batch are selected such that the current workloads on the machines are nearly equivalent to the globally calculated ratios[358].

5.2.1.3. Optimization of an arbitrary objective function with a given number of batches

So far approaches have been described which intend to minimize the number of batches and which attempt to minimize the makespan. These result in partitions of the set of J orders into L batches with the value of L being an outcome of the procedure and not a given. In the following discussion, it will be assumed that the *number of batches* L has been externally *fixed* in advance. Consequently, the new task is to find an exhaustive partition of the set of J orders into L mutually

---

357 **Kuhn** (1990), p. 67

358 A computational comparison between a modified variant of the *Rajagopalan* procedure with several alternative approaches is presented by **Kuhn** (1990), pp. 219-248.

exclusive batches while attempting to maximize or minimize a particular objective function. This way of looking at the problem is useful for those approaches to pre-release planning in FMSs in which the number of batches is successively changed, so that for each value of L it is important to know the optimal batch structure[359].

- *Kuhn*[360]

proposed a cluster analytical procedure for the determination of the optimal batch structure which can be implemented in either its *deterministic* or a *stochastic* version. It is possible to follow any objective function at all.

5.2.1.3.1. A deterministic improvement method

The starting point for the deterministic improvement method for solving the SEF model [see figure (188)] is an initial partition of the set of J orders into batches which is feasible within the tool magazine constraints. A feasible initial partition can, for example, be generated with one of the heuristic procedures described in section 5.2.1.1. Several "neighbors" of this solution are then generated

---

Procedure SEF-CLUST-D
Iteration 0: *Initialization*
Find an exhaustive partition of the order set.
Iteration 1: *Move or exchange*

Step 1: Consider *order j*
 	
    Step 2: Consider *batch l*
 	
    Move:
    Move order j into batch l and compute the change of the objective function's value, if the move is feasible.
 	
    Exchange:
    Exchange order j with any other order currently assigned to batch l; compute the change of the objective function's value, if the exchange is feasible.
 	
    Save the solution with the largest improvement in the value of the objective function as the currently best solution.
 	
    Repeat step 2 for all batches l.
 	
Perform the solution change that results in the largest improvement of the value of the objective function.
 	
Repeat step 1 until, after J consecutive trials, no further improvement of the value of the objective function is achieved.

Figure 188: Deterministic batch improvement procedure

---

359 see section 5.4.4.
360 **Kuhn** (1990), pp. 167-188; for an efficient general procedure for grouping objects see **Dorndorf/Pesch** (1993).

by moving an order j into every other batch or exchanging order j for orders currently assigned to other batches. From among the feasible solutions resulting from the moves or exchanges, that with the largest improvement in the value of the objective function is taken and stored for the next iteration. If no improvement is found the current solution is retained. The process is repeated for each order in the set of orders consecutively until a run of J trials fails to produce a change in the batch structure.

Since the form of the objective function is of no special importance in this procedure, any objective function could be used. The only requirement is that for each partition of the orders into batches it must be possible to determine a value for the objective function and to identify its feasibility. It is possible to reduce the number of generated solutions by introducing problem-specific search rules. However, this will not be discussed here in any detail[361].

The quality of the solution that can be achieved with the SEF-CLUST-D procedure depends partially on the initial partition of the set of orders. Hence, one way of improving the solution is to run the algorithm several times starting from different initial solutions and to take the best of the local optima found. This will be explained with reference to the general problem of minimizing a hypothetical multi-modal objective function Z with two variables X and Y. Figure (189) shows an example of an arbitrary objective function along with its various contour lines.

The figure shows that aside from the *global* minimum G, there is also a *local* minimum L. If the search for the optimal solution starts at point A, the local minimum L will be reached, and it may not be possible to leave this "valley", since no "uphill" moves are accepted. If the search starts at point B, however, it will lead directly to the global optimum G.

5.2.1.3.2. A stochastic improvement method

One important characteristic of deterministic improvement methods is that once a "valley" has been reached, there is no possibility of getting away from the local optimum. One way out of this dilemma can be, as described above, to run the deterministic search procedure several times starting from a number of randomly selected initial solutions. This increases the amount of computing time, however. In addition, many steps in the procedure are calculated over again even when the shape of the objective function leaves no doubt. It is to be expected that all initial solutions near point B or in the south-western part of the topology shown in figure (189) will lead to the global optimum G[362].

A *stochastic search procedure* can also avoid becoming trapped in a local optimum by sometimes accepting a move into a solution's neighborhood with an unfavorable change in the value of the objective function. This makes it possible to leave a "valley" in the topology of the objective function.

---

361 **Kuhn** (1990), pp. 172-173

362 Solution points from which the application of a deterministic improvement procedure leads to the same local or global optimum will be called the **dominated area** of the optimum.

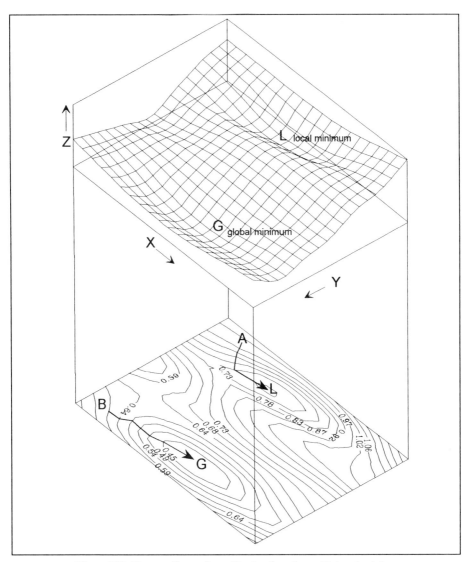

Figure 189: Contour lines of an objective function with local minima

A kind of *stochastic search procedure* which has been frequently discussed in the last few years is the *simulated annealing* approach which has had some significant successes in solving numerous combinatorial optimization problems[363].

---

[363] **Laarhoven/Aarts** (1987), pp. 77-152 and the literature cited therein; **Eglese** (1990). For an application of simulated annealing to job scheduling in an FMS see **Lee/Iwata** (1991).

This approach works roughly as follows. If in one step no reduction in the value of the objective function is achieved, an unfavorable solution is accepted with a certain probability. The probability of acceptance depends on how much the value of the objective function is increased, and it becomes smaller as the procedure continues. Thus, the probability that very poor solutions will be accepted in the early stages of the *stochastic search procedure* is relatively high, but over time worse solutions are more frequently rejected. Equation (225) describes the probability of acceptance as a function of the increase in the objective function's value between two neighbor solutions l and j, ΔZ_{lj}, assuming a given parameter τ (temperature) which is systematically decreased as the procedure progresses.

$$\text{Acceptance probability} = e^{-\Delta Z_{lj}/\tau} \qquad (225)$$

Figure (190) illustrates the acceptance probability as a function of ΔZ_{lj} for three values of the parameter τ. The probability of acceptance for smaller values of τ declines very quickly. This means that the smaller the parameter τ, the less frequently an increase in the value of the objective function will be accepted.

Reducing τ step-by-step causes the acceptance probability to approach zero. Hence, the procedure terminates as soon as no further improvement can be found in the neighborhood of the current solution.

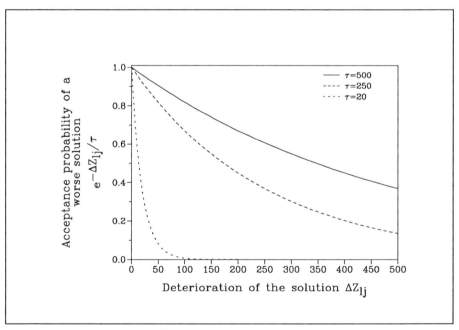

Figure 190: Acceptance probability as a function of the increase of the value of the objective function

The following basic choices must be made for any implementation of a simulated annealing approach. Aside from the *initial solution* and the termination criterion, a *construction rule* for the set of neighbor solutions must be provided. Furthermore, the initial value of the temperature (parameter τ) and a *cooling function* determining how the parameter τ is reduced in each step must be defined.

The cooling function and the number of neighbor solutions generated in each step are mainly influenced by the specific structure of the problem under consideration[364]. Figure (191) describes the simulated annealing procedure as suggested by *Kuhn*[365] for the solution of the batching problem.

Procedure SEF-CLUST-S
Iteration 0: *Initialization*
Initialize T_0; compute an initial solution
Iteration 1: *Change the current solution*
Step 1: Generate neighbor solutions With respect to solution 1 randomly generate a neighbor solution j and compute the corresponding change of the value of the objective function, $\Delta Z_{1j}=Z_j-Z_1$. If $\qquad \Delta Z_{1j}<0 \qquad\qquad$ (*solution is improved*) or $\qquad \exp(-\Delta Z_{1j}/T_1)\geq RAN$[366], $\qquad$ (*solution is worse, but accepted*) make the new solution the current solution. If a stationary situation is reached, go to step 2; otherwise repeat step 1. Step 2: Reduce the parameter T $\qquad T_{1+1}=T_1-\Delta T_1$ If a given termination criterion is met, STOP; otherwise repeat step 1.

Figure 191: Stochastic search procedure for batching (simulated annealing procedure)

The deterministic improvement method SEF-CLUST-D can be used to find the neighbor solutions. In the SEF-CLUST-D procedure the neighbor solution j of another solution 1 is the batch structure in which the largest decrease (or the smallest increase) in the objective function, ΔZ_{opt}, results from a move of order j into every other batch or an exchange of order j with orders currently assigned to other batches. In this way J different neighbor solutions result for each solution 1. The progress of the SEF-CLUST-S procedure is thus basically identical to the representation given in figure (188). It only has to be decided whether or not a batch structure with a *worse* value of the objective function should be accepted.

---

364 Eglese (1990)
365 **Kuhn** (1990), p. 176
366 RAN is a random number distributed uniformly in the interval [0,1].

Aside from this adjustment in the procedure, the initial temperature τ_0 and the termination criterion must be set. The SEF-CLUST-S procedure is identical to the SEF-CLUST-D procedure for $\tau_0 = 0$, because here no decreases in the solution value would be accepted.

The development of the values of the objective function for a numerical example, not explained in any more detail here, is shown in figure (192). These were calculated for different values of the parameter τ_1. The procedure starts with $\tau_0 = 1000$. As it continued on τ_1 was decreased by $\Delta\tau_1 = 20$ after J trails until finally $\tau_1 = 0$ was reached. The range of values of the objective function found in a single iteration is shown in figure (192) for each value of τ_1. As the value of the parameter τ declines, i.e. as the procedure progresses, the range of values of the objective function decreases and the quality of the best batch structure found up to that point improves.

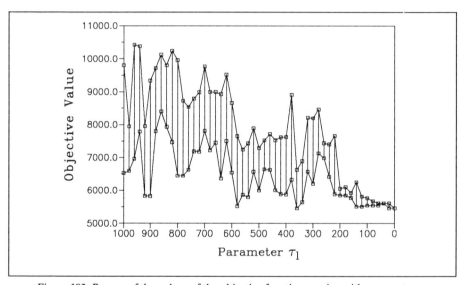

Figure 192: Ranges of the values of the objective function varying with parameter τ_1

Kuhn has shown in a comprehensive numerical investigation that the SEF-CLUST-S procedure can only produce good results when high initial temperatures (parameter τ_0) and a slow reduction in the probability of acceptance are used. A sufficiently high initial probability of acceptance is necessary to leave a deep local optimum, since this requires that a relatively large deterioration of the objective function value be accepted. A slow reduction in the probability of acceptance is necessary so that a new balanced state of the procedure for every value of the parameter τ_1 can be found. Otherwise it is possible that the procedure might not be able to find its way out of an unfavorable region in which it could become stuck.

In summary is can be stated that the stochastic search procedure for batching problems is superior to the deterministic improvement procedure. It is particularly useful when, due to a steeply sloping objective function, only few optimal or near optimal solutions exist.

5.2.2. Release of Flexible Batches

When releasing orders into the FMS in flexible batches, the batching process is re-initiated the moment the set of not yet completed orders has changed. *Reasons* for changing the batch structure include,

- the *arrival of new orders* (*order release by the PPC system*) and
- *the completion of an order* processed in the FMS.

Periodic batch planning with fixed planning intervals is no longer possible since the times of the changes in the set of not yet completed orders can not be precisely predicted and are not equidistant from one another. Due to the relatively frequent planning runs, the amount of work involved in planning for flexible batches is greater since in each planning run all the orders not yet processed in the FMS must be included in the re-optimization. Yet, the quality of the solution can be expected to be better than with fixed batching. A flexible release strategy does, however, increase the danger that relatively frequent tool exchanges may be necessary - in accordance with the requirements of the changing batch structures. Various approaches have been suggested to deal with building batches under the conditions of a continuous release process.

- *Stecke and Kim*[367]

formulate a model whose objective is to *maximize the utilization of the machines*. It is assumed here that *different machine groups*, i.e. groups of machines with identically tooled machines, are given. A planning situation is analyzed in which, aside from the determination of the batch structure (assignment of the orders to batches), the relationship of the various workpiece quantities of each type that will simultaneously circulate in the FMS must be determined. *Stecke and Kim* assume that each order includes several workpieces, with an *order size* normally being greater than 1. It is further taken into consideration that the number of workpieces of a certain type (order) which can circulate simultaneously in the FMS at any one time is limited by the availability of the order-specific fixtures f_j. The objective is to maximize the

- *utilization of all machines*.

Stecke and Kim replace this objective, however, with what they consider as its equivalent: *balancing the workloads at the machines*. This is attempted by mini-

---

367 **Stecke/Kim** (1988); for a similar model without tool consideration see **Stecke/Kim** (1986), (1989), (1991)

mizing the weighted positive and negative machine workload deviations from predetermined target workloads. The decision variables in the model are the batch structure and the workpiece type mix, i.e. the relative numbers of workpieces of each type to be produced simultaneously in the FMS. According to the planned mix, the orders of a batch are manufactured until the order size of a workpiece type has been produced. Following that a new plan is generated using updated data excluding the order that has just been completed[368]. When the order arrival process is dynamic, orders released by the central PPC system in the meantime can be integrated into the new plan.

The decision model for the simultaneous determination of the *batch structure* and the *workpiece type mix* is as follows:

Model SEV-SK

$$\min Z = \sum_{m=1}^{M} \underbrace{a_m^+ \cdot d_m^+ + a_m^- \cdot d_m^-}_{} \qquad (226)$$

⌊ weighted positive and negative machine workload deviations from target workloads

subject to

$$[\sum_{j \in J_0} b_{jm} \cdot x_j] - d_m^+ + d_m^- = g_m \qquad\qquad m=1,2,\ldots,M \qquad (227)$$

⌊ target workload of machine group m

⌊ total processing time at machine m of all workpieces of order j

$$x_j \le f_j \qquad\qquad\qquad j=1,2,\ldots,J \qquad (228)$$

⌊ number of fixtures available for order j

$$\sum_{t=1}^{T} \sigma_{tm} \cdot y_{tm} \le h_m \qquad\qquad m=1,2,\ldots,M \qquad (229)$$

$$\sum_{j \in J_0} \sigma_{jtm} \cdot x_j \le J \cdot y_{tm} \qquad\qquad t=1,2,\ldots,T; \ m=1,2,\ldots,M \qquad (230)$$

$$x_j \ge 1 \qquad\qquad j \in J_1 \qquad (231)$$

$$x_j \ge 0 \text{ and integer,} \qquad\qquad j \in J_0 \qquad (232)$$

$$d_m^+, d_m^- \ge 0 \qquad\qquad m=1,2,\ldots,M \qquad (233)$$

$$y_{tm} \in \{0,1\} \qquad\qquad t=1,2,\ldots,T; \ m=1,2,\ldots,M \qquad (234)$$

where:

---

368 **Stecke/Kim** (1988), (1989), (1991)

Data:

j	-	order index ($j = 1,2,...,J$)
m	-	machine index ($m = 1,2,...,M$)
t	-	tool index ($t = 1,2,...,T$)
b_{jm}	-	processing time of a workpiece of order j at machine m
f_j	-	number of fixtures available for order j
g_m	-	target workload of machine m
a_m^+	-	weighting factor for a positive deviation from the target workload at machine m
a_m^-	-	weighting factor for a negative deviation from the target workload at machine m
J_0	-	set of orders not yet assigned to a batch
J_1	-	set of orders for which processing has started, but not yet been completed
σ_{tm}	-	number of tool magazine slots required by tool t at machine m
σ_{jtm}	=	$\begin{cases} 1 \text{ , if order j requires tool t at machine m} \\ 0 \text{ , otherwise} \end{cases}$
h_m	-	tool magazine capacity of machine m

Variables:

d_m^+	-	positive deviation from the target workload at machine m
d_m^-	-	negative deviation from the target workload at machine m
x_j	-	number of workpieces of order j circulating in the FMS simultaneously
y_{tm}	=	$\begin{cases} 1 \text{ , if tool t is assigned to machine m} \\ 0 \text{ , otherwise} \end{cases}$

The set of orders which must be considered in a planning step consists of two subsets: the set J_0 includes those orders which have already been released for processing in the FMS by the PPC system but whose *processing at that moment has not yet started*. The set J_1, on the other hand, includes those orders which have *started but not yet completed processing*. The objective function (226) balances workloads as much as possible by minimizing weighted machine over- and underloads. Weighting allows differences in importance of the machines to be accounted for. Nothing is said as to how the weighting scheme is established. The over- and underloads with respect to predetermined target workloads are defined in equations (227). The target workloads, which can be different for each group of identically tooled machines, are calculated by *Stecke and Kim* in a previous planning stage using the classical CQN model for universal pallets[369]. They take into consideration the fact that machine groups of different sizes perform differently under stochastic conditions[370].

The constraints (228) limit the number of workpieces of each type that can circulate in the FMS at any one time to the number of fixtures which are available for this workpiece type. The limited tool magazines at the machines are represented in the constraints (229). Constraints (230) assure that the required tools are made available at the machines. With the inequality (231) it is guaranteed that for the orders in the set J_1, from which some workpieces are already being

---

369 **Stecke/Kim** (1989), p. 25; see also sections 3.1.1.1. and 5.3.1. Two iterative procedures for finding the workload allocation among the machine groups of different sizes that maximizes throughput are described by **Kim** (1988), pp. 25-30; see also **Lee/Srinivasan/Yano** (1991a)

370 see also section 5.3.1.

processed in the FMS, the processing of at least one workpiece will be continued. Together these constraints form the interface between two successive planning stages. Neglecting the constraints (231) could lead to an order already assigned to a batch and partially processed being suddenly removed from the batch.

The SEV-SK model could also be used when *fixed batches are released*. In this case, all the released orders in the set J_1 would have to be fully processed before the remaining orders could be partitioned into a new group of batches. Since the order sizes are not considered in the SEV-SK model, it is possible that orders of quite different sizes could be put together to create a batch. The danger of this is that machines which are primarily used to process orders that are completed early may end up with a very low utilization at the end of the makespan.

The basic structure of the SEV-SK model is a linear mixed-integer optimization model with multiple objectives. It aims at the minimization of the weighted absolute deviations in the workloads on the machines from the externally predetermined target workloads. *Stecke and Kim* solve the model with a standard algorithm for mixed-integer linear optimization. They suggest that the integer constraints may be relaxed in order to shorten computing time. The continuous values of the decision variables are later rounded to the closest integer values[371].

The quality of the solution of this model depends to a large degree on the absolute values of the target machine workloads g_m. These are found using the relative workload distribution among the stations as calculated with the help of the classical CQN model. The relative workloads can be used to derive the target workloads for the individual stations from the available workload capacity of the FMS during the planning horizon.

Obviously, the objective of balancing workloads on the machines cannot be achieved when the target workloads (227) are most fully satisfied at a station other than the one where the tool magazine constraints (229) are binding. An example for such a situation is shown in figure (193).

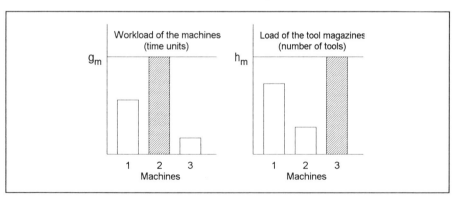

Figure 193: Machine workload vs. tool magazine load

371 **Stecke** (1987), p. 12; **Stecke/Kim** (1988), p. 19

The capacity of the *tool magazine* at machine 3 is exhausted, whereas the *utilization of the machine* is still relatively low. In contrast, the tool magazine at machine 2 still has some space available, although the machine itself is fully utilized. In this situation, in which a machine is not a bottleneck in respect of both the workload capacity and the tool magazine capacity, achieving the target workload for machine 2 does not lead to a balanced workload at the machines, although a solution with a balanced workload may exist.

The example demonstrates that with respect to the objective of achieving a balanced workload at the machines, the externally predetermined target workloads g_m at the stations are quite significant, though the weights of the over- and underloads from this target value may be important as well.

A second group of modelling approaches attempts, assuming a case with flexible batching, to minimize the tool setup time associated with a change from one batch to another. The objective of these approaches to batching is

- *the minimization of the number of tool switches*

between all the orders released by the PPC system. Among the researchers considering this objective are

- *Tang and Denardo*[372]

as well as

- *Bard*[373]

and

- *Oerlemans*[374].

The solution procedures developed, however, can only be used for *single-machine* problems.

- *Jaikumar and van Wassenhove*[375]

describe a simple heuristic procedure for the same problem but with several identical machines.

Further reading for section 5.2.:

Kuhn (1990)
Oerlemans (1992)
Rajagopalan (1985), (1986)
Sawik (1990)
Stecke (1989)
Stecke/Kim (1986), (1988), (1989), (1991)
Tang/Denardo (1988a), (1988b)

---

372 **Tang/Denardo** (1988a)
373 **Bard** (1988)
374 **Oerlemans** (1992), pp. 125-154; **Crama/Kolen/Oerlemans/Spieksma** (1994)
375 **Jaikumar/Van Wassenhove** (1989), pp. 75-76

5.3. SYSTEM SETUP PLANNING

System setup planning refers to the preparation of an FMS for processing the orders assigned to the next batch. The structure of the system setup problem is illustrated in figure (194).

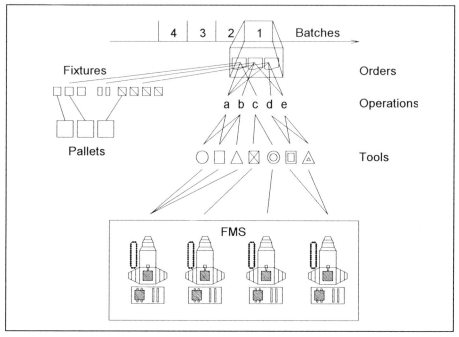

Figure 194: The system setup planning problem

An order can include various workpieces on which a variety of different operations must be performed. Each operation requires one or more tools with which the tool magazines must be supplied before processing can begin. The workpieces are clamped on pallets for which workpiece type-specific or order-specific fixtures must be mounted. When a specific fixture is mounted on a general purpose pallet this pallet then becomes a workpiece type-specific special pallet.

System setup planning, therefore, includes two central tasks:

- *To provide the tool magazines at the machines with the required tools (loading).*

- *To assign workpiece-specific fixtures to the pallets circulating in the FMS.*

- **Tooling of the machines**

The primary task of setting up an FMS is to provide the local tool magazines with the required cutting tools for processing the workpieces. In the batching models discussed in the previous section different machine types or different machine groups had been assumed. The process plans clearly indicated at which machine a workpiece had to be processed. If, as is assumed in this section, the FMS also includes *identical* machines which can be alternatively used to carry out an operation, it is necessary to find the optimal assignment of the operations to the identical machines. This also determines the set of tools to be provided to each of the machines.

In principle, this problem could be disaggregated to the level of the individual workpieces. This will not be done here, however. Instead it is assumed that all workpieces combined in an order (workpieces of a particular type) are treated equally with respect to the assignment of their associated operations to the machines. The operations required for each order are the smallest entities which will be studied.

Let O_j represent the set of different operations which are required to process a particular order j. Then the set of different operations that are required to be performed for batch l, O, can be calculated using equation (235).

$$O = \bigcup_{j \in J_1} O_j \tag{235}$$

Each of these operations must be assigned to at least one machine. If the tool magazine capacities are limited, then for large batches it may be possible that no feasible solution exists, i.e. one in which all the orders are processed without having to change the setup of the FMS.

If an FMS contains several different machine types, each one with identical machines, then the setup problem for the tool magazines can be solved for all the machines of one group independent of the other machine groups, as long as their technical capabilities do not overlap, i.e. when they are truly different.

• Assignment of the fixtures to pallets

After the machines have been provided with the required tools, the next planning phase is dedicated to the assignment of workpiece-specific fixtures to the pallets. This depends on how the orders have been combined into batches, and it defines the number of workpieces of a given type that can circulate simultaneously in the FMS. This in turn significantly influences the production rate (number of completed workpieces per unit time) of a workpiece type. Assigning fixtures to pallets is made more difficult by the fact that workpiece-specific fixtures are often only available in limited quantities. If at any time all the fixtures of a specific type are being used, it must be determined whether it makes sense to prepare any free pallets by attaching fixtures of a different type to them. This would cause the production rate of the product type now assigned a larger number of pallets to increase, while the production rate of other product types would decrease[376].

---

376   see section 3.1.1.2.3.

Both

- *Stecke and Kim*[377]

and

- *Solot*[378]

present approaches which, after appropriate modifications, could be applied to the solution of this problem. The issues associated with the assignment of fixtures to pallets will not be discussed in any further detail here, however.

In the following the problem of loading the tools into the tool magazines and the closely associated assignment of operations to the machines will be reviewed. Two different strategies are suggested in the literature. In the first one, groups of *identically tooled machines* are selected from the larger set of all the identical machines (pooling with tool duplication), and operations are then assigned to these machine groups[379]. The creation of machine groups requires that identical sets of tools be made available to the machines of a group.

The second approach does not build machine groups. Instead the *operations are assigned directly to the identical machines*. Here the multiple provision of identical tool sets is either explicitly excluded through the formulation of a decision model, or it results from the assignment of the operations to the machines.

5.3.1. Machine Pooling

If identical machines of an FMS are partitioned into identically tooled machine groups, then all machines of a group can be used alternatively to perform a particular operation. The advantage of machines being able to easily replace each other becomes clear when a machine breaks down since the *routing flexibility* of the workpiece types is increased. However, with machine grouping it is necessary to provide several tools of the same type (sister tools, tool duplication), since a tool assigned to a machine has to be present there without interruption. This is a main drawback of machine pooling, particularly when the tools are expensive.

In addition, machine grouping limits the batch of orders to be simultaneously processed in the FMS to fewer different workpiece types. The number of different orders with different tool requirements combined in a batch affects whether the tool magazine capacities of the machines are large enough as to provide room for all the tools required while still allowing for some of the magazines to be identically tooled. Therefore, the possibility of grouping machines has already to be considered in the batching phase. The issues involved in machine pooling will be explained with the help of figures (195) and (196).

---

377 **Stecke/Kim** (1986); **Stecke** (1987)
378 **Solot** (1990a)
379 **Stecke** (1983); **Stecke** (1986); **Stecke/Kim** (1988); **Mazzola/Neebe/Dunn** (1989)

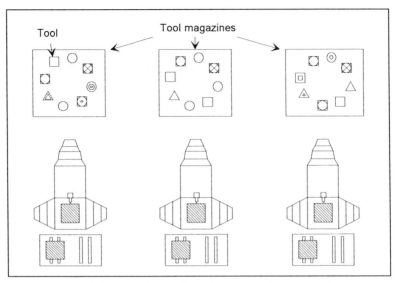

Figure 195: No machine pooling (3 machines with different tools)

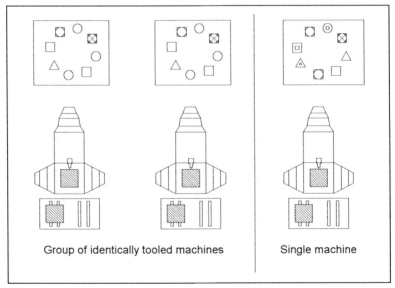

Figure 196: Machine pooling (2 machines with identical tools)

It is assumed in figure (195) that a batch contains so many different orders that, due to the tool requirements, every one of the identical machines must be equipped with a different tool set. From the point of view of the workpieces, this reduces the *routing flexibility* since the path they have to follow through the FMS is fixed due to the assignment of tools to the machines.

In contrast, the batch providing the basis for the tooling shown in figure (196) contains orders with a limited diversity in their tool requirements. This allows two of the three machines to be equipped with identical tools and thus to build a homogeneous machine group.

The *objective of machine pooling* is to group the machines so as to maximize the production rate of the workpiece types assigned to a given batch. Technical constraints (tool magazine capacities) must be taken into consideration. Both

• *Stecke and Morin*

and

• *Stecke and Solberg*[380]

have used the classical CQN model to show that the production rate of an FMS can be increased when as few machine groups as possible are created. This argument is plausible since several identically equipped machines can operate as parallel servers which, in the classical CQN model, are supplied from a single *common queue*.

If the minimum number of groups is known, then the machines should be formed into groups such that the sizes of the groups are as unequal as possible. If, for example, five identical machines are to be divided among two machine groups, then one group should be assigned four machines while the other should be assigned only one. In this way, the number of parallel servers in one group is maximized.

Figure (197) shows a simplified CQN representation of an FMS with three machines. Two different variations are considered: in the first the machines are not grouped, i.e. all machines have different sets of tools; and in the other the machines are grouped, i.e. two machines are provided with identical tools.

If all machines are equipped with different tools, then they must be modelled as three independent queueing systems each having a single server fed by a dedicated queue. This implies that machine 2 can be idle while a workpiece waits in front of machine 1. If instead two machines are identically equipped with tools, then they can be modelled as a single queueing system with two parallel servers that are supplied from a common queue. A machine can only be idle in such a constellation when the common queue is empty.

Table (88) summarizes the data required to solve the CQN models for the described examples. The average transportation time is assumed to be zero ($b_M = 0$) for both cases. In order to retain the same workpiece flow which would apply without machine pooling, the arrival probability $p_{(1+2)}$ must be adjusted after combining machines 1 and 2 in a single group with identically tooled machines. Therefore, the arrival probabilities at the stations 1 and 2 were added in table (88).

---

380 **Stecke/Morin** (1985); **Stecke/Solberg** (1985); also **Stecke/Kim** (1988)

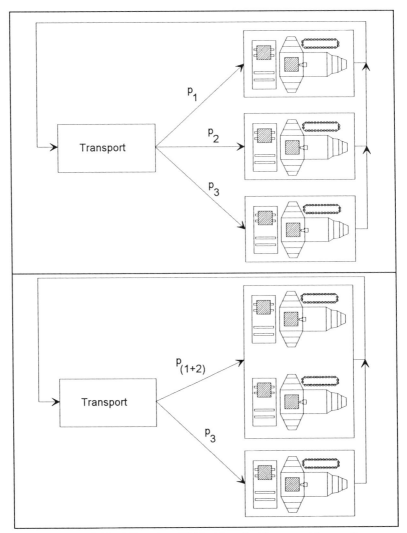

Figure 197: Modelling of an FMS with and without machine pooling

Without machine pooling				With machine pooling			
m	S_m	b_m	p_m	m	S_m	b_m	p_m
1	1	1	0.33	1+2	2	1	0.67
2	1	1	0.33				
3	1	1	0.33	3	1	1	0.33

Table 88: Data of the FMS considered

Figure (198) illustrates the development of the production rate of the FMS as a function of the number of pallets for both constellations. The production rate of the FMS without machine pooling is less than that of the FMS in which two of the machines have been provided with identical tools. This is true because of the three different queues in the first case: it is possible that one machine may be idle although several pallets are still waiting in the other queues. This effect diminishes as the number of pallets increases, since the probability that such a situation may arise decreases.

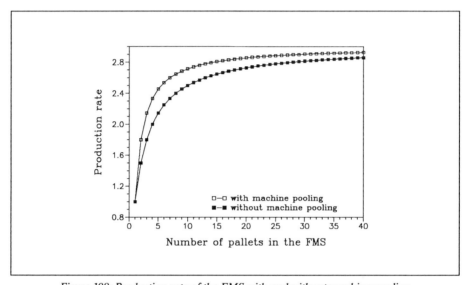

Figure 198: Production rate of the FMS with and without machine pooling

The production rate of a machine group is greater than the sum of the production rates of the individual machines in the group. This, therefore, presents a *further optimization problem* in determining the optimal distribution of the workload among the different machine groups[381]. The machine groups can, due to their higher production rate, process more workpieces per period than the individual machines. It makes sense, therefore, to shift the workload towards the more productive machine groups and to adjust the arrival probabilities for the improved performance of the machine groups.

The simplified FMS from figure (197) can help to explain this process more clearly. Figure (199) shows the development of the production rate of the FMS resulting from variations in the workload distributions at each machine in machine group 1 (machines 1 and 2) for several different numbers of pallets.

---

381 **Stecke** (1983), pp. 279-281

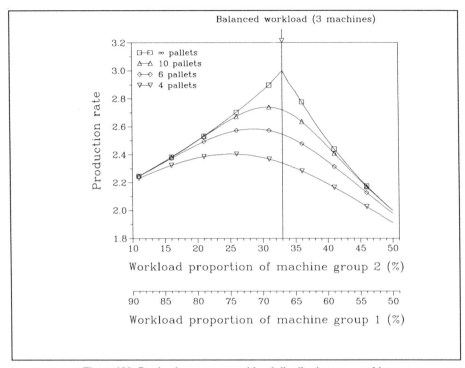

Figure 199: Production rate vs. workload distribution per machine

If the arrival probabilities p_m for the three machines are evenly distributed based on the number of machines (i.e. $p_{(1+2)}=0.667$, $p_3=0.333$) and if the *number of pallets is finite*, the maximum production rate will *not be reached*. In order to achieve the maximum production rate, machine group 1 must be assigned a higher arrival probability. In this way the relatively more efficient machine group is preferentially supplied with workpieces. This has a positive effect on the production rate. If, for example, 4 pallets are circulating in the FMS, then the maximum production rate will be achieved when the machine group 2 (machine 3) takes on 25% and the machine group 1 75%[382] of the total workload. Figure (200) presents this aspect of the problem from another three-dimensional point of view.

As indicated by the line connecting the greatest production rates (the solid line) in figure (200), the optimal workload distribution deviates more and more from the evenly distributed workload per machine (the dotted line) as the number of pallets circulating in the FMS is reduced.

Therefore, when the sizes of the machine groups are unequal, it is advantageous to unbalance the workloads at the machines so that the machines in a machine

---

382   This is equivalent to a workload of 37.5% per machine in group 1.

group have a relatively large workload in comparison to the individual machines. However, the assumptions underlying the classical CQN model must hold.

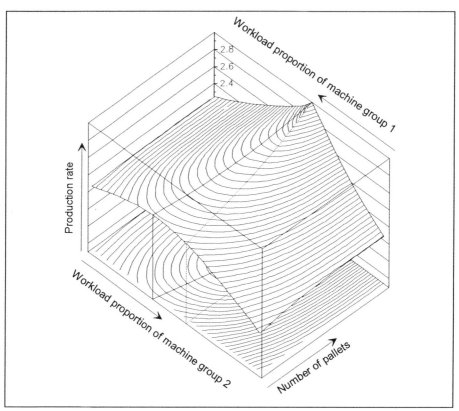

Figure 200: Production rate vs. workload distribution per machine for different numbers of pallets

• *Stecke*[383]

has proposed a procedure for optimal machine pooling in which first integer upper and lower bounds of the number of machine groups are calculated. If the upper and lower bounds are different, the minimum number of groups (lower bound) is calculated by a simple heuristic procedure[384] (similar to the SEF-KUHN procedure[385]). In a second step, the machines are assigned to groups such that the range in group size is as large as possible.

The workload assigned to the machines is largely ignored in the *Stecke* approach. It is first known when the operations are assigned to their machine groups (or

383   **Stecke** (1986), pp. 374-375.
384   section 5.2.1.1.
385   **Stecke** (1983), pp. 277-278

machines)[386]. The problem remains that machine pooling requires that an appropriately large number of (duplicate) tool sets be available.

Overall, the usefulness of the concept of machine pooling, as discussed here and in detail in the literature, must be seen in a critical light since it contradicts the flexibility intended to be an integral part of the FMS by fitting several machines with identical tools. Under certain conditions, it may be necessary and useful to have the tools required for an operation available at a number of machines. This means, however, that only this one operation - not all operations assigned to the machines - has the freedom to choose among a number of machines. Partitioning machines into independent machine groups thus seems appropriate only in exceptional cases, such as when large numbers of identical workpieces are to be manufactured. Otherwise, it is possible that a decision may be made about duplicate tooling in the operation/machine assignment, as described in the next section.

It must also be considered that the relationships demonstrated by *Stecke* and many other authors are only true under stochastic conditions. During the operation of an FMS workpieces are not released based on the stationary behavior of the FMS. Instead release is usually based on the current workload on the machines, so the effects described here will be much less severe - if they are present at all. An unbalanced workload per machine for a system of groups of pooled machines of unequal sizes could even, under deterministic conditions, lead to worse results than a balanced workload distribution.

Further reading for section 5.3.1.:

Co/Biermann/Chen (1990)
Gray/Seidmann/Stecke (1990)
Kim/Yano (1992)
Lee/Srinivasan/Yano (1991a), (1991b)
Mazzola/Neebe/Dunn (1989)
Stecke (1983), (1986), (1987)
Stecke/Kim (1986), (1989)
Stecke/Morin (1985)
Stecke/Solberg (1985)

5.3.2. Assignment of Operations and Machines

This section treats the assignment of tools to the identical machines to assure that all required operations of the selected orders in a batch can be performed. The workpieces of an order are processed according to a particular process plan that may include one or more operations. We use the term *operation lot* to describe a specific order, *with respect to a particular operation o*, including n_o identical workpieces [see figure (201)]. Except when explicitly otherwise indicated, the

---

386   see section 5.3.2.

term operation will be used as a synonym to operation lot. The central subject of the analysis is the assignment of operation lots to the identical machines. The result of this planning phase is the actual tooling of the local tool magazines and the determination of which machines will process the workpieces of an operation lot.

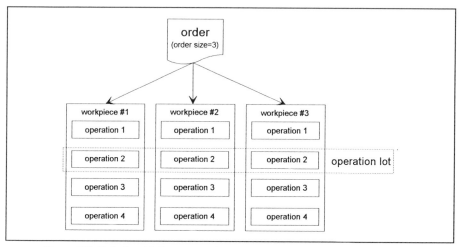

Figure 201: Relationship between order, workpiece, operation and operation lot

Figure (202) offers an overview of the data structure of the problem considered. Again the entity-relationship model is used as a descriptive tool. There is a 1:m relationship between orders (ORDER) and workpieces (WORKPIECE). The orders and the operations (OPERATION) are in an m:n relationship since one order can call for several operations, and one operation may be performed on several different orders. An operation lot can be formed by reinterpreting the type of rela-tionship[387] OPORD between the orders and the operations. There is an m:n relationship between the operation lots and the machines (MACHINE) since workpieces in one operation lot can often be assigned to several different machines (lot splitting). After solving the operation/machine assignment problem, the attributes of the relationship types OPORD-MACH-TOOL and OPORD-MACH provide the tooling of the tool magazines and the assignment of the operations to the machines.

The tools needed to carry out an operation are generally present at the machine before processing begins so that no unnecessary delays are caused while the FMS is running. The infinite ability of basically identical machines to replace each other applies only up to the moment when the machines acquire special-ized technical capabilities, i.e. when they are provided with a unique set of tools. The original given *machine flexibility* of the FMS is thus restricted after this planning phase.

---

387   see **Scheer** (1989), p. 24

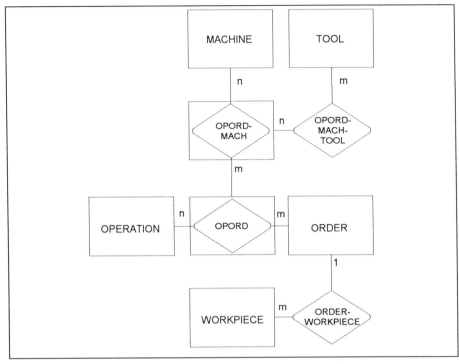

Figure 202: Data structure for operation/machine assignment

The overriding objective of this planning phase is to process the orders of a batch as *quickly as possible*. This allows the FMS to be available for processing further orders as early as possible. If it is assumed that the FMS is a bottleneck in a particular production segment, then this can directly affect the production quantity and thereby also the economic efficiency of production.

A number of financial and technical objectives are discussed in the literature in connection with the suggested modelling approaches for operation/machine assignment:

- *Minimization of the relevant costs*

  If the variable production costs are dependent on the operation/machine assignment, the minimization of these *costs* is a reasonable objective. Such a situation can, for example, exist when an operation in the FMS can be carried out at different machines using differently priced tools.

- *Minimization of the deviations between the target and the assigned workload*

  When this objective is pursued the idea is to achieve a balanced workload on the equipment, to minimize the makespan, and to maximize the production rate. If the FMS includes several machine groups of unequal size an unbalanced (rather than balanced) workload per machine maximizes expected production - assumed the stochastic conditions of the classical CQN model are given. Arguments for the reasonableness of this objective were discussed in the previous section 5.3.1.

- *Minimization of the greatest machine workload*

  Pursuing this objective also implies attempting to minimize the makespan. Such a formulation is particularly useful when the operations have different processing times at the identical machines.

- *Minimization of the number of required tools*

  The number of tools needed to process the orders in a batch can be influenced by assigning operation lots which are similar in their tool requirements to a single machine. This would tend to reduce the number of tool changes between the central and local tool magazines, and possibly reduce the number of tool changes inside the machine[388].

In the following sections the most important models found in the literature for operation/machine assignment will be presented. It will be distinguished between,

- *Models without tool constraints,*
- *Models with simplified tool constraints,* and
- *Models with tool constraints considering common tool usage.*

These model variations can be further differentiated with respect to tool duplication:

- *Single tooling* and
- *Multiple tooling.*

In addition, the models can be distinguished according to the objective functions used.

It is assumed for all cases that every operation can be performed at any machine, as long as the machine has been equipped with the necessary tools. If an operation/machine assignment is not allowed, this can be accounted for by an infinite processing time of the operation at the machine.

---

388 Tool change is not necessary if two consecutively processed workpieces require the same tool.

5.3.2.1. Models without tool constraints

In the simplest case the operation/machine assignment problem can be represented as a *generalized assignment problem*[389], when the constraints associated with limited tool magazines are ignored.

- *Kusiak*[390]

has designed such a model for a case in which the capacity of the machines per period in the FMS is limited, and in which variable costs of c_{om} are incurred due to the assignment of operation lot o to a machine m.

Model AGMA-KUS1

$$\min Z = \sum_{o=1}^{0} \sum_{m=1}^{M} c_{om} \cdot \pi_{om} \tag{236}$$

subject to

$$\sum_{o=1}^{0} \pi_{om} \cdot b_{om} \leq g_m \qquad\qquad m=1,2,\ldots,M \tag{237}$$

$$\sum_{m=1}^{M} \pi_{om} = 1 \qquad\qquad o=1,2,\ldots,0 \tag{238}$$

$$\pi_{om} \in \{0,1\} \qquad\qquad m=1,2,\ldots,M;\ o=1,2,\ldots,0 \tag{239}$$

where:

Data:

m	-	machine index (m = 1,2,...,M)
o	-	operation lot index (o = 1,2,...,O)
b_{om}	-	processing time of operation lot o at machine m
c_{om}	-	variable costs of processing operation lot o at machine m
g_m	-	capacity of machine m (time units)

Variables:

$$\pi_{om} = \begin{cases} 1, \text{ if operation lot o is processed at machine m} \\ 0, \text{ otherwise} \end{cases}$$

The objective function (236) describes the costs associated with a particular operation/machine assignment. The constraints (237) assure that the workload assigned to machine m per period does not exceed the available capacity of the machine throughout the planning period. Equation (238) guarantees that every operation is assigned to exactly one machine.

---

389 In contrast to the 1:1 assignment considered in the linear assignment problem, in the general assignment problem a 1:n assignment is possible; **Fisher/Jaikumar/Van Wassenhove** (1986)
390 **Kusiak** (1985b), p. 126

As a special type of combinatorial problem, a whole series of exact and heuristic procedures are available for the solution of the generalized assignment problem[391]. If the size is not too large, the AGMA-KUS1 model can be solved with a standard algorithm for binary optimization. Consider *example 5-2* with 2 machines and 8 operation lots. The data for this example have been summarized in table (89). As the capacities and processing times are the same, the two machines differ only in their variable costs.

o	Costs c_{o1}	c_{o2}	Processing times b_{o1}	b_{o2}
1	1	2	30	30
2	1	2	12	12
3	1	2	20	20
4	1	2	9	9
5	1	2	16	16
6	1	2	2	2
7	1	2	17	17
8	1	2	26	26

m	Machine capacity g_m
1	80
2	80

Table 89: Data for model AGMA-KUS1 (example 5-2)

The tableau of the binary linear program for the AGMA-KUS1 model is given in table (90).

	$\pi 11$	$\pi 21$	$\pi 31$	$\pi 41$	$\pi 51$	$\pi 61$	$\pi 71$	$\pi 81$	$\pi 12$	$\pi 22$	$\pi 32$	$\pi 42$	$\pi 52$	$\pi 62$	$\pi 72$	$\pi 82$	RHS
Costs	1	1	1	1	1	1	1	1	2	2	2	2	2	2	2	2	0
D.1	30	12	20	9	16	2	17	26									<= 80
D.2									30	12	20	9	16	2	17	26	<= 80
D.3	1								1								= 1
D.4		1								1							= 1
D.5			1								1						= 1
D.6				1								1					= 1
D.7					1								1				= 1
D.8						1								1			= 1
D.9							1								1		= 1
D.10								1								1	= 1
BOUND	0	0	0	0	0	0	0	0	0	0	0	0	0	0	0	0	
BOUND	1	1	1	1	1	1	1	1	1	1	1	1	1	1	1	1	

Table 90: LP tableau for example 5-2

This binary linear program has the optimal solution shown in table (91) with a minimal objective function value of 10. As was to be expected, the less expensive machine 1 is assigned as many operation lots as possible.

Practical applications of the AGMA-KUS1 model present numerous difficulties, however. The costs of the assignment of an operation lot o to each machine m, c_{om}, have to be calculated. Yet, the determination of the variable costs associated with the use of different machines is often quite difficult.

---

391 Fisher/Jaikumar/van Wassenhove (1986)

Machine	Operation	Processing time
1	2 3 4 5 6 7	12 20 9 16 2 17
Used capacity Unused capacity		*76* 4
2	1 8	30 26
Used capacity Unused capacity		*56* 24

Table 91: Optimal solution for example 5-2

The parameter c_{om} should only include the costs directly associated with the assignment of an operation to a machine. In practice, however, the unit of association is often a *machine hour rate*, which already includes proportionalized overhead costs. These cost rates are *not usable* for the AGMA-KUS1 model. It is generally found that in an FMS the relevant costs c_{om} are the *same for all identical machines*. Thus all feasible solutions of the AGMA-KUS1 model would be equally good with respect to the objective function (236). Another problem is that a workload limit for each machine g_m must be externally predetermined. This assumes that the duration of the planning period is known.

- *Afentakis*[392]

gets around the problem of determining the cost rates by pursuing the *objective of minimizing the greatest machine workload* in a model with constraints similar to those included in model AGMA-KUS1 [see equation (240)].

$$\min Z = \max_{m} \{g_m\} \tag{240}$$

Afentakis expands the problem of assigning operation lots to the machines by adding the assumption that the *material flow system* cannot directly connect every combination of two machines, and that *precedence relations* exist between the operations. With the constraints (241) these new aspects are taken into consideration.

$$\pi_{om} \le \sum_{j \in \phi_m} \pi_{nj} \qquad\qquad n \in \theta_o \tag{241}$$

where:

θ_o -   set of predecessor operations of operation o
ϕ_m -   set of machines from which machine m is directly reachable

---

392 **Afentakis** (1986), p. 514

Afentakis solves the problem with the following procedure. He constructs an un-directed graph in which every node represents a possible assignment of an operation to a machine. Two nodes are connected by an edge if these two assignments *cannot* both be realized at the same time. Hence, a feasible assignment of operations to machines corresponds with a *maximal independent set of nodes* in the graph. An independent set of nodes in a graph is a set of nodes such that no two nodes of the set are connected[393]. *Afentakis* suggests achieving the objective of minimizing the maximum machine workload by determining the value of the objective function (240) for every maximal independent set of nodes and selecting the best solution.

It often makes sense to *split an operation lot* to allow several workpieces of the same type (order) to be processed simultaneously on several identical machines. In this case the binary decision variables π_{om} should be replaced with continuous or integer variables u_{om} that describe the machine-dependent lot size of an operation o at the machine m. The equations (238) and (239) of the AGMA-KUS1 model would then have to be replaced with the constraints (242) and (243).

$$\sum_{m=1}^{M} u_{om} = n_o \qquad\qquad o=1,2,\ldots,O \qquad\qquad (242)$$

$\llcorner$ number of operations (workpieces) of operation lot o processed at machine m

$$u_{om} \geq 0 \qquad\qquad o=1,2,\ldots,O; \; m=1,2,\ldots,M \qquad\qquad (243)$$

The resulting model has the basic structure of a *generalized transportation problem*[394]. The *lot size* of the *operation lot* o is indicated by n_o and the variable u_{om} represents the number of operations (workpieces) of operation lot o that are assigned to the machine m. Equation (242) guarantees that the entire operation lot n_o is assigned and processed at anyone of the machines. The inequality (243) describes the non-negativity constraints of the operation assignment. Non-integer values are now also allowed. It can be assured in another constraint that these variables be integers.

• *DeLuca*[395]

has also formulated a model whose objective function is the minimization of the *greatest machine workload* [objective function (240)].

The fundamental problem with all of the models described in this section is that they all *fail to consider the limitations of the tool magazine capacities* - a severe drawback considering their application for short term system setup planning in an FMS. They are, therefore, only useful in the first phase of the examination of the operation/machine assignment problem.

---

393 The problem of determining the maximum number of independent nodes in a graph is described by **Syslo/Deo/Kowalik** (1983), pp. 399-404.
394 The generalization arises through the additional arc parameters b_{om} in equation (237); **Eisemann** (1964).
395 **DeLuca** (1984), p. 324

5.3.2.2. Models with simplified tool constraints

The limitations of the tool magazine capacities can, in simplified form, be integrated into the generalized assignment models already discussed in the previous section by adding a further group of constraints. These are described by equation (244).

$$\sum_{o=1}^{0} \sigma_o \cdot \pi_{om} \leq h_m \qquad\qquad m=1,2,\ldots,M \qquad (244)$$

$\quad\uparrow$
$\quad\llcorner$ total number of tool magazine slots required at machine m

where:

σ_o - number of tool magazine slots required for operation lot o

π_{om} = $\begin{cases} 1\text{, if operation lot o is processed at machine m} \\ 0\text{, otherwise} \end{cases}$

h_m - tool magazine capacity of machine m

Integrating the tools into the model in this way neglects the possibility that a tool may be used by several operation types assigned to a machine (tool commonality), and that it only has to be taken into the tool magazine once. If a tool is needed by three types of different operation lots assigned to a machine, for example, equation (244) would suggest that it takes up three separate slots in the tool magazine. Hence, the solution of this model will result in an underutilization of the tool magazines.

To illustrate this the example 5-2 has been expanded to include the tool requirements and tool magazine capacities shown in table (92).

o	Costs c_{o1}	c_{o2}	Processing times b_{o1}	b_{o2}	Tool requirement σ_o
1	1	2	30	30	5
2	1	2	12	12	6
3	1	2	20	20	4
4	1	2	9	9	10
5	1	2	16	16	3
6	1	2	2	2	10
7	1	2	17	17	4
8	1	2	26	26	5
m	Machine capacity g_m		Tool magazine h_m		
1	80		25		
2	80		25		

Table 92: Data for example 5-3

In order to solve the modified problem, the LP tableau shown in table (90) must now be adjusted for two more constraints [see table (93)].

	π11	π21	π31	π41	π51	π61	π71	π81	π12	π22	π32	π42	π52	π62	π72	π82	RHS
D.11	5	6	4	10	3	10	4	5									<= 25
D.12									5	6	4	10	3	10	4	5	<= 25

Table 93: Simplified tool constraints added to the LP tableau for model AGMA-KUS1 (example 5-3)

The *optimal solution* is summarized in table (94). The value of the objective function is 12 in this solution. Compared to the solution of the AGMA-KUS1 model, introducing the tool constraints has caused the distribution of the operation lots, and thus the workload per machine, to shift from the less expensive machine 1 to machine 2.

Machine	Operations	Processing times	Tools
1	2	12	6
	3	20	4
	6	2	10
	8	26	5
Used capacity		*60*	*25*
Unused capacity		20	0
2	1	30	5
	4	9	10
	5	16	3
	7	17	4
Used capacity		*72*	*22*
Unused capacity		8	3

Table 94: Optimal solution for example 5-3

One can directly expand the AGMA-KUS1 model by allowing recourse to the exchange of the machine-specific *tool sets* parallel to processing. In this case, the local tool magazine at machine m is organized with the help of *tool cassettes* or discs. If required it is possible to exchange a tool cassette for a new one with different tools from outside the machine. There are some *setup costs* associated with this exchange, however.

• *Kusiak*[396]

has designed a model that integrates this possibility. He also provides for the possibility that the workpieces in an operation lot may be directed to several machines (*lot splitting*). This option is modelled using two types of assignment variables. The integer variables u_{om} define the number of workpieces in operation lot o that are processed at the machine m (*machine-specific lot size*). The binary variables π_{om} describe whether or not at least one workpiece of an operation lot is assigned to a machine. The simultaneous processing of several identical workpieces at different machines is only possible when several identical sets of tools are available at the various machines. Thus the problem of tool duplication emerges. In its simplest form, the model reads as follows:

396 **Kusiak** (1985c); see also **Kuhn** (1990), pp. 73-74

Model AGMA-KUS2

$$\min Z = \sum_{o=1}^{O} \sum_{m=1}^{M} c_{om} \cdot u_{om} + \sum_{m=1}^{M} c_m \cdot z_m \qquad (245)$$

— costs for a tool magazine exchange at machine m

— processing costs

subject to

$$\sum_{m=1}^{M} u_{om} = n_o \qquad\qquad o=1,2,\ldots,O \qquad (246)$$

— size of operation lot o

— number of workpieces of operation lot o processed at machine m

$$\sum_{o=1}^{O} b_{om} \cdot u_{om} \leq g_m \qquad\qquad m=1,2,\ldots,M \qquad (247)$$

$$\sum_{o=1}^{O} \sigma_o \cdot \pi_{om} \leq h_m \cdot z_m \qquad\qquad m=1,2,\ldots,M \qquad (248)$$

— number of tool magazine slots required for operation lot o at machine m

$$u_{om} \leq n_o \cdot \pi_{om} \qquad\qquad o=1,2,\ldots,O;\ m=1,2,\ldots,M \qquad (249)$$

$$u_{om} \geq 0 \text{ and integer} \qquad\qquad o=1,2,\ldots,O;\ m=1,2,\ldots,M \qquad (250)$$

$$z_m \leq Z_m \text{ and integer} \qquad\qquad m=1,2,\ldots,M \qquad (251)$$

$$\pi_{om} \in \{0,1\} \qquad\qquad o=1,2,\ldots,O;\ m=1,2,\ldots,M \qquad (252)$$

where:

Data:

m	-	machine index ($m = 1,2,\ldots,M$)
o	-	operation lot index ($o = 1,2,\ldots,O$)
σ_o	-	number of tool magazine slots required for operation lot o
b_{om}	-	processing time of a single workpiece of operation lot o at machine m
c_m	-	setup costs for a tool magazine at machine m
c_{om}	-	variable costs of operation lot o at machine m
h_m	-	tool magazine capacity of machine m
g_m	-	capacity of machine m
n_o	-	lot size of operation lot o
Z_m	-	maximum number of tool magazine exchanges at machine m

Variables:

$$\pi_{om} \quad = \begin{cases} 1 \text{ , if a workpiece of operation lot o is processed at machine m} \\ 0 \text{ , otherwise} \end{cases}$$

u_{om} - number of workpieces of operation lot o processed at machine m (machine-specific lot size)

z_m - number of tool magazine exchanges required at machine m

The objective function (245) minimizes the sum of all costs associated with the assignment of operations to the machines, including setup costs, when the tool magazines are exchanged. The equations (246) guarantee that all n_o workpieces of an operation lot are assigned and processed at a machine. The constraints (247) assure that the workload capacities of the machines are not exceeded. The constraints (248) limit the number of tools that can be assigned to the tool magazines and define the number of required tool magazine exchanges (z_m). It is assumed that always the complete tool set is exchanged. The tool requirements of the machine m when at least one workpiece of operation lot o is assigned to the machine are defined on the left side. The number of slots available for tools is given on the right side. If $z_m > 1$, then the tool set at machine m must be exchanged. The inequality (249) describes the relationship between the assignment variables π_{om} (at least one workpiece of operation lot o is processed at machine m) and the variables u_{om} (machine-specific lot size).

Kusiak suggests that a standard algorithm for linear optimization should be used to solve the model (neglecting the integrality constraints). The non-integer variables can be rounded off afterwards[397].

Continuing the example 5-3, the *exchange of tool cassettes* shown in model AGMA-KUS2 is now integrated into the example, while the lot splitting option is not considered. It is only necessary that the objective function from the AGMA-KUS1 model be replaced with that of the AGMA-KUS2 model, and that the additional constraints represented by the equations (248) and (251) be added.

The capacity of the tool magazines at both machines is now limited to 20 tools. Furthermore, there are three exchangeable tool cassettes for each machine, and the setup costs for each tool cassette are assumed to be 5. The LP tableau of the resulting linear program is shown in figure (95).

	$\pi 11$	$\pi 21$	$\pi 31$	$\pi 41$	$\pi 51$	$\pi 61$	$\pi 71$	$\pi 81$	$\pi 12$	$\pi 22$	$\pi 32$	$\pi 42$	$\pi 52$	$\pi 62$	$\pi 72$	$\pi 82$	z.1	z.2	RHS
Costs	1	1	1	1	1	1	1	1	1	2	2	2	2	2	2	2	5	5	
D.1	30	12	20	9	16	2	17	26											<= 80
D.2									30	12	20	9	16	2	17	26			<= 80
D.3	1								1										= 1
D.4		1								1									= 1
D.5			1								1								= 1
D.6				1								1							= 1
D.7					1								1						= 1
D.8						1								1					= 1
D.9							1								1				= 1
D.10								1								1			= 1
D.13	5	6	4	10	3	10	4	5									-20		<= 0
D.14									5	6	4	10	3	10	4	5		-20	<= 0
BOUND	0	0	0	0	0	0	0	0	0	0	0	0	0	0	0	0	0	0	BOUND
BOUND	1	1	1	1	1	1	1	1	1	1	1	1	1	1	1	1	3	3	BOUND

Table 95: LP tableau for example 5-4 (model AGMA-KUS2)

397 **Kusiak** (1985c), pp. 231-232

The optimal solution of example 5-4 calculated with a standard algorithm for integer linear optimization is given in table (96). The optimal value of the objective function is 25. This solution agrees with the optimal solution of the AGMA-KUS1 model (example 5-2). The problems arising from the limited tool magazines are offset by introducing three tool cassettes all together.

Machine	Operation	Processing time	Tool
1	2 3 4 5 6 7	12 20 9 16 2 17	6 4 10 3 10 4
Number of tool cassettes			2
Used capacity Unused capacity		*76* 4	*37* 3
2	1 8	30 26	5 5
Number of tool cassettes			1
Used capacity Unused capacity		*56* 24	*10* 10

Table 96: Optimal solution for example 5-4

Since it is possible with the constraints (251) to limit the number of tool cassettes available to a machine, it is also possible to at least roughly account for limited capacities in the tool supply system.

5.3.2.3. Models with tool constraints in consideration of common tool usage

In the operation/machine assignment models discussed up to now it has been assumed that each type of operation (operation lot) assigned to a machine would have to be provided with its own set of tools in the tool magazine. One important fact has been ignored: different operations sometimes need the same tools, and it is often sufficient to make only one copy of a tool available in the tool magazine.

The common usage of a tool by several operation lots (tool commonality) can be integrated into the mixed-integer programming models considered up to now by introducing an additional group of binary variables. If the *minimization of the greatest machine workload* is pursued as the primary objective, the following model results[398]:

---

398 **Kuhn** (1990), pp. 194-195

Model AGMA-KU

$$\min Z = \max_{m} \{g_m\} \tag{253}$$

subject to

$$\sum_{o=1}^{0} b_{om} \cdot \pi_{om} - g_m \leq 0 \qquad\qquad m=1,2,\ldots,M \tag{254}$$

⌞ current workload of machine m

$$\sum_{t=1}^{T} \sigma_t \cdot y_{tm} \leq h_m \qquad\qquad m=1,2,\ldots,M \tag{255}$$

⌞ number of tool magazine slots of type t required at machine m

$$\sum_{o=1}^{0} \sigma_{ot} \cdot \pi_{om} \leq E \cdot y_{tm} \qquad\qquad t=1,2,\ldots,T; \ m=1,2,\ldots,M \tag{256}$$

$$\sum_{m=1}^{M} \pi_{om} = 1 \qquad\qquad o=1,2,\ldots,0 \tag{257}$$

$$\pi_{om} \in \{0,1\} \qquad\qquad o=1,2,\ldots,0; \ m=1,2,\ldots,M \tag{258}$$

$$y_{tm} \in \{0,1\} \qquad\qquad t=1,2,\ldots,T; \ m=1,2,\ldots,M \tag{259}$$

where:

Data:

E	-	large number
m	-	machine index (m = 1,2,...,M)
o	-	operation lot index (o = 1,2,...,O)
t	-	tool index (t = 1,2,...,T)
σ_{ot}	=	$\begin{cases} 1 \text{, if operation lot o requires tool t} \\ 0 \text{, otherwise} \end{cases}$
σ_t	-	number of tool magazine slots required by tool t
b_{om}	-	processing time of operation lot o at machine m
h_m	-	tool magazine size at machine m

Variables:

π_{om}	=	$\begin{cases} 1 \text{, if operation lot o is processed at machine m} \\ 0 \text{, otherwise} \end{cases}$
y_{tm}	=	$\begin{cases} 1 \text{, if tool t is assigned to machine m} \\ 0 \text{, otherwise} \end{cases}$
g_m	-	workload of machine m

The objective function (253) describes the greatest machine workload, and the current workload is defined by inequality (254). The constraints (255) limit the number of tools that can be assigned to the tool magazines. If operation lot o is assigned to machine m, then the inequalities (256) guarantee that the binary variables y_{tm} of the relevant tools are equal to 1, and thus the necessary load into the tool magazine will be correctly represented. If the variable y_{tm} is determined based on the assignment of an operation lot to the machine, and thus the tool t is present at the machine m, then other operation lots that also need the tool t can use it without adding the same tool again. The equations (257) assure that every operation is assigned to exactly one machine.

- *Sawik*[399]

proposes a similar model in which an operation lot can be processed at several machines (lot splitting) and thus several copies of a tool must be available (tool duplication). The number of tool duplications is not limited, so in an extreme case it may be possible that every tool could have to be present at every machine.

- *Sarin and Chen*[400]

have designed another model in which, aside from the machine workload capacities g_m and the capacities of the tool magazines, the tool lives and the total workload on all the machines in the FMS, $\Sigma_m g_m$, are considered as constraints. *Sarin and Chen* choose the minimization of the variable production costs as the objective function. Its value is dependent on the assignment of the operation lots to the machines and the tools associated with that assignment. To solve the model they use a standard algorithm for mixed-integer linear optimization.

An heuristic procedure, that also assigns product types to dedicated pallet types, is described by

- *Mukhopadhyay, Maiti and Garg*[401].

The allocation of tools to machines is performed with a greedy heuristic based on processing times which for a workpiece differ by the machine and tool set used. The processing sequences of the individual workpieces, their assignment to machines and pallets and the scheduling of the AGV are based on priority values.

Introducing binary variables y_{tm} in the representation of the assignment of a tool t to a tool magazine at machine m is one way to account for the common usage of tools. A second way to accomplish this is by introducing *nonlinear constraints*, in which the potential tool slot savings associated with a particular assignment of operations to machines are defined using nonlinear functions and included in the tool magazine constraints.

- *Stecke*[402]

has proposed such a model in which various objectives are pursued.

399 **Sawik** (1990), pp. 180-181
400 **Sarin/Chen** (1987). A model and a solution procedure which take tool movements between the machines into consideration are presented by **Han/Na/Hogg** (1989).
401 **Mukhopadhyay/Maiti/Garg** (1991)
402 **Stecke** (1983), pp. 276-277; *Stecke* also includes a parameter to take the production ratio of an operation into consideration. This coefficient may be allowed for by the processing time b_{om} without changing the model structure; **Stecke** (1983), p. 279.

Model AGMA-ST

$$\min \text{ or } \max Z = f(\underline{\pi}) \tag{260}$$

    ↑ $(O{\times}M)$-Matrix of assignments of operations and machines

subject to

$$\sum_{o=1}^{O} b_{om} \cdot \pi_{om} \le g_m \qquad\qquad m=1,2,\ldots,M \tag{261}$$

$$\sum_{m=1}^{M} \pi_{om} = 1 \qquad\qquad o=1,2,\ldots,O \tag{262}$$

$$\sum_{o=1}^{O} \sigma_o \cdot \pi_{om} - TS_m(\underline{\pi}_m) \le h_m \qquad\qquad m=1,2,\ldots,M \tag{263}$$

    ↑ tool magazine space savings at machine m depending on the assignment of operation lots to machines

$$\pi_{om} \in \{0,1\} \qquad\qquad m=1,2,\ldots,M; \ o=1,2,\ldots,O \tag{264}$$

where:

Data:

m	-	machine index ($m = 1,2,\ldots,M$)
o	-	operation lot index ($o = 1,2,\ldots,O$)
σ_o	-	number of tool magazine slots required by operation lot o
b_{om}	-	processing time of operation lot o at machine m
g_m	-	capacity of machine m
h_m	-	tool magazine capacity at machine m

Variables:

π_{om}	=	$\begin{cases} 1, \text{ if operation lot o is processed at machine m} \\ 0, \text{ otherwise} \end{cases}$
$f(\underline{\pi})$	-	objective function depending on the matrix $\underline{\pi}$ of assignments of operation lots to machines
$TS_m(\underline{\pi}_m)$	-	tool magazine space savings as a nonlinear function of the assignments of operation lots $\underline{\pi}_m$ to machine m

Aside from the variables and constraints already familiar from the models discussed above, the objective function and the constraints (263) are especially interesting here. The latter limit the number of tools that can be assigned to a tool magazine. The quantity $TS_m(\underline{\pi}_m)$[403] describes a *nonlinear function* that includes the potential savings in tool magazine space due to the assignment of the operations to the machine m, $\underline{\pi}_m$. The potential for savings arises from the common usage of tools and the required positioning of these tools in the tool magazine at

---

403 **Stecke** (1983), p. 276; **Berrada/Stecke** (1986), p. 1320; **Stecke** (1992)

machine m. If, for example, two tools requiring two tool slots each are placed side by side a total tool slot requirement of three slots may result.

Stecke suggests a number of technical objectives[404] to express the general objective function f($\underline{\pi}$) in more concrete terms:

- Minimization of the *differences among the workloads* on the individual machines (balanced workload).

- If there are identically sized machine groups in the FMS: minimization of the *differences among the workloads assigned to the machine groups* (balanced workload).

- If there are machine groups of different sizes in the FMS: minimization of the *deviations between the target and assigned workload* (unbalanced workload).

- Minimization of *the number of movements from machine to machine*, or equivalently, maximization of *the number of consecutive operations on each machine*.

- Maximization of *tool magazine utilization*, i.e. fill the tool magazines as densely as possible.

- Maximization of any *linear function*, e.g. maximization of the sum of operation lot priorities[405].

Aside from the tool magazine constraints (263), most of the variations of the objective function in the AGMA-ST model are nonlinear as well. The formulation of the constraints (263) requires the setting of a target for the resulting space savings in the tool magazine for every possible combination of operations at a machine. The number of possible combinations can be derived from the sum of the binomial coefficients for each possible number of operation lots:

$$\sum_{o=2}^{0} \binom{0}{o}$$

With K=20 operation lots, already more than 1000000 different savings in tool slots can be found. The AGMA-ST model can, therefore, only be used when tool sets overlap for very few operations.

- *Berrada and Stecke*[406]

have developed an $\in$-optimal branch-and-bound procedure[407] for the solution of a special version of the AGMA-ST model (with the objective of minimizing the greatest machine workload).

---

404 **Stecke** (1983), p. 279

405 In this case in the objective function each assignment variable π_{om} is weighted in order to assign critical operations more often than non-critical operations.

406 **Berrada/Stecke** (1986), pp. 1321-1325. An exact branch-and-bound procedure for identical machines is proposed by **Kim** (1988), pp. 42-51.

407 see also **Kuhn** (1990), pp. 79-81; **Wilson** (1992)

The nonlinear formulation of the operation/machine assignment problem with common tool usage is only of theoretical value due to the considerable difficulty just in formulating the model and to the complications in finding an optimal solution afterwards.

Nevertheless, the solution of the *AGMA-KU* model can also be quite difficult. The use of exact procedures is almost impossible for real-life problems. Several heuristic procedures can be used to solve the operation/machine assignment problem, however. The most simple procedures sort the set of operations according to a particular criterion, and then assign them to machines which have also been selected according to a specific criterion. The selection criteria chosen depend on the objective to be pursued.

• **Minimization of the number of tool requirements**

A simple heuristic procedure to minimize the number of tools that have to be made available at the machines is described by

• *Kuhn*[408].

First, every machine is assigned one operation lot. The remaining operation lots are then assigned to machines so as to minimize the number of *additional tools*. The structure of the procedure is illustrated in figure (203). This heuristic is also used in a similar form in industrial practice.

Procedure DIFFWZG
Step 0: *Initialization*
Assign each machine an operation lot and update the tool magazine occupation of the machine.
Step 1: *Assignment of the next operation lot according to the criterion of the minimum number of additional tools*
For each operation lot not yet assigned find the number of additional tools required at each machine. Consider the unassigned operation lot with the minimum number of additional tools that may be assigned to the machine without violating the tool magazine constraints. If no such operation lot exists, go to step 2. Assign the chosen operation lot and update the tool magazine occupation of this machine. In case of a tie choose the machine with the smallest number of used tool slots. Repeat step 1.
Step 2: *STOP*
If there are some operation lots left unassigned, no feasible solution has been found.

Figure 203: Procedure DIFFWZG

Example 5-3 is used in order to present the DIFFWZG procedure more clearly; it is now supplemented by the tool identification numbers representing the tools required for the individual operations [see table (97)]. The capacity of both tool magazines is restricted to $h_m = 20$ (m = 1,2) tools.

o	Processing times b_{o1} b_{o2}	Tool slots σ_{o1}	Tool identification numbers
1	30 30	5	1 4 5 9 12
2	12 12	6	6 17 18 19 20 21
3	20 20	4	1 7 8 10
4	9 9	10	3 10 12 16 18 25 26 28 29 30
5	16 16	3	2 5 12
6	2 2	10	6 9 13 15 19 21 22 27 31 32
7	17 17	4	7 8 11 14
8	26 26	5	4 6 22 23 24

Table 97: Data for model AGMA-KU (example 5-5)

One operation lot is assigned to every machine. Based on the resulting tool magazine utilization, the number of additional tools associated with the assignment of each operation lot is then established.

Machine 1																						Capacity
Tool slot	1	2	3	4	5	6 7 8 9 10 11 12 13 14 15 16 17 18 19 20															21 22
Operation 1	1	4	5	9	12	Additional tools required														Σ	
3	*					7 8 10														3	
4						3 10 12 16 18 25 26 28 29 30														10	
5			*		*	2															1	←
6				*		6 13 15 19 21 22 27 31 32														9	
7						7 8 11 14														4	
8	*					6 22 23 24														4	

Machine 2																						Capacity
Tool slot	1	2	3	4	5	6	7 8 9 10 11 12 13 14 15 16 17 18 19 20														21 22
Operation 2	6	17	18	19	20	21	Additional tools required													Σ	
3							1 7 8 10													4	
4			*				3 10 12 16 25 26 28 29 30													9	
5							2 5 12													3	
6	*			*		*	9 13 15 22 27 31 32													7	
7							7 8 11 14													4	
8	*						4 22 23 24													4	

Figure 204: Determination of the additional tools (1st run)

As can be seen from figure (204), only one additional tool has to be added to the tool magazine when operation lot 5 is assigned to machine 1. Therefore, this assignment is made and the corresponding changes in the tool magazine utilization of machine 1 are effected.

The calculation of the number of additional tools based on the newly completed assignment is shown in figure (205).

Machine 1																					Capacity	
Tool slot	1	2	3	4	5	6	7 8 9 10 11 12 13 14 15 16 17 18 19 20													21 22		
Operation 1	1	4	5	9	12		Additional tools required Σ															
5			*		*	2	1															
3	*						7 8 10 3 ←															
4							3 10 12 16 18 25 26 28 29 30 10															
6				*			6 13 15 19 21 22 27 31 32 9															
7							7 8 11 14 4															
8	*						6 22 23 24 4															

Machine 2																					Capacity	
Tool slot	1	2	3	4	5	6	7 8 9 10 11 12 13 14 15 16 17 18 19 20													21 22		
Operation 2	6	17	18	19	20	21	Additional tools required Σ															
3							1 7 8 10 4															
4			*				3 10 12 16 25 26 28 29 30 9															
6	*		*			*	9 13 15 22 27 31 32 7															
7							7 8 11 14 4															
8	*						4 22 23 24 4															

Figure 205: Determination of the additional tools (2nd run)

After the operation lot 3 has been assigned to machine 1 in the second run, the procedure DIFFWZG is continued until all the operation lots have been assigned to a machine. Due to considerations of space, the remaining iterations are not depicted here.

The *final assignment* of the operation lots to the machines, according to the criterion *"minimum number of additional tools"*,[409] is represented in table (98). The operation lots are arranged vertically in the sequence in which they were assigned.

Tool magazine occupation machine 1																					Capacity		
Tool slot	1	2	3	4	5	6	7	8	9	10	11	12	13	14	15	16	17	18	19	20	21 22 23		
Operation 1	1	4	5	9	12																		
5			*		*	2																	
3	*							7	8	10													
7								*	*		11		14										
4				*										*		3 16 18 25 26 28 29 30							

Tool magazine occupation machine 2																					Capacity		
Tool slot	1	2	3	4	5	6	7	8	9	10	11	12	13	14	15	16	17	18	19	20	21 22 23		
Operation 2	6	17	18	19	20	21																	
8	*								22	23	24												
6	*			*		*	*						9 13 15 27 31 32										

Table 98: Tool magazine occupations according to procedure DIFFWZG
(example 5-5)

---

409 Instead of concentrating on the complement set of tools one may also use the intersection set (i.e. many common tools) as a sorting criterion. This will often yield better results. **Kuhn** (1990), pp. 156-157, p. 159; see also section 5.2.1.1.

The resulting distribution of the workload among the two machines is quite un-balanced in this example [see figure (206)]: machine 1 operates for 92 units of time, while machine 2 is only busy for 40 units of time.

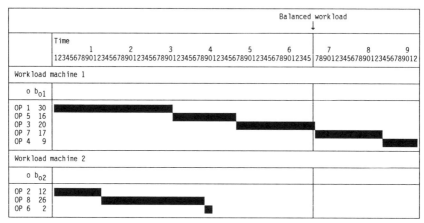

Figure 206: Workload of the machines according to procedure DIFFWZG
(example 5-5)

It appears that it would be useful to take the processing times into consideration when assigning operation lots to the machines. This will be done in the next section.

- **Minimization of the greatest machine workload**

The LPT rule[410] used for scheduling parallel machines in conventional job shops may also be used to minimize the greatest machine workload in FMSs, according to a suggestion of

- *Stecke and Talbot[411].*

The operation lots are sorted in order of non-increasing processing times and sequentially assigned to the machines with the current lowest workload[412]. Since the LPT criterion does not consider the number of tools required per operation, the feasibility of the assignment of an operation lot to a machine with respect to the tool magazine capacity must be reviewed when applying this rule.

If the operation lots from example 5-5 are sorted in order of non-increasing processing times the sequence would be {1,8,3,7,5,2,4,6}. If the operation lot is always assigned to the machine with the lowest workload, the assignment sequence of operation lots to the machines illustrated in table (99) will result.

---

410 Longest Processing Time
411 **Stecke/Talbot** (1985), pp. 76-85; see also **Ammons/Lofgren/McGinnis** (1985), p. 325. Several heuristic pro-cedures based on the LPT rule and the MULTIFIT algorithm [see **Coffman/Garey/Johnson**(1978)] are pro-posed by **Kim** (1988), pp. 52-62; see also **Kim/Yano** (1993)
412 **Baker** (1974), pp. 116-118

Assignment	Current workload of machine	
	1	2
	0	0
Machine 1 - Operation lot 1	0+30	
	30	0
Machine 2 - Operation lot 8		0+26
	30	26
Machine 2 - Operation lot 3		26+20
	30	46
Machine 1 - Operation lot 7	30+17	
	47	46
Machine 2 - Operation lot 5		46+16
	47	62
Machine 1 - Operation lot 2	47+12	62
	59	
Machine 1 - Operation lot 4	59+ 9	62
	68	
Machine 2 - Operation lot 6		62+2
		64

Table 99: Assignment of operation lots to machines according to the LPT rule
(example 5-5)

Figure (207) shows the resulting machine workloads.

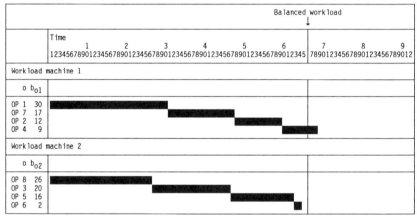

Figure 207: Workload of the machines according to the LPT rule
(example 5-5)

The tooling of the magazines, which was neglected in assigning the operation lots to machines, is shown for both machines in table (100).

Tool magazine occupation machine 1																				Capacity		
Tool slot																						
1	2	3	4	5	6	7	8	9	10	11	12	13	14	15	16	17	18	19	20	21	22	23
Operation 1																						
1	4	5	9	12																		
						7	8	11	14													
										6	17	18	19	20	21							
				*								*				3	10	16	25	**28**	**29**	**30**

(Operation rows for machine 1 listed at left: 1, 7, 2, 4)

Tool magazine occupation machine 2																				Capacity		
Tool slot																						
1	2	3	4	5	6	7	8	9	10	11	12	13	14	15	16	17	18	19	20	21	22	23
Operation 8																						
4	6	22	23	24																		
					1	7	8	10														
									2	5	12											
	*	*										9	13	15	19	21	27	31	32			

(Operation rows for machine 2 listed at left: 8, 3, 5, 6)

Table 100: Tool magazine occupation according to the LPT rule
(example 5-5)

It can be seen that the tools 28, 29, and 30 *exceed* the *capacity of the tool magazine* at machine 1. This is not surprising since in applying the LPT rule the tools had been completely ignored.

- *Kuhn*[413]

has proposed an approach in which the nonlinear generalized assignment model shown below is used for the solution of the AGMA-KU model, i.e. for the minimization of the greatest machine workload with respect to the limited tool magazine capacities.

Model AGMA-GAP

$$\min Z = \sum_{m=1}^{M} f(\pi_{om} | \pi_{om}=1) \tag{265}$$

subject to

$$\sum_{o=1}^{0} b_{om} \cdot \pi_{om} \le g_m \qquad\qquad m=1,2,\ldots,M \tag{266}$$

$$\sum_{m=1}^{M} \pi_{om} = 1 \qquad\qquad o=1,2,\ldots,0 \tag{267}$$

$$\pi_{om} \in \{0,1\} \qquad\qquad o=1,2,\ldots,0;\ m=1,2,\ldots,M \tag{268}$$

---

413 **Kuhn** (1990), p. 196; (1992b)

where:

Data:

m	-	machine index $(m = 1,2,...,M)$
o	-	operation lot index $(o = 1,2,...,O)$
b_{om}	-	processing time of operation lot o at machine m
g_m	-	capacity of machine m

Variables:

$$\pi_{om} = \begin{cases} 1 \text{ , if operation lot o is processed at machine m} \\ 0 \text{ , otherwise} \end{cases}$$

The constraints (266) limit the workloads assigned to the machines to externally predetermined maximum values. The equations (267) guarantee that every operation will be assigned to exactly one machine. The objective function (265) describes the minimization of the sum of all the required tool slots at all the machines. The nonlinear term $f(\pi_{om} | \pi_{om} = 1)$ gives the number of tool slots required due to a particular assignment of operation lots to machine m. The objective function is *nonlinear* since its terms $f(\pi_{om} | \pi_{om} = 1)$ are dependent on the solution of the model, i.e. the number of tool slots needed at a machine m are only known when the optimal assignment of the operations to the machines is completed. A similar model has been used by *Fisher and Jaikumar* for the solution of the vehicle routing problem[414].

If the unknown coefficients of the objective function (265) are approximated using linear coefficients d_{om}, the following linear objective function results:

$$\min Z = \sum_{m=1}^{M} \sum_{o=1}^{O} d_{om} \cdot \pi_{om} \tag{269}$$

This leads to a linear generalized assignment problem with the constraints (266)-(268) and the objective function (269), for which efficient algorithms exist[415]. The linear coefficients d_{om} have the task of producing groups of operations which may share some cutting tools.

Kuhn obtains the coefficients d_{om} as the additional number of tool slots that are needed for assigning operation lot o to machine m given a current assignment of operations to machines. This means that for every operation k he determines the increase in the number of tool slots needed at machine m, provided that the set of operations already assigned to machine m is enlarged by operation lot o. This is formally expressed in equation (270).

$$d_{om} = |T_{om} \backslash T_m| \qquad\qquad o=1,2,...,O; \; m=1,2,...,M \tag{270}$$

    ⌐   └ set of tools currently assigned to machine m

    └ set of tools required by operation o at machine m

---

414 Fisher/Jaikumar (1981), pp. 109-124
415 Fisher/Jaikumar/Van Wassenhove (1986)

The development of the SYSR procedure for the solution of the AGMA-KU model is outlined in figure (208)[416].

Procedure SYSR
Step 0: *Initialization*
Set n=0; Δg Find a feasible initial solution[417] for model AGMA-KU. Compute the resulting maximum workload g^n and set the workload bounds of all machines equal to $g_m^n=g^n$, (m=1,2,...,M).
Step 1: *Reduction of the capacities and computation of the coefficients of the linear objective function of model AGMA-GAP*
If the current workloads are within a tolerable range, go to step 3. Set n=n+1. Reduce the workload bounds at the machines: $$g_m^n=g_m^{n-1}-\Delta g \qquad\qquad m=1,2,\ldots,M$$ Compute new values d_{0m}^n.
Step 2: *Generation of a feasible solution*
Solve model AGMA-GAP. If after several parameter adjustments no feasible solution of model AGMA-KU has been found, go to step 3. If a feasible tool magazine occupation has been achieved, go to step 1. Otherwise adjust the coefficients of the objective function of model AGMA-GAP, d_{0m}^n and repeat step 2.
Step 3: *STOP*

Figure 208: Procedure SYSR for the solution of model AGMA-KU

A solution of the AGMA-GAP model with the approximate objective function may provide an assignment of operation lots to the machines that requires only a small number of tool slots within the workload bounds of the machines. Since the limited capacities of the tool magazines are not taken directly into account, the tool magazine constraints have to be checked for each solution of the AGMA-GAP model. If one of the constraints is *not met*, the procedure re-adjusts the coefficients of the objective function (d_{om}^*) and the AGMA-GAP model will be re-evaluated. This continues until a solution can be found which is feasible with respect to the tool magazine constraints.

To follow the original objective of *model AGMA-KU*, the bounds g_m of the machine workload are reduced after every generation of a feasible solution for the

---

416 more concisely **Kuhn** (1992b)
417 Here the procedure DIFFWZG may be applied.

considered problem. The iterative reduction of the parameter g_m distributes the workload more evenly among the machines. This process is continued until, even after repeated adjustments of the coefficients d_{om}, no feasible solution can be found.

The reformulation of the AGMA-KU model thus leads to a *parametric generalized assignment problem*. The parameter dependency affects both the quality of the solution and the computing time of the procedure. Since the procedure is an approximate approach, it is not strictly necessary to use exact GAP algorithms, heuristic algorithms may be appropriate[418]. Figure (209) shows how the solution develops in the SYSR procedure.

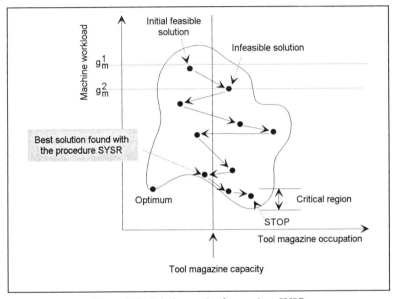

Figure 209: Solution path of procedure SYSR

The first solution is feasible with respect to the tool magazine constraints, but it can be assumed that workloads on the machines will be extremely unbalanced. Therefore, the workload bounds are decreased and the AGMA-GAP model is solved. The new solution violates the tool magazine constraints. After adjusting its objective function coefficients d_{om}, the AGMA-GAP model is solved until another feasible solution is found. This solution is also an improvement on the initial solution in terms of the minimization of the greatest machine workload. This process is continued in the following iterations until no further improvements in the solution are possible.

---

418 An heuristic procedure for solving the generalized assignment problem is described by *Martello and Toth*; **Martello/Toth** (1981); (1990), pp. 189-220.

Example 5-5 will be used to explain the SYSR procedure. The tool magazine occupation described in table (98) (19 tools at machine 1 and 17 tools at machine 2) is taken as the initial solution. The workload distribution for this initial solution is depicted in figure (210).

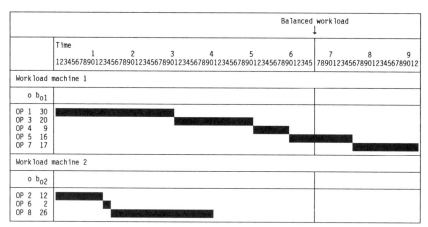

Figure 210: Machine workloads for the initial solution

This solution leads to an extremely uneven workload on the machines which induces a makespan of 92 time units. A completely balanced workload would be reached with 66 time units.

Machine 1 Tool magazine occupation

o	1	2	3	4	5	7	8	9	10	11	12	14	16	18	25	26	28	29	30	Additional tools	d_{o1}
OP 1	*			*	*			*			*										0
OP 2														*						6 17 19 20 21	5
OP 3	*				*	*		*													0
OP 4			*					*		*	*	*	*	*	*	*	*	*	*		0
OP 5		*			*			*													0
OP 6										*										6 13 15 19 21 22 27 31 32	9
OP 7				*	*			*			*										0
OP 8				*																6 22 23 24	4

Machine 2 Tool magazine occupation

o	4	6	9	13	15	17	18	19	20	21	22	23	24	27	31	32	Additional tools	d_{o2}
OP 1	*	*															1 5 12	3
OP 2		*			*	*	*	*										0
OP 3																	1 7 8 10	4
OP 4						*											3 10 12 16 25 26 28 29 30	9
OP 5																	2 5 12	3
OP 6		*	*	*	*			*		*	*			*	*	*		0
OP 7																	7 8 11 14	4
OP 8	*	*							*	*	*							0

Figure 211: Computation of the coefficients of the objective function of model AGMA-GAP

In the next step, the workload bound of the machines is slightly reduced (by one unit), i.e. to $g_m = 91$ ($m = 1,2$). The assignment of the operation lots to the machines is then processed with the AGMA-GAP model. Therefore, the values of the objective function coefficients d_{om} of this model have to be calculated. This process is shown in figure (211).

The additional tool requirements, based on the tooling at the tool magazines from the previous step, associated with the assignment of each operation to a machine is determined. These additional tool requirements yield the objective function coefficients d_{om} (o = 1,2,...,8; m = 1,2). If, for example, operation 2 is shifted from machine 2 to machine 1, 5 new tools would be required at machine 1 (tools 6, 17, 19, 20 and 21).

The configuration of the tool magazine shown in figure (212) is produced by the last solution of the AGMA-GAP model using the coefficients d_{om}. An asterisk "*" indicates that the required tool has already been assigned to the tool magazine.

Tool magazine occupation machine 1																				Capacity		
Tool slot	1	2	3	4	5	6	7	8	9	10	11	12	13	14	15	16	17	18	19 20	21	22	23
OP 1	1		4	5		9	12															
OP 3	*							7	8	10												
OP 4					*					*			3	16	18	25	26	28	29 30			
OP 7							*	*											11 14			

Tool magazine occupation machine 2																				Capacity		
Tool slot	1	2	3	4	5	6	7	8	9	10	11	12	13	14	15	16	17	18	19 20	21	22	23
OP 2	6	17	18	19	20	21																
OP 5							2		5	12												
OP 6	*			*			*		9	13	15	22	27	31	32							
OP 8	*													*					4 23 24			

Figure 212: Tool magazine occupations

In the new configuration 18 (19) different tools are required at machine 1 (2). The workload on the machines is illustrated in figure (213).

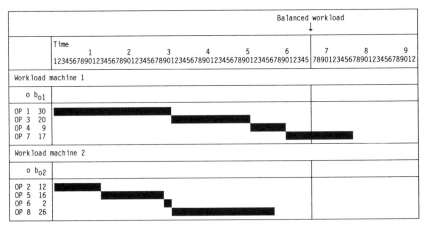

Figure 213: Machine workloads

As can be seen, the distribution of the workload between the two machines has become more balanced. The greatest assigned machine processing time is 76 units of time. Therefore, the workload bounds are reduced to $g_m = 75$ ($m = 1,2$) in the next step and, as shown in figure (214), new objective function coefficients d_{om} for the AGMA-GAP model are calculated.

Machine 1 — Tool magazine occupation

o	1	3	4	5	7	8	9	10	11	12	14	16	18	25	26	28	29	30	Additional tools	d_{o1}
OP 1	*		*	*			*			*										0
OP 2															*				6 17 19 20 21	5
OP 3	*					*	*		*											0
OP 4		*					*		*		*	*	*	*	*	*	*			0
OP 5				*					*										2	1
OP 6							*												6 13 15 19 21 22 27 31 32	9
OP 7						*	*		*	*										0
OP 8				*															6 22 23 24	4

Machine 2 — Tool magazine occupation

o	2	4	5	6	9	12	13	15	17	18	19	20	21	22	23	24	27	31	32	Additional tools	d_{o2}
OP 1	*	*		*	*															1	1
OP 2			*				*	*	*	*	*										0
OP 3																				1 7 8 10	4
OP 4					*				*											3 10 16 25 26 28 29 30	8
OP 5	*		*		*																0
OP 6					*	*		*		*		*	*				*	*	*		0
OP 7																				7 8 11 14	4
OP 8		*		*							*	*	*								0

Figure 214: Computation of the coefficients of the objective function of model AGMA-GAP

After solving the AGMA-GAP model once again, the tool magazines now contain 17 and 19 tools, and the workload assigned to each machine is more balanced; 62 and 70 time units for machine 1 and machine 2 respectively [see figure (216)].

Tool magazine occupation machine 1 — Capacity

Tool slot	1	2	3	4	5	6	7	8	9	10	11	12	13	14	15	16	17	18	19	20 ‖ 21	22	23
OP 3	1	7	8	10																		
OP 4			10	3	12	16	18	25	26	28	29	30										
OP 5					*								2	5								
OP 7		*	*												11	14						

Tool magazine occupation machine 2 — Capacity

Tool slot	1	2	3	4	5	6	7	8	9	10	11	12	13	14	15	16	17	18	19	20 ‖ 21	22	23
OP 1	1	4	5	9	12																	
OP 2						6	17	18	19	20	21											
OP 6			*		*				*		13	15	22	27	31	32						
OP 8		*			*										*		23	24				

Figure 215: Tool magazine occupations

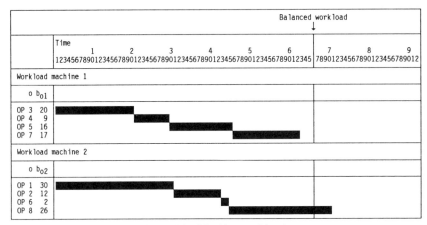

Figure 216: Machine workloads

The workload bounds are now reduced to $g_m = 69$ ($m = 1,2$), and the objective function coefficients are calculated again [see figure (217)].

Machine 1	Tool magazine occupation		
o	1 2 3 5 7 8 10 11 12 14 16 18 25 26 28 29 30	Additional tools	d_{o1}
OP 1	* * *	4 9	2
OP 2	*	6 17 19 20 21	5
OP 3	* * * *		0
OP 4	* * * * * * * * * *		0
OP 5	* * *		0
OP 6		6 9 13 15 19 21 22 27 31 32	10
OP 7	* * * *		0
OP 8		4 6 22 23 24	5

Machine 2	Tool magazine occupation		
o	1 4 5 6 9 12 13 15 17 18 19 20 21 22 23 24 27 31 32	Additional tools	d_{o2}
OP 1	* * * * *		0
OP 2	* * * * * *		0
OP 3	*	7 8 10	3
OP 4	* *	3 10 16 25 26 28 29 30	8
OP 5	* *	2	1
OP 6	* * * * * * * * * *		0
OP 7		7 8 11 14	4
OP 8	* * * * *		0

Figure 217: Computation of the coefficients of the objective function of model AGMA-GAP

The new solution of the AGMA-GAP model with workload bounds of $g_m = 69$ ($m = 1,2$) leads to an operation/machine assignment which is an unfeasible solution for the AGMA-KU model since at 21 required tools the tool magazine constraint at machine 2 is violated. Therefore, the linear coefficients in the objective function of the AGMA-GAP model have to be adjusted [see figure (218)].

o	Old values		New values	
	d_{o1}	d_{o2}	d_{o1}^{*}	d_{o2}^{*}
OP 1	2	0	2	0
OP 2	5	0	5	0
OP 3	0	3	0	3
OP 4	0	8	0	8
OP 5	0	1	0	1
OP 6	10	0	10	0
OP 7	0	4	0+**10**	4
OP 8	5	0	5	0

Figure 218: Coefficient adjustment[419]

After modifying the objective function coefficients, the AGMA-GAP model is solved again. A feasible solution results in which the machine workloads are 67 and 65 time units, and the tool magazines contain 20 and 19 tools for machines 1 and 2 respectively.

```
Tool magazine occupation machine 1                                    Capacity

Tool slot  1  2  3  4  5  6  7  8  9 10 11 12 13 14 15 16 17 18 19 20 ‖21 22 23

OP 1       1     4  5        9 12
OP 2                      6 17 18 19 20 21
OP 4             *         *              3 10 16 25 26 28 29 30
OP 5          *  *                                                  2

Tool magazine occupation machine 2                                    Capacity

Tool slot  1  2  3  4  5  6  7  8  9 10 11 12 13 14 15 16 17 18 19 20 ‖21 22 23

OP 3       1        7  8 10
OP 6                      6  9 13 15 19 21 22 27 31 32
OP 7          *  *                                        11 14
OP 8                *                          *              4 23 24
```

Figure 219: Tool magazine occupations

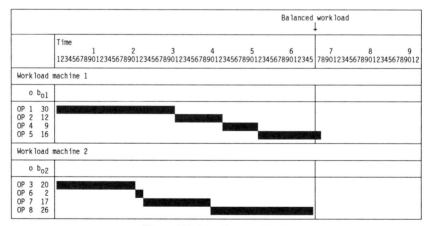

Figure 220: Machine workloads

---

419   The parameter adjustment is described in **Kuhn** (1992b).

This new solution, which is feasible with respect to the tool magazine constraints, is associated with a balanced workload that is not obtained with the LPT rule, even though the LPT rule ignores the limited tool magazines. The procedure is, therefore, terminated. The optimality of the obtained solution can be proved with a specialized implicit enumeration procedure developed by *Kuhn*[420]. This author has also performed a detailed numerical comparison of the implicit enumeration procedure and the heuristic procedures DIFFWZG and SYSR outlined in this section. It appeared that the DIFFWZG procedure achieved feasible operation/machine assignments but with poorly balanced workloads. The objective function value (i.e. the greatest machine workload) found was, on average, 35-40% greater than optimal. The SYSR procedure, on the other hand, achieved relatively good solutions in a remarkably small computing time, and they were an average of only 3% worse than the optimal solution.

One major problem in the SYSR procedure is that it is not known whether or not a feasible solution even exists while carrying out the procedure. This is particularly problematic when the workload bounds g_m have been chosen within or below the critical region marked in figure (209). Once the workload bounds are set so that the optimal solution has been excluded from the current solution space, then stepping back into the direction of the feasible region is not possible. The reduction of the workload bounds g_m by Δg thus becomes especially important. In order to approach the optimal solution as closely as possible, it is advantageous to choose a reduction step size Δg which is the smallest possible value that theoretically allows the objective function value to be improved.

Further reading for section 5.3.2.:

Berrada/Stecke (1986)
Kim (1988)
Kim/Yano (1993)
Kuhn (1990), (1992b)
Kusiak (1985b), (1985c)
Sarin/Chen (1987)
Sawik (1990)
Stecke (1983)
Stecke/Talbot (1985)

5.4. SIMULTANEOUS BATCHING AND ASSIGNMENT OF OPERATIONS AND MACHINES

In discussing the decision problems of *batching* and *operation/machine assignment* in sections 5.2. and 5.3., the key elements for a solution of the entire pre-release problem were analyzed. In this section several different approaches for an integrated treatment of the problems of *batching* and *operation/machine*

---

420 **Kuhn** (1990), pp. 210-217; (1992b)

assignment will be discussed. The integrated models of pre-release planning presented in the literature are intended to be used for a release process with *fixed batches*, and they also perform a *complete batching*, i.e. all the orders released by the PPC system for processing in the FMS are assigned to a batch.

The comprehensive decision problem of the pre-release planning of orders in an FMS can be generally characterized by the following *assumptions*.

- *Orders:*

  - Planning begins with a given set of J orders.
  - Every order j (j = 1,2,..,J) consists of n_j identical workpieces.
  - A set of O_j operations $\mathbf{O}_j = \{1,2,...,O_j\}$ have to be performed on a workpiece of the order j.
  - Every order is assigned a due date d_j.

- *Machines:*

  - The FMS consists of m = 1,2,..,M identical and/or complementary machines.
  - Every operation o can be alternatively performed at one of the machines from the set $\mathbf{M}_o$.
  - Every operation o is associated with a machine-dependent processing time b_{om}, m$\in \mathbf{M}_o$.
  - Every operation can be performed by only one machine at a time. A machine can execute only one operation at a time. The performance of an operation on a workpiece cannot be interrupted.

- *Tools:*

  - The necessary tools must be made available for the execution of an operation at machine m.
  - A tool t requires σ_t tool slots in a tool magazine.
  - Every machine m has a particular tool magazine capacity of h_m tool slots.
  - Only one workpiece at a time can be processed with a given tool. A workpiece may be simultaneously processed by several different tools[421].
  - A setup time s is needed for a major tool exchange. The setup time is independent on the number of tools to be exchanged.

The data structure (entity-relationship diagram) of the simultaneous batching and operation/machine assignment problem is illustrated in figure (221).

---

421 If multi-spindle drilling heads are used, several tools may get access to a workpiece simultaneously.

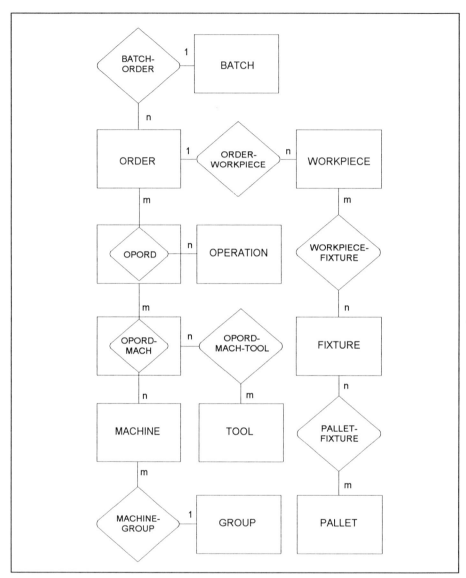

Figure 221: Data structure for simultaneous batching and operation/machine assignment

The decision model for pre-release planning which provides the basis for the following discussion is as follows:

Model SE-AGMA

$$\text{min or max } Z = f(L, \underline{x}, \underline{\pi}, \underline{y}) \tag{271}$$

     $\uparrow\ \uparrow\ \uparrow\ \uparrow$
       └ assignment of tools to machines
      └ assignment of operation lots to machines
     └ assignment of orders to batches
    └ number of batches

subject to

$$\sum_{l=1}^{L} x_{jl} = 1 \qquad\qquad\qquad j=1,2,\ldots,J \tag{272}$$

 └ assignment of order j to batch l

$$\sum_{m \in M_o} \pi_{oml} = x_{jl} \qquad\qquad j=1,2,\ldots,J; \ o \in O_j; \ l=1,2,\ldots,L \tag{273}$$

  └ processing of operation lot o of batch l at machine m

$$\sum_{j=1}^{J} \sum_{o \in O_j} \underline{\sigma_{ot} \cdot \pi_{oml}} \le E \cdot y_{tml} \qquad \begin{array}{l} t=1,2,\ldots,T; \ m=1,2,\ldots,M; \\ l=1,2,\ldots,L \end{array} \tag{274}$$

 └ number of tools of type t required by order j at machine m if it is assigned to batch l

$$\sum_{t=1}^{T} \sigma_t \cdot y_{tml} \le h_m \qquad\qquad m=1,2,\ldots,M; \ l=1,2,\ldots,L \tag{275}$$

 └ assignment of tool t to machine m with respect to batch l

$$x_{jl} \in \{0,1\} \qquad\qquad j=1,2,\ldots,J; \ l=1,2,\ldots,L \tag{276}$$

$$\pi_{oml} \in \{0,1\} \qquad\qquad \begin{array}{l} o=1,2,\ldots,O; \ m=1,2,\ldots,M; \\ l=1,2,\ldots,L \end{array} \tag{277}$$

$$y_{tml} \in \{0,1\} \qquad\qquad \begin{array}{l} t=1,2,\ldots,T; \ m=1,2,\ldots,M; \\ l=1,2,\ldots,L \end{array} \tag{278}$$

$$J \ge L \ge 0 \tag{279}$$

where:

Data:

j	-	order index (j = 1,2,...,J)
l	-	batch index (l = 1,2,...,L)
m	-	machine index (m = 1,2,...,M)
o	-	operation lot index (o = 1,2,...,O)
t	-	tool index (t = 1,2,...,T)

$$\sigma_{ot} = \begin{cases} 1, \text{ if operation lot o requires tool t} \\ 0, \text{ otherwise} \end{cases}$$

σ_t -   number of tool magazine slots required by tool t
E   -   large number
h_m -   tool magazine capacity at machine m
$\mathbf{M}_0$ -   set of machines available for operation o
$\mathbf{0}_j$ -   set of operations required to process a workpiece of order j

Variables:

π_{oml} = $\begin{cases} 1 \text{, if operation lot o of batch l is processed at machine m} \\ 0 \text{, otherwise} \end{cases}$

L   -   number of batches

x_{jl} = $\begin{cases} 1 \text{, if order j is assigned to batch l} \\ 0 \text{, otherwise} \end{cases}$

y_{tml} = $\begin{cases} 1 \text{, if tool t is assigned to machine m with respect to batch l} \\ 0 \text{, otherwise} \end{cases}$

The objective function of the SE-AGMA model is kept general since the decision models and solution approaches discussed in the literature pursue quite different objectives. The value of the objective function is dependent on the number of batches L, the partition of the orders into batches ($x_{jl} \mid x_{jl} = 1$), the assignment of operation lots to the machines ($\pi_{oml} \mid \pi_{oml} = 1$), and the tooling of the tool magazines at the machines ($y_{tml} \mid y_{tml} = 1$). The contents of the objective function could, for example, be expressed as the sum of the batch makespans and the orders' tardiness times. In this case, the defining equations for these values would have to be integrated into the system of equations[422].

The constraints (272) guarantee that every order is assigned to exactly one batch. The equations (273) define the interdependencies between the binary variables π_{oml} (operation/machine assignment) and x_{jl} (batching). The inequalities (274) guarantee that the necessary tools will be made available at the machine m if an operation o is assigned to that machine. The tool magazine capacities at the machines are represented in the constraints (275).

The SE-AGMA model assumes that any operation lot is exclusively assigned to one machine. This assumption is very restrictive. A multiple assignment of an operation to different machines would increase the routing flexibility of the workpieces in the FMS. As a result, system performance could be increased, especially when a machine breaks down. On the other hand, multiple assignment of operations implies that duplicate tool sets be present at different machines. Since most tools are quite expensive a trade-off between system performance and tool costs must be made. If duplicate tooling is allowed, the equations (273) of model SE-AGMA must be replaced with the constraints (280) and (281).

$$\sum_{m\in\mathbf{M}_0} u_{oml} = n_j \cdot x_{jl} \qquad\qquad j=1,2,\ldots,J;\ o\in\mathbf{0}_j;\ l=1,2,\ldots,L \qquad (280)$$

$\uparrow$ size of operation lot j

$$u_{oml} \geq 0 \text{ and integer} \qquad\qquad o=1,2,\ldots,O;\ m=1,2,\ldots,M; \qquad (281)$$
$$l=1,2,\ldots,L$$

---

422 see **Kuhn** (1990), pp. 108-112; see also **DeWerra/Widmer** (1991)

The variable u_{oml} describes the number of workpieces of the operation lot o from batch l that will be processed at machine m.

A number of different approaches for the solution of variations of the SE-AGMA model have been proposed. They differ in terms of the specification of the objective function and in the solution methodology they apply. They include:

- *Sequential priority procedures.*
- *Sequential iterative procedures.*
- *Hierarchical procedures.*
- *Integrated (simultaneous) procedures.*

The essential features of these approaches will be discussed in the following section.

5.4.1. The Whitney and Gaul Approach - A Sequential Priority Procedure

In spite of the high complexity of the problem of simultaneous batching and operation/machine assignment

- *Whitney and Gaul*[423]

have suggested a sequential priority procedure intended to make assignment decisions very quickly - in real time, if possible. Its basic principles are explained in figure (222). It is called a *sequential priority procedure* here because both planning steps (batching and operation/machine assignment) are fully executed for one order before the next order is considered. As in all priority procedures, the priority values determine the sequence in which orders are assigned to batches or in which operation lots are assigned to machines. This in turn determines the quality of the solution. *Whitney and Gaul* formulate priority values for the individual stages of the procedure that are dynamically updated after each treatment of an order[424]. They are supposed to correlate with the following objectives:

- High *utilization* of limited capacities (tool magazines, machine workloads).
- High *common usage of tools* by different operations.
- *On time completion* for all orders.

To solve the batching problem *Whitney and Gaul* determine a dynamic priority value $0 \leq ps_j \leq 1$ for each order j. The individual orders are assigned to a batch in order of non-decreasing priority values ps_j until no further orders can be assigned due to the limited tool magazine capacities at the machines. Following that, a new batch is begun and the procedure is repeated until all the orders have been assigned (*batching*).

---

423 **Whitney/Gaul** (1985)
424 *Whitney and Gaul* interpret the priority values as the probability that the remaining order set will not be successfully assigned; **Whitney/Gaul** (1985), p. 305.

After assigning an order j to a batch, the individual operations o of the selected order are assigned to the identical machines using another set of priority values $0 \leq ps_{om} \leq 1$ (*operation/machine assignment*).

Procedure WHITGAUL
Step 1: *Batching*
a) Determine priority values ps_j for all orders not yet assigned to a batch.   b) Assign the order with the lowest priority value ps_j that does not violate the tool magazine constraints to batch 1 and go to step 2.   If it is not possible to assign any order to the current batch, open a new batch and repeat step 1.
Step 2: *Operation/machine assignment*
a) Determine priority values ps_{om} for operation/machine assignment for all operations of an order assigned in step 1 to the batch 1.   b) Assign the operations of the order considered to the identical machines according to non-decreasing values ps_{om}.   c) If all orders are assigned, STOP; else go to step 1.

Figure 222: Procedure of Whitney and Gaul

The priority values ps_j for batching and ps_{om} for operation/machine assignment are calculated as described below.

• **Priority value ps_j (batching)**

The priority value for batching $0 \leq ps_j \leq 1$ of an order is made up of the individual priority values $0 \leq pt_j \leq 1$, $0 \leq pw_j \leq 1$ and $0 \leq pn \leq 1$. These stand for the cumulative advantages of assigning an order to a batch with respect to *balancing of the load on the tool magazine and the machining capacity* for the different machine types (pt_j), the *need to add new tools* (pw_j), and whether the orders' *due dates* will be met. High values for pt_j and low values for pw_j and pn indicate the satisfaction of the objectives. The individual priority values are combined to a total priority value ps_j, according to equation (282). A low priority value indicates that the order meets the mentioned objectives to a high degree.

$$ps_j = 1 - pt_j \cdot [1 - pw_j \cdot (1 - pn)] \qquad\qquad j \in J_0 \qquad\qquad (282)$$

```
        due date
      tool similarity
    balanced machine workload and tool magazine load
  assignment of an order to a batch
```

Combining the priority values in this way is based on the following considerations. The priority value pw_j, tool similarity, is weighted with the priority value (1-pn), meeting the due dates. When due dates are critical, the effect of the priority value pw_j on the total priority value ps_i is weakened, and the effect of the priority value pt_j is strengthened. The priority value pt_j is intended to balance the machine workloads and thus indirectly affects whether the due dates are met. *Whitney and Gaul* assume that when it is possible to complete all considered orders on time, orders which would bring many new tools into the batch could be preferred. If, however, meeting the due dates is not assured, then this criterion is neglected and balancing machine workload (capacity utilization) is assigned more weight. The individual terms of the priority values are determined as described below.

* *Balance load (pt_j)*

   The priority value pt_j should indicate the likelihood (priority value approaching 1) that an order j will contribute to balancing the loads of the resources (tool magazines and machines). *Whitney and Gaul* consider the *tool magazines* and the *machining capacities* of the machine groups to be limited. The priority value thus serves to balance the utilizations between individual machine groups. *Whitney and Gaul* interpret a machine group as all machines of one type which could be used to replace each other in the processing of a particular order. In the priority value pt_j the load (tool magazine loading and machine workload) at the individual machine groups is compared to the average load on all machine groups. If the individual loads are close to the average load the priority value pt_j will be high, whereas if the opposite is true the priority values will be lower.

* *Tool similarity (pw_j)*

   The priority value pw_j takes account of the degree to which the tool requirements of an order j can be met with the tools already present at a machine group. The priority value pw_j compares the number of common tools with the total number of tools required to process an order j. *Whitney and Gaul* take a positive view of an order which brings a large number of different tools into the batch. If the tool magazine capacity of a machine group is exceeded, the priority value pw_j is set to zero.

* *Meeting due dates (pn)*

   Whitney and Gaul do not consider the potential tardiness of an *individual order*, instead they consider only the probability that the *remaining set of orders* will be completed on time if the orders are selected randomly. The priority value pn is intended to estimate this probability. To determine the priority value pn *Whitney and Gaul* estimate the average remaining time before the due date of an order is reached (due date minus release date). The average remaining time of an order is compared to the estimate of the average amount of time required for processing an order. This relationship expresses the number of typical orders that can be processed during the available time window without exceeding the due dates. From this *Whitney and Gaul* build the priority value pn.

- **Priority value ps_{om} (operation/machine assignment)**

  The priority values ps_{om} are created for the operation set O_j of the selected order j in order to reach the most balanced loads possible on the machines in a machine group. The priority value of the operation/machine assignment $0 \leq ps_{om} \leq 1$ is made up of the individual criteria $0 \leq pt_m \leq 1$ and $0 \leq pw_{om} \leq 1$. This value seeks both a balanced workload on the identical machines (large pt_m value) and an efficient use of the tool magazine (small pw_{om} value). The two priority values are connected, as shown in equation (283); a lower value indicates a higher degree of objective achievement.

$$ps_{om} = 1 - pt_m \cdot (1 - pw_{om}) \qquad\qquad o \in O_j, \; m \in M_0 \qquad (283)$$

  └ tool similarity

  └ machine workload balancing

  └ operation/machine assignment

  - *Machine workload balancing (pt_m)*

    The priority value pt_m is the proportion by which the workload assigned to machine m lies below the workload of the bottleneck machine. The workload of an individual machine m is a result of the operation/machine assignment in the current batch and the processing time of the operation lot to be assigned.

  - *Tool similarity (pw_{om})*

    In the priority value pw_{om} the additional tools required by an operation o at the machine m are compared to the tool slots available in the tool magazine at machine m. If the tools required by an operation should be provided to several identical machines, then each operation of an individual workpiece of an order has to be considered separately instead of considering them as part of an operation lot. Thus, each individual operation is assigned with the help of the priority value ps_{om}.

Among the criteria proposed by *Whitney and Gaul*, the consideration of the orders' due dates pn is particularly problematic. This is a criterion based on the set of orders which have not yet been scheduled and is supposed to represent a measure of the potential that all the remaining orders will be completed on time. A clue as to *which order j should be selected* is not, however, part of the criterion pn. It is left up to chance to be sure that the orders with critical due dates are scheduled first.

It is also unclear why it is supposed to be advantageous when an order brings as many new tools as possible into the batch (priority value pw_j). *Whitney and Gaul*'s explanations on the subject have been contradictory up to now.

On a more general level, the use of a multi-dimensional priority value must be seen in a very critical light. The effect of a change in a priority value on whether an objective will be achieved is not transparent to the planner. It is possible that the combination of different objective criteria in one single priority value might generate solutions that are not better than those that had been randomly generated[425].

5.4.2. The Bastos Approach - A Sequential Iterative Procedure

Aside from the technical constraints, such as tool magazine capacities, the batch size can also have been limited by the length of planning period (time bucket). This is especially common when the pre-release planning process of the FMS has to be coordinated with the planning for the other production segments by the central PPC system.

• *Bastos*[426]

considers such a situation. Here the assignment of orders to batches and the assignment of operation lots to machines is to be determined in weekly intervals according to a rolling planning concept. In addition, the process plan for each workpiece type is to be selected from the set of possible process plans (route selection).

The central objective pursued is to minimize the makespan (the number of periods which are necessary to manufacture the complete set of orders) while considering the due dates and the tool magazine constraints. *Bastos* suggests a three level iterative procedure, in which the problems of batching, process plan selection, and operation/machine assignment are to be sequentially solved until a termination criterion has been satisfied [see figure (223)].

Procedure BASTOS
Step 1: *Determination of the minimum production quantities for each period*
Determine the minimum production quantities q_j of the orders for the current period with respect to the planned due dates.
Step 2: *Batching*
Find the current batch, i.e. the set of orders to be processed in the current planning period.
Step 3: *Route selection*
Determine the routes (process plans) to be used for the workpieces. This results in an assignment of operations to machines.

Figure 223: Procedure of Bastos

---

425 **Kuhn** (1990), pp. 235-248

426 **Bastos** (1988), pp. 235-236. Another approach which can be characterized as an iterative procedure is suggested by **Kim/Yano** (1992).

In the *first step* the production quantities are determined for all the orders that must be completed in the current planning period in order to meet their due dates. This is accomplished by applying a special *backward pass* time planning procedure. Beginning with the *last* period l=L in the planning horizon for which orders are available, those orders whose due dates d_j fall within this period are assigned to the batch that corresponds to that period. All orders that cannot be produced in period l, because of the limited capacity, are shifted to the previous period l-1. Here they are considered together with those orders whose due dates fall within the period l-1. This successive process continues until all the orders have been assigned to a particular period, i.e. assigned to the batch scheduled for production in that period. In order that this method can achieve a feasible solution, the PPC system must have predetermined the due dates very carefully. Otherwise, it may be possible that some orders could be left over at the end of the planning process since *Bastos* does not allow any order to fail meeting its due date.

The results of this first step are minimum production quantities per period which provide the basic inputs for the *second step* of the procedure. Here the production quantities to be manufactured in the current planning period are determined by solving the following binary linear optimization model (SE-BAS).

Model SE-BAS

$$\max Z = \sum_{j=1}^{J} \sum_{r \in R_j} a_{jr} \cdot x_{jr} \tag{284}$$

production quantity of order j using route r

set of alternative routes for order j

subject to

$$\sum_{r \in R_j} x_{jr} \geq x_{min(j)} \qquad\qquad j=1,2,\ldots,J \tag{285}$$

minimum production quantity of order j

$$\sum_{r \in R_j} x_{jr} \leq n_j \qquad\qquad j=1,2,\ldots,J \tag{286}$$

lot size of order j

$$\sum_{j=1}^{J} \sum_{r \in R_j} b_{jrm} \cdot x_{jr} \leq g_m \qquad\qquad m=1,2,\ldots,M \tag{287}$$

capacity of machine m

processing time for a workpiece of order j at machine m using route r

$$\sum_{j=1}^{J} \sum_{r \in R_j} \sigma_{jrm} \cdot y_{jr} \le h_m \qquad\qquad m=1,2,\dots,M \qquad\qquad (288)$$

tool magazine capacity at machine m

number of tool magazine slots required for order j at machine m using route r

$$x_{jr} \le E \cdot y_{jr} \qquad\qquad j=1,2,\dots,J;\ r \in R_j \qquad\qquad (289)$$

$$y_{jr} \in \{0,1\} \qquad\qquad j=1,2,\dots,J;\ r \in R_j \qquad\qquad (290)$$

$$x_{jr} \ge 0 \qquad\qquad j=1,2,\dots,J;\ r \in R_j \qquad\qquad (291)$$

where:

Data:

j	-	order index ($j = 1,2,\dots,J$)
m	-	machine index ($m = 1,2,\dots,M$)
r	-	route (process plan) index ($r = 1,2,\dots,R$)
σ_{jrm}	-	number of tool magazine slots required for order j at machine m if processed by route r
a_{jr}	-	weighting factor for route r of order j
b_{jrm}	-	processing time for a workpiece of order j at machine m if route r is used
E	-	large number
g_m	-	capacity of machine m
h_m	-	tool magazine capacity of machine m
n_j	-	size of order j
$x_{min(j)}$	-	minimum production quantity of order j
R_j	-	set of routes for order j

Variables:

x_{jr}	-	number of workpieces of order j, processed using route r
y_{jr}	$=$	$\begin{cases} 1, \text{ if order j is processed by route r} \\ 0, \text{ otherwise} \end{cases}$

The inequalities (285) guarantee that the minimum production quantity for order j from step 1 will be completed within the current period. The production quantities are limited by the constraints (286) according to which the number of workpieces to be manufactured in the next period must not exceed the updated remaining order size. The machining capacity constraints (287) limit the accumulated sum of processing times on each machine m. The limited tool magazine capacities are considered by the inequalities (288). The constraints (289) guarantee that if route (process plan) r is selected for at least one workpiece of order j ($x_{jr} > 0$), then the binary variable y_{jr} (route assignment) will be equal to 1. These constraints connect the periodic machine workload capacities and the tool magazine capacities.

In contrast to the formulation SE-AGMA, it is possible in the SE-BAS model to *split an order* and process it in different batches. Large orders could not otherwise be produced since the lengths of the planning periods are fixed (e.g. one week).

The objective function of model SE-BAS maximizes the sum of the weighted number of workpieces manufactured on a particular route. *Bastos* suggests that a particular workpiece type on a particular route be *heavily weighted*[427] if,

- many *pallets* are available for a single workpiece type,
- few alternative *process plans* are available,
- the relative *processing time* for a process plan is large, or
- the relative number of additional *tools* for a process plan is small.

The parameters of the tool magazine constraints (288) are adjusted dynamically based on the results of the previous planning stage. The tool magazine capacity h_m indicates how many tool slots are still available in the tool magazine. The tool slots requirement σ_{jrm} of a particular operation at machine m denotes the additional tools needed at this machine. This allows the observance of the tool similarity of the operations based on the tools already present in the magazine. The similarity among operations assigned during the application of the model is not taken into consideration, however.

In the *third step* the optimal process plans are selected for the orders or parts of orders assigned in the second step. Both steps two and three are carried out in an iterative way. The procedure is stopped when a predetermined termination criterion has been met.

One problem in this procedure is that tool changes are not allowed within a period. When the tool magazine constraints become binding too early it is possible that the machine capacity would not be fully utilized. Under these conditions a minimization of the makespan in the third step is of little use. The procedure is, therefore, only advantageous when the tool magazine constraints limit the number of different orders assigned to a batch, and when sufficiently large order sizes guarantee the usage of the available processing times per period.

5.4.3. The Mazzola et al. Approach - A Hierarchical Concept

Hierarchical approaches attempt to systematically coordinate the decisions in an FMS with the objectives prescribed by the central PPC system.

- *Mazzola, Neebe and Dunn*[428]

propose a planning structure in which it is assumed that the FMS is the bottleneck in the production environment [see figure (224)]. Orders with assigned due dates are passed on to the FMS computer from the central PPC system. These orders are created during the material requirements and lot size planning and due dates are assigned during the detailed capacity planning. Since the order-dependent setup costs are low due to the flexibility of the FMS, the order sizes may generally agree with the net requirements.

---

427 For the determination of the weighting see **Bastos** (1988), p. 235.
428 **Mazzola/Neebe/Dunn** (1989)

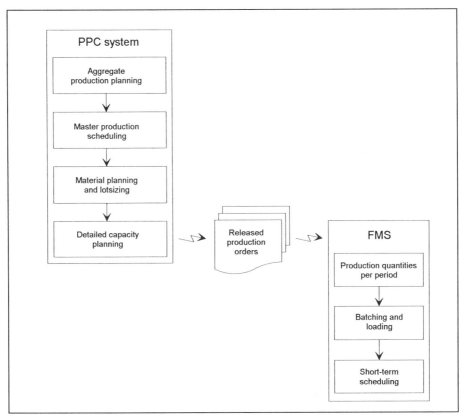

Figure 224: Hierarchical planning scheme

Mazzola, Neebe and Dunn have developed a two-level planning concept for pre-release planning of production orders which have already been assigned due dates. An overview of its structure is shown in figure (225). In the first step the timed production orders transferred from the PPC system to the FMS are distributed among the production periods based on the production capacities in the FMS. The problem structure corresponds to that of a generalized assignment problem with the planning periods being the *agents*. The central PPC system provides the earliest and latest possible completion times for each order.

Quantities that will cause the solution to have a specific structure can be used as coefficients in the model's objective function. If, for example, the objective is to finish processing of all orders as early as possible in order to provide maximum flexibility with respect to future demand variations, then the objective function coefficients should be quantified as a monotone non-decreasing function of the period index. In this case, the production quantities are scheduled as early as possible. If, on the other hand, the objective is to have the orders finished just in time, then the objective function coefficients should be quantified as a monotone non-increasing function of the period index. *Mazzola, Neebe and Dunn* have developed an heuristic procedure to solve this model.

Procedure MAZZOLA
Step 1: *Order selection*
Production orders released by the PPC system are assigned to production periods using a generalized assignment model.
Step 2: *Batching and system setup planning*
a) Determination of the minimal number of machine groups per batch given a fixed maximum number of batches. b) Successive assignment of operations to machine groups. c) Post-optimization: changing assignment of operations to batches in order to reduce the makespan.

Figure 225: Structure of the procedure of Mazzola, Neebe and Dunn

In the second step the *machines are partitioned into groups* with identically set up tool magazines, the *orders are combined into sequentially processed batches*, and the *operations are assigned to machines* for the next upcoming planning period (time bucket). Both limited tool magazine capacities and a limited number of fixtures are taken into consideration. The authors formulate a very large mixed-binary linear optimization model and suggest a two-level heuristic procedure for its solution. First it is attempted, under consideration of a predetermined maximum number of batches, to determine a *feasible machine grouping* and a *feasible allocation of tools*. In a subsequent optimization phase, after generating a feasible solution, the makespan of the batch is minimized.

In order to find an feasible initial solution *Mazzola, Neebe and Dunn* proceed as follows. The total number of tool slots needed for each machine type is determined. Dividing this number by the tool magazine capacity of the respective machine type provides a lower bound for the number of differently equipped tool magazines, and thus the number of different machine groups which are required for the considered machine type. *Mazzola, Neebe and Dunn* seek to minimize the number of machine groups, because fewer groups allow higher production rates to be achieved[429].

Using this initial partition of machines into groups, they start with the first batch and, using the LPT rule, assign the operations to machine groups with the lowest assigned workload but still having sufficient tool magazine capacity. The individual operations are considered independently of one another. Batching and operation/machine group assignment results in a feasible solution only when *all* the operations on a workpiece are assigned to a *single* batch. Otherwise, it might become necessary that a workpiece on which some operations have been carried out must be removed from the FMS and be brought back in as part of a subsequently processed batch. Furthermore the situation might arise that one opera-

---

429   **Stecke/Morin** (1985); **Stecke/Solberg** (1985); see also section 5.3.1.

tion has to be performed on a workpiece *before* its predecessor operation has been finished. Thus each time an operation is assigned, a workpiece's other operations must be assigned to the same batch. A batch is complete when no further operation or no further order can be assigned due to the limited tool magazine capacities. The procedure is continued until all operations have been assigned to machine groups and all orders have been assigned to batches. If it is not possible to stay within the maximum number of batches, the number of machine groups is increased and it will be again attempted to find a feasible assignment[430].

In the following optimization phase, *Mazzola, Neebe and Dunn* attempt to reduce the total makespan (makespan for all batches in the current time bucket) by transferring operations from each bottleneck machine group to an appropriate machine group with a strictly larger number of machines *within the same batch*. The bottleneck machine group in a batch is the machine group with the largest workload resulting form the assigned operations. This shifting of operations to larger machine groups, which are supposed to have larger capacity, is continued until the total makespan cannot be improved any further. In a secondary optimization phase the shifting of operations from bottleneck machine groups to nonbottleneck machine groups *in other batches* is tried.

A difficulty in the optimization phase is that when an operation is moved to another machine group, all the other operations of a workpiece also have to be moved to the new batch. Under such conditions the proposed procedure of choosing operations for moving and the selection of new batches is problematic.

Another significant problem with this approach is that the maximum number of batches has to be determined in advance. This number is likely to be the resulting batch number in the procedure, since the number of machine groups is inversely proportional to the number of batches and *Mazzola, Nebbe and Dunn* seek to minimize the number of machine groups per batch.

The number of orders that can be included in a single batch depends on the space required by the tools, the number of tool slots needed for each order, and the tool magazine capacities of the machines. Now assume an extreme case in which all machines of one type are identically tooled (a single machine group per machine type and batch). The number of tool slots available for a specific type of machines is then equivalent to the tool magazine capacity of a *single* machine. This involves that only a *minimum* number of orders can be assigned to a batch. Hence, a large number of batches results after having assigned all orders of the order pool. Minimizing the number of machine groups leads, therefore, to a large number of batches. The number of batches, however, has such a significant influence on the total makespan that it should be determined as a function of the objective being pursued.

---

430 A similar approach is proposed by **Shanker/Tzen** (1985) and **Shanker/Srinivasulu** (1989); see also **Kuhn** (1990), p. 90.

5.4.4. The Kuhn Approach - Integrated Batching and Operation/Machine Assignment

The common characteristic of all the previously discussed approaches is that the number of batches is a side product of the solution to the model and is not taken as a decision variable in the solution procedure itself.

- *Kuhn*[431]

has proposed an approach in which the interdependencies among the variables to be determined in the SE-AGMA model are integrated into a single procedure. The variables include:

- The *number of batches* to be created, L.
- The *assignment of the orders to the individual batches*, x_{jl}.
- The *assignment of the operation lots to the identical machines*, π_{oml}.

In this procedure the overall problem is partitioned into several subproblems that are systematically coordinated with each other. Each subproblem deals with one of the above-mentioned groups of decision variables. To solve the SE-AGMA model the following procedure is applied. In the first step of the procedure the *number of batches* L into which the set of J orders is to be partitioned is determined. Then the *batching* subproblem is solved. In a later step the *operation lots* for each batch are *assigned* to the identical *machines* [see figure (226)].

- **Determination of the number of batches**

The optimum number of batches L_{opt} lies between a minimum L_{min}, depending on the tool magazine capacities, and a maximum L_{max}, defined by the number of orders J to be assigned to batches. Thus the following is true:

$$L_{min} \leq L_{opt} \leq L_{max} = J \tag{292}$$

The optimum number of batches L_{opt} can be determined such that the optimum partition of orders for every possible number of batches is generated, and then the batch number with the best objective function value is selected. However, the determination of the optimal partition of orders with a given number of batches involves so much computing time that it would not be possible to determine the optimal partition for each possible batch number in real-life sized applications.

Kuhn, therefore, limits the number of batches to be analyzed in his procedure. He applies the following heuristic considerations in pursuing the objectives of minimizing the makespan and minimizing tardiness. If the number of batches is small then it can be expected that the operations, due to the increased importance of tool magazine constraints, must be assigned to machines at which a large number of the required tools is already available. This tool assignment may negatively affect balancing the workloads among the machines, however. It may

---

431 **Kuhn** (1990), pp. 116-120, 230-232

also be expected that in this situation the orders will be forced into batches which are not advantageous to the orders meeting their assigned due dates. An increase in the number of batches thus influences both the balance of workloads among the machines and the likelihood that the orders will be completed on time.

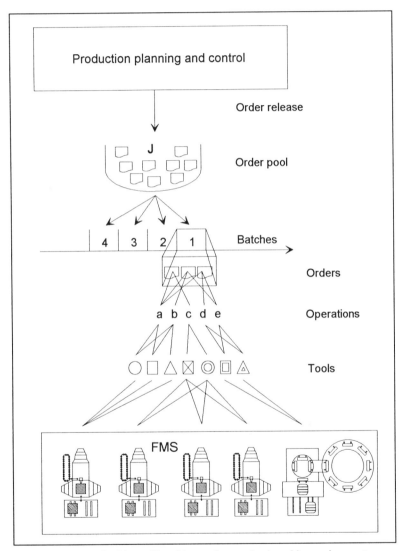

Figure 226: Problem of batching and operation/machine assignment

The positive effects of an increased number of batches are compensated with the fact that more batches also tend to require more setup periods between batches. This causes the makespan of the entire order set to be extended and may decrease the chances that the orders will be processed on time. It is to be expected that this also applies when setup changes are made simultaneously during workpiece processing, i.e. no setup time between batches. The decrease in the number of orders per batch (batch size) associated with an increasing number of batches makes workload balancing more difficult and thus the makespan may possibly be increased.

Furthermore, the total number of tools required may also increase as the number of batches increases. With an increasing batch number the mean number of orders per batch decreases. Thus, a lower number of different tools will be required per batch. This gives rise to the provision of several identical machines with duplicate tool sets so that identical workpieces can be processed in parallel.

Kuhn determines the optimal number of batches as follows. First he uses an heuristic procedure[432] to find the minimum number of batches L_{min}. Following that, while the objective function value decreases, the number of batches is increased until the objective function value rises. A qualitative example of the dependence of various components of the objective function on the number of batches is depicted in figure (227).

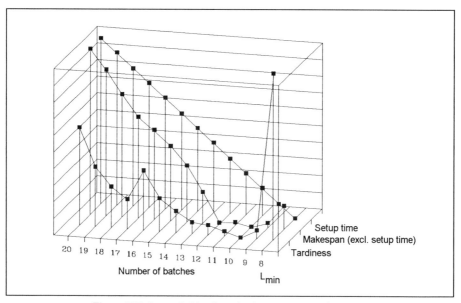

Figure 227: Several objective criteria vs. number of batches

---

432 **Kuhn** (1990), pp. 147-166; see also section 5.2.1.1.

- **Assignment of orders to batches**

In the second stage of the procedure, the optimal partition of orders for each given number of batches is generated. *Kuhn* uses the heuristic procedure SEF-CLUST which can be applied in both its deterministic and stochastic variations. Any objective function may be pursued during the progress of this procedure since an objective directed evaluation can be performed after each move or exchange of an order.

To determine the quality of an order partition *Kuhn* estimates the makespan of each batch using a closed queueing network model[433]. He then derives the total time for processing all batches and the resulting tardiness of the orders.

- **Assignment of the operation lots to the identical machines**

If the orders of a batch, and thus the operations to be performed, are known, the aim of the last planning stage is to assign the operations to the machines. The SYSR procedure is used to solve this problem. The procedure generates an operation assignment that minimizes the greatest machine workload. Since *Kuhn* sets the completion time of each order equal to that of its respective batch, minimizing the greatest machine workload takes account of the objectives of minimum makespan and minimum tardiness.

The overall concept of *Kuhn's* approach to solving the model SE-AGMA is illustrated in figure (228).

Procedure KUHN
Step 1: *Determination of an initial partition*
Determine a feasible operation/machine assignment with a minimum number of batches. One of the procedures described in section 5.2.1.1. may be used.
Step 2: *Improvement of a partition*
a) Use a variation of the local search procedure SEF-CLUST. b) If the objective function value can be improved compared to the value achieved with the last batch number, then increase the batch number by one. Go to step 2a). If an improvement cannot be achieved, then select the batch number with the best objective function value. Go to step 3.
Step 3: *Operation/machine assignment*
Determine for each batch and for each group of identical machines the optimal operation/machine assignment with procedure SYSR[434].

Figure 228: Procedure of Kuhn

---

433 **Kuhn** (1990), pp. 121-146; see also section 3.1.
434 see section 5.3.2.3.

Kuhn has carried out a detailed study comparing several variations of his own procedure with that of *Whitney and Gaul* and with two other procedures presented in the literature. Twelve different problem constellations with data sets resembling situations taken from industrial practical were studied. Detailed simulation models of the FMSs being studied were designed in order to evaluate the various pre-release planning concepts. The *Kuhn* approach proved itself to be distinctly superior[435].

Because of its modular structure, this concept can be adjusted to apply to different problem variations. In the form of the KUHN procedure described here [see figure (228)], the workload balance of the identical machines (SYSR procedure) is carried out subsequent to batching (SEF-CLUST procedure) (a sequential approach). It is possible, however, to solve the AGMA-KU model after any move or exchange during the SEF-CLUST procedure. This allows workloads to be balanced among the machines *during* batching (simultaneous approach). This variation can, under certain circumstances, lead to significantly improved results, but the additional computational has to be considered. An alternative would be to balance the workloads only for those machines which belong to the same bottleneck machine type. The modularity of the procedure allows both the computing time and the quality of the solution to be adjusted on a case by case basis as desired.

To close the discussion, the different approaches to pre-release planning discussed here and in the literature are summarized in table (101).

Further reading for section 5.4.:

Bastos (1988)
Chakravarty/Shtub (1986)
Co/Biermann/Chen (1990)
DeWerra/Widmer (1991)
Kim/Yano (1992)
Kuhn (1990)
Mazzola/Neebe/Dunn (1989)
Sawik (1990)
Whitney/Gaul (1985)

---

435   **Kuhn** (1990), pp. 235-248

Problem type	Without tool constraints	With tool constraints
Batching	Stecke/Kim (1986) Stecke/Kim (1989) Stecke/Kim (1991)	Rajagopalan (1985) Hwang (1986) Stecke/Kim (1988) Tang/Denardo (1988a), (1988b) Bard (1988) Hwang/Shogan (1989) Jaikumar/Van Wassenhove (1989) Kuhn (1990) Oerlemans (1992) Crama/Oerlemans (1993) Crama/Kolen/Oerlemans/ Spieksma (1994)
System setup planning	DeLuca (1984) Kusiak (1985b) Stecke/Talbot (1985) Afentakis (1986)	Stecke (1983) Kusiak (1985b), (1985c) Stecke (1986) Berrada/Stecke (1986) Sarin/Chen (1987) Kim (1988) Sawik (1990) Kuhn (1990), (1992b) Mukhopadhyay/Maiti/Garg(1991) Kim/Yano (1993)
Simultaneous pre-release planning		Whitney/Gaul (1985) Chakravarty/Shtub (1986) Bastos (1988) Kim (1988) Mazzola/Neebe/Dunn (1989) Co/Biermann/Chen (1990) Kuhn (1990) DeWerra/Widmer (1991) Kim/Yano (1992)

Table 101: Models for pre-release planning

REFERENCES

Afentakis, P., Maximum throughput in flexible manufacturing systems, in: Stecke, K. E. and R. Suri (Eds.), *Proceedings of the 2nd ORSA/TIMS Conference on FMS: Operations Research Models and Applications*, Amsterdam (Elsevier) 1986, pp. 509-520.

Agrawal, S.C., J.P. Buzen and A.W. Shum, Response time preservation: A general technique for developing approximate algorithms for queueing networks, in: *Performance Evaluation Review* 12(1984)3, pp. 63-77.

Akyildiz, I.F., Mean value analysis for blocking queueing networks, in: *IEEE Transactions on Software Engineering* 14(1988a)4, pp. 418-428.

Akyildiz, I.F., On the exact and approximate throughput analysis of closed queueing networks with blocking, in: *IEEE Transactions on Software Engineering* 14(1988b)1, pp. 62-70.

Akyildiz, I.F. and G. Bolch, Mean value analysis approximation for multiple server queueing networks, in: *Performance Evaluation* 8(1988), pp. 77-91.

Altiok, T. and H.G. Perros, Open networks of queues with blocking: Split and merge configurations, in: *IIE Transactions* 18(1986), pp. 251-261.

Altiok, T. and S. Stidham, The allocation of interstage buffer capacities in production lines, in: *IIE Transactions* 15(1983)4, pp. 292-299.

Ammons, J.C., Lofgren, C.B. and L.F. McGinnis, A large scale machine loading problem in flexible assembly, in: *Annals of OR* 3(1985), pp. 319-332.

Amoako-Gyampah, K., Meredith, J.R. and A. Raturi, A comparison of tool management strategies and part selection rules for a flexible manufacturing system, in: *IJPR* 30(1992), pp. 733-748.

Avonts, L.H. and L.N. Van Wassenhove, The part mix and routing mix problem in FMS: A coupling between an LP model and a closed queueing network, in: *IJPR* 26(1988), pp. 1891-1902.

Avonts, L.H., Gelders, L.F. and L.N. Van Wassenhove, Allocating work between an FMS and a conventional jobshop: A case study, in: *EJOR* 33(1988), pp. 245-256.

Baker, K.R., *Introduction to Sequencing and Scheduling*, New York (Wiley) 1974.

Banks, J. and J.S. Carson, II, *Discrete-Event System Simulation*, Englewood Cliffs (Prentice Hall) 1984.

Banks, J. and J.S. Carson, II, Process-interaction simulation languages, in: *Simulation* 44(1985)5, pp. 225-235.

Bard, J.F., A Heuristic for minimizing the number of tool switches on a flexible machine, in: *IIE Transactions* 20(1988), pp. 382-391.

Bard, Y., A simple approach to system modeling, in: *Performance Evaluation* 1(1981), pp. 225-248.

Bastos, J.M., Batching and routing: Two functions in the operational planning of flexible manufacturing systems, in: *EJOR* 33(1988), pp. 230-244.

Ben-Arieh, D., Knowledge based control system for automated production and assembly, in: Kusiak, A. (Ed.), *Modelling and Design of Flexible Manufacturing Systems*, Amsterdam (Elsevier) 1986, pp. 347-368.

Berrada, M. and K.E. Stecke, A branch and bound approach for machine load balancing in flexible manufacturing systems, in: *Man. Sci.* 32(1986)10, pp. 1316-1335.

Bidanda, B. and C.K. Muralikrishnan, Flexible fixturing for intelligent manufacturing, in: Kusiak, A. (Ed.), *Intelligent Design and Manufacturing: A Reference Book*, New York (Wiley) 1992, pp.205-232.

Boer, H., Hill, M. and K. Krabbendam, FMS implementation management: Promise and performance, in: *IJOPM* 10(1990)1, pp. 5-20.

Bonetto, R., *Flexible Manufacturing Systems in Practice*, New York (Hemisphere Publishing) 1988.

Bratley, P., Fox, B.L. and L.E. Schrage, *A Guide to Simulation*, New York (Springer) 1983.

Browne, J., Chan, W.W. and K. Rathmill, An integrated FMS design procedure, in: *Annals of OR* 3(1985), pp. 207-237.

Browne, J., Dubois, D., Rathmill, K., Sethi, S.P. and K.E. Stecke, Classification of flexible manufacturing systems, in: *The FMS Magazine* (1984)April, pp. 114-117.

Bruell, S.C. and G. Balbo, *Computational Algorithms for Closed Queueing Networks*, New York (North-Holland) 1980.

Bruell, S.C., Balbo, G. and P.V. Afshari, Mean value analysis of mixed multiple class BCMP-networks with load dependent service stations, in: *Performance Evaluation* 4(1984), pp. 241-260.

Buzacott, J.A., Modelling flexible manufacturing systems, in: Archetti, F., Lucertini, M. and P. Serafini (Eds.), *Operations Research Models in Flexible Manufacturing Systems*, Wien (Springer) 1989, pp. 123-134.

Buzacott, J.A. and J.G. Shanthikumar, Models for understanding flexible manufacturing systems, in: *AIIE Transactions* 12(1980), pp. 339-350.

Buzacott, J.A. and J.G. Shanthikumar, Design of manufacturing systems using queueing models, in: *Queueing Systems* 12(1992), pp. 135-214.

Buzacott, J.A. and J.G. Shanthikumar, *Stochastic Models of Manufacturing Systems*, Englewood Cliffs (Prentice Hall) 1993.

Buzacott, J.A. and D.D. Yao, On queueing network models of flexible manufacturing systems, in: *Queueing Systems* 1(1986), pp. 5-27.

Buzen, J., Computational algorithms for closed queueing networks with exponential servers, in: *Communications of the ACM* 16(1973), pp. 527-531.

Canada, J.R. and W.G. Sullivan, *Economic and Multiattribute Evaluation of Advanced Manufacturing Systems*, Englewood Cliffs (Prentice Hall) 1989.

Canals, D. and M. Frabolot, How to design, schedule and pilot FMS with simulation: a case study, in: Warnecke, H.-J. and R. Steinhilper (Eds.), *Proceedings of the 7th International Conference on Flexible Manufacturing Systems*, Berlin (Springer) 1988, pp. 371-372.

Carrie, A., *Simulation of Manufacturing Systems*, Chichester (Wiley) 1988.

Cavaille, J.-B. and D. Dubois, Heuristic methods based on mean-value analysis for flexible manufacturing systems performance evaluation, *Proceedings of the IEEE Conference on Decision and Control*, Orlando, Florida 1982.

Chakravarty, A.K. and A. Shtub, Production planning with flexibilities in capacity, in: Stecke, K.E., and R. Suri (Eds.), *Proceedings of the 2nd ORSA/TIMS Conference on Flexible Manufacturing Systems: Operations Research Models and Applications*, Amsterdam (Elsevier) 1986, pp. 333-343.

Chandra, J. and J. Talavage, Intelligent dispatching for flexible manufacturing, in: *IJPR* 29(1991), pp. 2259-2278.

Chandy, K.M. and D. Neuse, Linearizer: A heuristic algorithm for queueing network models of computing systems, in: *Communications of the ACM* 25(1982)2, pp. 126-134.

Chen, I.J. and C.-H. Chung, Effects of loading and routeing decisions on performance of flexible manufacturing systems, in: *IJPR* 29(1991), pp. 2209-2225.

Co, H.C. and S.K. Chen, Design of a model generator for simulation in SLAM, in: *Eng. Costs and Prod. Econ.* 14(1988), pp. 189-198.

Co, H.C. and R.A. Wysk, The robustness of CAN-Q in modelling automated manufacturing systems, in: *IJPR* 24(1986), pp. 1485-1503.

Co, H.C., Biermann, J.S. and S.K. Chen, A methodical approach to the flexible-manufacturing-system batching, loading and tool configuration problems, in: *IJPR* 28(1990), pp. 2171-2186.

Co, H.C., Jaw, T.J. and S.K. Chen, Sequencing in flexible manufacturing systems and other short queue-length systems, in: *JMS* 7(1988)1, pp. 1-9.

Co, H., Wu, A. and A. Reisman, A throughput-maximizing facility planning and layout model, in: *IJPR* 27(1989), pp. 1-12.

Coffman, Jr., E.G., Garey, M.R. and D.S. Johnson, An application of bin-packing to multiprocessor scheduling, in: *SIAM Journal on Computing* 7(1978)1, pp. 1-17.

Crama, Y. and A.G. Oerlemans, A column generation approach to job grouping for flexible manufacturing systems, in: *EJOR* (1993) forthcoming.

Crama, Y., Kolen, A.W.J., Oerlemans, A.G. and F.C.R. Spieksma, Minimizing the number of tool switches on a flexible machine, in: *IJFMS* 6(1994)1 forthcoming.

Dallery, Y., On modelling flexible manufacturing systems using closed queueing networks, in: *Large Scale Systems* 11(1986), pp. 109-119.

Dallery, Y. and Y. Frein, An efficient method to determine the optimal configuration of a flexible manufacturing system, in: *Annals of OR* 15(1988), pp. 207-225.

Dallery, Y. and Y. Frein, An efficient method to determine the optimal configuration of a flexible manufacturing system, in: Stecke, K.E. and R. Suri (Eds.), *Proceedings of the 2nd ORSA/TIMS Conference on Flexible Manufacturing Systems: Operations Research Models and Applications*, Amsterdam (Elsevier) 1986, pp. 269-282.

Dallery, Y. and B. Gershwin, Manufacturing flow line systems: A review of models and analytical results, in: *Queueing Systems* 12(1992), pp. 3-94.

Dallery, Y. and K.E. Stecke, On the optimal allocation of servers and workloads in closed queueing networks, in: *OR* 38(1990), pp. 694-703.

DeLuca, A., Optimal production planning for FMS: An "optimum batching" algorithm, in: Warnecke, H.-J. (Ed.), *Proceedings of the 3rd international Conference on Flexible Manufacturing Systems*, 11.-13. 9. 1984, Boeblingen, pp. 323-332.

Denning, P.J. and J.P. Buzen, The operational analysis of queueing network models, in: *Computing Surveys* 10(1978)3, pp. 225-261.

DeWerra, D. and M. Widmer, Loading problems with tool management in flexible manufacturing systems: A few integer programming models, in: *IJFMS* 3(1991), pp. 71-82.

Diehl, G.W., *A Buffer-Equivalency Decomposition Approach to Finite Buffer Queueing Networks*, Ph.D. Diss., Harvard University 1984.

Dorndorf, U. and E. Pesch, Fast clustering algorithm, in: *ORSA Journal on Computing* (1993) forthcoming.

Duffau, B. and E. Bloche, Modelisation and simulation of production units, in: *Proceedings of the 3rd European Conference on Automated Manufacturing*, Amsterdam (North-Holland) 1985, pp. 305-315.

Dupont-Gatelmand, C., A survey of flexible manufacturing systems, in: *JMS* 1(1982), pp. 1-16.

Eglese, R.W., Simulated annealing: A tool for operational research, in: *EJOR* 46(1990), pp. 271-281.

Eisemann, K., The generalized stepping stone method for the machine loading model, in: *Man. Sci.* 11(1964)Sept., pp. 154-176.

ElMaraghy, H.A., Simulation and graphical animation of advanced manufacturing systems, in: *JMS* 1(1982), pp. 53-63.

Erschler, J., Lévêque, D. and F. Roubellat, Periodic loading of flexible manufacturing systems, in: Doumeingts, G. and W.A. Carter (Eds.), *Advances in Production Management Systems*, Amsterdam (North-Holland) 1984, pp. 401-413.

Erschler, J., Roubellat, F. and C. Thuriot, Steady state scheduling of a flexible manufacturing system with periodic releasing and flow time constraints, in: *Annals of OR* 3(1985), pp. 279-300.

Escudero, L.F., An inexact algorithm for part input sequencing and scheduling with side constraints in FMS, in: *IJFMS* 1(1989), pp. 143-174.

Fisher, M.L. and R. Jaikumar, A generalized assignment heuristic for vehicle routing, in: *Networks* 11(1981), pp. 109-124.

Fisher, M.L., Jaikumar, R. and L.N. van Wassenhove, A multiplier adjustment method for the generalized assignment problem, in: *Man. Sci.* 32(1986)9, pp. 1095-1103.

Fishman, G.S., Statistical considerations in the simulation of flexible manufacturing systems, in: Archetti, F., Lucertini, M. and P. Serafini (Eds.), *Operations Research Models in Flexible Manufacturing Systems*, Wien (Springer) 1989, pp. 153-183.

Floss, P. and J. Talavage, A knowledge-based design assistant for intelligent manufacturing systems, in: *JMS* 9(1990)2, pp. 87-102.

French, S., *Sequencing and Scheduling: An Introduction to the Mathematics of the Job-Shop*, Chichester (Wiley) 1982.

Gordon, J.J., The evaluation of normalizing constants in closed queueing networks, in: *OR* 39(1991), pp. 863-869.

Gordon, W.J. and G.F. Newell, Closed queueing systems with exponential servers, in: *OR* 15(1967), pp. 254-265.

Graves, S.C. and B.W. Lamar, An integer programming procedure for assembly system design problems, in: *OR* 31(1983), pp. 522-545.

Graves, S.C. and C.H. Redfield, Equipment selection and task assignment for multiproduct assembly system design, in: *IJFMS* 1(1988), pp. 31-50.

Graves, S.C. and D.E. Whitney, A mathematical programming procedure for equipment selection and system evaluation in programmable assembly, in: *Proceedings of the 18th IEEE Conference on Decisions and Control*, Fort Lauderdale, Florida (1979), pp. 531-536; cited from Graves/Lamar (1983).

Gray, A.E., Seidmann, A. and K.E. Stecke, *A Synthesis of Tool-Management Issues and Decision Problems in Automated Manufacturing*, Working Paper, University of Rochester, W.E. Simon Graduate School of Business Administration, Rochester, New York, July 1990.

Greenwood, N.R., *Implementing Flexible Manufacturing Systems*, London (Macmillan) 1988.

Gross, D. and C.M. Harris, *Fundamentals of Queueing Theory*, 2nd Ed., New York (Wiley) 1985.

Gupta, Y.P., Evans, G.W. and M.C. Gupta, A review of multi-criterion approaches to FMS scheduling problems, in: *IJPE* 22(1991), pp. 13-31.

Gutenberg, E., *Grundlagen der Betriebswirtschaftslehre. Erster Band. Die Produktion*, 24th Ed., Berlin (Springer) 1983 (in German).

Hackstein, R., CIM-Begriffe sind verwirrende Schlagwörter - Die AWF-Empfehlung schafft Ordnung, in: AWF-Ausschuß für Wirtschaftliche Fertigung e.V. (Ed.), *PPS 85*, Proceedings, Böblingen 1985 (in German).

Han, M.-H., Na, Y.K. and G.L. Hogg, Real-time tool control and job dispatching in flexible manufacturing systems, in: *IJPR* 27(1989), pp. 1257-1267.

Harrison, P.G., On normalizing constants in queueing networks, in: *OR* 33(1985), pp. 464-468.

Haupt, R., A survey of priority rule-based scheduling, in: *ORS* 11(1989)1, pp. 3-16.

Hax, A.C. and D. Candea, *Production and Inventory Management*, Englewood Cliffs (Prentice-Hall) 1984.

Hertz, D.B., Risk analysis in capital investment, in: *HBR* 42(1964)1, pp. 95-106.

Hespos, R.F. and P.A. Strassmann, Stochastic decision trees for the analysis of investment decision, in: *Man. Sci.* 11(1965), pp. B244-259.

Hildebrant, R.R., *Scheduling Flexible Machining Systems when Machines are Prone to Failure*, Ph. Diss., Massachusetts Institute of Technology, Cambridge, MA 1980.

Hitz, K.L., *Scheduling of Flexible Flow Shops*, Working Paper LIDS-R-879, Laboratory for Information and Decision Systems, Massachusetts Institute of Technology, Cambridge, Massachusetts 02139, January 1979.

Hitz, K.L., *Scheduling of Flexible Flow Shops II*, Working Paper LIDS-R-1049, Laboratory for Information and Decision Systems, Massachusetts Institute of Technology, Cambridge, Massachusetts 02139, October 1980.

Hopp, W.J. and M.L. Spearman, Throughput of a constant work in process manufacturing line subject to failures, in: *IJPR* 29(1991), pp. 635-655.

Hwang, S.S., A constraint-directed method to solve the part selection problem in flexible manufacturing systems planning stage, in: Stecke, K. E. and Suri, R. (Eds.), *Proceedings of the 2nd ORSA/TIMS Conference on FMS: OR Models and Applications*, Amsterdam (Elsevier) 1986, pp. 297-309.

Hwang, S.S. and A.W. Shogan, Modelling and solving an FMS part selection problem, in: *IJPR* 27(1989), pp. 1349-1366.

Irani, S.A., Leung, L.C. and W.S. Snyder, Multi-machine replacement for sequential implementation of a hybrid flexible manufacturing system, in: Stecke, K.E. and R. Suri (Eds.), *Proceedings of the 2nd ORSA/TIMS Conference on FMS: Operations Research Models and Applications*, Amsterdam (Elsevier) 1986, pp. 233-243.

Jackson, J., Networks of waiting lines, in: *OR* 5(1957), pp. 518-521.

Jaikumar, R. and L.N. Van Wassenhove, A production planning framework for flexible manufacturing systems, in: *JMOM* 2(1989), pp. 52-79.

Jones, A.T. and C.R. McLean, A proposed hierarchical control model for automated manufacturing systems, in: *JMS* 5(1986)1, pp. 15-25.

Kakati, M. and U.R. Dhar, Investment justification in flexible manufacturing systems, in: *Eng. Costs and Prod. Econ.* 21(1991), pp. 203-209.

Kalkunte, M.V., Sarin, S.C. and W.E. Wilhelm, Flexible manufacturing systems: A review of modelling approaches for design, justification and operation, in: Kusiak, A. (Ed.), *Flexible Manufacturing Systems: Methods and Studies*, Amsterdam (North-Holland) 1986, pp. 3-25.

Ketcham, M.G. and J. Watt, Parametric simulation for flexible assembly systems, in: *JMS* 8(1989), pp. 115-125.

Kim, Y.-D., *An Iterative Approach for System Setup Problems of Flexible Manufacturing Systems*, Ph.D. Diss., Department of Industrial and Operations Engineering, University of Michigan, Ann Arbor, MI, 1988.

Kim, Y.-D. and C.A. Yano, An iterative approach to system setup problems in flexible manufacturing systems, in: *IJFMS* 4(1992), pp. 183-209.

Kim, Y.-D. and C.A. Yano, Heuristic approaches for loading problems in flexible manufacturing systems, in: *IIE Transactions* 25(1993)1, pp. 26-39.

Kimemia, J.G. and S.B. Gershwin, Network flow optimization in flexible manufacturing systems, in: *Proceedings of the 1978 IEEE Conference on Decision and Control*, 1979, pp. 633-639.

Kimemia, J.G. and S.B. Gershwin, *Multicommodity Network Flow Optimization in Flexible Manufacturing Systems, in: Complex Material Handling and Assembly Systems*, Final Report, Vol. II, No ESL-FR-834-2, MIT, Laboratory for Information and Decision Sciences, Cambridge, MA, 1980.

Kimemia, J.G. and S.B. Gershwin, Flow optimization in flexible manufacturing systems, in: *IJPR* 23(1985), pp. 81-96.

Kiran, A.S., Schloffer, A. and D. Hawkins, An integrated simulation approach to design of flexible manufacturing systems, in: *Simulation* 49(1989)Febr., pp. 47-52.

Kistner, K.-P., *Betriebsstörungen und Warteschlangen - Die Erfassung störungsbedingter Stauungen mit der Warteschlangentheorie*, Opladen (Westdeutscher Verlag) 1974 (in German).

Kleinrock, L., *Queueing Systems: Volume 1: Theory*, New York (Wiley) 1975.

Kochikar, V.P. and T.T. Narendran, A framework for assessing flexibility of manufacturing systems, in: *IJPR* 30(1992), pp. 2873-2895.

Köhler, R., *Produktionsplanung für flexible Fertigungszellen*, Münster (Lit Verlag) 1988 (in German).

Kouvelis, P. and A.S. Kiran, The plant layout problem in automated manufacturing systems, in: *Annals of OR* 26(1990), pp. 397-412.

Krinsky, I. and J. Miltenburg, Alternate method for the justification of advanced manufacturing technologies, in: *IJPR* 29(1991), pp. 997-1015.

Kuhn, H., *Einlastungsplanung von flexiblen Fertigungssystemen*, Heidelberg (Physica) 1990 (in German).

Kuhn, H., Einlastungsstrategien für ein FFS, in: Bühler, W., Feichtinger G., Hartl, R.F., Radermacher, F.J. and P. Stähly (Eds.), *Operations Research Proceedings 1990*, Berlin (Springer) 1992a, pp. 440-447 (in German).

Kuhn, H., *A Heuristic Algorithm for the Loading Problem in Flexible Manufacturing Systems*, Working Paper, Technical University of Braunschweig, Department of Production and Operations Management, Braunschweig, Germany 1992b.

Kusiak, A., Flexible manufacturing systems: a structural approach, in: *IJPR* 23(1985a), pp. 1057-1073.

Kusiak, A., Loading models in flexible manufacturing systems, in: Raouf, A. and S.I. Ahmad (Eds.), *Flexible Manufacturing*, Amsterdam (Elsevier) 1985b, pp. 119-132.

Kusiak, A., Planning of flexible manufacturing systems, in: *Robotica* 3(1985c), pp. 229-232.

Kusiak, A., Application of operational research models and techniques in flexible manufacturing systems, in: *EJOR* 24(1986)3, pp. 336-345.

Kusiak, A., *Intelligent Manufacturing Systems*, Englewood Cliffs (Prentice Hall) 1990.

L**aarhoven van, P.J.M. and E.H.L. Aarts**, *Simulated Annealing: Theory and Applications*, Dordrecht (Kluwer) 1987.

Law, A.M. and S.W. Haider, Selecting simulation software for manufacturing applications: practical guidelines & software survey, in: *IE* 31(1989)5, pp. 33-36.

Law, A.M. and W.D. Kelton, *Simulation Modeling and Analysis*, New York (McGraw-Hill) 1982.

Law, A.M. and M.G. McComas, Pitfalls to avoid in the simulation of manufacturing systems, in: *IE* 31(1989)5, pp. 28-31, 69.

Lazowska, E.D., Zahorjan, J., Graham, G.S. and K.C. Sevcik, *Quantitative System Performance*, Englewood Cliffs (Prentice-Hall) 1984.

Lee, H.F., Srinivasan, M.M. and C.A. Yano, An algorithm for the minimum cost configuration problem in flexible manufacturing systems, in: Stecke, K.E. and R. Suri (Eds.), *Proceedings of the Third ORSA/TIMS Conference on Flexible Manufacturing Systems: Operations Research Models and Application*, Amsterdam (Elsevier) 1989, pp. 85-90.

Lee, H.F., Srinivasan, M.M. and C.A. Yano, Some characteristics of optimal workload allocation for closed queueing networks, in: *Performance Evaluation* 13(1991a), pp. 255-268.

Lee, H.F., Srinivasan, M.M. and C.A. Yano, The optimal configuration and workload allocation problem in flexible manufacturing systems, in: *IJFMS* 3(1991b), pp. 213-230.

Lee, Y.-H. and K. Iwata, Part ordering through simulation-optimization in an FMS, in: *IJPR* 29(1991), pp. 1309-1323.

Leimkühler, F., Economic analysis of computer integrated manufacturing systems, in: Rembold, U. and R. Dillmann (Eds.), *Methods for Computer Integrated Manufacturing*, Berlin (Springer) 1984, pp. 453-482; see also in: Rembold, U. and R. Dillmann (Eds.), *Computer-Aided Design and Manufacturing - Methods and Tools*, 2nd Ed., Berlin (Springer) 1986, pp. 401-444.

Lenz, J.E., MAST: A simulation tool for designing computerized metalworking factories, in: *Simulation* 38(1983)2, pp. 51-58.

Lenz, J.E., *Flexible Manufacturing: Benefits for the Low-Inventory Factory*, New York (Marcel Dekker) 1989.

Leung, L.C. and J.M.A. Tanchoco, A profit maximization model for machine/part assignment in a manufacturing system, in: *Eng. Costs and Prod. Econ.* 10(1986), pp. 57-67.

Liberatore, M.J. (Ed.), *Selection and Evaluation of Advanced Manufacturing Technologies*, Berlin (Springer) 1990.

Little, J.D.C., A proof of the queueing formula $L = \lambda \cdot W$, in: *OR* 9(1961), pp. 383-387.

Magee, J.F., How to use decision trees in capital investment, in: *HBR* 42(1964), pp. 79-96.

Maleki, R.A., *Flexible Manufacturing Systems: The Technology and Management*, Englewood Cliffs (Prentice Hall) 1991.

Mao, J.C.T., Decision trees and sequential investment decisions, in: *Cost and Management* 4(1968), pp. 18-23.

Martello, S. and P. Toth, An algorithm for the generalized assignment problem, in: Brans, J.P. (Ed.), *Operational Research '81*, Amsterdam (North-Holland) 1981, pp. 589-603.

Martello, S. and P. Toth, *Knapsack Problems - Algorithms and Computer Implementations*, Chichester (Wiley) 1990.

Mazzola, J.B., A.W. Neebe and C.V.R. Dunn, Production planning of a flexible manufacturing system in a material requirements planning environment, in: *IJFMS* 1(1989)2, pp. 115-142.

Mellichamp, J.M. and A.F.A. Wahab, An expert system for FMS design, in: *Simulation* 48(1987)5, pp. 201-208.

Mellichamp, J.M., Kwon, O.-J. and A.F.A. Wahab, FMS Designer: An expert system for flexible manufacturing system design, in: *IJPR* 28(1990), pp. 2013-2024.

Menga, G., Bruno, G., Conterno, R. and M.A. Dato, Modeling FMS by closed queueing network analysis methods, in: *IEEE Transactions on Components, Hybrids, and Manufacturing Technology* 7(1984)3, pp. 241-248.

Meredith, J.R. and N.C. Suresh, Justification techniques for advanced manufacturing technologies, in: *IJPR* 24(1986), pp. 1043-1057.

Mertins, K., Entwicklungsstand flexibler Fertigungssysteme: Linien-, Netz- and Zellenstrukturen, in: *ZwF* 80(1985)6, pp. 249-265 (in German).

Miltenburg, G.J., Economic evaluation and analysis of flexible manufacturing systems, in: *Eng. Costs and Prod. Econ.* 12(1987), pp. 72-92.

Miltenburg, G.J. and I. Krinsky, Evaluating flexible manufacturing systems, in: *IIE Transactions* 19(1987), pp. 222-233.

Morton, T.E. and T.L. Smunt, A planning and scheduling system for flexible manufacturing, in: Kusiak, A. (Ed.), *Flexible Manufacturing Systems: Methods and Studies*, Amsterdam (North-Holland) 1986, pp. 151-164.

Mukhopadhyay, S.K., Maiti, B. and S. Garg, Heuristic solution to the scheduling problems in flexible manufacturing system, in: *IJPR* 29(1991), pp. 2003-2024.

Murata, K. and M. Tajima, Rationalisierung, Flexibilisierung und Mechatronisierung der Produktion in japanischen Unternehmen, in: Adam, D., Backhaus, K., Meffert, H. and H. Wagner (Eds.), *Integration und Flexibilität - Eine Herausforderung für die Allgemeine Betriebswirtschaftslehre*, Wiesbaden (Gabler) 1990, pp. 249-268 (in German).

Nemhauser, G.L. and L.A. Wolsey, *Integer and Combinatorial Optimization*, New York (Wiley) 1988.

Neupert, H., GRAFSIM - Grafisch interaktiver Simulator für flexible Fertigungssysteme mit Werkzeuglogistik, in: Feldmann, K. and B. Schmidt (Eds.), *Simulation in der Fertigungstechnik*, Berlin (Springer) 1988, pp. 377-390 (in German).

Newman, W.E., Boe, W.J. and D.R. Denzler, Examining the use of dedicated and general purpose pallets in a dedicated flexible manufacturing system, in: *IJPR* 29(1991), pp. 2117-2133.

Nof, S.Y., M.M. Barash and J.J. Solberg, Operational control of item flow in versatile manufacturing systems, in: *IJPR* 17(1979)5, pp. 479-489.

Oerlemans, A.G., *Production planning for flexible manufacturing systems*, Dissertation no. 92-08, Faculty of Economics and Business Administration, University of Limburg, Maastricht 1992.

Ohashi, K. and K. Hitomi, Analysis of flexible machining cells for unmanned production, in: *IJPR* 29(1991), pp. 1603-1613.

O'Keefe, R., Simulation and expert systems - A taxonomy and some examples, in: *Simulation* 46(1986)1, pp. 10-16.

O'Keefe, R. and J. Haddock, Data-driven generic simulators for flexible manufacturing systems, in: *IJPR* 29(1991), pp. 1795-1810.

Padmanabhan, S., A tandem expert support system as justification for a flexible manufacturing system, in: *JMS* 8(1989), pp. 195-205.

Pegden, C.D., Shannon, R.E. and R.P. Sadowski, *Introduction to Simulation Using SIMAN*, New York (McGraw-Hill) 1990.

Pidd, M., *Computer Simulation in Management Science*, 2nd Ed., Chichester (Wiley) 1988.

Pritsker, A.A.B., *Introduction to Simulation and SLAM II*, 3rd Ed., New York (Halsted Press) 1986.

Proth, J.M. and H.P. Hillion, *Mathematical Tools in Production Management*, New York (Plenum) 1990.

Rajagopalan, S., *Scheduling Problems in Flexible Manufacturing Systems*, Working Paper, Graduate School of Industrial Administration, Carnegie-Mellon University, Pittsburgh, PA 15213, September 1985.

Rajagopalan, S., Formulation and solutions for parts grouping and tool loading in flexible manufacturing systems, in: Stecke, K.E. and Suri, R. (Eds.), *Proceedings of the 2nd ORSA/TIMS Conference on FMS: OR Models and Applications*, Amsterdam (Elsevier) 1986, pp. 311-320.

Ranta, J. and I. Tchijov, Economics and success factors of flexible manufacturing systems: The Conventional Explanation Revisited, in: *IJFMS* 2(1990), pp. 169-190.

Rao, P.P. and R.P. Mohanty, Searching for definitions and boundaries in flexible manufacturing systems, in: *Production Planning & Control* 2(1991), pp. 142-154.

Rathmill, K. and P. Cornwell, Trends in the application of simulation to FMS design, in: Szelke, E. and J Browni (Eds.), *Advances in Production Management Systems 85*, Amsterdam (North-Holland) 1986, pp. 99-115.

Reeve, J.M. and W.G. Sullivan, A synthesis of methods for evaluating interrelated investment projects, in: Liberatore, M.J. (Ed.), *Selection and Evaluation of Advanced Manufacturing Technologies*, Berlin (Springer) 1990, pp. 112-138.

Reiser, M., A queueing network analysis of computer communication networks with window flow control, in: *IEEE Transactions on Communications* 27(1979)8, pp. 1199-1209.

Reiser, M., Mean-value analysis and convolution method for queue-dependent servers in closed queueing networks, in: *Performance Evaluation* 1(1981), pp. 7-18.

Reiser, M. and S.S. Lavenberg, Mean-value analysis of closed multichain queueing networks, in: *Journal of the ACM* 27(1980)2, pp. 313-322.

Rolston, L.J. and R.J. Miner, MAP/1 tutorial, in: *Proceedings of the 1985 Winter Computer Simulation Conference*, San Diego (Society for Computer Simulation) 1985.

Sarin, S.C. and C.S. Chen, A mathematical model for manufacturing system selection, in: Kusiak, A. (Ed.), *Flexible Manufacturing Systems: Methods and Studies*, Amsterdam (North-Holland) 1986, pp. 99-112.

Sarin, S.C. and C.S. Chen, The machine loading and tool allocation problem in a flexible manufacturing system, in: *IJPR* 25(1987), pp. 1081-1094.

Sawik, T., Modelling and scheduling of a Flexible Manufacturing System, in: *EJOR* 45(1990) pp. 177-190.

Scheer, A.-W., *Enterprise-Wide Data Modelling - Information Systems in Industry*, Berlin (Springer) 1989.

Scheer, A.-W., *CIM - Computer Integrated Manufacturing - Towards the Factory of the Future*, 2nd Ed., Berlin (Springer) 1991.

Schmidt, G., *CAM: Algorithmen und Decision Support für die Fertigungssteuerung*, Berlin (Springer) 1989 (in German).

Schroer, B.J., Tseng, F.T., Zhang, S.X. and J.W. Wolfsberger, Automatic programming of manufacturing simulation models, in: *Proceedings of the 1988 Summer Simulation Conference*, San Diego (Society for Computer Simulation) 1988.

Schweitzer, P., Approximate analysis of multiclass closed networks of queues, in: *Proceedings of the International Conference on Stochastic Control and Optimization*, Amsterdam 1979, pp. 25-29.

Schweitzer, P.J., Seidmann, A. and S. Shalev-Oren, The correction term in approximate mean value analysis, in: *Operations Research Letters* 4(1986), pp. 197-200.

Secco-Suardo, G., *Optimization of closed queueing networks*, Research Report ESL-FR-834-3, MIT, Electronic Systems Laboratory, Cambridge, MA, 1978.

Secco-Suardo, G., Workload optimization in a FMS modelled as a closed network of queues, in: *Annals of the CIRP* 28(1979)1, pp. 381-383.

Seidmann, A., Schweitzer, P.J. and S. Shalev-Oren, Computerized closed queueing network models of flexible manufacturing systems: A comparative evaluation, in: *Large Scale Systems* 12(1987), pp. 91-107.

Seidmann, A., Shalev-Oren, S. and P.J. Schweitzer, An analytical review of several computerized queueing network models of FMS, in: Stecke, K.E. and R. Suri (Eds.), *Proceedings of the 2nd ORSA/TIMS Conference on Flexible Manufacturing Systems: Operations Research Models and Applications*, Amsterdam (Elsevier) 1986, pp. 369-380.

Sethi, A.K. and S.P. Sethi, Flexibility in manufacturing: A survey, in: *IJFMS* 2(1990), pp. 289-328.

Shalev-Oren, S., Seidmann, A. and P.J. Schweitzer, Analysis of flexible manufacturing systems with priority scheduling: PMVA, in: *Annals of OR* 3(1985), pp. 115-139.

Shanker, K. and A. Srinivasulu, Some solution methodologies for loading problems in flexible manufacturing systems, in: *IJPR* 27(1989), pp. 1019-1034.

Shanker, K. and Y.-J.J. Tzen, A loading and dispatching problem in a random flexible manufacturing system, in: *IJPR* 23(1985), pp. 579-595.

Shanthikumar, J.G. and D.D. Yao, On server allocation in multiple center manufacturing systems, in: *OR* 36(1988), pp. 333-342.

Sharit, J., Eberts, R. and G. Salvendy, A proposed theoretical framework for design of decision support systems in computer-integrated manufacturing systems: A cognitive engineering approach, in: *IJPR* 26(1988), pp. 1037-1063.

SIEMENS AG (Ed.), *GRAFSIM - Simulationssystem für Fertigungseinrichtungen - Systembeschreibung*, München 1988, Best.-Nr. 6ZB5450-0AA01-0BA0 (in German).

Silver, E.A. and R. Peterson, *Decision Systems for Inventory Management and Production Planning*, 2nd Ed., New York (Wiley) 1985.

Solberg, J.J., A mathematical model of computerized manufacturing systems, in: *Proceedings of the 4th International Conference on Production Research*, Tokio, 1977.

Solot, P., A heuristic method to determine the number of pallets in a flexible manufacturing system with several pallet types, in: *IJFMS* 2(1990a), pp. 191-216.

Solot, P., A concept for planning and scheduling in an FMS, in: *EJOR* 45(1990b), pp. 85-95.

Solot, P. and J.M. Bastos, MULTIQ: A queueing model for FMSs with several pallet types, in: *JORS* 39(1988), pp. 811-821.

Solot, P. and M. van Vliet, *Analytical Models for FMS Design Optimization: A Survey*, Working Paper ORWP 90/16, Ecole Polytechnique Fédérale de Lausanne, Département de Mathématiques, Chaire de Recherche Opérationelle, Lausanne 1990.

Stam, A. and M. Kuula, Selecting a flexible manufacturing system using multiple criteria analysis, in: *IJPR* 29(1991), pp. 803-820.

Stecke, K.E., Formulation and solution of nonlinear integer production planning problems for flexible manufacturing systems, in: *Man. Sci.* 29(1983)3, pp. 273-288.

Stecke, K.E., Design, planning, scheduling and control problems of flexible manufacturing systems, in: *Annals of OR* 3(1985), pp. 3-12.

Stecke, K.E., A hierarchical approach to solving machine grouping and loading problems of flexible manufacturing systems, in: *EJOR* 24(1986), pp. 369-378.

Stecke, K.E., *Procedures to Determine Part Mix Ratios in Flexible Manufacturing Systems*, Working Paper No. 448 R, Division of Research, Graduate School of Business Administration, The University of Michigan, Ann Arbor, Michigan, July 1987.

Stecke, K.E., Algorithms for efficient planning and operation of a particular FMS, in: *IJFMS* 1(1989), pp. 287-324.

Stecke, K.E., Planning and scheduling approaches to operate a particular FMS, in: *EJOR* 61(1992), pp. 273-291.

Stecke, K.E. and I. Kim, A flexible approach to implementing the short-term FMS planning function, in: Stecke, K. E. and Suri, R. (Eds.), *Proceedings of the 2nd ORSA/TIMS Conference on FMS: OR Models and Applications*, Amsterdam (Elsevier) 1986, pp. 283-295.

Stecke, K.E. and I. Kim, A study of FMS part type selection approaches for short-term production planning, in: *IJFMS* 1(1988)1, pp. 7-29.

Stecke, K.E. and I. Kim, Performance evaluation for systems of pooled machines of unequal sizes: Unbalancing versus balancing, in: *EJOR* 42(1989), pp. 22-38.

Stecke, K.E. and I. Kim, A flexible approach to part type selection in flexible flow systems using part mix ratios, in: *IJPR* 29(1991), pp. 53-75.

Stecke, K.E. and T.L. Morin, The optimality of balancing workloads in certain types of flexible manufacturing systems, in: *EJOR* 20(1985)1, pp. 68-82.

Stecke, K.E. and J.J. Solberg, *The CMS Loading Problem*, Report No. 20, School of Industrial Engineering, Purdue University, West Lafayette, Indiana, 1981a.

Stecke, K.E. and J.J. Solberg, Loading and control policies for a flexible manufacturing system, in: *IJPR* 19(1981b)5, pp. 481-490.

Stecke, K.E. and J.J. Solberg, The optimality of unbalancing both workloads and machine group sizes in closed queueing networks of multiserver queues, in: *OR* 33(1985)4, pp. 882-910.

Stecke, K.E. and F.B. Talbot, Heuristics for loading flexible manufacturing systems, in: Raouf, A. and S.I. Ahmad (Eds.), *Flexible Manufacturing*, Amsterdam 1985, pp. 73-85.

Steudel, H.J., SIMSHOP: A job shop/cellular manufacturing simulator, in: *JMS* 5(1986)3, pp. 181-189.

Subramanyam, S. and R.G. Askin, An expert systems approach to scheduling in flexible manufacturing systems, in: Kusiak, A. (Ed.), *Flexible Manufacturing Systems: Methods and Studies*, Amsterdam (North-Holland) 1986, pp. 243-256.

Suresh, N.C., Towards an integrated evaluation of flexible automation investments, in: *IJPR* 28(1990), pp. 1657-1672.

Suresh, N.C., An extended multi-objective replacement model for flexible automation investments, in: *IJPR* 29(1991), pp. 1823-1844.

Suresh, N.C. and J.R. Meredith, Justifying multimachine systems: An integrated strategic approach, in: *JMS* 4(1985), pp. 117-134.

Suresh, N.C. and J. Sarkis, A MIP formulation for the phased implementation of FMS modules, in: Stecke, K.E. and R. Suri (Eds.), *Proceedings of the Third ORSA/TIMS*

Conference on Flexible Manufacturing Systems: Operations Research Models and Applications, Amsterdam (Elsevier) 1989, pp. 41-46.

Suri, R., A concept of monotonicity and its characterization for closed queueing networks, in: *OR* 33(1985), pp. 606-624.

Suri, R. and G.W. Diehl, A variable buffer-size model and its use in analyzing closed queueing networks with blocking, in: *Man. Sci.* 32(1986)2, pp. 206-224.

Suri, R. and R.R. Hildebrant, Modelling flexible manufacturing systems using mean-value analysis, in: *JMS* 3(1984)1, pp. 27-35.

Suri, R. and C.K. Whitney, Decision support requirements in flexible manufacturing, in: *JMS* 3(1984)1, pp. 61-69.

Swamidass, P.M. and M.A. Waller, A classification of approaches to planning and justifying new manufacturing technologies, in: *JMS* 9(1990), pp. 181-193.

Syslo, M.M., Deo, N. and J.S. Kowalik, *Discrete Optimization Algorithms with Pascal Programs*, Englewood Cliffs (Prentice Hall) 1983.

Taha, H.A., *Operations Research - An Introduction*, 4th Ed., New York (MacMillan) 1989.

Talavage, J. and R.G. Hannam, *Flexible Manufacturing Systems in Practice - Applications, Design, and Simulations*, New York (Marcel Dekker) 1988.

Tang, C.S. and E.V. Denardo, Models arising from a flexible manufacturing machine, part I: Minimization of the number of tool switches, in: *OR* 36(1988a), pp. 767-777.

Tang, C.S. and E.V. Denardo, Models arising from a flexible manufacturing machine, part II: Minimization of the number of switching instants, in: *OR* 36(1988b), pp. 778-784.

Tempelmeier, H., Kapazitätsplanung für Flexible Fertigungssysteme, in: *Zeitschrift für Betriebswirtschaft* 58(1988), pp. 963-980 (in German).

Tempelmeier, H., Template-based automatic generation of SIMAN IV simulation models, in: Schmidt, B. (Ed.), *Modelling & Simulation, Proceedings of the 1990 European Simulation Multiconference*, Nürnberg, Ghent (Society for Computer Simulation) 1990, pp. 210-215.

Tempelmeier, H., *Simulation mit SIMAN - Ein praktischer Leitfaden zur Modellentwicklung und Programmierung*, Heidelberg (Physica) 1991 (in German).

Tempelmeier, H., Design of machining systems, in: Kusiak, A. (Ed.), *Intelligent Design and Manufacturing: A Reference Book*, New York (Wiley) 1992a, pp. 303-325.

Tempelmeier, H., *Material-Logistik - Grundlagen der Bedarfs- und Losgrößenplanung in PPS-Systemen*, 2nd Ed., Berlin (Springer) 1992b (in German).

Tempelmeier, H. and Th. Endesfelder, Der SIMAN MODUL PROZESSOR - ein flexibles Softwaretool zur Erzeugung von SIMAN-Simulationsmodellen, in: *Angewandte Informatik* 29(1987)3, pp. 104-110 (in German).

Tempelmeier, H. and H. Kuhn, *The Influence of the Material Handling System on the Performance of a Flexible Manufacturing System*, Working Paper, Technical University of Braunschweig, Department of Production and Operations Management, Braunschweig, Germany 1990.

Tempelmeier, H., H. Kuhn and U. Tetzlaff, Performance evaluation of flexible manufacturing systems with blocking, in: *IJPR* 27(1989), pp. 1963-1979.

Tempelmeier, H., H. Kuhn and U. Tetzlaff, Performance evaluation of flexible manufacturing systems with starving, in: Fandel, G. and G. Zäpfel (Eds.), *Modern Production*

Concepts - Theory and Applications, Proceedings of an International Conference, Fernuniversität Hagen, 20.-24. August 1990, Berlin (Springer) 1991, pp. 584-600.

Tetzlaff, U., *Optimal Design of Flexible Manufacturing Systems*, Heidelberg (Physica) 1990.

Tetzlaff, U., *Tool Blocking in Flexible Manufacturing Systems*, Working Paper, George Mason University, Department of Decision Sciences & MIS, Fairfax, Virginia 1992a.

Tetzlaff, U., Selection of manufacturing equipment for flexible production systems, in: Kusiak, A. (Ed.), *Intelligent Design and Manufacturing: A Reference Book*, New York (Wiley) 1992b, pp. 233-255.

Tijms, H.C., *Stochastic Modelling and Analysis: A Computational Approach*, New York (Wiley) 1986.

Tou, J.T., Design of expert systems for integrated production automation, in: *JMS* 4(1985)2, pp. 147-156.

Troxler, J.W. and L. Blank, A comprehensive methodology for manufacturing system evaluation and comparison, in: *JMS* 8(1989)3, pp. 175-183.

Van der Wal, J., Monotonicity of the throughput of a closed exponential queueing network in the number of jobs, in: *ORS* 11(1989), pp. 97-100.

Van Doremalen, J.B.M, *Approximate analysis of queueing network models*, Diss., Technical University Eindhoven, Eindhoven 1986.

Van Looveren, A.J., Gelders, L.F. and L.N. Van Wassenhove, A review of FMS planning models, in: Kusiak, A. (Ed.), *Modelling and Design of Flexible Manufacturing Systems*, Amsterdam (Elsevier) 1986, pp. 3-31.

Villa, A. and S. Rossetto, Towards a hierarchical structure for production planning and control in flexible manufacturing systems, in: Kusiak, A. (Ed.), *Modelling and Design of Flexible Manufacturing Systems*, Amsterdam (Elsevier) 1986, pp. 209-228.

Vinod, B. and T. Altiok, Approximating unreliable queueing networks under the assumption of exponentiality, in: *JORS* 37(1986), pp. 309-316.

Vinod, B. and J.J. Solberg, Performance models for unreliable flexible manufacturing systems, in: *OMEGA* 12(1984)3, pp. 299-308.

Vinod, B. and J.J. Solberg, The optimal design of flexible manufacturing systems, in: *IJPR* 23(1985), pp. 1141-1151.

Voß, S., The two-stage hybrid-flowshop scheduling problem with sequence-dependent setup times, in: Fandel, G., Gulledge, T. and A. Jones (Eds.), *Recent Developments and New Perspectives of Operations Research in the Area of Production Planning and Control*, Proceedings of a DGOR/ORSA Conference, Fernuniversität Hagen, June 25-26, 1992, Berlin (Springer) 1993.

Wang, W. and R. Bell, A knowledge based multi-level modelling system for the design of flexible machining facilities, in: *IJPR* 30(1992), pp. 13-34.

Warnecke, H.-J. and J.-H. Kölle, Production control for new work structures, in: *IJPR* 17(1979)6, pp. 631-641.

Watson, H.J. and J.H. Blackstone, Jr., *Computer Simulation*, 2nd Ed., New York (Wiley) 1989.

Whitehouse, G.E., *Systems Analysis and Design Using Network Techniques*, Englewood Cliffs (Prentice Hall) 1973.

Whitney, C.K. and T.S. Gaul, Sequential decision procedures for batching and balancing in FMSs, in: *Annals of OR* 3(1985), pp. 301-316.

Whitney, C.K. and R. Suri, Algorithms for part and machine selection in flexible manufacturing systems, in: *Annals of OR* 3(1985), pp. 239-261.

Widmer, M. and P. Solot, Do not forget the breakdowns and the maintenance operations in FMS design problems, in: *IJPR* 28(1990), pp. 421-430.

Wilson, J.M., Approaches to machine load balancing in flexible manufacturing systems, in: *JORS* 43(1992), pp. 415-423.

Y**ao, D.D. and J.A. Buzacott**, Modeling a class of state-dependent routing in flexible manufacturing systems, in: *Annals of OR* 3(1985), pp. 153-167.

Yao, D.D. and J.A. Buzacott, Models of flexible manufacturing systems with limited local buffers, in: *IJPR* 24(1986)1, pp. 107-118.

Yao, D.D. and J.A. Buzacott, Modeling a class of flexible manufacturing systems with reversible routing, in: *OR* 35(1987), pp. 87-93.

Yao, D.D. and J.G. Shanthikumar, Some resource allocation problems in multi-cell systems, in: Stecke, K.E. and R. Suri (Eds.), *Proceedings of the 2nd ORSA/TIMS Conference on Flexible Manufacturing Systems: Operations Research Models and Applications*, Amsterdam (Elsevier) 1986, pp. 245-255.

Yao, D.D. and J.G. Shanthikumar, The optimal input rates to a system of manufacturing cells, in: *INFOR* 25(1987)1, pp. 57-65.

Z**ahorjan, J., Eager, D.L. and H.M. Sweillam**, Accuracy, speed, and convergence of approximate mean value analysis, in: *Performance Evaluation* 8(1988), pp. 255-270.

Zhuang, L. and K.S. Hindi, Mean value analysis for multiclass closed queueing network models of flexible manufacturing systems with limited buffers, in: *EJOR* 46(1990), pp. 366-379.

Zijm, W.H.M., Flexible manufacturing systems: Background examples and models, in: Schellhaas H. et al. (Eds.), *Operations Research Proceedings 1987*, Berlin (Springer) 1988, pp. 142-161.

ABBREVIATIONS

ACM	Association for Computing Machiney
AIIE Transactions	Transactions of the American Institute of Industrial Engineers
EJOR	European Journal of Operational Research
Eng. Costs and Prod. Econ.	Engineering Costs and Production Economics
HBR	Harvard Business Review
IE	Industrial Engineering
IEEE Transactions	Transactions of the Institute of Electrical and Electronics Engineers
IIE Transactions	Institute of Industrial Engineers Transactions
IJFMS	International Journal of Flexible Manufacturing Systems
IJOPM	International Journal of Operations & Production Management
IJPE	International Journal of Production Economics
IJPR	International Journal of Production Research
JMOM	Journal of Manufacturing and Operations Management
JMS	Journal of Manufacturing Systems
JORS	Journal of the Operational Research Society
Man. Sci.	Management Science
OR	Operations Research
ORS	Operations Research Spektrum
ORSA	Operations Research Society of America
TIMS	The Institute of Management Science

NOTATION

Indices

c	-	pallet type index (c = 1,2,...,C)
b	-	station size class index (b = 1,2,...,B)
e	-	index of the bottleneck station
h	-	period index (h = 1,2,...,H)
j	-	order index (j = 1,2,...,J)
k	-	product type index (k = 1,2,...,K)
l	-	batch index (l = 1,2,...,L)
m	-	station index (m = 1,2,...,M)
M	-	index of the transportation (MHS) station
o	-	operation index (o = 1,2,...,O)
t	-	tool index (t = 1,2,...,T)

Data and decision variables

Δ_m	-	relative increase in the production rate
θ_m	-	technical availability of station m
θ_o	-	set of predecessor operations of operation o
τ	-	parameter used in the simulated annealing procedure (temperature)
ϕ_m	-	set of machines from which machine m is directly reachable
Ω_{1m}	-	mean length of phase 1 at station m under Coxian distributed service times
Ω_{2m}	-	mean length of phase 2 at station m under Coxian distributed service times
α_k	-	production ratio of product type k with respect to the total production rate of the FMS
α_m	-	probability that phase 2 is reached at station m under Coxian distributed service times
β_k	-	production ratio of product type k with respect to the production rate of its product group (pallet type)
γ_m	-	binary variable for the inclusion of station m in the FMS
γ_{bm}	-	binary variable for the definition of the size class of station m
λ_{cm}	-	mean arrival rate of a workpiece of pallet type c at station m
$\mu_m(n)$	-	service rate of station m with n workpieces at station m
π_{om}	-	binary variable for the assignment of operation lot o to machine m
π_{oml}	-	binary variable for the assignment of operation lot o, machine m and batch l
σ_o	-	number of tool slots required for operation lot o
$\sigma\{.\}$	-	standard deviation
σ_t	-	number of tool slots required for tool t
σ_{ot}	-	binary coefficient which is set to 1 if tool t is required for operation lot o
σ_{tm}	-	number of tool slots required by tool t at machine m
σ_{jrm}	-	number of tool slots required with the production of order j using route r at machine m
σ_{jtm}	-	binary coefficient which is set to 1 if tool t is required by order j at machine m

$A_m(.)$	-	station specific auxiliary function
$A_{cm}(.)$	-	mean number of workpieces at station m seen by an arriving pallet of type c (arrival average)
AI_{mh}	-	investment expenditure for a resource of type (station) m in period h
AO_{krh}	-	operating expenses in period h associated with the production of a unit of product type k using route r
a_m^-	-	weighting factor for a negative deviation from the target workload of machine m
a_m^+	-	weighting factor for a positive deviation from the target workload of machine m
$a_m(.)$	-	station specific auxiliary function
a_{jr}	-	weighting factor for route r of order j
$\underline{B}$	-	matrix of the mean processing times at the stations
$\underline{B}^s$	-	matrix of the modified mean processing times at the stations
B_m	-	number of size classes of station m
B_{ZL}	-	mean disposal trip time (incl. idle trip time)
BV_m	-	mean backlog processing time at station m
BZ_{mj}	-	increase of processing time of a workpiece at the transition from station m to station j caused by blocking at station m
b_M	-	mean transportation time (without idle trips and disposal trips to the central buffer)
b_m	-	mean processing time of a workpiece at station m
b_m^a	-	mean completion time of a workpiece at station m
b_m^{a*}	-	adjusted mean completion time of a workpiece at station m
b_m^s	-	adjusted mean processing time at station m
b_Z	-	mean disposal trip time to the central buffer
b_{cm}	-	mean processing time of a workpiece of pallet type c at station m
b_{cm}^b	-	mean processing time of a workpiece at station m with respect to pallet type c, as used in the $(M/M/S_m)$ model
b_{jm}	-	processing time of a workpiece of order j at machine m
b_{km}	-	mean processing time of a workpiece of product type k at station m
b_{om}	-	processing time of operation lot o at machine m
b_{jrm}	-	processing time of a workpiece of order j at machine m using route r
b_{kmr}	-	mean processing time at station m of a workpiece of product type k using route r
$bl_m(n)$	-	mean blocking time of a workpiece at station m with n workpieces in the FMS
br_{cm}	-	mean residual service time of a workpiece of pallet type c at station m
bv_m	-	backlog processing time at station m
C	-	number of pallet types
C_N	-	fixed costs of a universal pallet
C_m	-	fixed costs of a resource (machine, setup area, vehicle, etc.) of station m
C_{bm}	-	total fixed costs of station m if station m belongs to size class b
CB	-	central buffer
CB_{om}	-	variable load and unload costs of operation o at station m
CO_{kr}	-	variable production costs if product type k is produced using route r
CO_{om}	-	variable production costs if operation o is assigned to station m
CV_m^a	-	coefficient of variation of the completion time at station m
CV_{cm}^a	-	coefficient of variation of the completion time with respect to pallet type c at station m
c_m	-	setup costs for a tool magazine at machine m

c_{om} -   variable costs of production of operation lot o at machine m

$\underline{D}$ -   matrix
D -   mean flow time
$D(.)$ -   mean flow time of a workpiece through the FMS
$D_c(.)$ -   mean flow time of a workpiece of pallet type c through the FMS
$D_m(.)$ -   mean flow time of a workpiece at station m
$D_{cm}(.)$ -   mean flow time of a workpiece of pallet type c at station m
d_j -   due date of order j
d_m^- -   negative deviation from the target workload at machine m
d_m^+ -   positive deviation from the target workload at machine m
d_{mj} -   matrix element
d_{om} -   estimated number of additional tools at machine m upon assignment of operation lot o

E -   big number
$E\{.\}$ -   expected value
e_h -   net cash flow in period h

$F_L(.)$ -   idle trip factor
F_Z -   proportion of disposal trips to the central buffer
$F_{Z'}$ -   proportion of disposal trips to the central buffer if the central buffer is of unlimited size
f_j -   number of fixtures available for order j
$f_m(.)$ -   station specific auxiliary function
f_{ko} -   proportion of workpieces of product type k running through the o-th operation

$\underline{G}$ -   matrix of the normalization constants
$g(N,M)$ -   normalization constant
g_m -   capacity or target workload of machine m (in time units)

H -   number of periods (planning horizon)
$H(\mathbf{J}_1)$ -   makespan of batch I (as a function of the set of orders $\mathbf{J}_1$)
h_m -   capacity of the tool magazine of machine m
$h_m(.)$ -   station specific auxiliary function

i -   discount rate

J -   number of orders
$\mathbf{J}_0$ -   set of orders not yet assigned to a batch
$\mathbf{J}_1$ -   set of orders for which processing started but which have not yet reached the planned production quantity
$\mathbf{J}_l$ -   set of orders assigned to batch I

K -   number of product types
K_0 -   present value
$\mathbf{K}_c$ -   set of product types which require pallet type c
KF_m -   correction factor for station m

L -   number of batches
L_m -   mean starving time

l_m	-	starving time (stochastic variable notation)
l_{kr}	-	marginal relative flow time change of the workpieces of product type k using route r
l_{om}	-	load and unload time for operation o at station m
M	-	number of stations; index of the transportation station
M_M	-	number of stopping-places in the FMS
M_o	-	set of machines being able to perform operation o
$MTTF_m^*$	-	service time of a repair order at the dummy station m^* (mean time to failure of machine m)
$MTTF_m$	-	mean time to failure of machine m
$MTTR_m$	-	mean time to repair of machine m
m_{ko}	-	station number of the operation in the o-th position of the process plan of product type k
N	-	number of universal pallets in the FMS
N^b	-	lower bound of the number of pallets
N_c	-	number of special pallets of type c
N_{max}	-	maximum allowed number of pallets in the FMS
$\underline{N}_{max}$	-	vector of the maximum allowed numbers of pallets at the stations
$N_{max(m)}$	-	maximum allowed number of pallets at station m
$N_{max(CB)}$	-	capacity of the central buffer
N_{SB}	-	minimum total number of pallets for blocking
n	-	number of pallets
$\underline{n}$	-	vector of the spatial distribution of pallets among the stations
$\underline{\underline{n}}$	-	matrix of the spatial distribution of pallets of different pallet types among the stations
n_m	-	number of pallets at station m (waiting or in process)
$\underline{n}_m$	-	vector of the number of pallets of different pallet types at station m (waiting or in process)
n_j	-	lot size of order j
n_o	-	lot size of operation lot o
0	-	number of operations
0_j	-	number of operations of order j
$P\{.\}$	-	probability
$P\{n_m\}$	-	probability that n pallets are at station m
$P_m\{.\}$	-	station specific probability
P_m	-	number of local buffer spaces at station m
P_Z	-	availability of the central buffer
PB_{cm}	-	probability that upon arrival of a pallet of type c all machines at station m are busy
p_m	-	relative arrival frequency of a workpiece at station m
P_{cm}	-	relative arrival frequency of a workpiece of pallet type c at station m
pn	-	priority value
ps_j	-	priority value of order j
ps_{om}	-	priority value of operation o with respect to machine m
pt_j	-	priority value of order j
pw_j	-	priority value of order j
pw_{om}	-	priority value of operation o with respect to machine m
$Q_M(.)$	-	mean number of workpieces in the transportation system (waiting or in transport)
$Q_m(.)$	-	mean number of workpieces at station m (waiting or in process)

$Q_m(n-1)$ - mean number of workpieces at station m with n-1 workpieces in the FMS (waiting or in process)

$Q_{cm}(.)$ - mean number of workpieces of pallet type c at station m (waiting or in process)

QW_{cm} - length of the queue of pallet type c at station m

q_k - planned production quantity of product type k

q_{kr} - proportion of the production quantity of product type k produced using route r

R_j - set of routes available for order j

R_k - number of routes available for product type k

RB_{cm} - mean residual service time of a workpiece at a busy station m upon arrival of a pallet of type c

RB_j - mean residual service time of a workpiece at station j

r_{jm} - transition probability of workpieces between stations j and m

S_m - number of machines, setup areas, transportation vehicles, etc. at station m

S_m^b - minimum number of resources required at station M

$S(N,M)$ - set of states of the FMS

$S'(N,M)$ - set of states of an FMS with limited local buffers

s - setup time between two batches

T - number of tools

T_A - expected transportation time of the processed workpiece

T_L - mean transportation time (incl. idle trip time)

T_m - mean transportation delay of a workpiece en route to station m

T_m - set of tools assigned to station m

T_{Wm} - waiting time of the processed workpiece at station m

T_{ZL} - total transportation time (incl. idle trip times and disposal trip times)

T_{om} - set of tools required for operation o at station m

$TS_m(\pi_m)$ - nonlinear tool slot saving function

t_m - transportation delay of a workpiece en route to station m (stochastic variable notation)

t_{ko} - deterministic processing time of the o-th operation of product type k

u_{om} - number of workpieces of operation lot o assigned to machine m

u_{oml} - number of workpieces of operation lot o in batch l assigned to machine m

U - total number of central buffer spaces required

$U_m(.)$ - utilization of station m

$U_{cm}(.)$ - utilization of station m with respect to pallet type c

$V\{.\}$ - variance

v_M - mean total number of operations performed on a workpiece in the FMS or mean number of transportation processes required to produce a workpiece

v_m - mean number of operations performed on a workpiece at station m

v_{cM} - mean number of transportation processes required to produce a workpiece of pallet type c

v_{cm} - mean number of operations performed on a workpiece of pallet type c at station m

v_{km} - mean number of operations performed on a workpiece of product type k at station m

v_{kmr} - mean number of operations at station m performed on a workpiece of product type k using route r

W_T - length of the relevant queue

W_{Tm}	-	corrected queue length of the transportation system with respect to station m
W_{TAm}	-	number of workpieces waiting for transportation to stations other than station m
W_{cm}	-	mean waiting time of a pallet of type c at station m
WO_{cm}	-	mean residual service time of a workpiece at station m upon arrival of a pallet of type c (arrival average)
WO_{cm}^a	-	adjusted mean residual service time of a workpiece at station m upon arrival of a pallet of type c (generally distributed processing times)
$W1_{cm}$	-	mean total processing time of all workpieces waiting at station m upon arrival of a pallet of type c (arrival average)
w_m	-	mean workload of station m
w_m^*	-	standardized mean workload of station m
w_{FS}	-	total workload of the FMS
w_{kmr}	-	mean workload of station m with respect to route r of product type k
X	-	mean production rate
$X(.)$	-	mean production rate of the FMS
X_{min}	-	minimum production rate of the FMS
$X_c(.)$	-	mean production rate of the FMS with respect to pallet type c
$X_{min(j)}$	-	minimum production rate of order j
$X_m(.)$	-	mean production rate of station m
X_{cm}	-	mean production rate of station m for pallet type c
X_{kh}	-	planned production rate for product type k in period h
x_j	-	number of concurrent workpieces of order j in the FMS
x_{jl}	-	binary variable for the assignment of order j and batch l
x_{jr}	-	production quantity of order j using route r
x_{kr}	-	production quantity of product type k using route r
x_{om}	-	proportion of the production quantity of operation o produced at station m
x_{krh}	-	production quantity of product type k produced in period h using route r
y_{jr}	-	binary variable for the assignment of order j and route r
y_{om}	-	proportion of production quantity of operation o loaded or unloaded at station m for the first time
y_{tm}	-	binary variable for the assignment of tool t and machine m
y_{tml}	-	binary variable for the assignment of tool t, machine m and batch l
$Z(.)$	-	value of the objective function
$Z_1, Z_2, \ldots$	-	values of the objective function
Z_l	-	value of the objective function in iteration l
Z_m	-	maximum number of tool magazine exchanges for machine m
ΔZ_{lj}	-	change in the value of the objective function in iteration l induced if a neighboring solution is chosen
z_m	-	number of tool magazine exchanges required at machine m
$z_m(n)$	-	binary variable for the description of the fact that station m is fully occupied when n workpieces circulate in the FMS
z_{mh}	-	number of machines added to station m in period h

AUTHOR INDEX

SUBJECT INDEX